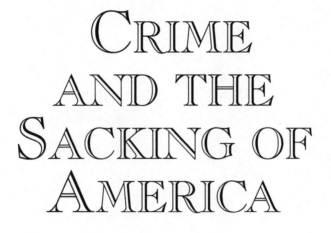

CRIME
AND THE
SACKING OF
AMERICA

CRIME AND THE SACKING OF AMERICA

THE ROOTS OF CHAOS

ANDREW PEYTON THOMAS

BRASSEY'S
Washington • London

Library of Congress Cataloging-in-Publication Data

Thomas, Andrew Peyton.
   Crime and the sacking of America: the roots of chaos/Andrew Peyton Thomas.
     p. cm.
   Includes bibliographical references and index.
   ISBN 0-02-881107-0
   1. Crime—United States. 2. Crime prevention—United States.
   I. Title.
   HV6789.T44   1994
   364.973—dc20   94-21266
                                                 CIP

10 9 8 7 6 5 4 3 2 1

Printed in the United States of America

To Ann,
my wife

Contents

Preface

On June 5, 1993, my hometown paper, the *Arizona Republic,* ran on its front page an article titled "Study Finds High Minority Arrest Rate." Like similar articles that were concurrently turning up in newspapers across the country, the gist of the story was simply a confirmation of what most Americans had previously sensed without statistical authority: many American youth run afoul of the law early and often. This particular article reported that criminal justice researchers from Arizona State University had found that over 70 percent of black males in metropolitan Phoenix have a criminal record; that is, have had formal charges brought against them in county juvenile courts before they turn eighteen. The local reaction to these findings was identical to that received by comparable studies of high black crime rates in large American cities "back East." Implicit in the article was the same mixture of concern and, to some degree, condescension from many whites toward the apparent inability of the black community to behave itself.

Only later in the article was the diligent reader treated to the real news in the study. It turned out that Mexican–American juveniles had been disciplined in high numbers as well. Just under 43 percent of all adolescent Latino males are prosecuted by the Maricopa County juvenile justice system. There was more. Only a fraction behind them were whites. Currently in Phoenix, one of America's largest and fastest-growing cities, an estimated 38.9 percent of all white males are formally charged with at least one crime before they reach their eighteenth birthday. True, the types of crimes were not specified, and the figures were only an estimate for all boys between the ages of eight and seventeen. Yet there it is. Close to half of all Phoenix juveniles are either criminal offenders or, it would seem, close enough to criminal activity to get themselves prosecuted.

These findings stunned many local leaders and activists, who had apparently believed whites to be immune to such trends. When told of the statistics, for instance, the head of the Arizona ACLU commented, "*Even for the Anglo kids,* that percentage is astronomical." (Emphasis added.) He concluded: "Is there no one in our society who isn't breaking laws?"

This question, put somewhat clumsily by one whose organization bears some responsibility for its premise, is the urgent subject of this book. I fear that we are witnessing the death of our civilization. We live in a time of random lawlessness that, I believe, is unprecedented in human history. It is a period and condition that I call throughout this book the Great Havoc, as there is no existing term to describe it. This conclusion is simply a matter of mathematics. A democratic nation in which an emerging majority of citizens are unwilling to obey the law cannot survive. Although Arizona's individualistic culture lends itself to exceptionally high delinquency rates, evidence is mounting daily that the crime coursing through Phoenix streets is scarcely confined to Barry Goldwater's libertarian lodestar. Nations, of course, rise and fall, the speed of their decline depending on the vigor with which they are defended. We must acknowledge that America is not above the latter fate, all the more so given the current exponential decay. Unless drastic changes are made soon, some of which cut to our very soul, it seems doubtful that the United States can remain a stable, viable society very far into the twenty-first century. The crime in our urban cores is only a taste of things to come for our entire country. The above–mentioned ACLU official, and the rest of us, had better believe it.

As we examine the roots of this havoc, a word about the terms used in this book is in order. Writers sometimes balk at existing ideological labels because they prefer to be creative or to pretend to be more moderate than they really are. I reject the typical usage today of the words "liberal" and "conservative" for different reasons. Both liberalism and conservatism, as practiced in modern America, are by historical standards a loose, rather arbitrary collection of various interest groups. These groups might be summed up, with admitted hyperbole, as libertines, public employees' unions and anti-white bigots on the Left; materialistic antitax rich folk and yuppies, poseur patriots and antiminority bigots on the Right. There are honorable people on both sides of the current political spectrum. Yet both camps, when their views are considered as a whole, share a poisonous obsession with individual rights. Infecting both liberalism and conservatism today is what I view as America's most significant political development of our time: the acceptance of radical individualism, first theoretically and subsequently in political and social practice. For purposes of clarity I call this radical-individualist philosophy libertarianism when embraced by the Right, ultraindividualism or social atomism on the Left. The former is popular with the American people generally, the latter with influential academics and opinion leaders. Both grow from the same philosophical seed, and are more or less the same theory defended differently by two factions with divergent motives.

This book is an attempt to integrate philosophy with a detailed, documented analysis of how philosophy has realized itself in modern America—namely, in the sacking of the American Republic. Although this is an unorthodox undertaking, I know of no other way to demonstrate the philosophical antecedents of the dour statistics that daily fill our newspapers.

I hope that the people who have helped me write this book, often unknowingly, will be spared criticism for its contents. I list them only to express my gratitude, not to draft them for my defense under a hopeful strategy of strength in numbers; the blemishes in this book, sadly, are all mine. I am grateful for the assistance of the following people and institutions: the library resources of Harvard University and the Harvard Law School, the University of Missouri–Columbia, Arizona State University, and the Phoenix Public Library; Mead Data Central for access to its incomparable Nexis service; Jessica Wainwright of the Literary Group for her unflagging assistance in getting the book published and the author compensated, a job made more difficult by my choice in political philosophy; my editor, Ted Johnson, for his excellent if humbling insights; and my publisher, Franklin D. Margiotta of Brassey's, who saw something worth publishing in this stream of impertinence, improved it through alternating criticism and encouragement and even paid me a little for it.

Special thanks go to members of the Harvard Law School faculty who refused, on ideological grounds, to supervise my third-year paper when I proposed various crime-related theses that are now expounded as chapters in this book. Because of the self-censorship that would have been necessary to satisfy their requirements, the result of those efforts, had they agreed, might well have been an analysis bathed in half-truths—which, I am afraid, are legion at that institution. All the same, I am grateful for the chance to have attended there, and for the hillbilly quota that allowed me to.

I am especially grateful for my family and their diverse help: my mother, for her love and practical wisdom through the years; my father, for the martial ardor and love of philosophy that he imparted, and for his research assistance; my brothers-in-law, Prudencio "Sukie" Estrada, Marcos "Sensen" Estrada, and Jesus "Popo" Estrada, for helping me better understand urban Latino culture and life in general; Eva Estrada, my sister-in-law, for her education on American education and, specifically, Lakewood High School.

Finally, I thank Ann, my wife and general mentor in life. She was the only person to review the work before it was mailed off back East to prospective agents, and the one who endured what was necessary to make it a reality. *¿Qué he hecho?*

You hear, O Lord, the desire of the afflicted;
you encourage them, and you listen to their cry,
defending the fatherless and the oppressed,
in order that man, who is of the earth, may terrify no more.
                                          Psalms 10:17–18

Introduction:
America's Model City

September 8, 1992. It was the first day of preschool for twenty-two-month-old Sarina Basu, and her mother, Pam Basu, left with her from their home in Howard County, Maryland, that morning in the family BMW bound for that destination. A block away Ms. Basu stopped at a stop sign. Two young men from nearby Washington, D.C., Rodney Eugene Solomon and Bernard Eric Miller, approached the driver's side of the vehicle. Over the next several minutes the pair would, in the course of their offense, manage almost single-handedly to crowd a new, horrible crime into an American vocabulary already laden with such recent additions: "carjacking." Witnesses would later describe the two as assaulting Basu repeatedly through the window with "their fists balled," the two "just nailing her."[1] Basu screamed and struggled to retrieve her daughter from the car. In the process she became entangled in a seat belt. As the two drove off the car dragged Basu, her body "flopping. . . like a rag doll." The vehicle left in its wake a mile-and-a-half-long "bloody streak" in the road. After tossing her daughter unharmed into the street, Solomon and Miller attempted to dislodge Basu's body by ramming the car into a barbed–wire fence around a nearby cattle farm. Her body was later found entwined and hanging in the barbed wire. The two men "appeared to be calm" as they departed the scene.[2]

July 10, 1993. Angry that a fellow patron of a packed music hall had bumped into him on the dance floor, an unidentified sixteen-year-old male began a shoving match inside the WUST Radio Music Hall in the Shaw section of Northwest Washington. His complaints not redressed, the youth then pulled out a handgun.

He aimed at the other young man and shot him point–blank in the chest. As the youth ran through the crush of people toward the hall's exit, he fired indiscriminately into the crowd, seriously injuring four others. "It hurts to see young people destroying themselves . . . [but] this kind of thing is happening throughout the city," commented the Reverend Melvin Robinson, whose Master's Child Glorious Church of God shared the hall building, which subsequently bore a bullet hole in its facade.[3]

September 25, 1993. Four armed young men emerged from the woods around the playground at Weatherless Elementary School in Southeast Washington. They singled out and stalked one twenty-six-year-old, Kervin Brown, as they approached the crowd watching a pickup football game. "Come here, Kervin. Where you going, Kervin?" taunted the four as he began to run. They opened fire, one youth with a gun in each hand, and continued shooting as they stood over Brown's body. Fatally wounded as well was four-year-old Launice Smith, struck in the head and hand as she played nearby. Police concluded that the slayings were due to a war between rival neighborhood drug gangs known as the Greenway and Ridge Road crews.[4]

Three incidents, three snapshots in time over a little more than a year, all in and around our nation's capital. They are admittedly but a footnote to the recent explosion of crime in Washington, D.C., a full accounting of which would redden these pages. But they are also typical of a new, terrifying social phenomenon in the United States—a generation of "stone killers," generally young men, emerging across the country. They are criminals apparently wholly lacking in conscience, for whom murder carries no more remorse than grocery shopping. These young men, whose ranks are growing rapidly in number and notoriety, have stained the nation's sidewalks and focused our attention on crime as has nothing else in our history. Their viciousness and the increasing frequency of their appearance on the national scene have led Americans to wonder what possibly could have brought about such mindless brutality. We are right to be worried. In the moments that we do not spend locking doors, turning on alarm systems and loading firearms for self-protection, we do well to take time to ponder the origins of this crisis, and the foreboding that we feel about America's future should current trends continue.

The reason for the growth of crime in America and its capital city is not nearly as unclear as we sometimes assume in despair. The reason, in fact, is inside all of us, if only we have the courage to probe our darkest nature. While many Americans, particularly in academia and government, often explain crime as "caused" by things beyond the individual's control, we do so only by overlooking an essential social fact: committing a crime is an intensely personal decision. It is arguably the *most* personal of decisions. Crime is the most extreme form of selfishness. By definition, crime involves the taking of something that does not belong to the offender; namely, the lives, belongings, rights or peace of others. Whatever the matter being appropriated, crime's first prerequisite is a decision to revolt against one's family, community and society. Thus, to the extent that social factors are responsible for one's choosing to commit a crime, their culpability rests in their lowering of one's regard for the welfare of others. Everything that society does to encourage selfishness directly or indirectly encourages crime.

The forces that have driven this individualistic breakup are not the societal injustices that we are accustomed to pointing to. They are rather the ideas that have rationalized the natural, occasionally brutal self-obsession of man. Civilization was created to constrain egoism. We therefore cannot expect our recent, ill-advised glorification of this instinct, evident in both popular attitudes and law, to be free of uncomfortable consequences. Many have blamed the frenetic events of the 1960s as the starting point for these trends. But while some of its intellectual leaders have seemed at times to think otherwise, that decade's merry, mass overturning of custom was only the implementation of independently conceived theories centuries in the making. First in theory and then in practice, the self became king. By persuading us to wage a form of low-intensity warfare on one another, to view others merely as either obstacles to or sources of self-indulgence, these ideas have allowed the atomizing of American society. The community has disintegrated into a fine powder of self-interested individuals lacking sympathy for one another's concerns and fidelity to the common social web that we call law.

The unprecedented crime wave that has resulted, a Great Havoc rupturing both Washington, D.C., and the rest of U.S. society, features three major themes, or, if you will, three overarching explanations for the momentous events of our day. The three parts of this book are devoted to their discussion. They are the inability of all levels of government to win a war prosecuted against woes that are intellectual and spiritual in origin; the common attempt to explain crime as due to various external causes rather than as the result of personal decisions by responsible individuals; and the confusion and apathy of many Americans, who look to illusory solutions for a crime crisis that sprouts from our very souls. Washington, D.C., in fact, provides an important case study reflecting the above three themes of the present undoing, an analysis relevant to the entire nation. For while we would prefer to think otherwise, Washington's decline is not some strangely bloody departure from our Republic's generally favorable social trends. Washington's sacking by America's home-grown barbarians is a classic example of how an entire civilization can be lost to the chaotic individualism that percolates within us all, and that spills forth rapidly when society no longer resolves to contain it.

The first theme of the current time of troubles is our government's intrinsic inability to solve a crime crisis arising, if inadvertently, from the attitudes and values of the population it works for. American government, from the District of Columbia to the country's least populous corners, currently relies upon three main institutions to combat crime: police, courts and prisons. These three components of the criminal justice system form a triad of forces opposing society's criminal foes. The crime surge of recent years has placed great stress on this system, with many unkind results. One consequence is that American government today is unable to consistently bring offenders to justice. Criminals, whose business is capitalizing on weakness, have recognized and taken advantage of the opportunities that this breakdown presents.

The criminal justice triad deployed by Washington, D.C., has buckled from the sheer volume of offenders. Although the District has the highest number of police officers per capita of any city in the nation,[5] it continues to spin out of lawful control. In Washington today, only one out of four cases of murder, society's most serious crime, results in a conviction.[6] Even Mayor Sharon Pratt Kelly's federally rejected proposal in 1993 to order the National Guard into the District's mean streets, a revival of Mayor Marion Barry's same exasperated suggestion several years before,[7] held little promise of stemming the tide. Washington courts must process some 14,000 serious criminal cases a year. This overload forces delays in pending prosecutions and often damages them irreparably because of loss of testimony or evidence.[8] The District has also been unable to build enough new prisons or convert enough existing structures for incarceration to keep up with the number of convicted offenders, despite substantial federal outlays for that purpose.[9]

Apparently in part because of discouragement over these trends, the more experienced D.C. cops have resigned from the force in large numbers over the past several years. In 1992 about 25 percent of D.C.'s policemen had been hired within the prior two years.[10] Many of these newer officers, hired hastily and given preferential treatment if they had attended Washington high schools, were functionally illiterate and were sworn in without even criminal background checks.[11] A series of arrests and indictments of dozens of these younger officers has been the result.

By the time of Mayor Barry's arrest for inhaling crack cocaine in 1990, a watershed in the District's history, America had begun to felicitously call Washington, D.C., its murder capital. The District in 1990 achieved the highest per capita murder rate of any American city, a title it still retains. Between 1987 and 1990, D.C.'s murder rate almost doubled.[12] By 1991 the District was averaging two homicides a day; the body count from 1987 to 1991 was more than 3,000 people killed.[13] From 1989 to 1990 alone, the number of rapes in Washington rose 66 percent.[14] Washingtonians during those years were more likely to be killed at the hands of their countrymen than were citizens of El Salvador, Lebanon or Northern Ireland. District residents were also estimated in 1989 to spend more money on cocaine than on food and drink.[15] Today the city confronts genuine anarchy.

The federal government has fared no better than District officials in dealing with this crisis. Despite a declaration of war on crime nationwide and specifically in Washington, D.C., federal policymakers have had to similarly confront in short order the inherent limits to combating multiplying vices with the flimsy resources of democratic government. Federal politicians have recently begun to respond in earnest to public demands for sterner crime control. Generally their policy proposals revolve around expanding the federal criminal justice triad. Legislation recently offered in Congress would, for example, create federal college scholarships for future police officers; enact a "three strikes and you're out" statute, which would mandate lifelong incarceration in federal prisons for all three-time serious offenders; expand the death penalty to cover a wide range of new offenses, including genocide; and, as a less creative but perennially popular solution, establish more federal courts and penitentiaries.

Although the latest stack of anticrime initiatives contains some thoughtful and fresh approaches, all of them, it would appear based on recent history, stand to reap a harvest of dashed hopes and essentially unabated crime. A preview of their likely failure came from the federal government's recent ill-fated nomination of Washington as a "model city" in the War on Drugs. In 1989 drug "czar" William J. Bennett announced at President Bush's behest that D.C.'s crime rate was "so glaring, so out-of-control," that the administration would make the District a test case for its strategy for winning the War on Drugs. Victory was thought attainable through the expansion of police, courts, and prisons.[16] Bush had entered office that year with the District crime rate having risen 15 percent the prior year, and almost 40 percent in certain neighborhoods, such as Anacostia.[17] The administration ordered nearly $100 million in emergency aid earmarked for increased expenditures on the D.C. triad. One year later the returns came in: America's capital was still firmly in the enemy's hands. Washington's murder rate, still the nation's highest, was actually climbing. The violent crime rate had jumped 5 percent, almost as much as in the previous year.[18] For his part, Bennett gracefully accepted the blame, and resigned before the year was out. Some doubts remained about whether the Barry administration had used the resources effectively; perhaps, it was thought, a better-managed battle plan would have worked. But at least for the seasoned observers heading the executive and legislative branches of the federal government, for whom continued crime control follies might cause unemployment, such hopes were not persuasive. There would be no more talk of Washington or anyplace else as a model city in the battle against criminal despotism. Crime in the District, and the nation, continued to soar. And Washington, D.C., began to look like a different sort of model city—a glimpse into the future for the rest of the American Republic.

We must not, however, heap all our criticisms on the politicians, for there is plenty to go around. Our government has proved ill equipped to handle this crisis because it takes its orders, ultimately, from a sovereign people; and we ourselves have not been thinking or behaving very responsibly of late. There is, then, a second important theme to the lawlessness of our day: theories and ideas that either directly advocate or take a lenient view of criminality. Many of our nation's criminologists and political theorists, continuing an intellectual tradition established in the French Enlightenment, have lately subscribed to a philosophy that we may call ultraindividualism or social atomism. This philosophy defends theoretically the extreme egoism in today's society, yet, somewhat curiously, holds individual offenders not responsible for their crimes. Most of these researchers and thinkers have also come to see as their main professional undertaking the investigation of the causes of crime. Reflecting this Enlightenment heritage, many of these theories have sought to locate the causes of crime in impersonal entities or inanimate objects. Poverty, guns and drugs have become the most frequent foci of concern.

The theater where these ideas have culminated most starkly is the inner city. Indeed, we must rack our brains and dust off many chronicles of history to find a more direct, or more tragic, realization of antisocial notions conceived outside the affected class of citizens. The disintegration of the family and abandonment of children out of parental self-interest; the resulting, often violent, disaffection of children; racial balkanization; other social afflictions made possible by a proliferation of individual liberties at the expense of civic responsibilities: Washington's pathologies all trace their origins to these intellectual roots.

The future of the nation's capital—and, we will see, potentially of the American Republic in its entirety—can be seen in the crime-scarred faces of its children. The flight of adults from family responsibilities is the main ingredient of this fragmentation. Americans have lately forgotten that the family was created for the stability and safety of the race, and that any temporary, individual enjoyment that we may get from this arrangement's disbandment carries a duly severe penalty. Left by their fathers to be raised by single, overextended mothers, children learn from the cradle our current self-interested conception of citizenship and its antisocial tendencies. Washington proves the point well. Nearly 50 percent of the District's children report domestic violence. Roughly 30 percent examined by the National Institute of Mental Health show "clinically deviant" signs of depression, fear or hyperactivity, almost three times the national average.[19] A recent trend among D.C.'s preteen children is planning their own funerals. One eleven-year-old girl hoped to be buried in her prom dress. "I want to be dressy for my family," she explained.[20]

Gangs and their drug subculture often fill this void of family. What follows is a psychotic version of *Oliver Twist* that would have shocked even Dickens' jaded sensibilities, as armed neighborhood drug dealers become local father figures. For inner-city children these new values have warped a normal feature of adolescence, peer pressure, into a force of incalculable destruction. A record number of children seventeen years old or younger are now arrested in D.C. on murder or weapons charges. In the three years from 1986 to 1988, 43 juveniles were arrested for homicide; in just 1989 and 1990, 129 were arrested.[21] Twenty-four percent of District defendants charged with homicide in 1988 were sixteen to eighteen years old at the time of the crime. Just two years later that percentage had risen to 34 percent.[22]

The symbiosis of delinquency and drugs has been crucial to this upswing. Youth gangs are now one of the main agents of criminality in the District.[23] Although drugs per se are often seen as the culprit for Washington's wave of violence, District police have concluded that murders in the city typically owe less to the illegal narcotics trade than to a culture of bellicose greed and "disrespect for life" that has accompanied the current crime surge.[24] D.C. prosecutors attribute much of the drop in conviction rates to the fear of teenage assailants "whose callousness intimidates witnesses."[25] Even among girls, the arrest rate for serious crimes increased 57 percent in just one year, 1991.[26]

A 1992 study provided a more complete assessment of the dimensions of the crisis. Research conducted by the National Center on Institutions and Alternatives that year found that 42 percent of Washington's black men aged eighteen to thirty–five were under criminal justice supervision, that is, in jail, on probation or parole, or out on bond or outstanding warrant.[27] The study estimated that as many as 70 percent of Washington's black men have been arrested by the time they turn thirty-five, and about 85 percent are arrested at some point in their lives. And while its authors insisted that the study revealed merely that the criminal justice system, by replacing the "social safety net . . . [with] a dragnet," was "criminalizing people we should be treating in other ways,"[28] there was another, more direct conclusion. For D.C.'s children, society has altogether imploded. As former police chief Maurice Turner observed, "In this town, the weapons have always been out there; it's the behavior of the young people that's changed."[29] Asked to give back to a family and society that in many cases have deserted them, the District's children have responded, with some justification, by pointing a gun with one hand and raising their middle finger on the other.

There is a third and final important theme to the Great Havoc, one which, like the other two, suggests that U.S. crime rates will continue to zigzag upward for the foreseeable future. And let us admit this third truth frankly: we are still not willing to do what is necessary to pull back from the edge. We can lay some of the blame for this complacency on human nature, which compels Americans, like all other peoples, to embrace ideas and government policies that require as little self-evaluation or change in lifestyle as is thought possible. Gun control, victims' rights and other popular anticrime proposals capitalize on this tendency directly. So too does the assumption that the current Havoc, what we have come to describe as the "crime problem," can be solved merely by hiring more police and constructing more prisons. The idea behind this approach, stripped to its essence, is to forcibly subdue the more enthusiastic, criminal participants in the popular extreme individualism. This helps us to avoid broader soul-searching, and the recriminations that would come from realizing that the clues to halting the chaos lie within us all, in the selfish values that we as a people have lately adopted.

Yet we know that such "get tough" programs, in the end, cannot by themselves bring our national tale of woe to a happy ending. These policies, while useful in the short run, are doomed to failure, if only because a nation practicing self–government cannot employ enough policemen to ensure order if a majority of its citizens no longer view the rule of law—or, more to the point, anything—as a moral absolute. Increasingly, we do not want anyone telling us what we can and cannot do, including the government. Criminals simply join in this national chorus with a bit more fervor.

We must recognize that if government does not wield these essential powers, or if it lacks public support, other, less trustworthy fellows will fill the void. Thus it is that while state and local police expenditures rose more than sevenfold from 1970 to 1991, and the U.S. prison population tripled over the same period, crime rates continued to skyrocket.[30] The criminal justice triad alone cannot do the job. We must look elsewhere for solutions.

Instead, we too often look for scapegoats. One of the worst is white Americans' common perception of crime as a "black thing," a troubling aberration unique to the inner city. Ghetto residents are thought of sympathetically, but nonetheless strictly, as unfortunate members of an urban community with pathologies fundamentally different from the rest of society. The Republic is ultimately safe, it is assumed, because whites are in the majority and remain good law-abiding types themselves.

The residents of Washington must be excused the smile that might well come over their lips upon hearing such analysis. For it is becoming clear that for all the well-documented problems in the ghetto, our inner cities are but the first major tracts of this Republic to be surrendered to criminals. The crime that today grips the nation's capital is lapping at the borders of middle-class white society as well, despite confident suburban denials.

Those Americans fortunate enough to view Washington, D.C., at a distance, and who conclude that their own communities will be magically spared such happenings, should bear in mind two immensely important facts. First, the juvenile crime rate. The crime rate among white juveniles, while hitherto well below that of African-Americans, is now growing *twice as fast* as the black juvenile crime rate is growing, juveniles being the age group that is the most crime-prone and predictive of future crime rates. The FBI recently noted in its *Uniform Crime Reports* that during the 1980s, juvenile crime increased 27 percent. For blacks the juvenile crime rate rose 19 percent; for whites it rose 44 percent, or *more than double* the rate of growth among blacks.[31] The FBI noted that juvenile crime rates are soaring not only among "minority youth in urban areas," but also among "all races, all social classes and lifestyles."[32] From 1990 to 1991 juvenile crime in suburban counties grew 5.2 percent. Violent crime rose 11.8 percent in that one year. Close to 80 percent of these offenders were white. Crime in rural Midwestern states with almost exclusively white populations has also risen dramatically in recent years.[33] An estimated 38.9 percent of white males in metropolitan Phoenix have a criminal record before they turn eighteen.[34] Indeed, between 1965 and 1991 the violent crime rate among *white* Americans rose nearly *250 percent.*[35] The number of fifteen-to-nineteen-year-olds of all races is expected to rise 23 percent over the next decade, further aggravating these trends.[36] If, as appears likely, the black community is reaching its saturation point for criminal violence, while whites are only beginning to succumb to the same trends, this erosion of the crime gap between the races should continue; and crime rates will continue to soar. The ghetto is proving to be color-blind.

A second fact to remember is equally enlightening: the only reason that Washington, D.C., has not slid into complete and permanent chaos is that the rest of society, via the federal government, is still capable of and committed to dispatching enough force to the city to maintain at least a semblance of order. Should the rest of America fall to the criminal forces now strangling the inner cities, these Americans, unlike Washingtonians, will have no one to save them from themselves. Of course, we only kid ourselves by pointing optimistically to occasional downward blips in crime rates that, overall, have only one credible trajectory—up, in a big way. While some cite, for instance, very recent crime figures as hopeful evidence that we have turned a corner (the violent crime rate rose only 1.1 percent in 1992), Washington's recent agonies again provide relevant perspective. The District's murder rate declined in 1992. But those who hailed the capital's progress were chastened a year later when the rate resumed its climb.[37] We must look at broad trends, and their direction is unmistakable. In view of all this, especially the growing menace of white juvenile crime, it was of more than passing interest that recently, authorities in one well-off suburban Virginia county outside Washington reported that the number of juvenile arrests rose 42 percent over the prior year. Local authorities termed this a "disturbing" increase, which, it turned out, was mirrored throughout the rest of the D.C. suburban region. Indeed, the District was the only area jurisdiction to report a decrease in juvenile arrests during that period.[38]

For all of our animated attempts to think otherwise, those of us looking with horror and amazement at Washington, D.C., should not see a unique display of anarchy and bloodshed confined to the ghetto. We see instead a true "model city" for the modern United States, a portent of things to come for the nation as a whole should we not heed the social lessons carved into the precocious faces of our capital city's children.

PART ONE

MARCHING AS TO WAR

CHAPTER ONE

The Slain Leviathan

[C]ovenants, without the sword, are but words.

—Thomas Hobbes

So this is how it all ends.

As the twentieth century sears its final momentous years into the tablets of recorded human existence, Americans should, by most superficial measures, be jubilant. Our Republic is capping off what arguably qualifies as the most remarkable century of national ascent in history. Having entered the 1900s an immature, cloistered society more concerned with subduing Indians than policing the globe, our nation has grown up fast—and impressively. The United States began this century an underdeveloped nation struggling to find a competitive niche in an international economy still dominated by the Old World; it ends it with unprecedented economic supremacy in a truly global market. This was in large part a function of her military skills. America, alone among nations, reaped huge profits from the two world wars, profits that her victories allowed her to keep. America's bumptious egalitarian culture soon captivated the postwar world, thanks largely to her near monopoly on the entertainment industry, and only the grumpiest cultural chauvinists complained.

America's principal external foe during this century was also disposed of in due course. Unable to put away her shield to return to the previously all-consuming business of national self-improvement, the Republic reluctantly wielded it again when threatened by her most potent foreign adversary to date—a nuclear-armed Marxism hatched from the writings of an ungrateful ward of capitalist England. America managed to wind up even this titanic struggle in the relatively short span of a half century, her Soviet adversary crumbling into quarreling new nation-states. Even after expending trillions of dollars in support of this enterprise, America finds herself at the end of the Cold War flush with one-fourth of the world's gross domestic product, roughly twice the amount of her nearest rival, Japan. The democratic ideas once under siege now seem so irrepressible that some scholars, borrowing from the same philosophical heritage that spawned the previously mighty enemy Marxism, talk of the "end of History." America, it seems, can now simply give a content sigh and relax, basking in her glory as world savior and reaping a handsome profit to boot.

But History, it seems, has not finished frolicking just yet. Something in the triumphant nation is amiss. It is evident in the public opinion surveys that show Americans are decidedly unimpressed by our recent accomplishments. Seventy percent of Americans believe the nation is "off track."[1] Seventy-six percent of us think that the United States is in a "moral and spiritual decline."[2] Beneath this national pessimism, reflecting in part Americans' famous penchant for self-analysis, lies an undeniable despair about the future of the land. The Republic's victories abroad are being spoiled by a nagging sense of impending calamity at home. We sense, it would seem, that our nation is slowly being torn apart. Unlike the official, abrupt dissolution of the Soviet Union and Warsaw Pact, America's domestic implosion does not reveal itself in a single instance or act. Mostly we must listen for the indicative groans of decay around us, occasionally punctuated by especially abominable acts of violence that drive home the full dimensions of the crisis.

Quietly underlying the brutality that most conspicuously reveals these trends is a seductive revolution in the way Americans think about one another. That is, we think about each other less, if at all, compared to years past. The ancient cultural prohibitions against self-indulgence that formerly tied Americans together in a community of mutual concern have been summarily repealed. The effects have been diverse but always vivid. The most immediately visible manifestation of this change has, naturally enough, been sensual. The antisocial excitement of the senses by narcotics and hallucinogens is but the most notorious form assumed by this newly released egoism. Less fearsome, because it does not flare up as quickly into armed aggression, has been the disbandment of the family, the oldest and most stabilizing of human institutions. Rising illegitimacy and divorce rates provide proof of a society that no longer resolves to provide children with fathers, who are biologically entrusted with teaching boys, the future recruits for the criminal class, proper behavior and citizenship. The materialism of the day, evident in middle-class "yuppie" culture, is another sign of decline. The objects of shared national purpose that formerly gave us a common, cohesive mission—i.e., attachment to family, community, and religion—have given way to a new emphasis on pursuing individual possessions and entertainment. A rising crescendo of statistics makes these facts undeniable. Perhaps the most revealing datum is one suggesting that Americans literally cannot stand to live with one another: almost 40 percent of American adults are not married.[3] We live isolated lives because we have forgotten how to live together happily. Once self-interest takes precedence over love and the common good, no two people can stand to be in the same room with each other, much less cobble together a viable society. In these social developments and others we see the replacement of the former social contract of unity and self-preservation in favor of a new one, unwritten and undiscussed but nevertheless almost universally practiced, to silently dissolve the civilization which makes such accords possible.

Crucial to all of this was the decline of religion—not just the Judeo-Christian tradition that guided earlier Americans, but all worship of the divine, of a Being more important than one's own ego. Religion is vital for providing an internal, omnipresent deterrent to antisocial conduct through the fear of supernatural punishment, and the subsequent creation of conscience. Equally essential is religion's unique capacity to compel a surrender of at least overt selfishness. A higher power must be obeyed and propitiated through a taming of the otherwise predominant self-absorption that eventually nibbles away at society. The prosperity of the post–World War II era made celestial concerns seem less important, and the opportunities for vice more abundant. A new set of ideas gave Americans a new master: our own tumultuous appetites. And ideas, it has been shown, have consequences.

Both the political Left and Right, as currently constituted, have contributed to this decomposition of the American Republic. Ultra-individualism or social atomism, the theory of radical individualism dominant on the Left, is one intellectual impetus behind these phenomena. Sprouting from the classical liberalism of the British philosophers Thomas Hobbes and John Locke, which provided for a basic, limited conception of individual rights, ultraindividualism has broadened this principle to view society and the government that sustains it as existing primarily for safeguarding an expanding range of individual entitlements. Prominent on the American Right is a related theory, libertarianism. It is a strain of British liberalism that argues for much the same outcome. Ultraindividualists emphasize personal fulfillment based on individual liberties. Often these are rooted in sexual, ethnic or occasionally criminal self-expression. Many members of this philosophical camp also deny that criminals are individually responsible for their actions. Libertarians similarly focus on individual rights, but mainly those concerning economic self-gain. This is to be achieved by limiting the role and size of government. Libertarians leave out of their creed an apology for criminals, and are thus generally more popular with the American public, whose lives and property would otherwise be at criminals' mercy. Democrats often identify with ultraindividualism, Republicans with libertarianism, although the lines have become more blurred of late. Both parties can at least agree that success in politics today requires prominent appeals to such corrosive self-interest in their respective platforms and initiatives.

And, of course, there is crime—the most spectacular evidence of this breakdown. That we lack even a basic agreement over what constitutes crime gives further notice of our fragmentation. Most Americans tend to view crime as a parasitic phenomenon, something that need only be plucked from the skin of an otherwise healthy body politic with the scalpel of more effective law enforcement. They typically term the most obvious signs of social disunity the crime problem, suggesting that such disorders developed independently from the society suffering them. Crime, it follows, can be rolled back merely with more marshals and jails, instead of significant changes in culture and soul. Other Americans, concentrated in academia, government and the press, take an opposite view. They believe crime to be essentially a disease that certain individuals contract from society. For some the cause of crime is poverty, or drugs, or racism; for others it is a combination thereof or a result of other factors. These two factions enjoy amity in their shared assumption that black Americans are uniquely susceptible to criminality, and fundamentally different in this regard from other groups. But as the crime rate among white Americans continues to rise, and as crime spills out from the barriers that white society has attempted, both intellectually and physically, to erect around the inner city, no rationalization can obscure the nature of the events we are experiencing.

In America today a crime of some sort occurs every two seconds. Somewhere in America property is stolen every 4 seconds; a burglary is committed every 10 seconds; someone is assaulted every 29 seconds; a woman is raped every 46 seconds.[4] An increasing proportion of the crime in America is violent. The violent crime rate has risen 560 percent since 1960.[5] The number of violent crimes committed annually is at an all-time high.[6] Nearly one-third of crimes today involve violence.[7] Each year, one out of four households is the target of a violent crime or theft.[8] Eighty-three percent of children born in 1975 will be victims or intended victims of violent crimes at least once in their lifetimes. Fifty-two percent will be victims of such crimes more than once.[9]

Murder is becoming one of America's most popular methods of dispute resolution. A citizen of automobile-dependent Los Angeles is more likely to die from a bullet wound than from a traffic accident. Since 1990 more than 90,000 Americans have been murdered, more than twice the number of American fatalities in the Vietnam War.[10] A resident of a large American city today is more likely to be a victim of homicide than the average U.S. soldier in World War II.[11]

Like most social dysfunctions, crime is regressive. Lower-income Americans are from two to three times more likely to be prey to a violent crime than middle- and upper-income people.[12] Blacks are 41 percent more likely and Latinos 32 percent more likely than whites to be violently victimized.[13] While 27 percent of white Americans believe crime to be a "real problem" in their neighborhood, 49 percent of African-Americans cite the same concern.[14]

Violent crime is worse in today's bureaucratized major cities than in the government-starved frontier towns of a century ago. Observed one historian for Wichita State University, an institution in one of Wyatt Earp's former jurisdictions, the dusty, chaotic streets of the nineteenth-century Wild West were safer than modern America's urban cores. "Homicide in cattle towns was rare, and homicide by gunplay was almost nonexistent," he noted.[15]

Crime disrupts the lives of more than just its immediate victims. Crime's multiplier effect on the economy, for instance, is enormous and growing. Although private crime control industries (security-systems vendors, security-guard firms, gun manufacturers) have done a brisk business in the wake of the current crime surge, the economy as a whole has taken it on the chin. One "conservative" estimate found that crime costs American businesses $128 billion annually in direct losses, litigation expenses and security outlays. This represents about 69 percent of all after-tax corporate profits in America. Since companies pass virtually all of these costs on to the consumer through higher prices, the estimated annual "crime tax" that results is $1,376 for every American household. The direct cost of crime consumes 2.3 percent of America's entire gross domestic product,[16] diverting money into security apparatuses and insurance that could otherwise be invested in research and development to improve the nation's international competitiveness. One source estimates the average psychological cost of crimes against Americans at $16,000 per assault, $19,200 per robbery and $54,000 per attempted or completed rape,[17] which, if included in the calculations, would make the nation's total loss to crime of still greater proportions. When all of the direct and indirect financial costs are taken into account, crime costs Americans an estimated $425 billion a year.[18]

Many Americans lose their jobs or employment prospects as a direct result of crime. One New York public policy group found that 26 percent of the city's small businesses said they had trouble hiring workers because of crime. Eighteen percent said crime had caused their sales to suffer; 17 percent were open fewer hours; 14 percent had employees who had quit because of crime; and 12 percent rejected proposed business expansions.[19]

Obviously but importantly, crime is also a big hassle. Sixty percent of Americans limit the places they will go by themselves because of fear of crime.[20] Twenty-two percent limit the places or times that they will work, a figure that rises to 33 and 37 percent for blacks and Latinos.[21] Crime forces people to purchase and use cumbersome locks and security devices; the locksmith industry does a brisk business unlocking cars whose keys are accidentally left inside. Checkout lines at grocery stores are longer because of time-consuming procedures for thwarting bad checks. Drug smuggling often makes passing through customs and immigration checkpoints a half-day ordeal. And in a hundred other small ways during the day, the ever present threat of crime makes Americans' lives more complicated and less pleasant.

Nevertheless, we not only put up with all of this, but seem to prefer to adapt to rising crime rates rather than to make the seemingly greater sacrifices necessary to reduce them. Others of us find it difficult even to address forthrightly the reasons for our condition, especially those of us who are uncomfortable with holding offenders individually responsible for their crimes. Thus, the subject must be changed. Sometimes this is accomplished by bringing up white-collar crime; it is proposed that middle-class society cannot properly condemn inner-city street criminals as long as crimes by the rich, such as price-fixing and pollution, are committed. This argument does, in one sense, register an important and valid point: lawlessness in the United States is today so widespread that no social class is above its reach, especially given the continued steep climb in white crime rates. But the retort to this line of reasoning could be supplied by any rape victim: there is a big difference between paying a dollar a week more for gasoline because of an illegal trust among oil companies and being forced at gunpoint to take a man's penis in one's mouth. Short of all-out war, violent crime is simply the most degrading and unbearable experience to which a human being can be subjected. Yet too many of us are more attentive to other concerns, even as large pockets of metropolitan areas are ceded daily to the criminal element. This neglect has produced a genuine sort of second-class citizenship for the residents of these abandoned areas, citizens whose political system is now essentially anarchy tempered by vigilantism.

For all our reluctance to make the sacrifices essential for preventing the growth of crime, Americans overwhelmingly recognize the present Great Havoc as the calamity that it is. From the beginning of this spasm of violent crime in the early 1960s, polls have consistently revealed crime to be the public's second-biggest political worry. Some interpretation of the polling data is in order, given that crime has frequently been subsumed under labels that divert the culpability for offenses from individuals to external events or other, nonhuman entities. But whether the term is riots, urban disorder, drugs or, most recently, guns, violent crime repeatedly surfaces as the runner-up for top political priority. The only concern to edge out crime, at least in periods of financial downturn, is the economy,[22] the imperial issue in modern American politics, and itself an indicator of the materialistic origins of America's crime crisis. Crime grows in large part because the most important concern to a majority of Americans is economic self-interest. This materialism inevitably trickles down to the lower classes, whose decisions in life have left them few opportunities to reach relative economic prosperity through legitimate means. The surge in crime reinforces Americans' devotion to economic security by destroying lower-class neighborhoods, thus heightening the desire to escape the ensuing perils by moving to the suburbs and other, more upscale areas. All the while politicians of both major parties exploit this egoism with a self-interest of their own, one that we must expect from faithful listeners to modern America's *vox populi*.

Remarkably constant through all of this is crime's durability as a dominant issue among an electorate whose intellectual opinion leaders sometimes seem vexed by this mere recognition of the problem. Even in 1968, when American involvement in Vietnam was at its peak and most journalists had focused on the war during that year's presidential campaign, the main concerns in the election, as evidenced by polls and the election's outcome, were the economy and crime/riots.[23] Americans today, when asked about their own circumstances, fear crime more than severe economic dislocation. Reflecting this ranking of dreads was a poll taken just prior to President Clinton's inauguration in January 1993, following an election in which appeals to materialistic self-interest among recession-weary Americans provided the dominant campaign theme for all three major candidates. The poll found that while 34 percent and 29 percent of Americans "worry a lot" about losing health insurance or their jobs, 36 percent fear becoming a crime victim.[24] A more recent poll determined that 62 percent of Americans say they are "truly desperate" about crime and personal safety, up from 34 percent only five years before.[25]

Even the citizens of a liberty-indulgent land such as the United States generally recognize that government's first and most basic duty to its citizens is to provide for the order that makes other, less vital freedoms possible. In recent years American government at all levels has, by this standard, been an undeniable failure. The current turmoil, indeed, threatens all the benefits that flow from organized living. Improved education, a cleaner environment and all the other welcome luxuries of civilization are simply impossible without the underlying foundation of the rule of law. And while most of us instinctively understand that the public is ultimately responsible for

restoring order—namely, by altering popular attitudes and habits—
we can still rightly expect government to lead the way out of this
morass, and to ensure that those citizens who are less enchanted
with the rule of law are compelled to mend their ways as well.

Of course, this notion of crime control as government's foremost
duty, and the corresponding conception of the right of personal security as the citizen's core civil liberty, did not originate in this crime-
beset age that belatedly recognizes their renewed appeal. These ideas
are literally as old as civilization itself. In America these principles
stretch back to the British philosophy that made law and order the
bedrock of government, while simultaneously laying as the cornerstone for legitimate government its protection of individual rights—
rights that would, at times, prove turbulent in practice. It was this
heritage that the Founders of the American Republic memorialized in
the founding charter of our government, a heritage that must be
understood to fully grasp the extent of our State's forsaking of its
most fundamental obligation.

Crime, we will see, has been a perennial American preoccupation,
largely because of what it means to be an American.

PEACE THROUGH GOVERNMENT: A HISTORY
OF AMERICA'S WAR OF ALL AGAINST ALL

When European settlers began clustering in communities along the
eastern shores of North America, crime was both the most and the
least of their worries. Crimes against persons and property, the only
behavior that our relativistic age recognizes as criminal, were almost
nonexistent in those small towns of caring, vigilant neighbors and
strict Christian precepts. Indeed, the whole reason why the earliest
European-Americans had time to affix scarlet letters to adulterers
was that there was so little else to punish. As an everyday phenomenon, crime as we define it hardly occurred. But they enjoyed this
freedom from crime only because their shared notions of community
and faith provided a potent internal and external repellent to antisocial conduct. Many of these seventeenth-century pioneers had
recently escaped the English Civil War. They knew firsthand the
potential for chaos once obedience to these communal principles
broke down. The fate of their own precarious civilization on the
edge of a vast, unexplored wilderness rested on whether loyalty to
God, family and community, as enforced by the criminal code,
would overcome the designs of selfish conquest that lurk in the

heart of every man, and that had been set loose in their homeland's fratricidal struggle. To them, effective criminal justice was not one of several equally deserving concerns in the cafeteria of public policy. Criminal justice was certainly not subordinate to economic prosperity. It was supreme. It meant life or death.

Their countrymen back in the British Isles were drawing similar conclusions from the Civil War. Their conclusions, though, were more secular, and thus more revolutionary, than those of the North American colonists. British political philosophers were preparing for a dramatic departure from past Western thought, a break which the colonists would enshrine, somewhat incongruously, in the founding government documents adopted after their rebellion against the British Empire. These otherwise diverse theories shared the notion of a social contract entered into upon mankind's hypothetical exit from the State of Nature. This idea, whose roots extended back to the Sophists of ancient Greece, held that a society is not just unless its institutions would have been selected and established by its citizens had they created their society from scratch. To envision this sort of primitive constitutional convention, these theorists pictured untamed men emerging from a presocietal forest, the State of Nature, in order to set up a government, institute the rule of law and thereby beget civilization and all its comforts. Thus, for instance, a society whose government denied freedom of religion was, by this theory, unjust because rational people creating a society after leaving the State of Nature would surely desire and safeguard such a right. These British philosophers differed as to which rights they thought essential enough for their denial to render society unjust. But as a theoretical device for scrutinizing the fairness of political institutions, the social contract was firmly embedded in the thinking of America's governing class by the time of the American Revolution. Indeed, the unique historical circumstances of the founding of the English colonies seemed to many Americans to represent the very incarnation of this theory. Early charters of self-government such as the Mayflower Compact, which established the earliest political institutions in the colonies, appeared to be real-life social contracts designed to repulse the sylvan State of Nature surrounding them.

The idea of the social contract held significant—and, as it turns out, disturbing—implications for the citizen's relations with the State. A contract enumerates rights and duties held by the contracting parties. While such legal instruments, as entered into by private parties, were very common at the time of the Constitution's framing, the idea of a contract between government and governed was unheard of. The whole notion seemed like treason. Prior to the writings of the social-contract theorists, the concept of political rights held by individuals against the State was simply alien to most men. Up to that time Western societies had been preoccupied with instituting a safe, stable civilization following the disorder of the Dark Ages. Both Church and State agreed that society should be regarded as an irreducible single unit. Typically society was looked upon as either a big family with a fatherly leader in church or government, or a single organism of which all citizens were parts. Under this conception of the State, the idea of individual rights made no sense. Children could not claim liberties against their father; feet could not brandish rights against the brain. The persuasiveness of the social-contract/individual-rights theory is evidenced by the fact that the medieval Englishman's incomprehension of rights is itself equally incomprehensible to Americans today.

The theory of the social contract found an especially receptive audience in the North American colonies. The philosopher who blended these dual views into a social fabric that would one day swaddle the infant American Republic was Thomas Hobbes. Like most philosophies, Hobbes's can best be understood as a reaction to the events of his time. Hobbes was born in April 1588. He entered a society that was bracing itself for the arrival of the Spanish Armada, a naval force dispatched by Spain's King Philip II to settle once and for all which nation would rule the seas (and thus the developing overseas colonies, including those in the Americas). We are told by Hobbes and his biographers that his mother was so racked by the national apprehension that she gave birth to him prematurely. Hobbes later explained that he was thus born "a twin with fear," and understandably "abominated his country's enemies and loved peace."[26] The English Civil War later deepened his obsession with peace and its domestic prerequisite, order. As he saw Parliament turn against Crown and both sides subsequently enlist contending forces to spoliate the nation's countryside, a fight that culminated in the beheading of the English monarch over a century before France would behead her own, a horrified Hobbes reacted by expounding a political theory that justified order at seemingly any price. In 1651, following the war, he published this theory in his greatest work, *Leviathan*.

Never has a thinker been so radical in trying to prohibit radicalism. Hobbes offered a political philosophy that sought to abolish civil insurrection by making fidelity to the law the keystone of the nation's political structure. He did so with an original and extraordinary twist. He proposed that the individual be absorbed into a slavish society wholly obedient to the State, but based this surrender of the self on a frank appeal to the grossest sort of atomistic self-interest. The State deserved loyalty not because of patriotism or love of a theoretically extended family, but because, and only as long as, the State faithfully served the selfish desires of its citizens. From this grand *quid pro quo* arose the modern notion of rights. Rights were to be guaranteed by the State as long as individuals honored their own corresponding duty to obey the law. But whereas later theorists would discard Hobbes's limited conception of rights in favor of a more generous grab bag, Hobbes thought it best to concentrate on fundamentals. He recognized exactly one civil right: the right of personal security.

Colored by the terrifying anarchy of civil war, Hobbes's philosophy was built on what many Americans today would consider a highly negative conception of human nature. Hobbes saw man as inherently selfish. Thus, he concluded that life in a State of Nature unhindered by a common government was not a refreshing, pastoral existence in a peaceful commune. It was hell. Or, to use his synonym, it was war. With no government to deter them, men reverted to their basest, most egoistic instincts, murdering and brutalizing one another, plundering each other's families and possessions with no moral scruples; since, Hobbes insisted, there *was* no morality in the State of Nature. He observed: ". . . during the time men live without a common power to keep them all in awe, they are in that condition which is called *war;* and such a war as is of every man against every man. . . . In such condition, there is no place for industry, because the fruit thereof is uncertain: and consequently . . . no society, and which is worst of all, continual fear, and danger of violent death; and the life of man, solitary, poor, nasty, brutish, and short."[27]

Small wonder, then, that the weaker competitors in this earliest warfare sought to escape. One of the more obvious means of terminating the chaos, and the one they chose, was hiring a bodyguard. This was the genesis of government. Government was designed to inspire "awe" in the outlaw revelers by using force against combatants who refused to lay down their arms, and to deter a relapse into this former state by threatening like force against future aggressors. However, this method of "getting themselves out from that miserable condition of war" was not without its costs. The agreement entailed reciprocal obligations from the societal trailblazers who had retained the sovereign's services. They were required to show absolute allegiance to the new ruler. Only in return for this loyalty would the sovereign uphold the citizen's lone cognizable right of personal security.

Hobbes described the metamorphosis of the presocietal right of nature to the civil right of personal security as a mass, simultaneous swapping of one liberty for another. As part of the "mutual transferring of right" known as the social contract, those emerging from the State of Nature agreed to surrender their right of self-preservation, or right of nature, enjoyed in the State of Nature (and akin to a right of vigilantism) in exchange for the State's promise to uphold the rule of law. Hobbes believed that this mass surrender would inevitably occur once men tired of the bacchanalia of violence and saw the advantages of life under a common ruler. "The passions that incline men to peace are: fear of death; desire of such things as are necessary to commodious living; and a hope by their industry to obtain them."

It is "reason" itself that "suggesteth" the necessary arrangement for the transferring of rights to the State: the drafting of "convenient articles of peace upon which men may be drawn to agreement."[28] These contractual terms were to provide "more than consent, or concord; it is a real unity of them all in one and the same person, made by covenant of every man with every man. . . ." Thus did Hobbes try to preserve the "real unity" of the traditional, organic political regimes of his time by clinging to the optimistic notion that the rights-armed individuals executing the social contract still came together in "one and the same person." "This done," Hobbes continues, "the multitude so united in one person is called a COMMONWEALTH; in Latin, CIVITAS." All will have agreed to trade their right of nature, or absolute right of self-defense, for a right of personal security within the commonwealth premised on unquestioning subservience to the common sovereign. Who, then, is to be the sovereign selected pursuant to this contract? He is to be the "great LEVIATHAN, or rather, to speak more reverently, of that mortal god to which we owe, under the immortal God, our peace and defence."[29]

In an age that almost prides itself on unfamiliarity with Scripture, the reference to the Leviathan seems old-fashioned and befuddling. To Hobbes's countrymen, however, no explanation was necessary, nor was one given. The Leviathan was the term used in the Book of Job to denote an unidentified species of aquatic beast. Many

Englishmen at the time thought it to mean a sea monster; modern scholars believe it may have been a crocodile. What is clear is that it signified an "awe-inspiring" creature that scared wayward men into submission. It was this "mortal god" to which men desperate to escape the terrors of the State of Nature paid homage under Hobbes's theory. And it was to be perpetual homage: "[N]one of his subjects, by any pretense of forfeiture, can be freed from his subjection."[30] Hobbes presented only two scenarios in which men were permitted to violate this contract. One was if the Leviathan threatened the subject with death. The second opt-out provision was if the Leviathan failed to uphold the citizens' right of personal security. As Hobbes saw it, "the definition of *injustice* is no other than *the not performance of covenant*."[31] A Leviathan that failed to maintain order by inspiring "awe" had failed to live up to its end of the agreement—was therefore literally unjust—and deserved to perish.

Tellingly, Hobbes's theory is best remembered today for inaugurating the modern infatuation with rights, even though, if that was Hobbes's intention, he had a rather poor understanding of how to prevent civil disunity. The first generation of Americans saw other elements of Hobbes's philosophy more to their liking. The Founders of the American Republic, particularly the subgroup who framed the U.S. Constitution, believed in a "conception of mankind [that] has justifiably been termed Hobbesian."[32] Of course, few Americans in the late eighteenth century could bear the thought that subjects were morally forbidden to rebel against their ruler except in the narrow circumstances Hobbes listed. They preferred the less pinched version of Hobbesian thought offered by a later Englishman, John Locke. Locke's influence in the colonies was profound. Thomas Jefferson called him one of "the three greatest men the world had ever produced," and proposed that his *Second Treatise on Civil Government* be required reading at the University of Virginia, which he founded. Samuel Adams wrote his thesis at Harvard on Locke's theories. Visiting England, Benjamin Franklin told Locke's countrymen that his thoughts had spurred many of their North American colonists into insurrection against the empire.[33] The language of the Declaration of Independence, Constitution and Bill of Rights is expressly Lockean.

Locke lived in happier times, and felt free to reject some of Hobbes's gloomier assessment of man. Locke wrote his most important political works in the wake of the Glorious Revolution of 1688, a bloodless coup that established once and for all Parliament's supremacy over the king. Locke's *Second Treatise on Civil Government*, published in 1690, was in many respects a literary welcome mat for the newly installed limited monarchs, whom Parliament had invited from Holland and who took the throne after agreeing to an explicit social contract recognizing Parliament's predominance. Locke could afford to be more charitable.

Still, his conception of man and life in the State of Nature is not nearly as rosy as many of his present-day admirers would contend. Locke's State of Nature lacks Hobbes's graphic description of men constantly at each other's throats. Indeed, at one point he directly took issue with Hobbes: ". . . here we have the plain difference between the state of Nature and the state of war, which however some men have confounded, are as far distant as a state of peace, good will, mutual assistance, and preservation; and a state of enmity, malice, violence and mutual destruction are one from another." Locke based this disagreement with Hobbes, though, on an odd semantic quibble. "Men living together according to reason without a common superior on earth, with authority to judge between them, is properly the state of Nature. But force, or a declared design of force upon the person of another, where there is no common superior on earth to appeal to for relief, is the state of war."[34] Was Locke being a Pollyanna, or just ornery? Since he conceded that the common element in both the State of Nature and the supposedly distinct "state of war" is the lack of a "common superior," the difference between the two, if at all meaningful, is only temporary. The lack of a "common superior" would surely act as a massive inducement to anarchy, making the State of Nature but a brief phase before its more opportunistic members turn the wilderness into the Hobbesian nightmare of the "war of all against all."

Although most students of Locke conclude from these and other scattered remarks that his vision of the State of Nature was the opposite of Hobbes's, they should read on. For what Locke lacked in consistency, he generally made up for in hardheaded, empiricist* realism. Elsewhere Locke made clear that his earlier, apparent sim-

---

*Empiricism is the philosophy that considers all knowledge to be based on the senses and human experience. The empiricist contends that the reader knows of this book's existence because he sees and touches it. Locke started the modern British empiricist tradition, which has been highly influential in America.

Empiricism's main philosphical foe is rationalism. Rationalism teaches that some ideas are innate, present since birth, not learned from sensory experience. For instance, some rationalists defend belief in God as arising from an innate knowledge of God's existence.

This is a long-running feud that goes back to Aristotle and Plato, respectively.

plemindedness was just an inept sally at Hobbes, with whom he actually had much in common. For one thing, Locke similarly recognized a broad natural right of self-preservation in the State of Nature. Surely this would be unnecessary in a harmonious communal utopia. Indeed, this right was all the more indispensable for Locke given that, unlike Hobbes, he recognized a code of natural laws binding in the State of Nature despite the lack of a common rights enforcer. Lacking a "common superior," responsibility for enforcing the natural law devolved upon individual inhabitants of the State of Nature, "whereby every one has a right to punish the transgressors of that law to such a degree as may hinder its violation." Absent a common sovereign, men were obliged to mete out self-help, vigilante justice against violators of the natural law. "For the law of Nature would, as all other laws that concern men in this world, be in vain if there were nobody that in the state of Nature had a power to execute that law, and thereby preserve the innocent and restrain offenders."[35]

This seems awfully harsh for a land of "men living together according to reason" in a state of "peace, good will, mutual assistance, and preservation." It turns out that Locke's conception of the State of Nature is not at all a blissful vision of happy campers. Like Hobbes, Locke recognized that a natural right of self-preservation was vital because it was inevitable that men would resort to "declared designs of force" on each other. Locke even conceded at different points in his *Second Treatise* that life in the State of Nature and the "enjoyment" of one's rights are in fact "very uncertain and constantly exposed to the invasion of others." This "condition which, however free, is full of fears and continual dangers" is a "very unsafe, very insecure" existence. Ultimately life in the State of Nature is so intolerable that it leads men to "join in society . . . for the mutual preservation of their lives, liberties and estates, which I call by the general name—property."[36] This instability derived in turn from a lack of uniform punishment for wrongdoing; presocietal men were unequally equipped to "punish the offender" by serving as their own "executioner of the law of Nature."[37]

Such "executioners," while sometimes "awe-inspiring," were necessarily unorganized and ineffective because of an absence of unity of command. Although Locke thought this rough justice acceptable in the short run, it was a poor substitute for equal justice under law, the kind a common sovereign could provide. This criminality and strife could be eliminated only by a public authority capable of enforcing the natural law with independence and detachment, an umpire to officiate the game of life and mediate disputes impartially. Locke observed that "in the State of Nature every one has the executive power of the law of Nature." This made for poor neighbors. Locke explained, "I doubt not but it will be objected that it is unreasonable for men to be judges in their own cases, that self-love will make men partial to themselves, and their friends; and, on the other side, ill-nature, passion, and revenge will carry them too far in punishing others, and hence nothing but confusion and disorder will follow, and that therefore God hath certainly appointed government to restrain the partiality and violence of men."[38] "Confusion and disorder," "partiality and violence"—all because of "self-love": Hobbes could hardly have said it better himself. Locke likewise concurred with Hobbes as to the solution for this lawlessness. "[C]ivil government is the proper remedy for the inconveniences of the state of Nature, which must certainly be great where men may be judges in their own case."[39]

Where Hobbes and Locke agreed, then, was that personal security, obtained through order, was the baseline of rights for any society. Whether to escape the "war of all against all" or the tyranny of "impartial" vigilantes, men leaving the State of Nature did so mainly to gain and preserve certain freedoms from encroachment by their covetous, self-interested neighbors. For Hobbes, man's quest for the good life ended upon reaching a State which provided this bare right of personal security. For Locke, man's devotion to the State was not required unless the magistrate also recognized the distinct, broader rights package of life, liberty and property, only the last term of which Jefferson modified in the Declaration of Independence. Whereas Hobbes allowed for disobedience only when the lone right of personal security was neglected, Locke saw a right of revolution to depose rulers who failed to safeguard his wider panoply of liberties. Hence Locke's popularity in the North American colonies, whose citizens had ample domestic order in which to suffer the deprivation of other basic rights. In the end, both thinkers viewed the right of personal security as primary, the foundational right on which other freedoms might be constructed. For both, the thought that the right of personal security was somehow optional or less important than secondary rights, such as freedom of speech or criminal procedural rights, would have been dismissed with a puzzled chuckle.

It was left to Sir William Blackstone, England's greatest jurist, to certify the right to personal security thus defined as a legally actionable right under British law. Blackstone's masterful, sweeping synthesis of the British common law was influential in part because it was so unlawyerlike—clear, concise and understandable to the aver-age reader. Lincoln taught himself law by studying Blackstone's *Commentaries on the Laws of England.* Twenty-five hundred copies of his *Commentaries* were sold in America prior to the Constitutional Convention in 1787,[40] and his writings have had a towering influence on American law to this day.

Blackstone sought to analyze the right of personal security more fully and have it safely deposited in the laws of the British Empire. He did this by explicitly writing Hobbes and Locke's right of personal security into the endlessly rolling parchment of the common law. This right rested on one of Blackstone's most important, if underrecognized, contributions to legal theory: his concept of primary or principal rights. In this age of rights relativism, we tend to group all rights, especially all constitutional rights, together as equally important. Blackstone saw this as an invitation to chaos. He recognized instead three basic rights, which he called "absolute," and which took precedence over other rights that he termed "relative." Thus, while rights such as freedom of assembly and the right against self-incrimination can be helpful political additions to an exceptionally advanced society, they necessarily "result from, and are posterior to, the formation of states and societies; so that to maintain and regulate these is clearly a subsequent consideration." Blackstone wrote an intriguing synthesis of Hobbes and Locke in listing the "three principal or primary" rights of man that the State must concentrate on preserving: "the right of personal security, the right of personal liberty, and the right of private property." Of these, the right of personal security, which "consists in a person's legal and uninterrupted enjoyment of his life, his limbs, his body, his health, and his reputation," is plainly the most important, since the others are "posterior to" the State's ability to provide the order on which the right to personal security and all other rights are based.[41]

This commonsense distinction between primary and secondary rights is now often lost on us. We have been led to believe by the ACLU and other extreme individualists that, simply put, all rights have equal rights; all have equal claim to our loyalties and to our government's protection. Frequently Americans think and speak as if we enjoy inalienable rights, equal in importance, to everything from low interest rates to government-sponsored medical care to space research. There are many unfortunate by-products of this mind-set. As Amitai Etzioni noted in his call for a ten-year moratorium on the minting of new rights, the current "incessant issuance of new rights, like the wholesale printing of currency, causes a massive inflation of rights that devalues their moral claims."[42] This confusion is also a primary reason for our present decomposition. Understanding Blackstone's basic hierarchy of rights is essential, for if this society of innumerable choices is to survive, we must ultimately prioritize. We must put first things first. We must do so by sifting through the layers of secondary liberties that have been piled on top of the indispensable, foundational right of personal security outlined by Blackstone and defended philosophically by Hobbes and Locke. The notion of personal security as the basis of all other freedoms was part of the common intellectual inheritance bestowed upon the first Americans. The Founders of the American Republic accepted the idea without amendment, making it the cornerstone of a political system that, because of its devout, rights-centered individualism, would always need it.

It was not long after the Revolution when Americans' devotion to ordered liberty, as conceived by these theorists, received perhaps its severest test. The Articles of Confederation, adopted after the Revolution as the Republic's first Constitution, was a document only an extreme civil libertarian could love. It provided for such a radical decentralization of authority that the thirteen new states were effectively separate countries, in a relationship much like America's current relationship with Canada, Germany and other members of NATO. While such independence from the federal government may sound delightful in the present era of general federal bungling, post-Revolutionary Americans found that it crippled the national government's ability to respond effectively when harassed by armed adversaries. The Southern Confederacy would discover this intrinsic shortcoming in the following century. In 1786 it was the North's turn.

In the fall of that year, because the end of the Revolution and the return of veterans to the labor force, postwar deflation and a bloated labor pool made many of the farmers and small landholders in western Massachusetts unable to pay their debts and taxes. When the courts became overly efficient in processing foreclosures on their land, the farmers adopted a two-step approach for redress of grievances. First, they petitioned the state legislature for debt and tax relief. When these efforts were of no avail, they then endeavored to rid the area of one of the more obnoxious pestilences imported (as stowaways) from Great Britain, whom they blamed for many of their woes: lawyers. A widely circulated letter, which Professor Charles Warren noted "accurately summed up" the farmers' grievances, listed a series of demands that included abolition of the courts of common pleas and a grant of authority to constables so that "a large swarm of lawyers will be banished from their wonted haunts, who have been more damage to the people at large, especially the farmers, than the common, savage beasts of prey."[43]

When the farmers' demands were ignored, things soon began to turn ugly. In the winter of 1786 the Massachusetts legislature, goaded by influential creditor interests, doubled state taxes in an effort to retire the Massachusetts debt. A groundswell of armed opposition erupted. Debt-saddled veterans dusted off their muskets to take up arms against what they felt to be a new, homegrown tyranny. Some two thousand insurgents united to enforce their demands. Rallying around Captain Daniel Shays, a local hero of the Revolution, the armed bands closed the courts in western and central Massachusetts by force, at one point sealing off the state's Supreme Judicial Court. Debt collections and foreclosures were terminated at gunpoint. Lacking any real power under the Articles of Confederation, federal authorities at first offered no resistance to this stunning threat to the stability of the young Republic.

Finally, when the federal arsenal at Springfield was menaced, the national government was prompted to take action. Yet even then the response from the federal Leviathan was ominously toothless. As the revolt quickly overwhelmed local sheriffs and constables, Governor James Bowdoin pleaded with federal authorities to send in troops to restore order. The problem, federal officials explained to the governor, was that the Articles of Confederation did not authorize such assistance. By the time the federal government finally rationalized the constitutionality of intervention and appealed for forces from the other twelve states, the uprising had already engulfed most of Massachusetts. The rebellion was put down only after private subscription in eastern Massachusetts managed to raise enough state militia forces to allow General Lincoln to disperse the "Shaysites."

Clinton Rossiter has described "the celebrated Shays Rebellion" as "one of the few events in American history that was as important in fact as it has become in legend."[44] Its effect on Americans of that era was well summed up by fellow historian Gordon Wood: "Shays' uprising in 1786 was only the climactic episode in one long insurrection, where the dissolution of government and the state of nature became an everyday fact of life. Indeed, it was as if all the imaginings of political philosophers for centuries were being lived out in a matter of years in the hills of New England."[45] Right before their very eyes, Americans were witnessing the raw reality of what was previously an exclusively theoretical State of Nature. Prominent federal officials trembled at its perceived approach. John Marshall, who later became Chief Justice of the U.S. Supreme Court, wrote at the time, "All is gloom in the Eastern States, Massachusetts is rent into two factions, and an appeal, I fear, has by this time been made to the God of battles." Secretary Knox reported to George Washington that "this dreadful situation has alarmed every man of principle and property in New England. . . . What is to afford us security against the violence of lawless men?"[46] As New England splintered into the war of all against all, Shays and his comrades-in-arms laid threadbare the federal government's utter inability to uphold the citizenry's most basic freedom, that of personal security. With the introduction of anarchy to large expanses of the new Republic, the brittle constitutional order cracked for the whole nation to see.

No one was more aghast at the State of Nature's appearance in rural New England than Mr. Washington. He wrote that he was "mortified beyond expression" at the "commotions" in western Massachusetts. The old soldier recognized the threat to the young nation that this uprising posed. "Commotions of this sort, like snowballs, gather strength as they roll, if there is no opposition in the way to divide and crumble them." Without prompt corrective action, he warned James Madison, the future for the young Republic was dim. "We are fast verging to anarchy and confusion!"[47]

Washington's plan of action was simple. He offered no sociological blueprint for eradicating the financial travails of Massachusetts farmers or otherwise conducting well-intentioned social programs. He proposed a stern alternative: suppress the rebellion with any necessary force, and then strengthen the federal government with powers that would allow it to avert similar crises in the future. While he desired to know the reasons for the rebellion, he had no patience with those who indecisively wrung their hands because they could not pinpoint the causes of the upheaval; "to trace the causes would be difficult," he told the Marquis de Lafayette. He reiterated the need for a "call for decision":

Know precisely what the insurgents aim at. If they have *real* grievances, redress them if possible; or acknowledge the justice of them, and your inability to do it in the present moment. If they have not, employ the force of government against them at once.

"If government shrinks, or is unable to enforce its laws," Washington admonished, "fresh manoeuvres will be displayed by the insurgents, anarchy and confusion must prevail, and every thing will be turned topsy turvey in that State; where it is not probable the mischiefs will terminate."[48]

In the short run a swift, aggressive reaction was essential; ultimately the nation had to replace the tattered political regime with one whose institutions could muster an effective response to such uprisings. He asked Madison, "What stronger evidence can be given of the want of energy in our governments than these disorders? If there exists not a power to check them, what security has a man for life, liberty or property?" The solution, he felt, was a "General Convention to revise and amend the foederal [sic] Constitution"; "the thinking part of the people of this Country" had already "appointed . . . delegates to meet at Philadelphia . . . to revise and correct the defects of the federal System."[49] Deferring to the father of their country and the manifest perils of inaction, Madison and the rest of the nation hurried to overhaul the constitutional order and thereby banish the State of Nature once again to the trifling realm of philosophers.

As Washington and most historians agree, Shays' Rebellion and the resulting apprehension over domestic tranquillity were the main reasons for the calling of the Constitutional Convention in 1787. The fear of seeing the State of Nature pop up in their own backyard sent almost every state scurrying to expedite delegates to Philadelphia. By early May only Rhode Island had failed to send a delegation to the assembling Constitutional Convention. If the delegates had any doubts as to why they were there, the introductory remarks at the Convention quickly removed them. In the Convention's opening speech, Governor Edmund Randolph of Virginia stated that the "rebellion . . . in Massts" was the reason for the Convention, and he listed as one of the defects in the Articles of Confederation "that the [federal] government could not check . . . a rebellion in any [state,] not having constitutional power Nor means to interpose according to the exigency."[50] Madison, who wrote the Virginia Plan, which ultimately became in amended form our present Constitution, criticized

the rival New Jersey Plan proposed by William Paterson for its failure to address these anxieties. "Will it secure the internal tranquillity
of the States themselves?" Madison asked the alternative plan's
authors. "The insurrections in Massts. admonished all the States of
the danger to which they were exposed. Yet the plan of Mr. P. contained no provisions for supplying the defect of the Confederation
on this point."[51] The records of the Convention are weighted with
references to Shays' Rebellion and the urgent need to craft a document that could prevent such criminal violence in the future. One
law professor counts thirty-five such references,[52] as compared to a
handful of allusions to the need for the civil liberties contained in
the First Amendment.

Madison, Alexander Hamilton and John Jay supplied a fuller
explanation of the Framers' thinking in *The Federalist Papers*, a
series of pro-Constitution newspaper columns published in New
York following the Convention. The fear of Shays-like civil disturbances and an ensuing Hobbesian existence uniformly darkens the
trio's writings. Hamilton, for example, took a bleak view of man
straight out of *Leviathan,* observing that "men are ambitious, vindic-
tive and rapacious," something to be borne in mind when addressing
the "dangers" of "domestic factions and convulsions." Jay observed
in *Federalist* No. 3, "Among the many objects to which a wise and
free people find it necessary to direct their attention, that of providing for their *safety* seems to be the first." Madison's case for a muscular federal government charged with defending the common order
was based on a Hobbesian critique of man's natural vices. "What is
government itself but the greatest of all reflections on human
nature?" Madison asked. "If men were angels, no government would
be necessary." In *Federalist* No. 51, Madison reiterated Hobbes's
premonitions in arguing that the principal aim of the new government was to avoid the proliferation of the sort of "factions" that had
just ransacked Massachusetts. He embraced the "great principle of
self-preservation," as well as the natural law articulated by both
Hobbes and Locke, "which declares that the safety and happiness of
society are the objects at which all political institutions aim and to
which all such institutions must be sacrificed."[53]

So wrote the authors of what Hobbes would recognize as our
"convenient articles of peace," the U.S. Constitution. The chief
object of this document was to bind all its signatories and the people
they represented to a government enlisted to annihilate the State of
Nature. Government's energies were to be concentrated on that

objective; as Madison put it, personal security under the rule of law was the "aim . . . to which all institutions must be sacrificed." Nothing less would do. That the Framers of the Constitution viewed the right of personal security as the most important of American freedoms, of course, does not mean that they were foes of civil liberties. Indeed, they invented them; Madison, for instance, went on to draft the Bill of Rights. What the Framers rejected was the modern notion of the egalitarianism of rights. Society, they realized, could not afford to view all rights as created equal, for none took precedence over the primary right of personal security. A country that ignored this basic Blackstonean distinction did so at its peril. Inevitably such a society would incur the "topsy turvey" chaos from which Washington recoiled, chaos that sent a nation scrambling to a national convention to prevent its recurrence. Having witnessed the State of Nature once, they had no desire to entice it again. The Framers put first things first.

Present-day America has abandoned these old truths, with the predictable results. Our nation has disregarded the warnings of Hobbes, Locke and Blackstone that were so diligently heeded by early, post-Shays America. The Framers' careful selection and ranking of the civil liberties to be protected by the federal government has been turned into a "topsy turvey" rights regime that has invited the current explosion of criminal violence. The hardy distinction between primary and secondary rights has given way, first in the judiciary and later in the public psyche, to a profound misunderstanding of government's most basic duties. Americans today often assume that all individual rights, especially all constitutional rights and their judicial gloss, may make equal demand on our affections and enforcement efforts. Government, we have come to think, should not be so stingy as to concentrate on the basics. And we somehow manage to be surprised by the inevitable results of this mentality.

We must take a moment from self-flagellation, though, to note that this erroneous conception of rights is primarily the doing of the judiciary, the undemocratic branch of American government. Judges have hastened America's individualistic troubles by writing hundreds of new rights into law, often through their interpretation of the Constitution. These additions are always, by necessity, at the expense of the less inspiring right of personal security. The First Amendment is one prolific source of these new liberties. Thus, written into the Constitution at present is a conception of freedom of speech so broad that it protects even the most direct assaults on the community, such as flag- and cross-burning and calls to armed confrontation. A more direct trade-off with the primary right of personal security occurs when the rights of the accused are expanded, rights that the Framers frankly termed criminals' rights. The numerous procedural safeguards for criminal defendants contained in the Bill of Rights, designed to ensure basic due process and freedom from torture, have been annotated so frequently and expansively in recent years that the enforcement of the Constitution itself has been severely hampered. Two of the three governmental authorities that modern Americans charge with law enforcement, the police and courts, have lost in this flux some of their traditional methods of keeping the peace. The other main component of twentieth-century criminal justice, the prisons, has likewise experienced greater instability because of the judicial interpretation of the Eighth Amendment's proscription of cruel and unusual punishment. This interpretation has inadvertently imposed a genuinely Hobbesian State of Nature on American inmates, conditions probably beyond even the worst trepidations of our Republic's founders.

Consistent with the spirit of the age, some have proposed as the solution to the modern Shays' Rebellion writ large that yet another constitutional right be manufactured—a constitutional right of personal security.[54] As with many of the new rights of the accused, this right's existence in the Constitution's text is not to be found; however, unlike these other liberties, the right of personal security was not included because its insertion was considered superfluous. The rights in the Bill of Rights were, as Blackstone put it, "posterior to" a stable society in which the protection of personal security was the chief concern of government. Such a right is implicit in the State's very existence. Yet this right's exclusion from the Constitution makes its certification as a constitutional right just as inappropriate and disquieting as the new criminals' rights it is intended to offset. Such a right would also be unworkable. As Professor Laurence Tribe, a leading ultraindividualist legal scholar, remarked in a rare moment of lucidity, the citizen possessing such a right "may be unable to gauge with any specificity exactly how much service she is receiving, how much she has a right to expect, or when a harm she suffers can be attributed to government."[55] It is a telling sign of our intellectual state that the creation of an extra constitutional right, intended to serve as an counterpoise for the broadening of criminals' rights, is often our preferred strategy for restoring order to a society already swimming in liberty.

It is now clear that no new constitutional right can undo the damage. The Leviathan is slain. Our "convenient articles of peace" lie shredded, useful only for the papier-mâché constitutionalism of the nation's judges. The various "factions" of the Framers' depiction have responded to the reduced costs of criminality, like the rational human beings they are, by taking over entire neighborhoods and cities. The prospective horrors at which the Framers cringed are now a way of life in large sections of urban America, their residents left to the war of all against all despite the Constitution's luminous promise to the contrary. And the "anarchy and confusion" continue to spread well beyond the line of defense erected around America's ghettos by a white society convinced of its exemption from such pathologies. As America experiences the worst national crime rates ever recorded, a creeping State of Nature casts its shadow over the land.

In assessing the nation's prospects for holding off these trends without radical introspection and reforms—in short, without sacrifices of the soul—it is necessary to examine the triad of forces that the nation deploys as a short-term deterrent to the criminal element: the police, courts and prisons. The following three chapters are dedicated to this purpose. This analysis is, if nothing else, essential for understanding how ineffectively tools of government can remedy a crisis of the spirit, and just how poorly they are currently standing up to America's flirtation with the jungle.

CHAPTER TWO

The Police: Crime Control by Other Means

It is well that war is so terrible—we should grow too fond of it.

—General Robert E. Lee

When Americans get irked enough over a matter to elevate it mentally from a nuisance to a problem, we often blurt out one of those penetrating expressions that lay bare the dynamism and occasional recklessness that define our national temperament: "Do something!" The exclamation point is not optional. A matter that is pressing enough to trigger such a remark is, to the American mind, something that should have been addressed and resolved yesterday. When the problem perturbing the public is crime, particularly violent street crime, "doing something" means enacting a government policy that immediately reduces the amount of visible lawlessness. This inevitably means the use of force against offenders, a projection of society's determination to give as good as it gets from the criminal element. In late-twentieth-century America the regiment-of-choice for this mission is the police. Armed and conspicuously organized along paramilitary lines, the police are policymakers' most forceful and flashy method of vanquishing the criminal forces arrayed against our civilization. These uniformed public servants are dispatched to launch military-style offensives in what politicians are apt to mislabel, sometimes for self-serving reasons, a "War on Crime."

This obstinate human desire for order that the police help to satisfy finds a formidable competitor for the American people's affections in our fondness for the rule of law. A society under the rule of law must center its attempts to subdue offenders on its criminal justice system. This system provides the legal process by which a free people purges itself of enemies of the common order, and which places limits on the role of brute force in the law enforcement regime. Jeremy Bentham, a citizen of a nineteenth-century British society also dedicated to this reconciliation of law and order, believed that the legal system's supremacy in the democratic crime control regime relegated the police to a supporting role. He affirmed the division of crime control strategies that his fellow Englishmen had come to accept: "justice," which he equated with the criminal justice process, and "prevention," a category under which he placed the police.[1] The police, he suggested, amounted to justice plus—judicial commands backed by force, to be applied when useful in forcibly quelling domestic disturbances that threaten the ultimate authority of the judicial system.

Bentham's treatment of the police finds an intriguing parallel in the definition of war offered by the great Prussian strategist Karl von Clausewitz. Clausewitz's most famous observation was that war does not represent the collapse of normal political dealings, but is rather politics "by other means."[2] The police, to extend the War on Crime analogy, serve much the same function, albeit with all its obvious limitations. The police are that extra element of the criminal justice system that gives modern law enforcement its punch, and that allows the legal process to issue verdicts on guilt or innocence that are more than hollow proclamations.

The parallel to Clausewitz notwithstanding, the martial image that an armed police force unavoidably evokes would, in any case, probably make declarations of a War on Crime irresistible to the frustrated generals occupying many of the nation's elected offices. From its inception the modern police force has prompted comparisons to frontline troops entrenched in deadly and decisive combat with the forces of anarchy. With so many armed men in distinctive uniforms

brashly patrolling city neighborhoods, such a force had all the bearing of a domestic army, which in fact was no small cause for alarm
when the first bobbies and cops began policing freedom-loving
Anglo-Saxon societies. Yet even such deep-seated fears were no
match for the potent appeal of the military analogy. After overcom-
ing the apprehensions associated with a quasi-domestic army and
steering through Parliament in 1829 the bill authorizing the creation
of the first modern police force, British Prime Minister Robert Peel
appointed a distinguished military officer, Charles Rowan, as one of
the London force's two police commissioners. Rowan organized the
department as a paramilitary force with army-style training and discipline, impressing upon the new department an unmistakable military demeanor that seemed to confirm British suspicions about the
warlike nature of the force. Rowan's application of military techniques to domestic policing was soon transplanted to America, and
was perpetuated in Great Britain by Rowan's successor, E. Y. W.
Henderson, another military officer.[3]

Like the nation from which it had violently parted only a few
decades before, America in the early 1800s followed much the same
route. Americans' distrust of standing armies proved insufficient to
discourage its new chiefs of police from adopting the military airs of
the London force, on which they relied as a model when establishing
their police departments. Grover Whalen, an early New York City
police commissioner, openly relished the military flavor of his new
position, to the point of placing a bronze figurine of Napoleon on
his desk.[4] The notion of policeman-as-soldier solidified under the
command of a subsequent New York police commissioner, Teddy
Roosevelt, whose eagerness to lead troops into desperate battles
infused New York's Finest with the same zeal and pugnacity that
later propelled their commissioner up San Juan Hill. President
Woodrow Wilson declared at one point that every policeman had
the "sacred duty of a soldier."[5] By then few Americans, even outside
his ambitious chain of command, would have taken issue with him.
Until a few years before World War II, all the top posts of the
nation's state police forces were reserved for young military
officers.[6]

It took some time, and the rude prodding of a burgeoning criminal
class, to expose the fraud of the military analogy. The comparison's
most glaring shortcoming is the fact that the police, by enforcing the
rule of law "by other means," are bound by the central political principles they are executing. In Anglo-American societies, the core prin-

ciple of law is due process, the grand strategy of selective engagement that dictates which enemies the police may combat. Due
process, of course, is beyond the pale of even the most scrupulous
ethics of warfare. In this domestic war, one is not permitted simply
to fire away at the enemy. Indeed, a policeman cannot even assume
that a person who is dressed and behaving like the enemy is to be
treated as such, unless the officer has accumulated enough evidence
to give him probable cause to act on his intuitions. Even after gathering sufficient evidence, the policeman is restricted to merely
arresting the enemy. The officer must then comply with complicated
judicial directives as to the enemy's treatment, after which he hands
him over to other authorities responsible for ultimately meting out
punishment. If in fact we have declared a full-scale War on Crime,
this is surely an odd way to wage it.

It is bad enough that many politicians offer this misleading
metaphor to a public desperate for results. But even more tragic are
the exaggerated expectations that this warfare generates among the
American people, and the consequent blow to police-community
relations that it delivers. In war, as General George Patton once
barked, Americans love a winner and will not tolerate a loser.
Politicians' invocation of the term "war" to mobilize support for
their crime control strategies encourages Americans to apply to the
nation's law enforcement establishment the same hopes for total victory that they are accustomed to seeing fulfilled in wartime. The
police dutifully attempt to live up to these unrealistic demands. Yet
they invariably fall short, because of both inadequate resources and
an unrealistic grand strategy often formulated by judges. The
police's frustrations at falling short of the mandatory smashing victory have led them to invoke a different military scenario to describe
their sense of despair and failure. They find themselves embroiled in
a domestic Vietnam, a conflict in which the troops are ordered to
fight under a grand strategy that renders them fundamentally incapable of winning.

They can find an even more accurate allegory in an earlier failed
war effort, appropriately enough, right here at home. The Supreme
Court's power to modify the prime ingredient of grand strategy in
this conflict, due process, has indeed lent the War on Crime a resemblance to a Vietnam-style debacle. In both struggles, political leaders
provided the war's generals with impracticable objectives, objectives
that, in the current war, are often unreachable because of rules of
engagement that effectively favor the enemy. Compounding these

grand-strategic shortcomings is police leaders' mismanagement of the forces under their command. Police chiefs compose the echelon of command that B. H. Liddell Hart called "generalship";[7] in the War on Crime, the decisions of these leaders constitute strategy per se. Clinging to outmoded crime control tactics, inefficient deployment of forces and other strategic mistakes, many American chiefs of police have failed to wield the forces at their command effectively. Unlike the situation in Vietnam, then, where U.S. forces arguably never lost a battle yet were eventually compelled to withdraw because of political, grand-strategic mistakes, the troops enlisted for the War on Crime find themselves answering to both uninformed lawyer-leadership at the grand-strategic level and misguided generalship. This double-layered formulation of faulty strategy suggests another American war effort as a more apt description of the plight of today's police officer: a latter-day Pickett's Charge, in which the troops find themselves waging a losing battle in a war they cannot win.

"UP, MEN, AND TO YOUR POSTS."

The defeatism of today's policeman is something quite unlike the confident *élan* of previous generations of officers. The creation of the modern police in the early nineteenth century was heralded optimistically as a signal development in the human quest for order, a seemingly overdue departure from the previous, less successful attempts to curb the chaotic impulses that simmer within every society. Medieval England, for instance, had a different institution. The Norman conquerors imported a system of private law enforcement from the Continent that revolved around a collective approach to domestic security. Under the frankpledge, Englishmen who did not own property were grouped into tithings (ten households) and hundreds (ten tithings) and organized for required community self-defense within this framework. Twentieth-century Americans would recognize the frankpledge as mandatory service in a Neighborhood Watch program. All able-bodied men over the age of fifteen were also subject to compulsory service in the *posse comitatus*. The posse was summoned to pursue fleeing criminals when either the sheriff invoked the power of the county or a citizen raised the hue and cry. Supported by the constable, the unpaid, conscripted citizen who served as the reluctant workhorse of the medieval law enforcement regime, this Norman system of community self-defense stood essentially unchanged until the 1800s.

English colonists in North America, for all their later sampling of revolutionary notions, never seriously tampered with this inherited law enforcement regime. Neighbors were still considered primarily responsible for each other's safety. The frankpledge along with its growing inadequacies crossed the Atlantic intact. By the seventeenth century public apathy had so undermined the constable-watchman system in English cities, particularly the night watch, that hired substitutes were necessary. Londoners' lack of interest in the faltering frankpledge resulted in a sharp increase in London crime rates by the early nineteenth century. The public's clamor for greater safety, without greater law enforcement duties on their part, instigated Prime Minister Peel's introduction in Parliament of the Metropolitan Police Act in 1829. The act proposed the formation of the world's first publicly financed police force devoted to *preventing* crime rather than apprehending offenders after the fact. Peel managed to overcome British concerns about the establishment of a standing army and secure the bill's passage. And after public complaints over urban disorder grew loud enough to drown out protests over a domestic security force, New Yorkers relented and instituted in 1845 a police program modeled after the London force. Within twenty years almost every major American city had adopted a similar system. The London police department was credited with a substantial reduction in crime immediately following its establishment,[8] providing Americans with further grounds for optimism.

One of the prime reasons for the new regime's efficacy was its incorporation of the so-called beat system. In the late eighteenth century Henry Fielding and his half brother John formed a network of neighborhood patrolmen called the Bow Street Runners. The force was partially subsidized by the government and charged with propping up the decrepit frankpledge. The Fieldings assigned each runner a "beat," a specific London neighborhood to which the runner was to confine his patrolling. Combining the direct deterrent effect of a police presence with the informal social controls of smaller English communities, the beat system integrated the two approaches to yield a highly effective repellent to crime. Fearing that a neighborhood officer of the law might be in the vicinity, criminals were more likely to move on to another area. Emboldened by the presence of a law enforcement official whom they considered an auxiliary neighbor, residents of the protected zone were more likely to volunteer information about criminal activities in the neighborhood. The beat system thereby provided an intelligence network which, for the first time, made it possible for law enforcement personnel to realistically aspire to prevent crime. Peel, among others, saw the potential. After the eponymous prime minister secured the employment of London's "bobbies," the city's police force accepted as its prime directive the ferreting out of crime before it actually occurred, mainly through getting to know members of the community and encouraging their cooperation.

With popular demands for a citizens' police force combined with widespread expectation of parochialism from its public servants, America presented fertile ground for the beat system. The beat system commanded near-universal loyalty for almost a century. The first conversion from the system occurred in 1905, with the seemingly unexceptional appointment of August Vollmer as chief of police of Berkeley, California. Vollmer was the first chief to order part of his force to patrol city neighborhoods in some of the new automobiles sputtering down American roads.[9] Other police chiefs tried to copy his apparent success; within a few decades patrol cars had replaced the beat system in every major American city. By the 1950s rapid advances in communications technology seemed to further suggest that an "omnipresent police force" had finally become technologically feasible by linking a vast communications network to patrol cars.[10] Policemen who had spent their entire careers walking beats and getting acquainted with the residents and ne'er-do-wells in their neighborhoods were soon taken off the streets and assigned to squad cars, at a time when, uncoincidentally, crime began its great surge.

Under the patrol-car system, the police were reduced to the role of constables prior to the creation of the London force in 1829: a reactive force limited to solving crimes after the fact rather than preventing them through preemptive strikes. The foot patrolman's familiarity with the community and its residents had made this prevention possible. Since around 87 percent of police activity in urban high-crime areas is initiated by telephone calls from ordinary citizens,[11] the patrol-car system has thus largely forfeited the elements of surprise and initiative. A 1974 study by the Police Foundation found that increases in police-car patrols had no detectable effect on crime rates. And while the study's authors, headed by George Kelling, cautioned that the research did not support an indictment of the police's overall value as an institution,[12] many critics of the police subsequently paid less attention to the miscalculations of the patrol-car strategy than to the very concept and effectiveness of policing.

Police chiefs have only recently been persuaded to reinstitute the more fruitful beat system, giving it the trendy new title "community policing." The only element in this refurbished foot-patrol system that is even arguably new is the police ministation. A practice with roots in nineteenth-century Prussia and the modern Japanese *koban* system, the ministation of today's police departments is a small-scale precinct house located in a high-crime neighborhood, often in one of the unused storefront properties abundant in such areas. This new, improved beat system is yielding a growing number of success stories. Baltimore County, Maryland, brought back foot patrols in the late 1980s and instantly cut overall crime rates in participating neighborhoods by 12 percent. In Newport News, Virginia, robbery, auto theft and burglary dropped a full 25 to 50 percent in neighborhoods where the enhanced beat system was implemented.[13] In response to gang violence and drive-by shootings in South-Central Los Angeles, police set up barricades creating culs-de-sac and saturated the area with officers on bicycles. The result: a 67 percent drop in gang-related drive-by shootings, a 10 percent drop in street crimes, and a 14 percent drop in school truancy.[14] Bob Burgreen, San Diego's chief of police, judged the system "enormously successful" and subsequently established foot patrolling in every neighborhood of his city. The useful parochialism that explains community policing's success was succinctly expressed by one foot-patrol officer in Lansing, Michigan: "This is my neighborhood, and I'll be damned if anybody is going to do those things to my neighborhood."[15]

In 1991, when foot patrols were restored in New York subways and midtown Manhattan, similar results were witnessed. Assistant Chief of Police Thomas Walsh commented that he had "never seen such a sharp decrease in robbery anywhere in the city before." The number of robberies fell 18 percent in one year, apparently without simply diverting criminals to other neighborhoods. Perhaps the biggest compliment given the beefed-up foot-patrol system came from an admitted "convict and street hustler" in *The New York Times*. When asked why crime had plummeted in midtown, the twenty-eight-year-old man replied, "Too many cops in sight—it's intimidating. . . . People are saying, 'Damn, how am I going to get paid?'"[16]

Yet despite such evidence of the value of community policing, our elected officials have too often not rewarded these encouraging trends at budget time. While in 1960 there were three police officers for every violent crime in America, by 1990 there were three violent crimes for every police officer.[17] Moreover, even when criminals are convicted, police routinely watch them promptly return to the streets through the penal system's revolving door. Mark Kleiman of Harvard's Kennedy School of Government calculated that the average robbery in 1958 earned a sentence of roughly 389 days; this had plunged to 115 days by 1986. For burglary, punishment dropped from 61 to 21 days over the same period.[18] Thus, just as police leaders' growing renunciation of the patrol-car strategy has now finally made it possible for increased government expenditures to translate into reductions in many categories of street crime, too often the fight has been abandoned at the grand-strategic level.

Still, the policeman's frustrations with disinterested politicians and an alienated citizenry are usually not his greatest source of pessimism and irritation. These emotions are saved for the judicial system. As borne out by polls of policemen, judge-crafted "technicalities," rules barring the use of certain police-procured evidence at trial, are the grand-strategic decisions that police complain of the most. These have come in the form of broader judicial interpretations of the liberties in the Bill of Rights, particularly those of the Fourth and Fifth Amendments.

Probably none of these recent constitutional entitlements puts policemen in a foul mood faster than the exclusionary rule. The Fourth Amendment forbids "unreasonable searches and seizures," and, toward that end, requires that search warrants be issued only "upon probable cause." Thus, if a policeman finds incriminating evidence after entering one's home without a search warrant, or with a warrant but without the necessary probable cause, that search is unconstitutional except in rare, limited circumstances. The policeman and the government he works for have always been liable in monetary damages for that constitutional violation. But beginning in the 1914 case of *Weeks v. United States*,[19] the Supreme Court decided to draft its own means of further upholding the Fourth Amendment. The Court forbade the use of such unconstitutionally obtained evidence in court, even when the evidence established the criminal guilt of the defendant. The judge-conceived "exclusionary rule" holds that all evidence that policemen obtain through an unconstitutional search or seizure is inadmissible in court against a defendant whose Fourth Amendment rights were thereby violated.

In 1961 the Court applied this rule to state as well as federal courts in *Mapp v. Ohio*.[20]

Curiously, one of the *Mapp* Court's two rationales for the rule, the deterrence of police misconduct, appears to be empirically unsupportable. Studies have emerged showing that policemen often disregard the rule, hoping to obtain incriminating evidence while evading judicial reproach.[21] One researcher concluded after examining motions to suppress in Chicago over a twenty-one-year period that, as far as he could tell, police "are not deterred by the exclusionary rule at all."[22] Police, it seems, are willing to run the risk of the evidence's exclusion and *Mapp*'s other discomforts in order to fulfill their public duties as they perceive them. At times this means rounding up evidence, when necessary, by other means.[23]

The *Mapp* Court's biggest mistake was its defense of the exclusionary rule on empirical rather than rationalist, rights-based grounds. This exposed the rule to the kind of pressure that simple, old-fashioned facts can bring to bear, especially on inventions conceived without reference to research data or everyday experience. Of course, the standard criticism of the exclusionary rule—that it "handcuffs" police—is, while an understandable reaction to the exclusion of probative evidence, less an attack on the exclusionary rule than on the underlying principle embodied in the Fourth Amendment. That is, since the amendment prohibits unreasonable searches and seizures and thus necessarily places certain evidence out of reach, it is this constitutional restriction on police power that is ultimately responsible for removing certain proof of wrongdoing from the scope of proper police searches. That much of the irritant, at least, must not be laid at the doorstep of the exclusionary rule. The exclusionary rule merely attempts to defend the Fourth Amendment's integrity, albeit, in fairness to the rule's critics, in a crude, peremptory manner. There are other, more valid objections to the rule. It fosters perjury among policemen, consumes limited judicial resources, contributes to court delays, and excludes incriminating evidence that is usually reliable and highly probative.[24] The rule inordinately benefits guilty defendants. While, by definition, it provides no remedy for innocent citizens who suffer illegal searches, the practice offers guilty defendants a bargaining chip for a reduced sentence. Indeed, exclusion of evidence under the exclusionary rule often forces the prosecution to dismiss all charges against such parties.[25] Professor Dallin Oaks found that the exclusionary rule compelled prosecutors to dismiss

charges in one-fourth of all weapons cases and one-third of all narcotics cases.[26] Those who do not escape punishment altogether still
may benefit from reduced sentences, as prosecutors generally enter
into plea bargains when they fear their evidence will not survive
Mapp's scrutiny.[27]

Although it forged the police into a more professional force, the
exclusionary rule, for the above reasons, has had trouble making
friends among its blue-uniformed servants. Few officers appear to
have accepted the rule as legitimate. Jerome Skolnick found that the
typical policeman in the post-*Mapp* era feels that he has been saddled with broad, ill-defined duties.[28] Albert Reiss and David Bordua
observed that policemen often view judges' decisions to dismiss
charges as a "rejection of their decisions," causing the policeman to
feel "dishonored" and puzzled at the court's leniency.[29] Judging
from public opinion polls and the variety and profitability of *Dirty
Harry*-type movies glorifying the circumvention of such technicalities, discontent with the exclusionary rule is not confined to the
police station. In fact, like too many other American exports these
days, the exclusionary rule has found no buyers overseas. Every
other criminal justice system in the world has rejected the rule save
for the Philippines, a former American colony that will undoubtedly
rid itself of this final vestige of Yankee imperialism once crime
becomes enough of a problem.

If the exclusionary rule has any competitor for the American
policeman's vexation, we must look for it among the other recent
judicial annotations to the Bill of Rights. The courts' expansion of
liberties listed in the Fifth Amendment has further precluded the use
of certain generally probative evidence at trial. This has been accomplished through a sharp curtailment of the police's traditional powers of interrogation. In the 1966 case of *Miranda v. Arizona*,[30] the
Supreme Court held that before questioning a suspect, policemen
are constitutionally obligated to inform him of his Fifth Amendment
right against self-incrimination and Sixth Amendment right to counsel. The Court provided to that effect a set of instructions to guide
police in sharing this information.

Those who question *Miranda*'s importance in the overall scheme
of crime control do have a point; but let us also hear the policeman
out. *Miranda* has utilitarianism on its side: If suspects are ignorant of
their constitutional rights, who is better positioned to inform them,
as a purely practical matter, than the police? Even so, if *Miranda* was
originally limited to the mere idea that cops should give free legal

advice to detainees, *Miranda* has, in its three decades of life, matured into something much more. Elsewhere in the Court's decision lay the reasons for this untoward growth. Under the Court's reasoning, an officer's failure to recite the new rules, a suspect's "*Miranda* rights," prior to questioning was presumed to constitute compulsion violative of the Fifth Amendment upon the officer's *very first question* of the suspect. This made any confessions following that question inadmissible in court. Unlike prior cases, which had required evidence of "physical violence or other deliberate means calculated to break the suspect's will,"[31] *Miranda* adopted a per se rule of compulsion. Interrogations of any suspect who had not been read his rights were, as such, compulsive and unconstitutional, conceivably even when an officer simply asked the offender his name. The Rehnquist Court has since *expanded* the *Miranda* rule. Recent cases now effectively bar the use of all post-arraignment confessions not made in the presence of the accused's attorney unless the accused specifically declines the assistance of counsel.[32]

Given its limitations on society's main means of law enforcement, *Miranda* inevitably meant more than a symbolic rebuke to rebellious police officers. The decision had an immediate and significant effect on the number of confessions that police obtained. This result was observed in studies of police departments in Philadelphia, Pittsburgh and New York County immediately after *Miranda*.[33] Again, however, like the decrease in convictions that Oaks and others documented after *Mapp*, the unstated target of critics touting these studies is the underlying Fifth Amendment right against self-incrimination. *Miranda*, after all, merely served to inform offenders of their constitutional rights; it did not create them. The right against self-incrimination is the gravamen of their complaint, not *Miranda*'s attempt to publicize it. But the policeman's riposte to this truth has merit as well, and must carry the day. The extra entitlements created by *Miranda* had previously eluded generations of diligent judges for a reason. These liberties lack a basis in the Fifth Amendment's text or history, presumably because the Framers did not think them wise. For a rights-engrossed society, the last thing that policemen, of all people, should be obliged to do is inform criminal suspects of their right not to confess their offenses. Conceived with high motives, *Miranda* and its later interpretations have nonetheless further complicated the police's already arduous tasks, and vindicated, at least in a narrow sense, the lamentation that he who increaseth knowledge, increaseth sorrow.

Lacking strategic and logistical support from elected officials and judges, today's police forces have bravely sought to hold their ground all the same. As Sparrow, Moore and Kennedy observed in their important study of the police, cops have concluded, based on this lack of political succor, that they "are hopelessly shackled by unrealistic constraints foisted on [them] by civil liberties groups, thanks to the fecklessness of politicians."[34] A few remarkable generals have led a counterattack. This small group of unorthodox police chiefs has devised new strategies to cope with the constraints recently imposed by all three branches of government. The most innovative of these attempts to disengage from the present-day Pickett's Charge comes from an unlikely figure: a black, Jewish chief of police in the cradle of the Confederacy, Chief Reuben Greenberg of Charleston, South Carolina. Acknowledging his lack of political and judicial assistance with laudable frankness, Chief Greenberg now directs his officers in drug-infested areas to limit themselves to the goal of the earliest police, pure deterrence. Instead of trying to arrest offenders and vainly hope for their successful prosecution and punishment, Charleston cops content themselves with merely interfering with drug dealing, literally inserting themselves physically between drug dealers and their clients to prevent any exchanges. The strategy has enjoyed happy results thus far. Chief Greenberg claims that at least 30 percent of Charleston drug dealers were forced out of business shortly after the policy's enactment.[35]

Clever though it is as a response to diminishing police resources, Chief Greenberg's strategy is not one in which a society under the rule of law can take much pride. His approach amounts to a strategic shrug, an admission that apprehension and punishment are no longer feasible goals for the American criminal justice system. A society that accepts such apathy effectively abandons criminal punishment as a central aim of government, and the pursuit of justice as a unifying social goal. In short, such a society has lost the will to fight. In Chief Greenberg's microcosmic struggle against the Great Havoc, his strategy of pure deterrence is an eloquent but sobering commentary on the state of our criminal justice system. This undoubtedly sorrowful concession to the enemies of our civilization poignantly reveals the extent to which today's police officer finds himself in a losing crusade.

OCCUPYING POWERS

To his colleagues, one word best described Officer John Glenn Chase—"idealistic."[36] Chase had made it clear from his first day on the Dallas police force that, in his own small way, he hoped to improve the lives of Dallas residents victimized by spiraling crime rates, particularly residents of the inner city. On the cold morning of January 23, 1988, the young officer was ordered to perform a related but far more mundane task, one common to American policemen in the 1980s: patrol-car duty. Observing a motorist committing a minor traffic violation in an inner-city neighborhood, Chase pulled over the driver and walked out of his car to speak to him. As Chase began to question the driver, a thirty-four-year-old homeless black man, Carl Williams, walked up to the officer and irately demanded that Chase let the driver go. A fight ensued, during which Williams managed to grab Chase's .44 caliber revolver and force the twenty-five-year-old white officer to lie on his back. By this time, a crowd of residents from the predominantly black neighborhood had assembled around the two men, watching the argument rapidly escalate into a life-or-death struggle. None of the bystanders attempted to intervene. And then, a voice from the gathering crowd rose above the din.

"Shoot him!"[37]

Others joined in. "Shoot him! Shoot him!"

As the chants grew louder, the officer begged for the crowd to stop. His pleading soon ended, abruptly. Williams had fired three bullets into Chase's face. Two other officers arrived several minutes later to find their colleague dead. Williams, who turned out to have had a history of mental problems, died after the officers were forced to shoot him in self-defense. The cheering finally stopped.

Although there were much broader lessons to be drawn, many whites saw in this murder merely confirmation of evils unique to black Americans. The reaction of local black elected officials did little to discourage this grim assumption. For years prior to Chase's public execution, Dallas's black elected officials had suggested that the large number of African-American suspects shot by police was proof that they had been deliberately targeted in a pattern of police discrimination. When the two black members of the city council, Al Lipscomb and Diane Ragsdale, declined to attend Chase's funeral, many Dallas policemen were indignant. Dallas police chief Billy Prince seemed to sum up their attitude when he remarked, "I can't

help but believe that the almost constant barrage of criticism directed toward the good men and women of this department contributed
in some way to this officer's tragic death."[38]

Less clear was the extent to which average African-Americans
shared the views imputed to them. Subsequent man-on-the-street
interviews of Dallas blacks by The New York Times indicated that
they were far more sympathetic toward and appreciative of the
police than had been suggested. These results squared with the atti-
tudinal rift, increasingly documented in national polls, between
blacks and black political leaders on many major political issues.
However, a poll by the Dallas Morning News published several days
after Chase's murder showed that while 57 percent of whites rated
police conduct as excellent, only 15 percent of blacks and 26 percent of Latinos gave the same rating. Thus, while most black citizens
deplored Chase's murder, they appeared to share some of the same
misgivings toward the predominantly white police force voiced by
local black elected officials. This distrust, it would seem from polls
and recent history, is shared by blacks nationwide.

Dallas's sanguinary separatism mirrored the strains in police-community relations that have occurred throughout the country. Some
of the first empirical indications of a widening divide between police
and residents of the inner city came in a survey by the President's
Commission on Law Enforcement and Administration of Justice in
1967. The commission reported that while the public as a whole
overwhelmingly rated law enforcement as "good" or "excellent,"
nonwhites, especially blacks, were a good deal more critical of the
police. Nonwhites were more than twice as likely as whites to think
that the police were doing a "poor" job.[39] One year later the Kerner
Commission's report on the origins of the nation's urban riots found
"deep hostility between police and ghetto communities."[40] In later
studies race has proved a more accurate predictor of negative attitude toward the police than age, gender or socioeconomic status.[41]

A major reason for this disparity, the widespread belief among
blacks that police still widely discriminate on the basis of race, initially seems supported by the disproportionately high number of
African-Americans arrested. This is a number even higher than what
could be reasonably expected based on blacks' higher-than-average
share of the crime rate. However, studies suggest that this differential exists because blacks, disproportionately the victims of black
crime, on average demand arrests more often than white com-
plainants.[42] These researchers found evidence of discriminatory atti-

tudes among police, but for various, somewhat curious reasons, little to indicate that these attitudes affected arrest patterns. Indeed, Albert Reiss found that fully three-fourths of all white policemen made "prejudiced remarks" about blacks, yet that both white and black cops were most likely to use excessive force against members of their own race.[43] Similarly, James Q. Wilson concluded in his study of deadly force that departmental policies governing proper self-defense techniques, rather than racial or ethnic considerations, are primarily responsible for the frequency of shooting deaths of suspects.[44]

Much black dissatisfaction with law enforcement may in fact stem from a *lack* of police, especially among inner-city blacks. The National Advisory Commission on Civil Disorders found that African-Americans in Harlem and South-Central Los Angeles cited inadequate police protection as their main reason for resentment toward the police. This reason was offered more often than police brutality, harassment or other complaints.[45] Wilson also concludes that the police's failure to provide effective law enforcement is the primary reason for this disgruntlement. He notes the Kerner Commission's finding that a majority of African-American respondents feel that police "don't come quickly." Wilson points out in addition that the stratum of black Americans who are the most critical of the police are those in the highest income level,[46] who are presumably removed from most ghetto crime.

The average white policeman, in any event, has little interest in wading through this sea of data to figure out why he encounters animosity in the inner city. Although most residents of even the most crime-ravaged neighborhoods are law-abiding, this is sometimes lost on the white cop. It is surely hard for him to ignore the inner-city riots that erupt periodically in supposed retaliation for police misconduct, from New York City to Los Angeles to Miami's Liberty City. Rather than seeing such unrest as a natural display of Americans' traditional distrust of law enforcement, the white policeman frequently interprets such disorders as an expression of collective, murderous revolt by the black community against him and his friends.

The response of many black political leaders to such disorder does little to discourage this dismal conclusion. We have seen in recent years far too many black politicians who treat such criminal unrest as a legitimate method of protest, and who even, at times, publicly sympathize with such offenders. The reaction of many African-

American politicians to the Rodney King Riots in April 1992 was a reminder of this tendency. While most offered at least a brief disclaimer of the violence, many such leaders stated that the parties responsible for the revolt were police and various ill-defined forms of socioeconomic injustice. Jesse Jackson called the riots a "terrible rainbow of protest,"[47] attributing a political motive to crimes that, in the vast majority of cases, was plainly lacking. Benjamin Hooks of the National Association for the Advancement of Colored People interpreted the riots not as an ominous return of the State of Nature, but as proof that African-Americans were "fed up" with mistreatment. Congressman Maxine Waters returned to her constituency in South-Central Los Angeles, found her campaign office burned and concluded that the riots had been caused by the failure to sufficiently expand federal social spending programs in the 1980s.[48] Policemen searched in vain for any sign that these figures did not condone the worst anti-police riots in our nation's history.

An omen of the riots in southern California came from New York several years before, with much the same public justifications for the unrest. In November 1986 New York police attempted to arrest Larry Davis, a Bronx drug dealer, at his sister's apartment. As they tried to enter the premises to arrest him on murder charges, Davis shot six officers. Although none died, one policeman lost an eye, and his head was filled with scores of irretrievable shotgun pellets. When Davis was tried before a jury of ten blacks and two Latinos in 1988 on charges of attempted murder, the jury acquitted Davis not only of attempted murder, but also of aggravated assault. They ruled that he had acted in justifiable self-defense. Davis's legal defense, provided by attorney-activist William Kunstler, argued that the conviction of officers in another police precinct for drug dealing, together with the shootings of several blacks in the city by police, created a climate in which Davis could reasonably fear for his life when police attempted to take him into custody. Davis was convicted only on charges of illegal-weapons possession.

There were no riots in the Bronx following the verdict, but jubilation. "People at my job jumped up in elation when they heard he was acquitted," recounted Gloria Thomas, a forty-one-year-old South Bronx resident. "I feel he did what he had to do," she concluded.[49] Throughout the South Bronx Thomas's sentiments were echoed. "I'm glad he got acquitted," said Willie Daly, sixty-three. "He's a hero to me," added Jothern Smith, eighteen. "He stood up for himself." Indeed, when the police finally caught Davis seventeen days after he managed to escape from the scene of the shootout, residents of a South Bronx housing project chanted "Lar-ry! Lar-ry!" as he was spirited into a police car. "We were hoping he wouldn't get caught," Thomas added. There was even a street dance named after him. With talk that he could convert his new local celebrity status into a book and movie deal, Davis expressed the hope following his acquittal that he could be portrayed by actor Eddie Murphy.[50]

Although cop-killers are not, as a rule, treated so leniently (of course, few have the services of Mr. Kunstler), such celebrations must disperse any doubt that Davis's actions were widely applauded in his neighborhood. The message that these residents of the South Bronx had for cops was the same that, twenty years before, James Baldwin had ascribed to Harlem residents in one vivid, enduring passage from *Nobody Knows My Name*:

> [The police's] very presence is an insult, and it would be, even if they spent their entire day feeding gumdrops to children. They represent the force of the white world, and that world's criminal profit and ease, to keep the black man corraled up here, in his place. The badge, the gun in the holster, and the swinging club make vivid what will happen should his rebellion become overt. . . . [The policeman] has never himself, done anything to be hated—which of us has?—and yet he is facing, daily and nightly, people who would gladly see him dead, and he knows it. There is no way for him not to know it: there are few things under heaven more unnerving than the silent, accumulating contempt and hatred of a people. He moves through Harlem, therefore, like an occupying soldier in a bitterly hostile country; which is precisely what, and where, he is, and is the reason he walks in twos and threes.[51]

We must not end the analysis here, however, as many are wont to do for a variety of motivations. It is easy and customary to attribute this resentment of police to racial hostility, or to some uniquely intractable lawlessness on the part of black Americans. But we must dig deeper, beyond the superficialities to which matters of race too often lend themselves. Such public anger toward the police scarcely originated with African-Americans, nor are today's fragile police-community relations even primarily the result of racial conflict. The enmity toward police expressed by these inner-city blacks is simply the most brutally honest display of Americans' historic animosity toward law enforcement officials. American policemen, who by both trade and temperament are ardent realists, do not suffer illusions about the joys they stand to earn from enforcing the laws of a liberal democracy. They accept, even if they do not much enjoy, the public's displeasure toward a patrol force whose reason for being is the organized suppression of liberty; in this age, our ability to do whatever we desire. Popular animosity toward the government employees charged with preserving ordered liberty has especially deep roots in America. Here, the freedoms that police necessarily constrain are the single greatest source of pride-in-country. For Americans, limitations on individual freedoms often seem downright unpatriotic. We still want order, to be sure, but on our terms—that is, an incoherent mishmash of made-in-America clichés: "limited government" versus "law and order," and so on. The American policeman, as a result, is employed in an occupation that sandwiches him between the dueling appeals of liberty and order, a tension that the American public is often either ignorant of or indifferent to.

Obviously, this does not make for an ideal work environment. Policemen in other democratic societies have their share of problems, but nothing to rival American cops' expansive duties and dim prospects for success. Our police have never enjoyed the public habit of deference to authority that has greatly aided, for instance, British bobbies. Indeed, the earliest New York police complained that a cop's request for aid from bystanders was often "received with a guffaw."[52] New Yorkers in particular have always been less than accommodating toward their policemen. Their resistance to law enforcement traces back to the British attempts to use constables to suppress the Dutch inhabitants of newly annexed New Amsterdam. This prevailing contempt for officers of the law in the seventeenth century was pithily captured in the common, earthy epithet that one early Jerseyman hurled at a British law enforcement official: "Thou sheriff, thou turd."[53]

The self-imposed antiprofessionalism of early American policemen, the product of Jacksonian democracy's distaste for all elites, was designed in part to deal with the widespread discomfort with the police. Police were discouraged from being *too* successful in enforcing the law. By the 1850s both *The New York Times* and New York mayor Fernando Wood concluded that a democratic society, especially one acutely protective of individual freedoms, required a certain degree of inefficiency in law enforcement.[54] Policemen, by an unstated but ever present maxim, were expected to be fashionably lenient. Not only were they to honor the difficult enough duty of maintaining order in a uniquely individualistic democracy; they were also to estimate to whom the laws should be applied and with what vigor. Such was the tacit bargain that American society struck between competing considerations of individual freedom and the rule of law, between the guardians of the common order and an adamantly independent citizenry who wished to preserve the right to cut loose and break a law or two. This rough compromise has endured. It exposes itself most commonly today when policemen occasionally, glumly attempt to enforce the widely disregarded speed limits on U.S. roads. But this compromise held more or less for over a century, until the bumptious forces of criminality previously bottled up through social conventions and traditional police powers burst out upon society in the Great Havoc.

Although American police accept, as a practical matter, the inherited *modus vivendi* between a freedom-intoxicated society and that society's internal security force, they can hardly cherish their role as jugglers of the nation's highest social goals. For the police, these strains in police-community relations are more than an abstract collision of competing philosophical principles. They are a significant employment hazard. The dangers and unpleasantness of policing an often ungrateful and sometimes violent public would dispose anyone toward a reclusive existence. Since this is not possible for a public servant, policemen instead settle for an insular lifestyle and a professional fraternity rooted in absolute fidelity to fellow officers. Sparrow, Moore and Kennedy note, "Loyalty to colleagues counts above everything else."[55] It is the glue that binds officers together in a hazardous mission, engendered by the inherent perils of crime control and the isolation of an authoritarian figure in a democratic land. For the many Irish-Americans who still make up a large share of U.S. police forces, the traditional Irish hatred of informers and subversives—the quality that appealed to the nineteenth-century Anglo-Saxons who recruited them for the new American police departments[56]—still reinforces these institutional incentives for secrecy and solidarity. This nucleus of police values forms an unwritten code of conduct that, along with the camaraderie arising from joint service in life-threatening situations, cements the officers in a bond of fellowship that allows them to cope with a frequently antagonistic society.

The rift between police and community in America is thus preordained. It reflects this democracy's uneasiness with granting its domestic security force the necessary authorization to curtail the individual liberties that make criminal enterprise inevitable. Yet these tensions represent more than simply the inescapable clash between liberty and order. They derive from the reasons for the American police's very existence. The professional law enforcement establishment that set up shop in nineteenth-century American cities, far from essential to Americans' original conception of democratic government, was nowhere to be found in the Founders' blueprint for preserving domestic tranquillity. The creation of the American police force was a political response to the widespread unwillingness of nineteenth-century city-dwellers to cooperate in private ventures of community self-defense. The practical dissolution of collective law enforcement was evident in Boston by the turn of the century, when an apathetic population forced its elected officials to effectively scrap the frankpledge by employing constables and watchmen at public expense.[57] These limited attempts to bolster the delapidated constable-watchman structure through State intervention eventually yielded to a more profound rearrangement. Americans later repealed *in toto* the Norman system of collective security, which had humbly kept the Anglo-Saxon peace, at least in terms of crime control, for the better part of eight centuries.

The professional police, originally intended as a mere supplement to the frankpledge,[58] was soon seized upon by the public as completely replacing the prior system of private crime control. The concept of professional specialization, born of the Industrial Revolution, aided this change. The popular view of the police as a disconnected entity whose "job" was crime control was not far behind. Private citizens, relieved of their previous obligations, soon no longer felt that they were ultimately responsible for the safety of their neighborhoods. The Norman notion of community self-help as the center of crime control efforts unceremoniously dissolved. The basic features of the former system would not reemerge in the Northeast for over a century.

Beneath the shortsightedness and urbanization driving the community's flight from the frankpledge was also a radical shift in political philosophy, without which the police would have lacked a convincing rationale for their monopoly on crime prevention. Preparing the way for this new philosophy were the waves of immigration that began in the early 1800s, which swelled the population and fueled the crime rates of Northeastern cities. The stimulated nativism of city-dwellers, combined with the urbanization and subsequently heightened criminality that accompanied the Industrial Revolution, provided the impetus for shoring up the existing law enforcement regime with professional police.[59] Other, farther-reaching changes were also in the works. The Yankee heirs of the early American Republic, feeling inundated by swarms of lawless immigrants, became ripe for a theory of government that rationalized a lack of concern for their increasingly foreign fellowman. They found this new creed in the emerging British political philosophy of libertarianism.

Libertarianism was an outgrowth of the rights-based liberalism inaugurated by Hobbes. It was an elaboration of his departure from the organic conception of government toward a theory of justice anchored in an array of individual rights wielded against the State. As laid out in John Stuart Mill's revolutionary tract *On Liberty,* the new theory argued for maximum toleration of selected individual liberties and a corresponding reduction in government's proper role over the affairs of the people. Mill espoused an uncompromising individualism that rejected the idea that rights might be pruned if the community thought it vital for its well-being. His main premise was: "That the only purpose for which power can be rightfully exercised over any member of a civilized community, against his will, is to prevent harm to others. His own good, either physical or moral, is not a sufficient warrant." For society to justly prohibit any human conduct, "the conduct from which it is desired to deter [the individual] must be calculated to produce evil to someone else." Mill explained:

> The only part of the conduct of anyone for which he is amenable to society is that which concerns others. In the part which merely concerns himself, his independence is, of right, absolute. Over himself, over his own body and mind, the individual is sovereign.[60]

This sounded promising. Americans had always loved to rail against "government." This was especially so after Jefferson and Jackson gave philosophical and political validity to the nation's proud tradition of rugged individualism and instinctive distrust of the State and its agents. Many at the time did not seem to grasp that the theory might later be enlisted to overturn the Framers' view of the State as the repository and defender of the community's fundamental, stabilizing moral beliefs. Nor did they detect in this condition, which we might call rights-solitude, the pugnacious "solitary" life of Hobbes's war of all against all. At the time of its birth, libertarianism, advocated as a theoretical hedge against bloated government powers, seemed as if it could have sprung from the minds of the Founding Fathers.

But new, especially radical-individualist, philosophies have a demonstrated tendency to be commandeered by revolutionaries and driven to their logical extremes, often in short order. Just as the other major political philosophy contrived in the nineteenth century, Marxism, was invoked in violent insurrections within only a few years of its birth, libertarianism swiftly moved from advocacy of limited government to the preservation of a new regime of materialism and rough-and-tumble individualism. Thus, Hobbes begat Mill, who begat the philosophy of social Darwinism. Like Mill, the social Darwinists of the mid-1800s praised rights in absolute terms. But they spotted one particular bundle of liberties that they felt Mill had wrongly neglected to single out for special treatment: property rights. Social Darwinists offered a philosophy that properly viewed the unequal distribution of wealth in capitalist countries as largely reflecting differences in individual ability. However, in trying to draft government to shepherd this wealth, they argued that government's mission was safeguarding merely the basic rights of life, liberty and property. Theirs was the vision of the State as umpire. The State's employees were to supervise the contestants in the game of life by enforcing rules of fair play and defending the spoils of the victors. Any larger role for the State threatened this regime of sanctified selfishness. A nonlibertarian State might allow the people to enforce policies based on community values, which could lead to infringements of economic liberties by eradicating the promising new industries that would take root in an amoral political order. Laws against drug abuse and prostitution, for instance, could squash what would otherwise be thriving businesses.

A nonlibertarian regime could also permit the losers in this survival-of-the-fittest contest to be treated as something other than inferior members of the species. The community, to the extent it represented something more than a quaint throwback to Judeo-Christian pieties, endangered this unhampered individualism by potentially permitting less affluent citizens to be regarded as neighbors and fellow citizens. Libertarianism's marriage of Mill's rights-based liberalism to the concept of absolute economic liberties dominated American life in the century when the police force was created. Social Darwinist libertarianism resonated with the political, intellectual and business leaders of the time, who wanted a more secure philosophical basis for protecting the bounty that they had accumulated in this sanitized war of all against all.

To paraphrase Mill, egoism became "sovereign"—and a jealous, volatile sovereign at that. Each individual was the center of his own morally void universe, with money and rights constituting his core. It was a glorious system in the abstract, one that would move man's inner selfish half to leap with glee. But there were some details to be worked out. First, individualism was an unstable foundation for a new political order. Individualism is the seed of crime. Crime, to water the analogy, sprouts in gardens of overabundant liberty, and withers only when the community takes back the individual's philosophical and legal basis for waging war on his neighbors. There was also no place for religion of any meaningful sort in Mill's scheme. Religion provides the supernatural supplement to the comparatively weak dread of jail, and, among its many other benefits, it saves society many policemen.[61] Yet this too was to be forgone as part of libertarianism's price. The results were predictable for any who had eyes to see. Today, instead of inheriting the pleasant regime that Mill promised, America suffers from the "terrible individualism" of Dostoevsky's fears. Ours is a period of criminal havoc that he, through the character of Father Zossima, predicted would follow the West's rejection of God.[62]

The police, in turn, were to have their hands full in the new libertarian republic sketched by Mill. They were to serve, within this theoretical framework, as the flesh-and-bones umpires preserving the fairly earned wealth of society's elites. In addition to providing the newly established police with philosophical backing, libertarianism also supplied an intellectual basis for the rights-based atomism that, in America, had always threatened to pry apart police and community. Later generations of Americans would stop thinking of themselves as a community, and instead as a loose affiliation of self-centered individuals. Their only obligation toward the internal protection of society was to pay taxes to maintain the police force. A new, distorted notion of civic duty arose: "I pay my taxes and reasonably follow the rules of the game—now defend me!" But by accepting the centrifugal forces of radical individualism as a fundamental principle of government, Americans ensured that the losers in this game of life would make trouble for the winners. Eventually the losers would try to pillage the possessions of better-off competitors. Often the losers would do so by turning libertarianism against itself, claiming a "right" to a portion of the spoils. If that failed, they could always resort to crime. And under the prevailing relativism, they need not feel guilty about taking what was not lawfully theirs. After all, the other guy would do the same if he were in their shoes. In the war of all against all, that's life.

The policeman's role in American society took shape during this period; he assumed the status of umpire in this great and sometimes brutal contest. Indeed, the theory's vision of a society of individuals in constant conflict, and its implicit encouragement of antisocial activity, made crime more attractive than ever. Libertarianism's rationale for the police was thus self-fulfilling. While the policeman was handed the thankless task of preserving order in a tattered society, the losers in the game of life were simultaneously given a massive inducement to do battle. And the public in general was encouraged to regard the police in the same way modern sports fans view umpires: people to boo when the breaks are not going your way.

If the nation's police-community relations are to improve, there must once again be an America that can be properly called a community.

THE NORMAN RECONQUEST: THE COMMUNITY'S RESPONSE TO THE GREAT HAVOC

Of the many conflicting instructions that American police receive from politicians and the public, perhaps the one that best crystallizes the often self-defeating nature of their work is the familiar demand for "law and order." The upsurge in crime and the resulting frequent use of this term have made law and order a cliché, a cliché that can be misleading. Generally Americans invoke the term when they are clamoring for greater crime control—meaning, more order. We would do well to divorce the pair and stick to this latter word. Taken to its extreme—and that is where our libertarian judiciary invariably takes things—law undermines order. Law limits society's options for how it can dispose of its disorderly members. And sometimes, as with recent court rulings, law erodes the system by which a free society remains free.

It is order, the regime of legally enforced social stability that distinguishes civilization from barbarism, on which all of society's accomplishments are built. Human life itself is largely impossible without order; Saint Augustine recognized the establishment of "earthly peace," and its goal of a "well-ordered concord of civic obedience and rule," as the State's most pressing concern.[63] It is therefore no surprise that what James Q. Wilson calls the "order-maintenance function"[64] of the policeman is his most basic duty, both historically and necessarily. The policeman's role as society's janitor goes back to the earliest Norman watchmen. They were expected to ensure order through a myriad of tasks that ranged from halting riots to lassoing livestock running through English streets.

Wilson, in fact, believes the officer's order-maintenance obligations to be more than baggage from a bygone era. He views crime and order as inextricably linked. Wilson developed a thesis to that effect with George Kelling from which he has received much of his rightly earned fame as a leading criminologist and student of the police. Crime, he submits, is due less to a lack of police than to society's refusal to maintain order—or, more to the point, at least the appearance thereof—in the community. Ultimately crime arises from a lack of social tidiness. The community must be willing to do the simple things, such as property maintenance, that give neighborhoods the appearance of being inhabited by people who care enough about preserving order to be willing to roll up their sleeves and do the harsher things as well, such as punishing criminals. The crumbling of order and resulting self-destruction of the community start with broken windows not being fixed; next prostitutes and vagrants are allowed to loiter; soon delinquents and youth gangs realize they can act with impunity; and by then the neighborhood is well on its way toward disintegration. Instead of surrendering en masse to an armed invasion, neighborhoods slowly slide into the swamp of widespread crime. This happens, in the final analysis, because of subconscious decisions not to maintain the deterrent aura of order.[65]

The past three decades provide powerful evidence of this suspected correlation between disorder and crime. The most striking confirmation of this theory came following the Supreme Court's repeal of a status offense used for thousands of years for order-maintenance purposes, vagrancy. Vagrancy statutes have been enforced since at least ancient Athens, where Solon made idleness a crime. The British Statute of Laborers enacted in the fourteenth century codified this offense for the first time in a common-law jurisdiction. Although the statute was intended to deal with the flocks of recently freed British serfs roaming the countryside, vagrancy statutes later came to be accepted as an effective means of deterring crime by encouraging thrift and upholding order. The British Vagabond Act of 1774 treated idle and disorderly persons as one of three categories of vagrants, thus revealing the emerging conceptual amalgamation of vagrancy and disorderly conduct. The first Americans adopted similar legislation in all thirteen states. They also inserted a clause into Article 4 of their Articles of Confederation that exempted "paupers" and "vagabonds" from the guarantee of free movement between states.

All fifty states enforced vagrancy statutes until the 1972 Supreme Court decision in *Papachristou v. City of Jacksonville*.[66] In an opinion by Justice William O. Douglas, the Court effectively held vagrancy statutes per se unconstitutional because of their inherent vagueness and invasion of personal freedoms. Justice Douglas devoted much of his opinion to discussing the value of recreational walking, which he evidently equated with vagrancy. He stated that "'wandering or strolling' from place to place ha[s] been extolled by Walt Whitman and Vachel Lindsay," and claimed that Puerto Ricans have a distinct cultural affinity for vagabondism. Douglas also listed the health benefits of a late-evening stroll, including its ability to cure insomnia.[67]

If Justice Douglas genuinely wished for others to share the pleasures of nightly walking, his opinion was, as it were, a big step in the wrong direction. *Papachristou,* like *Mapp* and *Miranda* before it, limited police prerogatives and thus inevitably impaired their ability to maintain order. Currently *Papachristou* is interpreted as rendering unconstitutional virtually all antivagrancy statutes. Police efforts to bar known criminals or gangs from congregating on street corners, such as Newark's enhanced sweep operations pursuant to a law against "blocking pedestrian traffic," are now constitutionally suspect.[68] *Papachristou* took away the police's authority to disperse alcoholics, prostitutes and other distributors of disorder from neighborhoods threatened with social decay. Vagrancy, in short, became a constitutional right.

Papachristou also signaled an even more noteworthy, and troublesome, development. The case marked a watershed in America's attitude toward vagrants as a class. To understand the dimensions of this change, we must recognize, first of all, that Americans have not been sent this social subgroup as a unique curse from the gods. Every known society has documented and objected to disorderly individuals of this sort, who rebel against the customs and lifestyle of the masses in their particular era and milieu. The Court in *Papachristou* rejected this age-old social practice. By viewing vagrants as, in essence, mainstream members of American society, the Court offered a conception of vagrants as ordinary citizens who, being either down on their luck or insomniacs, deserved sympathy rather than a legal stimulus to behave differently. No longer the class of bohemian citizens who had drawn the ire of previous millennia of civilization, the vagrants of modern America became seen as victims of social neglect. Still, while *Papachristou* was the government's first official suggestion that vagrants deserved legal protection, even Justice Douglas in his wildest somnambulistic dreams could scarcely have foreseen what later budded from his efforts. His opinion would help lead to the invention of an entirely new word and concept to describe this category of people—the "homeless."

The confusion about the homeless phenomenon cannot be fully understood without analyzing the history of its defining term. The *Oxford English Dictionary* cites the first use of the term "homeless" in 1615.[69] For two centuries its exclusive meaning was "having no home or permanent abode," as expressed in Wordsworth's 1802 sonnet "Jones! as from Calais": "A homeless sound of joy was in the sky." In the mid-nineteenth century a few writers, such as Dickens in *Dombey and Son,* began to apply the term to the poor. But very few if any journalists pressed the term into similar service. And no one even conceived of using "homeless" as a synonym for vagrant. Indeed, a review of American periodical literature shows that in the extremely rare instances in which the media, for instance, applied "homeless" to the poor or destitute, they did so to describe people whose homes had been destroyed by a natural disaster or similar tragedy.

This conception held, that is, until the 1980s. It is informative to compare descriptions of vagrants prior to that decade to those immediately after. In his 1980 book on the police, for example, prominent sociologist Donald Black analyzed the class of people later popularly labeled the homeless and termed them residents of "skid row." He described them in the following illustrative manner: ". . . sociologically, skid row is not so much a matter of geography as of lifestyle, involving nomadism, unemployment, heavy consumption of alcoholic beverages, foraging, begging, and a principled rejection of conventional modes of existence."[70] This description is typical of both popular and academic attitudes toward vagrants up to that time. Prior to the 1980s every generation of Americans had frankly acknowledged the existence of a layer of society composed of people who were unwilling to accept the habits and responsibilities of average citizens. This, of course, was only to be expected. Some people are more individualistic than others, and prefer to live independently of all claims from other people, be they family, employers or society. Sometimes this lifestyle may very well be "principled," as Black and others termed it, in the sense that it is chosen because it is more personally agreeable. But a nation that sanctions such extreme individualism must expect to be penalized. All prior generations of Americans had realized this, and sought to combat this danger by stigmatizing vagrancy and related ways of life. They did so with a variety of labels for its participants, including "tramp," hobo," "bum," or the most universal and polite term, "vagrant."

Then came the 1980s, and an attempt by political activists to coin and propagate an entirely new view of this social subgroup. This conception of vagrants quarried the guilt of a prosperous American society that still felt certain misgivings about its materialism and self-centeredness. People living on the streets, Americans were told, were not there because of any "principled rejection of conventional modes of existence." A person would have to be *crazy* to choose to be homeless, it was said; and many Americans, with no relevant experience or point of reference to draw from, had to agree. From this grew the concept of homelessness. It was a vision of vagrancy that was designed, primarily, to discredit the federal fiscal policies of the era. The tax-cutting, government-shrinking practices of the 1980s were undoubtedly motivated at least in part by the electorate's materialism, as was alleged. The problem was that these policies had very little to do with the existence or growth of vagrancy.

The reasons for homelessness are now fairly well documented. Homelessness was not the result of poverty. The 1980s featured substantial economic growth at all wage levels, some of which, it is true, seemed to reflect the artificial multiplier effect of federal deficit spending. Government aid to the poor was also not nearly as parsimonious as is commonly thought. During the 1980s federal housing subsidies for low-income families rose in real terms by over 50 percent.[71] The engine behind homelessness, it seemed, was the fact that the homeless were people like us in at least one important respect— they responded to economic incentives. While the number of shelter beds rose in the 1980s from 98,000 to 275,000, the new beds were promptly occupied without any appreciable reduction in the available homeless population. In a 1988 survey of New York City's shelters, 90 percent of the families arriving at shelters were found to be receiving welfare benefits. Often they had previously been doubled up with friends or relatives or in cheap rented rooms before taking advantage of the city's offer of free housing.[72] New York officials are reaching the same conclusion in response to the ongoing "explosion" of requests for free emergency shelter in the 1990s.[73] The increased wealth of the 1980s gave government and private charities more revenue to devote to what became, as a whole, one of the more misdirected social causes of our time. The homeless, it should be noted in their defense, simply accepted the invitation.

In moments of candor, homeless rights' activists would confess deceit. In the words of one academic, homeless advocates had concealed a "nasty little secret" about the homeless. That secret was that the overwhelming majority of the homeless were single, able-bodied males who were either drug- or alcohol-dependent, or ex-cons and street hustlers.[74] The Cuomo Commission found that 80 percent of the New York homeless given urinalysis tested positive for illegal drugs, mostly cocaine.[75] Peter Rossi, a sociologist then with the University of Massachusetts, analyzed sixteen different studies and found that an average of 42.1 percent of the homeless had actually spent time in jail or prison.[76] The homeless were therefore not only carriers of disorder and a subsequent rise in crime; they frequently lived a life of crime themselves. Robert Hayes, director of the National Coalition for the Homeless, admitted that homeless advocates had sought to suppress these facts because they "feared that the public would lose its sympathy for the homeless."[77]

There were other reasons for the sudden rise in vagrancy. The deinstitutionalization of the mentally ill in the 1960s had contributed to vagrants' ranks. These citizens, once let loose, were too often forgotten and uncared for, and left to fend for themselves on increasingly dangerous city streets. In the 1980s the mentally disturbed were often included statistically with alcoholics and panhandlers in order to give the appearance of a larger homeless population. One of the most saddening and sordid spectacles of the era was the litigation pursued by civil rights lawyers representing the mentally ill homeless. These attorneys sought a judicially broadened right to vagrancy for souls who, in many cases, were unable even to comprehend their plight fully. The most famous figure in this legal strategy was Billie Boggs, the mentally ill New York street dweller who was celebrated at Harvard Law School in 1988 for having won the right to return to life on the New York streets. Soon thereafter she abandoned her job and professional care and reverted to her earlier street life of defecating on public sidewalks, shouting obscenities at passersby, and drug addiction.[78] Only the lives of the homeless activists themselves exposed more clearly the deception at the heart of the homeless movement. Typical was the movement's unofficial leader in the 1980s, Mitch Snyder. He became a professional activist after deserting his wife and children; fortunately they did not end up on the streets to become his clients. Snyder, among other questionable practices, often inflated figures about the number of homeless to obtain more federal funding.[79] In a fitting footnote to Snyder's life following his 1990 suicide, homeless activists seeking a more generous right-to-shelter law in Washington, D.C., placed an urn containing Snyder's ashes before the D.C. board of elections so that he could be "present" for their lobbying efforts. The article describing Snyder's posthumous appearance in *The Washington Post* was tellingly titled "Guilt Ploy Tried Again by Homeless."[80]

By lending credence to the idea that vagrants are people like us who have fallen through the cracks of a callous society, the concept of "homelessness" has added to a welter of competing, distracting issues in our crime control debate. We have spent our energies of late flattering ourselves into thinking America the first nation in history to rid itself of irresponsible, "skid row" elements. We have also, as a result, failed to seriously address the crime wave in which, it turns out, a significant number of the homeless have participated. This legitimation of the concept of homelessness has not been without its costs. It has effectively condoned urban disorder and made even more difficult the police's efforts to dredge out the ingredients of crime.

The surge in crime and disorder in the 1980s, exacerbated by these events, eventually provoked a counterrevolution, in the true sense of the word. The popular conceptual acceptance of homelessness contributed to a national schizophrenia not unlike that suffered by many of the deinstitutionalized mentally ill. Even as many Americans were accepting homelessness as a national failure, they became frightened at the same time by this government-sanctioned breakdown of order. In the tradition of the stubborn, sometimes raucous independence of their forefathers, many Americans resolved to take matters into their own hands. The 1980s saw not only the rise of the homeless phenomenon, but also a curious, simultaneous resurgence of vigilantism, the disorderly means of restoring order that has long tugged at the American imagination.

Always bubbling beneath an official government monopoly on the right to use force in defense of the common order, American vigilantism has been cast in uniquely populist terms that give it enduring appeal. Vigilantism in the United States lays claim to the grandest traditions of Western political thought. Drawing on the Hobbesian and Lockean principles that motivated the Framers, it asserts the right of the community to enforce justice itself when the government established for that purpose fails to honor this most fundamental duty. Vigilantism was Europe's universal system of justice following the collapse of the Roman Empire. Outlawry was the most frequent form of vigilantism. In practicing outlawry, the community would unite informally to punish criminals through the destruction of their property, banishment or death. This systematic vigilantism enforced European order for many government-deprived centuries. The first recorded instances of vigilantism in America took place before the political principles of the American Revolution could provide private defenders of the peace with an explicit philosophical basis for their efforts. In 1767 a group calling itself the Regulators launched a crusade against the roving criminal gangs preying on South Carolina. The leaders of the Regulators, like those of later vigilante movements, issued proclamations filled with appeals to God, country and the ultimate authority of positive law. But when the government lacked the resolve or resources to provide for public security, they maintained, the right of popular sovereignty entitled them to administer justice the old-fashioned way.

While postbellum Southern lynch mobs later twisted vigilantism into a defense of racial terrorism, in the rest of the country it retained its original, limited mission as a stand-in for the rule of law. Vigilantism was thought to be a substitute system for ensuring rough justice when law enforcement authorities were unavailable or impotent. This system was ready-made for the frontier. There, order was scarce and dependent on community action, and the ideology of rugged individualism made self-help law especially attractive. One newspaper writer reported this public backing of the practice when he noted, following an 1879 vigilante execution in Golden, Colorado, that "the popular verdict seemed to be that the hanging was not only well merited, but a positive gain for the county, saving at least five or six thousand dollars."[81] Legal scholars and judges widely endorsed vigilantism in limited application until as late as the early twentieth century. Vigilantism remained the standard regime of criminal justice on the frontier until the government, with its specialized police force and judicial system, was established firmly enough to persuade the community to rely on it for protection.

The return of do-it-yourself justice predictably came in the high-crime years of the late twentieth century, when government once again seemed unable to punish criminals effectively. At first vigilantism assumed relatively restrained forms. One example was the establishment, in the late 1960s and '70s, of organizations such as the Guardian Angels. Under the articulate leadership of young Curtis Sliwa, the Guardian Angels began in 1978 to outfit inner-city youths with distinctive red berets and charge them with the narrow mission of apprehending and detaining criminals until police arrived. The full magnitude of the growing vigilante movement did not register, however, until 1984, when a bespectacled, unassuming electronics engineer named Bernhard Goetz boarded a New York subway on December 22. His shooting of four black youths who had "asked" him for money while displaying a sharpened screwdriver outraged many of America's opinion leaders in government and in academia, but otherwise turned Goetz overnight into something of a national hero. A *New York Times* poll found that 52 percent of New Yorkers were generally supportive of Goetz's actions, with 28 percent not supportive.[82] Among African-Americans, a plurality, 45 percent, were supportive. Mayor Edward Koch received letters running eighty to one in favor of Goetz's actions. Goetz's supporters ranged from Roy Innis, the leader of the the Congress of Racial Equality, to comedienne Joan Rivers, who offered to help Goetz pay his $50,000 bail.[83]

Goetz's salvo, while not technically vigilantism (his actions were more in the nature of self-defense), reverberated throughout his crime-battered country, echoing the frustrations of a society whose leaders appeared unable to safeguard their most essential freedom. The demonstrations of public support that Goetz received suggested something else as well. Americans were starting, tentatively, to think and feel like a community again. Emerging was a new, if overdue and limited, awareness of community crime control responsibilities. Sometimes this new sense of duty assumed the form of coordinated community pressure on law enforcement officials to stiffen criminal penalties. One such reaction came in 1987, when residents of several northern California towns effectively quarantined their communities from Lawrence Singleton. He had been convicted of raping a teenage girl and leaving her for dead after hacking off her forearms with an ax, and had been released on parole before most residents thought it prudent. In one community proposed as his new home-town, an estimated 175 neighbors demonstrated against Singleton, carrying placards saying, "Get the Hacker Out!"[84] In 1994 another California hamlet, Alturas, was the scene of militant protests against the housing in their community of Melvin Carter, a parolee who had confessed to some one hundred rapes. At other times this vigilante backlash has come in more traditional forms: Black Muslims patrolling inner cities and occasionally roughing up suspects to the cheers of community residents; suburban neighbors in Michigan and elsewhere banding together to burn down local crack houses; the 1981 shooting of the reputed town bully in Skidmore, Missouri, by community leaders, after the criminal justice system failed to halt his terrorizing of town residents. Numerous examples could be cited of vigilante actions that seem far less justified, and that are typical of the sort of mob rule that comes to the fore when governmental crime control becomes toothless. We can expect much more of this until American government can once again effectively protect the right of personal security.

The best regime, of course, is one that avoids the radical practice of vigilantism by fusing policing with constructive community activism and self-restraint. One example was Detroit's recent reaction to the annual real-life Halloween horror of Devil's Night. In response to the local tradition of an arson festival on the nights preceding All Hallows Eve, Detroit residents in 1991 banded together with fire extinguishers, flashlights and radios in a massive display of community deterrence. With the help of police helicopters and a dusk-to-dawn curfew for youths under eighteen, the 4,000 volunteers cut the number of fires from 141 the prior year to 62.[85] Where such government assistance is unavailable, though, private citizens can only be expected to take care of such things themselves. On one thing more and more Americans of virtually every persuasion agree: vigilantism, while clearly no substitute for the rule of law, is better than no justice at all.

While Americans are increasingly reverting to self-help law enforcement and self-protection devices, including massive invest-ments in security systems (which, in the words of one top ACLU official, evoke "visions of 1984, Big Brother and all that stuff" when used in businesses),[86] there is only so much that private citizens can do without a coordinated government strategy for combating crime. In addition to political leadership, people need one of the things government is uniquely capable of providing—a common call to civic duty, backed by the force of law. One such program would be a restoration of the frankpledge, or required service in a Neighborhood Watch program. This might also be dubbed the crime control "draft." The able-bodied men of every household who did not have a criminal record would once again be subject to obligatory service for community crime surveillance. Properly strong criminal penalties would deter those who might be tempted to dodge this draft by committing a crime. Women should not be subject to such conscription for the same reasons that they have traditionally been spared combat duty; and, in any case, since men commit the vast majority of crimes, it only seems fair to assign them these corresponding responsibilities. They would be required to patrol their neighborhoods without weapons, armed only with walkie-talkies or other communications gear capable of informing police of any discovered criminal activity. Their sole duty would be to inform police of crimes in progress.

The returns from this reinstatement of the frankpledge along Neighborhood Watch lines could be vast. The probability of arrest for a crime in progress is about 33 percent, while a mere fifteen-minute delay reduces the probability to 5 percent.[87] One prominent criminologist, Herman Goldstein, has estimated that a 5 to 10 percent increase in citizen involvement could "possibly prove of much greater value in combating crime than a 50 or 60 percent increase in the number of police officers or an equally large investment in technical equipment."[88] Conscription into this mandatory Neighborhood Watch program would improve police response time, buttress law enforcement and fortify the citizen's attachment to the community—perhaps the best antidote to crime for young men today, who often lack any commitment to the society that sustains them.

A second practical reform with much the same likely results is legislation obliging witnesses to report crimes to the police and aid in their investigation. A statutory reporting requirement would also further reinforce the notion that the community is ultimately responsible for its own security. Since almost all crimes are committed in the presence of other people, this law would merely ensure that citizens not effectively abet offenders by not reporting them. Appropriate limited exceptions to this requirement would be made for members of an offender's family, the clergy, and so forth. A return to the misprision-of-felony requirements inherited from the British and subsequently abandoned, such a statute would invigorate and affirm the citizen's most basic duty to his fellowman: to inform police of a crime when he possesses firsthand knowledge of it and can reasonably do so without endangering himself. While such a requirement has a long history in British criminal justice, only three states currently have such a law on the books. All are essentially unenforced.[89]

It is a tribute to the influence that libertarianism has over present-day America that such minimal public obligations are sure to spark controversy. But until we submit to certain basic citizen crime-control responsibilities and actively assist the nation's beleaguered, outnumbered police forces, we will never reclaim our streets. *Never*. The crime epidemic that we face is simply too vast for outnumbered policemen to reverse by themselves. Only a new dedication to public service in defense of the common order can hope to make the War on Crime less of a rout. In this supreme conflict, where the frontline and the home front are the same battlefield, active community involvement presents the last hope of victory. News of such fresh troops, when and if enlisted, is sure to elicit cheers from the row of blue uniforms who must otherwise resign themselves to a siege that promises to end unpleasantly.

CHAPTER THREE

The Courts: Dueling Proxies

Without justice there are but litigants, the oppressors and the victims.

—Napoleon

"Perhaps we should give up. Nothing works. Nothing has ever worked in a free society like ours."[1]

So much for a rousing call to arms for America's War on Crime. And from one of its lieutenants? Say it ain't so. The distress expressed above is from a Tennessee district attorney, dejected because of the failure of the state's most recent "get tough" crime control legislation. Such pessimism could be forgiven of the average citizen, who has seen too many anticrime political promises go unfulfilled. But when this defeatism is articulated by one of the officers in the War on Crime's judicial theater of operations, a democratic society that still desires the rule of law should take notice. It is in the courts where due process, the core of grand strategy, is formulated and applied. If things are not going well there, a detached forum spared the travails of actually apprehending and holding violent offenders, then the war is going very poorly indeed.

The courts are often the forgotten leg of America's criminal justice triad. A nation partial to showy government programs quickly loses interest in the relatively tedious but essential business of determining the guilt or innocence of criminal defendants. We are too often impatient with the programs and institutions that fail to do something about crime *now,* preferably something "tough." The courts, in addition to appearing less tough than the other legs of the triad, suffer from the additional handicap of being, by comparison, rather boring; and thus too many Americans lack the necessary forbearance for the slow, stuffy processing of criminals through trials by jury. Our scarce crime control resources (made scarce by conscious political decisions to channel tax revenues into other government programs), the popular thinking goes, are better spent on the police and prisons. These involve the physical disciplining of criminals, and are therefore "tougher."

This disinterest in the nation's overwhelmed court system must lessen, and soon, if we are serious about regaining our ability to efficiently segregate the lawless from the lawful. In a society under the rule of law, criminal punishment is based on a just determination of guilt. This is a determination that in America, at least, courts are uniquely capable of providing. A shortfall in the judicial resources necessary for financing these daily adjudications means a breakdown in the entire crime control regime. The courts' current inability to handle their rising caseload and the reasons for the litigiousness choking the administration of justice in modern America, thus deserve our attention. There are important lessons to be learned here. Much of this legal mayhem, it turns out, has been accomplished not by criminals, but by a slightly less mischievous class of equally self-interested citizens: lawyers.

TRIAL BY BATTLE

The courtroom—often plush and paneled, and increasingly cramped—seemingly provides a poor arena for combat. But just as the gladiators and gunslingers of old meted out criminal justice as their societies defined it, today the American courtroom provides a less deadly, but every bit as consequential, battleground for the bodies and souls of the citizens under its domain. Before a select audience of his peers, an individual accused of a crime watches his fate decided by the decorous but critical shoot-out between prosecution and defense, who sit center stage. From this clash of rhetoric and evidence, circumscribed by the rules of criminal procedure that have developed over centuries of Anglo-American jurisprudence, emerges a verdict from the defendant's peers that determines whether the State may punish him for criminal wrongdoing. Only then may society truly get tough.

This inevitable collision of outlaws and society's defenders has taken a unique and peculiar form in the Anglo-American system of justice. Of course, the prosecution of accused offenders, by pitting State against citizen, per se institutionalizes a certain amount of social conflict. But this essential organized strife has reached, in the American criminal justice system, an extreme only slightly more progressive than the duels of olden times. American criminal justice has adopted, and is virtually synonymous with, a regime of supervised duels that the lawyers serving in them have named the adversary system. Unlike continental Europe, where the prosecution of the accused revolves around an impartial judge who actively supervises the proceedings much like a father settling a family quarrel, the United States clings to this British system of justice through lawyer warfare. The adversary system eschews the alternative, judge-centered criminal proceedings in favor of a judicially officiated match between lawyers. These hired guns are retained from the mercenary corps of today's bar associations to represent the State's and the accused's respective interests.

Here, in the miniature gladiator pits that are American courts, the outcome often depends on the fighting spirit of the lawyer-combatants. Reduced to an umpire, the judge presides over the proceedings as a detached figure restricted to settling disputes over which evidence the lawyers may present to the jury. Marshaling the (helpful) evidence and offering it to the jury with all his powers of oratory and drama, each attorney crafts and delivers the best representation of his client's interests. And just as the better gladiator or gunslinger prevailed in earlier, "primitive" judicial systems, the talents of the lawyer largely determine the jury's decision. The better-armed lawyer—that is, the one more skilled at obtaining the exclusion of damaging evidence or at simply charming the jury—usually emerges the victor, his client's interests secured and his bank account refreshed.

Although we often reflexively view America's political and legal institutions as the world's most enlightened, the Great Havoc has

helped to direct some otherwise uncritical eyes to the problems with
the adversary system. Chief among these is the fact that the adversary system is, when stripped of the legitimating sediment of tradition, a medieval institution reflecting medieval notions of justice.
The adversary system is the product of a young English nation grop-
ing for fair ways to identify and punish its criminals. This search
eventually took the singular form of the medieval trial. The English
of the Middle Ages believed that the most trustworthy method of
determining the guilt of the accused was to subject him to a trial.
This meant a physical test at times bordering on torture.

There were two types of trial, which were combined conceptually
over time. One was trial by ordeal. Since the medieval English
believed that God would intervene to protect innocents from harm,
they concluded that the surest way to find out whether a defendant
had committed one of the sins forbidden by the criminal code was to
subject him to mortal, or at least severe, danger, commonly by
requiring him to handle a piece of red-hot iron or plunge his hand
up to the wrist into boiling water.[2] Despite the biblical injunction
against putting God to the test, these trials were essentially community demands for a divine miracle to save the accused. Even if the
Almighty were to overlook this impertinence and grant such a sign,
the rescued individual might still be viewed as guilty—unharmed
only because of the powers of black magic and the like. When, for
instance, the ordeal of water was chosen and the accused was
accordingly submerged, sinking was viewed as a sign of innocence,
floating as proof of guilt. Thus, those who did not drown were
deemed guilty all the same, and subject to swift capital punishment
of a different sort. Accusation of a severe crime, in practice, frequently amounted to an automatic death sentence.

If trial by ordeal was only slightly more humane than a summary
execution, it did at least offer one escape route: trial by battle.
William the Conqueror himself introduced trial by battle, or combat,
to the British Isles. This system was largely an altered version of the
private war previously allowed between feuding families under the
pre-Norman reign of King Alfred. The institution of private war permitted a wronged party to battle the accused offender without the aid
of government, either personally or with a proxy. As the influential
British jurist Sir James Fitzjames Stephen recounts, William regarded
trial by battle "as a modified form of private war," which in fact "was
only private war under regulations." The early English practice
allowed one either to submit to the ordeal or to appeal to trial by bat-

tle with one's accuser. In addition, each of the parties could choose a proxy, "his man," to duel in his place. These rented champions of justice would, for the right price, stand in for the accused. From this clash of armor and flesh would emerge a decision that was thought to reflect God's judgment. This legal jousting match was the precursor of the modern criminal trial, and the knights-for-hire who served in it were the forerunners of today's attorneys.[3]

When the English later came to rely on the wisdom of the community to decide the accused's guilt, rather than a presumptuous testing of God's favors, trial by ordeal was transformed but not replaced. In the thirteenth century trials by ordeal fell into disuse, but the "trial" remained. The fate of the accused still hinged on an exchange between prosecution and defense. The verdict, however, came not from the death of the combatants, but from a judgment of the spectators—a jury chosen from the community.

Over the next five centuries the trial evolved into a more efficient and objective fact-finding process. Important to this advancement was the near-exclusion of lawyers. Records from the Old Bailey, England's main criminal court, indicate that in most felony trials during this period neither side was represented by counsel. Those lawyers who did participate were only minor, peripheral figures. Instead, the English judge, much like the judges on the European continent today, assumed functions now performed by lawyers. British judges would lead the questioning of witnesses and the presentation of evidence.[4] The judge's central role and relative activism were due in part to the lack of a recognized right of counsel for the accused, a limitation not similarly binding on the prosecution. Lawyers saw in this manifest injustice a chance to broaden their influence. In the 1730s they offered themselves as the levelers in this struggle for equal justice under law, capable of ending the imbalance by assuming the duties formerly held by the judge and enforcing the accused's right to counsel. Gaining control over these central procedures, especially the all-important role of presenting evidence to the jury, English barristers secured a crucial position in the criminal trial.[5] The outlines of the old trial by battle reemerged in a new clash of mercenary forces. The new lawyer-centered trial became fossilized and enshrined in Anglo-American courts, and remains intact.

Attorneys applied this same zeal to extracting a steadily rising price for their services from those they shielded from bodily harm. An English populace liberated from the menace of medieval justice soon found itself subjected to another ordeal: retaining an attorney. Popular resentment was not slow in coming. Long before Shakespeare's barbs pierced them from the nation's playhouses, lawyers were popularly judged a class of corrupt, opportunistic entrepreneurs who took advantage of the suffering of others by using the looming threat of punishment to extort money from the accused. Lawyers, as English Sophists, came to be seen as the classic sellers of truth that Socrates and Plato had inveighed against. The public obloquy that naturally followed worked its way into law when new English lands free of the bar were discovered and populated. The first laws of the Massachusetts Bay Colony, for instance, codified the widely held perception of lawyers as godless, materialistic scoundrels. In their Body of Liberties, a remarkable document that preceded the English Bill of Rights by over 40 years and the U.S. Bill of Rights by almost 140, the settlers clamped on an embargo of lawyers to widespread approval. Like several other colonies at the time, Massachusetts banned lawyers flatly:

> Every man that findeth himselfe unfit to plead his owne cause in any Court, shall have the Libertie to imploy any man against whom the Court doth not except, to help him, *Provided he give him noe fee, or reward for his paines.*[6] [Emphasis added.]

Yet lawyers were a wily prey. They retained their influence over America's legal system by holding on to a semimonopoly on the means of avoiding criminal punishment. The alliance of lawyers and politicians—and in America the later virtual merger of the two classes—ensured that the bar would continue to corner the market on these vital services and thereby dominate Anglo-American society in a way that no other profession ever has. But even such a durable arrangement, like the elite castes that have climbed to the top of other democracies, required at least a pro forma justification for its special status. The system's need for a convincing apologia was especially acute given that for seven centuries England had gotten along just fine without it.

Continental Europe, in fact, still follows this ancient regime. The Continent's communal-law system* offers a competing conception

---

*I coin this term because of the current lack of a better one. Despite its popularity, the term "accusatorial," often used to describe this competing system, was thought up by lawyers who clearly were no friend of the alternative, impoverishing system.

of justice production revolving around the judge rather than attorneys. By marginalizing lawyers and making State-appointed judges the main fact-finders, the communal-law system ensures that justice does not depend on the quality of representation from lawyers. This system provides for greater equality under law. Given this alternative regime, which beckons from the continent that invented the very concept of the rule of law, American lawyers have not been able to take their authority for granted. The lawyer-centered system has required an appealing name and an acceptable *post hoc* reason for being. Such was the origin of the term "adversary system" and the theory intended to validate it, the notion of truth-by-collision.

This concept, in which law students are still loyally drilled, captures well the legal profession's striking talent for inventing persuasive after-the-fact rationales to consolidate its economic gains. The theory behind the adversary system holds that the artificial combat of two attorneys rhetorically slugging it out is much more than a medieval anachronism. The institution is actually superior to the communal-law system. The adversary system generates a privately financed quest for truth that can produce more accurate legal conclusions than one conducted by the government. The struggle between opposing interests in the adversary system yields a more assiduous search for the facts, and hence a more just result, than the objective investigations overseen by the European magistrate. Each side under the adversary system more thoroughly scrutinizes the arguments and evidence of the other side, blasting holes in its opponent's position with independently collected evidence. The jury then decides which party's position is less frazzled. This defense of the adversary system also bears some superficial resemblance to the later marketplace-of-ideas defense of free speech. The philosophical basis for the adversary system is thus libertarianism applied to the judicial system: let each side buy the legal services of its choice from the free market, and may the best man win.

The defense rested; and by and large English-speaking peoples acquiesced, reluctantly acquitting lawyers of the popular charge of grand larceny. Americans in particular relented to this arrangement less because of widespread agreement than because of the power of lawyer-politicians, who made meaningful legal reform dishearteningly difficult. Today the adversary system's shortcomings generally go unnoticed and unqueried, except for an occasional question from quizzical law students, whose financial interest in viewing their future profession as honorable eventually clarifies the justice of it all.

America currently conducts more than 90 percent of the world's criminal jury trials, and nearly all of its civil jury trials.[7] As Professor Gordon Van Kessel has noted, this inherited system "is the most uncompromisingly adversary criminal trial structure in the world," a luxury for which "we pay a high price."[8]

The problems with this "extreme" system[9] remain much the same as those of centuries past. The most obvious is the adversary system's conception of lawyers as crusaders who, after being retained for a criminal trial, gallantly ride off in an objective search for the Truth without regard to their client's interests. The lawyer who conceived this defense of the adversary system must have had a twinkle in his eye. To the extent that this vision of legal errantry materializes at all in a criminal trial, it does so only in respect to the prosecution. Although the defense attorney is required by the bar's rules of professional responsibility to devote himself exclusively, and by practically any means short of fraud, to gaining his client's acquittal, the prosecutor is bound by the same professional rules to promote justice above the interests of his client, the State. While the defense attorney can concentrate on getting the best possible deal for his client, the governing ethical rules mandate that the prosecutor serve as a "minister of justice."[10] This means juggling his responsibilities to the government and his opponent. The prosecutor must, for example, reveal any exculpatory evidence to the defense, as well as any evidence that might argue for reduced punishment. The defense has no corresponding duties. In fact, defense counsel will face disciplinary sanctions if he reveals any incriminating evidence in return. Constrained only by the profession's liberal ethics canons, defense attorneys are the best example of legal philosopher Richard Wasserstrom's description of lawyers as "amoral technicians,"[11] a description approvingly quoted by his subjects ever since.

Applied to a criminal justice regime that institutionally already favors the defendant, the modern adversary system sanctions a unilateral quest for truth. The American legal system outfits the prosecutor for the dispassionate search for justice while requiring the defense to do everything he can to disrupt the prosecutor's mission. One Supreme Court justice often regarded as something of a hanging judge in criminal justice cases, recently retired Justice Byron White, has framed the defense's duty of obfuscation in constitutional terms. "Defense counsel," White stated, "need present nothing, even if he knows what the truth is. . . . If he can confuse a witness, even a truthful one, or make him appear at a disadvantage, unsure or indecisive, that will be his normal course."[12] Professor Van Kessel observes, "For defense attorneys, courtroom victory usually translates into obtaining an acquittal, and they often regard discovery of the truth as incidental or even irrelevant to this pursuit. In most criminal trials, discovery of truth is the last thing a defense lawyer desires."[13]

If it is not much of a shoot-out when the duelists are firing in opposite directions, the skirmish is even less sporting when the combatants are unequally armed. Truth, which is essential for justice, cannot consistently emerge from this demilitarized trial by battle when the two parties are unevenly matched. A fair clash of ideas is impossible when the talents of one side's counsel overwhelm those of the other. Yet such inequality of representation is today the norm in U.S. trials; it is, in fact, truly a defining characteristic of American criminal justice. Until the mid-nineteenth century caps on attorneys' fees discouraged such inequity. States set the maximum price that attorneys could charge their clients. This imposed a crude but sensible price control that lessened the harshness of economic life under a lawyer monopoly. Now, having secured the repeal of those restrictions, lawyers may charge as much as the market allows. The wealthy thus are able to hire the better attorneys, while poorer defendants are forced to rely on less talented State-appointed counsel. While we may be tempted, given our crime-beset age, to applaud this state of affairs, given that most criminals are poor and thus are represented by the worst lawyers, any society that styles itself a defender of equal justice under law clearly must do better than reserving its best advocates for the well-to-do.

While we know most inequalities of class in a capitalist country to be the result of wealth fairly earned, we must draw the line at this imbalance. Justice is different. The adversary system ingrains in our criminal justice process the most inflammatory sort of inequality, inherently favoring people of means at every stage of prosecution. Instead of a government-appointed, impartial judge sifting through the evidence and submitting the facts to the jury, lawyers largely determine the outcome. Perhaps not much has improved since the Middle Ages; today, as before, the winner is often the one with the most cash.

If this assessment seems harsh, then consider, as Exhibit A, the means used to bring about the bar's power and wealth. Aggravating these literal injustices is the fact that the American bar remains the last of the great, unregulated monopolies. Or, technically, it is the last of the great trusts, a guild ensuring limited monopolistic competition among a restricted number of competitors. Admission to the guild is made difficult to discourage competition. To practice law one must comply with several strict requirements, in particular, graduation from law school and passing the bar exam. These requirements often seem intended less to guarantee high-quality legal services than to hinder others from entering the profession. The pool of competitors thereby stays small enough to effectively keep lawyers' salaries overpriced (although, as word of this bounty has spread, the ensuing recent glut of new law graduates is challenging lawyers' traditional economic assumptions). Every state in the nation penalizes those who engage in the unauthorized practice of law, including those who can provide most of a lawyer's often-rote services for a lesser fee. The bar tries to make amends by encouraging its members to occasionally take clients *pro bono,* or free. But these are almost always the nonemployed poor, and this concession is purely voluntary. Caught between the rich, who retain the best lawyers, and the prideless poor, who accept the bar's legal charity, most Americans lack reasonably priced access to their nation's judicial system.

The medieval English who created the adversary system were not, of course, blind to these flaws, but saw them as a necessary trade-off. They were willing to accept the payment of what remains, in effect, protection money because the greatest source of injustice at the time was a tyrannical government. The prospect of capital or other severe corporal punishment for a criminal conviction far outweighed the indignity and sacrifice of paying for overpriced counsel. Only a lawyer could counter the vast resources used by the prosecution under this lawyer-designed system. The English tolerance of the adversary system and the lawyers' legal cartel is, given this dilemma, easily understandable. So too are the great safeguards implanted to guarantee fairness from this underlying system, such as the rights of due process and counsel. Employable by the citizen in his defense against overbearing government, these legal arms provided the medieval Englishman with his only means of self-defense against what was then the greatest peril to his liberty.

A public defender was half right when, in this vein, he frankly acknowledged that "rights are tools to work with."[14] The early English saw rights for what they really are: weapons. Rights are instruments for battering the State to ensure fair play when criminal punishment is threatened. To the extent that the State is coextensive with order, the rights of the accused thus may also serve as weapons for weakening society. Criminals wishing to cudgel the common order need look no further than the Constitution. Where most Americans see in this document prudent bulwarks against governmental monkey business, offenders see the makings of a new tyranny over which they can preside. Since criminals enjoy the same rights as law-abiding citizens prior to their conviction, these rights serve, in the criminal's hands, as weapons for fighting the community. Rights that were once vital for defending individual liberty from absolutism have become in this democratic age the criminal's means of undermining the same society that makes these rights feasible.

Left to hold the line against these empowered foes are the prosecutors. The most common prosecutor is the assistant district attorney, an employee of the state and local governments that prosecute some 90 percent of American crimes. Generally they are relatively young and inexperienced, and of average ability. They list the complaints common to government employees in positions of great responsibility: too much work for too little pay, in a job made more difficult by the very system they are trying to serve. As both lawyers and government employees, assistant DAs are members of two of America's most abhorred classes of citizens. Indeed, even the "sense of professional unity" that prosecutors were formerly able to count on from their fellow bar members among defense counsel has, like so much else of late, frayed with the atomism of the times; this former friendliness has yielded to what a former assistant U.S. attorney general likened to a "war . . . between the private bar and the prosecutors."[15] Yet like the policemen who generate such scarce gratitude from the society they protect, prosecutors console themselves with self-assurances about the value of the social services they render daily. These are services performed with relative effectiveness under demanding circumstances. Their lot was well summed up in Tom Wolfe's *The Bonfire of the Vanities* as that of "the garbage-collection service, necessary and honorable, plodding and anonymous."[16]

While prosecutors in recent years have had to cope with the various pressures that arise from chronic underfunding, defense lawyers over the same period have seen their fortunes steadily improve. Democracy's total victory over monarchy has eroded the original institutional advantages enjoyed by the State and prosecutors without any accompanying reduction in entitlements for the accused. All the procedural stumbling blocks that the Bill of Rights placed before the prosecutors of a newly emancipated America continue to benefit defendants, often at the expense of the community. This is so even though the original reason for such protections has in some cases completely vanished. Some of these constitutional safeguards, we have seen, have lately been expanded by the judiciary. Earned over centuries of epic battles against a previously despotic criminal justice system run by a king, the full basket of criminal procedural rights has been handed down without subtraction to present-day defense attorneys.

Other, nonconstitutional rights also come into play. One such criminals' right probably would have lapsed some time ago had lawyers not viewed it as a business asset. The attorney-client privilege is a rule of evidence that holds that communications between a lawyer and his client are "privileged," not admissible in court as evidence. The rule thus allows the defendant to confide his guilt to his attorney in preparing his defense. In doing so, the rule does more than bar otherwise admissible hearsay evidence from admission against the offender in court. The attorney-client privilege allows the attorney and client to identify and remedy the weak spots in the defendant's case, and, in the process, to conceal them from the jury. The defendant and his counsel, rather than cooperating to ensure justice, work together to seek what is, in the final analysis, an unjust acquittal.

Perhaps no right of the accused puzzles the public more. Many seem to recognize that this right is, for instance, the reason why the Mafia has "in-house" counsel who often help its members avoid successful prosecution. The bar has offered another *post hoc* explanation to clear up these questions; and indeed the history of the attorney-client privilege provides another discouraging example of the expedients used through the ages by an educated minority to get the better of the majority. Originally, the attorney-client privilege was held by the *attorney*. It was designed to spare attorneys from having to testify in court, which they thought to be unseemly and degrading. The absence of such a privilege was also not good for business. The potential disclosure of a client's confidences could deter prospective customers. The privilege was thus intended to guard legal income and, in the words of the jurist John Henry Wigmore, to uphold "the oath and the honor of the attorney."[17]

In the 1700s judges, apparently in response to public criticism, shifted the locus of the right. They began to hold that the privilege was vested in the client rather than the attorney. An instant counter-rationale was needed. Wigmore explains: "Doubtless the [privilege] would have fallen at the same time with the others of like origin had not a new theory, ample to sustain and even to enlarge it, by that time come to be recognized. That new theory looked to the necessity of providing subjectively for the client's freedom of apprehension in consulting his legal adviser." The rule "proposed to do this by removing the risk of disclosure by the attorney even at the hands of the law."[18] At times members of the bar have acknowledged the privilege's real rationale, as in 1981, when the American Bar Association admitted that the rule helped to promote the employment of lawyers.[19]

The intellectually omnipresent Jeremy Bentham, Esquire, has provided the most incisive critique of the attorney-client privilege. In his *Rationale of Judicial Evidence,* a multivolume endeavor that exhaustively scrutinized the common law's numerous exclusionary rules, Bentham scowled at the "lawyercraft" he saw. He concluded that that judge-made law was "law made by lawyers, never but for the benefit of lawyers." He pointed to the attorney-client privilege in particular as making attorneys "accessories after the fact" to crimes and judges "confederates on the bench." He saw the privilege as but one block in a structure of "liberty-oppressing and money-catching falsehoods," and pulled no punches in assessing the rule's standard rationale, that is, that a defendant's "confidences" should not be "reposed":

> Not reposed?—Well: and if it be not, wherein will consist the mischief? The man by the supposition is guilty; if not, by the supposition there is nothing to betray: let the law adviser say every thing he can have heard from his client, the client cannot have any thing to fear from it.[20]

With the attorney-client privilege having weathered the Benthamite storm, the only potential chink in this legal armor is the possibility that the defendant himself might be required to testify. Enter the right against self-incrimination. No one can question its pedigree. The right not to be forced to testify against oneself is a centuries-honored entitlement, one of the few explicitly included in the Fifth Amendment to the Constitution. But the right has become, it would seem, a bit too popular these days. One legal scholar has noted that while a British defendant's invocation of the right of silence is "exceptional," as a result of recent American court decisions the defendant's silence "is becoming the common practice in trials in the United States."[21]

The right against self-incrimination is one of those criminals' rights introduced in colonial days whose original justifications have crumbled with the oppression that prompted them. The right was first recognized as necessary to prevent unbounded inquisitions by English government officials at the behest of a monarch. Today, this rationale having lapsed, the right against self-incrimination has had to search for a new *raison d'être*. A new group of rationales, both utilitarian and metaphysical, has been offered in recent years. The right is currently defended as encouraging third-party witnesses to testify by removing the fear that they may be compelled to incriminate themselves.[22] But since district attorneys can provide the same incentive by granting immunity from criminal prosecution in exchange for the witness's testimony, this argument is clearly wanting. Others defend the right against self-incrimination on rationalist, libertarian grounds. These thinkers range from Professor Charles Fried, former solicitor general for President Reagan, who argues that requiring a criminal to confess his guilt at trial is an unacceptable invasion of privacy,[23] to Professor Wasserstrom, who claims that "required disclosure of one's thoughts by itself diminishes the concept of individual personhood within the society."[24]

If the notion of "individual personhood" remains ill-defined and even somewhat eerie, much clearer are the consequences of the right against self-incrimination's exercise. The option to decline to testify allows the guilty defendant to have it both ways. He can either take the stand if he thinks himself credible and capable of convincing the jury with a lawyer-aided version of events, or he can leave the matter entirely to his attorney. This choice is a fairly recent gift from the State. Until the late 1800s defendants were actually *forbidden* to testify, as a sensible extension of the right against self-incrimination. This prohibition was founded on the commonsense assumption that the defendant was highly likely to commit perjury. Wigmore reports that this rule was put in place as early as the 1500s, and that "by the time of James II, just before the Revolution, the court is found expressly repudiating the notion that the accused's statements are to be taken as testimony." Since, until the late 1800s, "criminal defendants were submerged in a large class of persons disqualified as witnesses because of interest," the right against self-incrimination was moot; the question of the right's scope "never arose." Prior to 1868 only fifteen reported federal cases mentioned the right.[25] As this prior prohibition was repealed, the offender found in the right against self-incrimination a means of enjoying all of its potential advantages with none of its drawbacks.

Wigmore put it well when he remarked of the right against self-incrimination, "Does the law wish to tolerate a device the purpose of which is to make law unenforceable?"[26] The settled answer to this query—in the affirmative—bears reexamination. European observers often remark on this "peculiar" removal of the accused as a "testimonial resource." They note that "the accused will virtually always be the most efficient possible witness at a criminal trial," given that "[e]ven if he has a solid defense, the accused has usually been close to the events in question, close enough to get himself prosecuted."[27] Yet the right now stands more solidly than ever. The right against self-incrimination meshes well with the relativism of our age, as valuable evidence is kept from the jury to serve a higher truth, even as the *absolute* legitimacy of the right is asserted.

Along with the attorney-client privilege and the right against self-incrimination, another rampart to this "castle of lawyercraft," as Bentham termed it,[28] are the common law's many other exclusionary rules of evidence. Once the common law accepted the principle, implicit in the very concept of the adversary system, that the search for truth is subordinate to other pursuits, the British bar soon applied this judicial philosophy to the fact-finding process. English jurists began to hold that certain kinds of evidence should be excluded from trials. This list of categories of barred evidence has, in recent years, been greatly lengthened as a result of courts' exclusionary additions to the Fourth and Fifth Amendments. In a seminal comparative analysis of the adversary system and the Continental communal-law system, Professor Mirjan Damaska concluded that the American preference for judicial relativism, as embodied in exclusionary rules, suggests "a conscious sacrifice of fact-finding accuracy for the sake of other values."[29]

One common-law exclusionary rule that did not arise from recent court rulings is that excluding evidence of past crimes committed by the defendant. Evidence of a criminal defendant's character was viewed as essential evidence throughout most of British legal history. Indeed, compurgation, or the summoning of witnesses to testify to the character of the accused, was at the center of early English justice.[30] While the British later recognized that such evidence, while enlightening, should not provide the trial's *only* testimony, evidence of past crimes remained fully admissible for centuries. Subsequently, another rule took its place. Reasoning that a defendant should not be tried on the basis of what he has done in the past, judges began to hold evidence of past crimes inadmissible. Wigmore observes that this axiom "has been so often judicially repeated that it is a commonplace."[31] This particular exclusionary rule precluded exceptionally useful evidence from trial, evidence that was admitted, for instance, in Old Bailey trials, and that juries rightly saw as highly instructive.[32] Studies of career criminals have established that while it is difficult to predict future criminal behavior, it is statistically more probable that a previously convicted person, especially one convicted many times, will commit a crime than a nonconvicted citizen.[33] By the same token, the lack of a criminal record serves as corroborating evidence for the innocence of the accused. Nonetheless, evidence of past criminality is now uniformly kept out of American trials.

The other rights that the accused offender may turn to are too numerous to treat satisfactorily in a brief survey of the current body of defendants' rights. Suffice to say that the American criminal often finds the rights currently available to provide more than ample weaponry. If given to reflection on these entitlements, Americans might still hold fast to many of them. And given our history, perhaps we should be forgiven for viewing them as the legal equivalent of the old, trusted muskets above the hearths of our colonial forefathers, similarly guarding against a tyrannical State. In fact, a recent poll found that 78 percent of Americans approve of the right to be read one's *Miranda* rights upon arrest,[34] a rule that unavoidably benefits offenders far more than law-abiding citizens. Perhaps, as this suggests, the judiciary was merely bowing to popular libertarian demand in minting some of these more recent criminals' rights. But in this era of dissolving government and war in the streets, Americans must begin to recognize these liberties for the service they lend the enemy. They constitute the battery of weapons used by offenders for avoiding punishment. When these rights are assembled and wielded by a skilled hired gun, a lawyer himself motivated by self-interested amorality, justice becomes the first casualty.

CROWDING OUT THE COMBATANTS

As we have seen, much intellectual and emotional energy is devoted these days to reassuring America's middle class that the surge in societal disorder originates in, and is largely confined to, the inner city.

However, the fraying and snapping of the ties that once held the nation together are not simply a ghetto phenomenon. While non-ghetto America has generally not yet succumbed to the open, random violence typical of the inner-city variety of atomism, the decline of society's former code of civility is just as undeniable among the white middle class. Of course, the form that this latter, middle-class disintegration assumes is, as we would expect, considered more civilized, since it is the middle class and its spokesmen in academia and government that define civilization and law. But disintegration it is. And this sort of disorder is spreading just as rapidly, and ominously, as ghetto violence.

Middle-class social decay typically comes in the form of a lawsuit. Disagreements that were formerly settled privately and informally—by mediation by churches, private agreements, or, most commonly, "lumping it"—are now referred to public courts, with the citizen's expectation of adjudication at public expense. Dickens, who thought his England had generated a uniquely unhealthy liking for legal redress of grievances, might be consoled by the example of the modern United States. Even defenders of the American bar admit, "It is now a commonplace that America is the most litigious nation on earth, indeed, in human history."[35] Patrick Atiyah, Oxford professor of English law, found that American lawyers have financially far outdone their barrister brethren, with three times as many lawyers per capita as in Great Britain, tort claims ten times higher, and product liability claims a hundred times higher.[36] Counting only insurance expenses (benefits paid out and insurance company overhead), the U.S. tort system cost $132 billion in 1991.[37]

Only the self-interest of another bloc of society checks this disorder. Lawsuits must compete for the same judicial resources that are straining to process the many criminal defendants streaming out of the ghetto. The competition for these scarce resources may well determine the survival of the rule of law in America. It is important, therefore, to examine the reasons for the growing civil input into the court system, if for no other reason than to better understand the reasons for the unacceptable criminal output.

Because the criminal courts are usually funded as a component of the legal system that includes civil courts, the economic incentives that coax lawyers to file civil suits can distort the allocation of judicial resources and siphon them away from criminal trials. Lawyers have monopolistic control over the legal system's civil input. Indeed, for plaintiffs' lawyers courts are not so much a public resource as a sort of business asset from which large profits can be obtained at very little cost. This power over the civil docket allows plaintiffs' attorneys to crowd out criminal proceedings.

With advantages like this, financial and otherwise, to be gained after only three years at a law school, it is not hard to understand why America has so many lawyers. The United States has more than twice the number of attorneys per capita as the closest industrialized nation, and more than four times the average of the thirteen leading industrialized nations.[38] The number of lawyers has risen from one for every 695 Americans in 1951 to one for every 418 in 1980; the ratio is estimated to be one lawyer for every 279 in 1995.[39] Indeed, the costs of paying claims and legal fees for insurance companies and other corporate defendants correspondingly rose from about 1.4 percent of gross domestic product in 1975 to 1.8 percent in 1984 to 2.3 percent in 1991—again, consuming roughly as much GDP as does crime.[40] The growth in these expenditures now outpaces that of major U.S. social programs such as welfare and Social Security.[41]

Before we further vivisect it, let us first give the current legal system its due. Americans do receive "justice" of sorts from this great crashing of rights; otherwise, no one would be filing lawsuits. However, the "justice" received rightly leaves us asking if there is not a better way. Our legal system too often favors the wealthy, the politically powerful and those who simply complain more vociferously. It is open to serious doubt whether these are qualities that should entitle someone to success in litigation. We must also wonder what will befall a nation that allows such pursuits to become all-consuming, and that expects its government to provide these services at a time when its efforts are urgently needed elsewhere—in particular, for law enforcement.

It was Alexander Solzhenitsyn, perhaps this century's greatest chronicler of deep-set American shortcomings, who best explained the social costs incurred by America's enchantment with litigation:

> A society based on the letter of the law and never reaching any higher fails to take advantage of the full range of human possibilities. The letter of the law is too cold and formal to have a beneficial influence on society. Whenever the tissue of life is woven of legalistic relationships, this creates an atmosphere of spiritual mediocrity that paralyzes man's noblest impulses.[42]

Delivered to a nation that, at the time, seemed to be losing the Cold War because of such defects of national character, Solzhenitsyn's 1978 commencement address at Harvard University struck a nerve. When, however, a number of Solzhenitsyn's admirers sought to reprint the speech, they discovered that even this scourge of American litigiousness had made some friends among the bar; he threatened to sue them for copyright violation.[43] If "man's noblest impulses" have their price in modern America, even for recent, otherwise principled immigrants, Solzhenitsyn was at least insightful in his description of the deformation of the American soul by the adversary system's subsidizing of strife, and the costs that we as a society incur. The tragedy of America's obsession with litigation stems from the same social dissolution fueling the nation's soaring crime rate: the growing tendency to resort to force for selfish purposes, through either a violent criminal act or the implicit threat of State-sponsored force undergirding a successful lawsuit. The two forms that this egoism assumes, crime and litigation, are fittingly forced to square off themselves in a court system that now lacks the resources to accommodate them both.

If criminals can be deterred, so can lawyers. The most obvious method of litigation deterrence is to increase the cost of litigation incurred by the lawyers themselves. Currently American attorneys bear very little direct expense for filing a lawsuit. Each side must pay its own attorney's fees, even when the lawsuit turns out to be groundless. The United States is the only nation with such a policy. Hence its name, the "American rule." Even the British, normally our mentors in the creation of uniquely unworkable legal devices, have not adopted this system. Like the rest of the world, they follow the rule that "the costs follow the event."[44] The losing party to a British lawsuit is obligated to pay the winning party's attorney's fees in addition to any judgment that may have been awarded. This "loser pays" rule, sometimes called the British rule, recognizes that a legal victory is not complete if a suit leaves substantial expenses uncovered. By requiring the defendant to pay his own legal fees, even to defend against frivolous actions, the American rule allows plaintiffs' attorneys to obtain settlements from corporations and other "deep pocket" defendants whose attorney's fees would outweigh the cost of going to trial. The American legal profession has thus become one of the world's few industries in which much of the capital is provided by the government free to the businessman, and where the costs are largely limited to lost time.

The American rule, as we might expect, has a colorful, circuitous history. The rule was the product of the bar's lobbying in the nineteenth century to overturn the centuries-old costs statutes inherited from the British, which limited the amounts that lawyers could charge their clients. As libertarianism crossed the Atlantic and won a foothold in America, many of the nation's judges saw in it a new theory to support the legalizing of lawyers' refractory tendency to ignore the costs statutes.[45] Usually judges overturned these laws as violative of freedom of contract, the rationale that a libertarian Supreme Court later used for overturning New Deal legislation in the 1930s. When judges failed to do so, the bar would use its political clout to obtain the same ends.[46]

The American rule, as jointly fashioned by judicial and legislative authorities, wove together irreconcilable principles pulled from two discrete philosophies. Lawyers, under the libertarian freedom of contract, obtained the repeal of price controls. As a token homage to the former regime, however, some of the old restrictions on cost recovery were left in place. That is, the restrictions now applied only to unsuccessful parties, so that the winners could not recover their attorneys' fees. For lawyers, it was the best of both systems. Attorneys were free to charge as much as they could command in the market. This made the better attorneys unaffordable for many Americans. Meanwhile, the new American rule allowed plaintiffs' lawyers to file suit without worrying about the cost. Defense counsel, of course, could be hired by the defendants in such suits, and without fear of nonpayment—now, regardless of price.[47]

Although the American rule is probably the main institutional reason for the rapid growth in litigiousness and the resultant crowding out of criminal cases from the court system, some critics of the current rule think they have found an even more powerful litigation lure: the contingency fee. The contingency fee allows a plaintiff's attorney to collect a percentage of the amount recovered from the defendant, in exchange for the risks associated with taking the case and possibly collecting nothing at all. While it allows the lawyer to hold a financial interest in the outcome of litigation, the contingency fee per se only promotes dubious suits to the extent that the lawyer need not fear having to pay the costs of unsuccessful litigation. Indeed, a prudent attorney will not waste his time on a case that has doubtful merit. The contingency fee arrangement allows citizens of modest means to gain access to the judicial system that they could not otherwise afford, given the repeal of the costs statutes. The contingency fee is, of course, unnecessary under a loser-pays system. Under that system the defense must pay in full the prevailing plaintiff's legal fees. The contingency fee system, which has arisen to deal with the untoward incentives of the American rule, is a major reason for the recent rise in litigation, and for the creation, as one observer put it, of "more overnight millionaires than just about any business one could name."[48] However, the contingency fee itself is often a person's only way of getting justice, given the flaws in the system.

The voluminous civil suits that result from these incentives place strains on the court system, strains that eventually result in a miscarriage of justice. One such outcome is plea bargaining. As civil suits compete for the judicial resources needed for criminal trials, this depletion of docket space creates a dilemma for the State and its agents in criminal law enforcement. They can either contribute to the problem by competing for space on crowded court dockets, or pare back the criminal caseload through legally permissible shortcuts to trials by jury. By trading recommendations for reduced sentences—which judges, who need to clear their own dockets, very rarely deny—in exchange for guilty pleas, prosecutors can relieve court congestion and their own workload at the same time. In return, criminals are punished less, or sometimes not at all.

There is a false choice at the heart of this debate. Plea bargaining is not the State's only means of handling the criminal caseload. It is rather the rationing of judicial resources kept artificially scarce through political decisions. Elected officials' failure to fund the court system sufficiently permits offenders to use the shortage of judicial resources as leverage for forcing the State into granting them reduced punishment.

What Dean Roscoe Pound called a "license to violate the law"[49] almost a century ago is today the overwhelming method of obtaining criminal convictions. At present over 85 percent of all felony convictions are the result of plea bargaining.[50] If, as is commonly assumed, plea bargaining is an indispensable aspect of democratic government, presumably we can find in Anglo-American law a long, distinguished history for the practice. It is instructive, therefore, to find in the history of plea bargaining the very opposite.

It is telling that plea bargaining did not exist until the mid-nineteenth century. Although the guilty plea has been available from the first stirrings of the common law, for centuries confessions of guilt were extremely rare. The earliest common law treatises to refer to the guilty plea suggest that judges at that time generally refused to accept it. Sir Matthew Hale wrote in 1680 that while the guilty plea was slowly becoming more common, judges usually responded to the plea by ignoring it. They advised "the party to plead and put himself upon his trial, and not presently to record his confession, but to admit him to plead."[51] A century later Blackstone reiterated the judicial opposition to the guilty plea. He stated that courts "generally advise the prisoner to retract it."[52] There were some reasonable concerns that motivated this odd policy of coercing guilty defendants to deny their guilt. These included questions about the truthfulness of the guilty plea, the lack of appointed counsel under English common law and the mandatory imposition of capital punishment for all felony convictions during that time.[53]

The judicial hostility to guilty pleas in America survived the Revolution and lasted for over a century. American criminal court records in the early 1800s show a very low rate of guilty pleas.[54] The Supreme Court's opinion in the 1878 *Whiskey Cases*[55] ossified this opposition, holding federal plea bargaining agreements to be null and void. State supreme courts during the same period similarly censured plea bargaining. Occasionally the practice was condemned as a violation of the constitutional right to a "speedy public trial";[56] usually plea agreements were struck down simply because, as one court put it, "[t]he law favors a trial upon the merits."[57] The Wisconsin Supreme Court in 1877 expressed the typical view from the bench when it called plea bargaining "hardly, if at all, distinguishable in principle from a direct sale of justice."[58]

But even such biting criticism from the judiciary could not thwart the institution's growth. By the late nineteenth century plea bargaining accounted for most criminal convictions.[59] Plea bargaining became even more commonplace following the crime surge of the 1960s, even though, as one scholar noted, prosecutors have had "to offer greater concessions simply to keep guilty plea rates constant."[60]

Eventually, even many judges endorsed the practice, to the point of making some of these prosecutorial concessions themselves. The Supreme Court has given variegated reasons for its recent acceptance of plea bargaining. In the 1971 case of *Santobello v. New York*,[61] the Court reversed its century-old *Whiskey Cases* decision in holding that plea bargaining "is not only an essential part of the process but a highly desirable part," implicitly deserving constitutional protection. The Court continued: "Properly administered, it [plea bargaining] is to be encouraged. If every criminal charge were subjected to a full-scale trial, the States and the Federal Government would need to multiply by many times the number of judges and court facilities."[62]

If this unsolicited budgetary advice for legislators went unappreciated, other observers took exception to the rest of the Court's reasoning. Studies by Dallin Oaks and Warren Lehman and by Peter Nardulli, as well as the successful prohibition of plea bargaining in Alaska and other jurisdictions, have all undermined the assumption that plea bargaining is necessary to prevent overcrowded dockets.[63] But recent court rulings have augmented both plea bargaining and its practitioners; the result, as one New York defense attorney explained, was "a simple matter of economics." A Massachusetts assistant attorney general added, "If guilty pleas are cheaper today, it is simply because Supreme Court decisions have given defense attorneys an excellent shot at beating us."[64]

Plea bargaining is not a long-lasting institution because of strong public support. Popular resistance to the practice remains considerable,[65] undoubtedly because plea bargaining runs counter to the most basic human understanding of criminal justice. At the heart of the rule of law lies the State's agreement to clearly inform citizens in advance about the activities it prohibits and the precise punishment they will receive for disobedience. Plea bargaining violates this sacred understanding between government and governed. By negotiating pleas, the State engages in favoritism of the worst sort. Plea bargaining allows lighter punishment for those criminals talented at deal-making, thereby sapping the law of its moral force. The practice also makes the law unpredictable and arbitrary, weakening society's ability to deter potential offenders by making the level of punishment uncertain and open to negotiation. Plea bargaining, in short, makes "justice" a hustle.

The practice endures, however, in large part because of the supreme difficulty of reforming an industry composed of and governed by the bar. Indeed, criminal lawyers "prefer the negotiation and plea process to the alternative of trial for the very reason that they can better control the former, and the outcome is more predictable." More important, private defense attorneys, whether they are paid by private clients or by the government, make more money disposing of cases by plea bargaining than by trial. Defense attorneys are in fact somewhat notorious for complaining about "losing money by going to trial."[66]

We should note that the breakdown in criminal justice that makes plea bargaining so commonplace is not at all an unmitigated windfall for the criminal defendant. As Professor Van Kessel notes, "In the past few decades, criminal jury trials have become so lengthy and complex that we cannot, or will not, provide them to the vast majority of defendants. Instead of offering a fair and expeditious procedure in which the trier of fact has the opportunity to hear substantially all relevant evidence and come to an informed decision, our system relies on pleas of guilty that entirely displace the trial."[67] One professor has even likened plea bargaining to the methods of torture formerly used in continental Europe.[68]

Even so, we cannot feel too sorry for the offenders denied their right to trial by jury. The infringement of that lone constitutional right has been more than made up for by the expansion of other, more efficacious liberties. With these subsequent legal arms, the offender may avoid not only having to go to trial, but, in too many cases, any punishment at all. He may use this expanded bundle of rights as leverage for sidestepping prosecution altogether, especially if he is an experienced offender who knows how the system works and how to work the system.

"PASSIVISM" AND OTHER DERELICTIONS OF DUTY

Seated in the center of this swirl of battle over the citizen's criminality is the judge. His seems, at first glance, a coveted post. The American judge is accorded all the prestige reserved for a lawyer, whose crowning, usually terminal, career point is the bench. Everyone stands when he enters the courtroom, quiets when he speaks and solemnly defers to his judgments as to the admissibility of evidence. The judge is also his own boss, able to set his own hours and secure the trappings of a comfortable occupation and lifestyle.

But perks are a cheap and bitter substitute for power, especially for one who, like the American judge, knows that his authority is truncated. He knows that for all the regalia of office that he sports, the adversary system dictates that his role is at best that of an umpire. Indeed, a libertarian designing a legal system from scratch could hardly have done a better job than the inherited adversary system. The system transforms the courtroom into a miniature manifestation of the libertarian ideal. In a trial the judge, reduced to a mere moderator, doubly represents the modern libertarian government, both literally as the government's highest-ranking employee in the courtroom and symbolically as a neutral government observer officiating a clash of individual rights. While the ultimate power over guilt or innocence rests in the jury, a cross section of and stand-in for the community, the lawyers mold the jury's conclusions. Counsel battle one another as artfully as their talents and implements of legal combat allow. With truth thought to emerge from the free exchange of barrages between the rights-bearing parties, the judge's opinions are irrelevant. Other than enforcing good manners and the evidentiary rules of the game, the judge, like the libertarian State, is not allowed to "impose his personal views," or in any other way "judge" anything of substance. The very term "judge" is indeed somewhat of a misnomer when applied to the adversary system.

His peripheral role in a trial does not, however, make the judge unimportant to the criminal justice system. It is the judge who ultimately determines how fast the court system digests cases, and thus how many criminal trials can be placed on the dockets. Despite the judge's vast control over the supply side of the judicial economy, researchers and policymakers plumbing the clogged criminal courts have only recently begun to pay attention to the judge's role in case processing. One of the first important studies of the judge's effect on the dockets was a 1985 survey by the National Center for State Courts. The study found that merely freeing up more space on the dockets, on either the supply side (increasing judicial resources) or the demand side (deterring frivolous litigation, reducing jury trials through plea bargaining), may do relatively little to lubricate the courts. The main determinant of case-processing time, the center concluded, is the judge.

Judges' relativistic work environment has apparently taken its toll on their work ethic. American courts, which feature the ironic combination of libertarianism administered by a bureaucracy, are beginning to acknowledge the globally vindicated truth that people work harder when they are held individually responsible for their productivity. When judicial productivity is publicized, the National Center for State Courts study found, judges become more industrious. In particular, when the pace of litigation in their courts is made public, judges often prove capable of handling a significantly higher number of cases.[69]

At the same time, the perceived erosion of judicial discipline has impelled another important reform, the return of determinate sentencing. Popular complaints of judges' excessive leniency in criminal sentencing are as old as the system of indeterminate sentencing itself, since it is this system, after all, that makes such judicial discretion possible. In the late nineteenth century, as a centerpiece of the reha-bilitationism advocated by the Progressive movement, most state leg-islatures voted to allow judges to weigh the differences among offenders. Judges could then punish them individually based on their own subjective conclusions as to the likelihood of rehabilitation. Formerly criminals had been sentenced according to a firm, prede-termined punishment. Under the new indeterminate sentencing regime, convicts were to receive loose estimates of incarceration time rather than rigid sentences. Thus, criminals who previously knew they would receive, for example, a ten-year sentence for a given crime were soon receiving sentences of "five to ten years." Parole boards could then release the offender within this five-to-ten year framework based on the offender's success at rehabilitation in prison.

Today's high crime rates have exposed the misconceptions behind the indeterminate sentencing system, sparking recent reform. The shortcomings of indeterminate sentencing eventually produced a bipartisan alliance of Left and Right. Many on the Left disliked the broad discretion that the system ceded judges and parole authorities. They feared the introduction of racial or class prejudice into such an open-ended sentencing process.[70] Conservatives, in turn, had their own list of objections. They questioned judges' ability to correctly identify repeat offenders, or recidivists; their hesitancy to imprison all but a small percentage of convicted felons; and the widely varying judicial philosophies of punishment. This union was finally consum-mated at the federal level in new sentencing guidelines for federal judges, which Congress passed in 1984 "without opposition."[71] The law proved most successful at eliminating disparities between judges of different regions. A growing number of states also adopted deter-minate sentencing guidelines during the 1980s, a development that the soon-estranged ideological camps credited with, respectively, swelling the prison population beyond humane limits and marginally shaving the crime rate for certain offenses during that decade. Recent statistics showing that approximately two out of three offenders on parole commit serious crimes within three years of their release has further undercut public support for parole.[72]

Determinate sentencing has also been helpful for securing truth-in-sentencing reforms. The policy of clearly informing potential criminals of the exact severity of the punishment they will receive, formerly indistinguishable from the very notion of the rule of law, lapsed in the twentieth century with the rise of plea bargaining and indeterminate sentencing. Advocates of the penal philosophy of deterrence argued that would-be offenders cannot be discouraged from committing crimes unless society tells them explicitly and specifically what evils they will encounter upon breaking the law. Other reforms designed to allow for less ambiguous criminal punishment, such as limitations on plea bargaining, are often of little value without an accompanying restraint on the power of judges, via discretionary sentences, to institute their own *de facto* plea bargaining system. The elimination of plea bargaining without accompanying sentencing guidelines for judges merely moves the locus of bargaining to the judiciary, where judges can award offenders who plead guilty reduced sentences regardless of the punishment deserved or their prospects for reformation. As witnessed by the pessimistic Tennessee DA quoted at the beginning of this chapter, states such as California and Tennessee that have banned or limited plea bargaining without instituting minimum sentencing requirements for judges have seen their reforms nullified.[73]

While crucial to establishing a more just system of criminal punishment, determinate sentencing and the like cannot tackle the underlying, predominant reasons for the crisis in the court system. Curtailing the power of judges is a relatively minor political struggle in an Anglo-American society. A reduction of their authority usually entails a corresponding increase in the power of attorneys. Our overloaded criminal court system cannot be seriously remedied without the dismantling of the adversary system, a radical but vital reform. The rights warriors in the bar must be disarmed, through either reductions in the stockpile of rights or a redistribution of certain rights to the judge—or, ideally, both. Admittedly, one faces better prospects of redesigning the Washington Monument than repealing the lawyer monopoly, and probably less chance of being called unpatriotic. Among other hurdles to reform, the Supreme Court has held on several occasions that the adversary system is constitutionally protected.[74] But if we are to get at the root of the current inequality and frustrated justice in the land, truly nothing less will do.

Just as Americans of a century ago became trustbusters, we must become—shall we say it?—barbusters, and for an even worthier cause: the survival of the rule of law in America. Again, we must recall that the communal-law regime provides a stable, tried-and-true alternative. The communal-law system represents little more than the legal system that preceded the bar's predominance in the

Anglo-American world. This regime features an activist judge who is primarily responsible for presenting evidence and, like his early English predecessors, takes an active role in the jury's deliberations. There the hearsay rule, the prohibition against evidence of past crimes and other exclusionary rules do not exist. The accused also lacks an expansive right against self-incrimination. The average criminal defendant in, for example, France has already fully confessed several times by the time he comes to trial. This, combined with the elimination of the time-consuming contentiousness of attorneys, allows communal-law trials to be completed much faster than trials in the United States.[75] The communal-law system is now practiced in various forms throughout virtually the entire non-Anglo world. The global marketplace of ideas has rejected the adversary system by a wide margin.

The most important distinction between the two systems is the communal-law system's reliance on the judge for its fact-finding process rather than on attorneys. Adversary-system jurisdictions presume that a judge should be uninformed of the facts of the case to be effective and impartial. In communal-law countries, by contrast, the judge is required to familiarize himself with the evidence. This factual background is important for the communal-law judge because he, rather than the lawyers, is responsible for selecting and introducing evidence to the jury. Since verdicts are ultimately based mostly on evidence, the lawyers under a communal-law system are, as a rule, unimportant. And, because the purchasing power of defendants increases with the power given to attorneys, a heightened role for the judge—meaning a paring-back of the adversary system to Continental limits—is thus a precondition for equal justice under law in America.

The hazards of handing the scales of justice to lawyers were recognized by many of the Britons who first witnessed it. Edmund Burke denounced the growing practice in his day of making the judge a side figure in the trial's fact-finding process:

> It is the duty of the Judge to receive every offer of evidence, apparently material, suggested to him, though the parties themselves through negligence, ignorance or corrupt collusion, should not bring it forward. A judge is not placed in that high situation merely as a passive instrument of parties. He has a duty of his own, independent of them, and that duty is to investigate the truth.[76]

But Burke, in decrying the "passive" role of his country's judges, was, as usual, taking on a losing cause. His thoughts were forgotten by a nation that, within a few years, produced the libertarianism that would provide belated philosophical support for the modern adversary system.

The communal-law judge could be the great equalizer in an American court system that is incapable of dispensing equal justice, because of both the recent strains on the system and the system's frank abuse by the bar. By vesting more power in the judge and making attorneys of limited value, communal-law countries go a long way toward ensuring that wealth cannot protect an individual from criminal punishment. The Kantian rights-based libertarians who often defend the current arrangement should recall Immanuel Kant's apothegm that "justice ceases to be justice if it can be bought for a price."[77] As criminals correctly calculate the limited risk of punishment they face from our court system, the community will continue to pay an additional price for these legal services—more crime. Until the American legal system is seriously and fundamentally reformed, our courts will remain an unmanageable institution where the prevailing, self-motivated system of law looks more and more like a prescription for no law at all. Such a state of affairs, among its many inconveniences, promises to be rather bad for business, at least for those accustomed to wearing a coat and tie.

CHAPTER FOUR

The Prisons: Social Burial

The object of war is not to annihilate those who have given rise to it, but to cause them to mend their ways.

—Polybius

Possibly no modern phenomenon would perplex the Founding Fathers more than this: the countryside, which most of them called home, is today less a place of residence than a receptacle for things society does not want. While most of us today, including the bulk of criminologists, are not particularly troubled by this twentieth-century exodus from country to city, the Founders of this Republic would be far less complacent. They, of course, viewed life in the countryside as the linchpin of national unity. Rural life provided a regime where local democracy reinforced the social controls of small towns, harnessing the centrifugal forces of a rights-based society that threatened to pull the country apart if given full rein. Jefferson predicted doom for the young nation if its traditional rural lifestyle gave way to the coarsening anonymity of an urban society. But as economic self-interest proved more potent to Americans than the ties of community and even family in the wake of the Industrial Revolution, more and more Americans were attracted into the nation's urban centers. The same stimulated self-interest among the new city-dwellers mandated that the unpleasant things they produced in the city be deposited in places where they no longer lived. Thus it is that the countryside has become the place where an urbanized America dumps its garbage and toxic waste and erects its institutions for incarcerating the most dangerous members of an increasingly urban, and increasingly violent, society.

Small, rural and destitute of political clout, Marion, Illinois, met all the requirements for the site of a new federal prison in the 1980s. Nestled where the cornfields of the Midwest give way to the rolling hills of Kentucky and the Ohio River Valley, and where the people speak with a drawling twang derivative of these overlapping regions, Marion was located away from the area's crime-generating big cities. When, in 1983, federal authorities selected Marion for a new federal penitentiary designed to house the federal prison system's most dangerous inmates, the people of Marion did not rebel against their elected officials as big-city folks often do when asked for a similar sacrifice. In Marion federal officials found a wary but dutiful recipient of society's offenders. There the nation could lock up its most violent, incorrigible criminals far from the urban centers that bred them, tucked away in an area where only the deer and the antelope need contend with the institution's aesthetic and spiritual ugliness.

Prior to October 1983 Marion was run like other maximum security prisons of our day; that is, the prisoners ran it. But following a three-year spasm of inmate warfare, capped off by the fatal stabbings of two guards and a week of riots, Marion Prison locked down. Inmates were isolated from one another in individual cells. And, almost instantly, Marion Prison reclaimed order. The smallest disturbances were immediately quashed; inmate violence became virtually nonexistent. The strict regimen seemed to have a deterrent effect as well. Out of 302 inmates rotated out in the four years following the lockdown, only 20 returned, making its recidivism rate substantially below that of other prisons. Several years later the federal government, duly impressed, chose the prison as the federal system's main warehouse for its most sociopathic inmates. Warden Gary L. Henman summed up the type of refractory offender and the new penal philosophy which his institution would follow: "For these men, there is no social medicine. We're not gonna cure them."[1]

Nathaniel Hawthorne once described prisons, from his comfortable abode just outside Boston, as the "black flower of civilized society."[2] He implied that prisons were weeds in the nation's garden, a symbol of society's culpability in fertilizing crime. But we must wonder whether Hawthorne would have felt the same guilt had he shared his thoughts with the rather unsympathetic fellows stored in the then new penitentiary at nearby Castle Island. He certainly never visited Marion. The trip, we can safely assume, would have done him good. The folks in Marion would have told him in their own unsophisticated way that the nastiness permeating their new prison was none of their doing. The unsightly penal complex of gray, squat buildings composing their skyline would billet these offenders far away from the long string of victims they left behind in places like Boston; and, in any case, it was the victims who should be polled for sentiments on national guilt. Cautiously but dutifully, the people of Marion would serve as the nation's custodians, picking up after a nation whose values and lenient criminal justice system had helped to create the people who ended up there.

Marion's patriotic duty did carry some hidden costs. As the prison officially became the new federal storage site for irreclaimable offenders, the national media converged on the Illinois hamlet to scrutinize what they termed the prison's "controversial" treatment of its inmates. The Marion federal penitentiary made news because, in attempting to meet the perceived needs of a uniquely pathological population, the authorities had chosen to isolate prisoners in individual cells. The conditions were not, all things considered, especially harsh. Each offender was still given reasonably comfortable quarters, as well as an individual television and radio, access to pornography and other amenities. But others judged Marion's hospitality more harshly. Amnesty International stated that the regimen "appeared to violate the United Nations standard minimum rules for the treatment of prisoners." The group concluded, "Certain conditions could, in their totality, amount to 'cruel, inhuman or degrading' treatment." Another "prisoners'-rights" advocate, attorney Jan Susler, denounced the Marion regimen as "psychological terror." The federal prison in Marion, these critics agreed, represented a "disturbing portent for the future."[3]

The new prison's system of enforced solitude was, in fact, not so much a portent of the future as a reappraisal of the discarded ways of the past. Marion Prison represented a return to some old penological practices, forgotten by a society that had hoped to make prisons, as such, obsolete. Prisons, in fact, are latecomers to Western penology. Although we often assume imprisonment to be as old a form of criminal punishment as the lash and the stockade, prisons are actually a relatively recent instrument of crime control. At the time of the framing of the U.S. Constitution, prisons as we know them did not yet exist. Their predecessor, the British gaol, was used up to that time merely as a temporary holding pen for defendants awaiting either trial or a more popular form of punishment, usually fines or corporal punishment. Prisons were almost never used as punishment per se. For one thing, they cost too much; for another, they hid the offender from public view, precluding the use of his example for the moral education of the people. Records from the Old Bailey, the main criminal court for eighteenth-century London, show that imprisonment accounted for only 2.3 percent of the sentences handed out between 1700 and 1774.[4]

It was not until the nineteenth century that the West broke sharply with traditional forms of incarceration, starting in Europe's most penally innovative society. The British experiment with imprisonment arose from one of the last great collaborations of Western intellectuals and Christian reformers. This alliance in turn reflected a joint mission based on the different principles held by each group—one secular, the other spiritual, but both scholarly. In the closing years of the eighteenth century, intellectuals witnessed, for a brief, fleeting moment, the normally squabbling movements of empiricism and the Enlightenment at peace long enough to conceive a body of thought that eventually earned the name "criminology."

Bentham, one of the founders of utilitarianism, applied his talents to analyzing the English criminal justice system of the 1800s, and became the leading intellectual force behind the reform of the archaic, brutal regime of his day. Unlike other intellectuals, however, he did not contend that the solution to inhumane punishment was less punishment. Bentham felt that the system simply needed some fine-tuning. He was, to use the criminological jargon of our day, an advocate of deterrence. He saw crime as the result of the offender's pragmatic calculation that the potential gains from the transgression outweighed the harms that society would impose when and if the offender was convicted. Crime is preventable, therefore, if society correctly estimates and imposes punishment with sufficient certainty and severity to deter the contemplated offense. Thus, Bentham's complaint with the jails of his time was not so much their barbarous living conditions. It was rather their failure to tailor the punishment they handed out to the narrow, justifiable aim of teaching prisoners that crime does not pay. He argued for a careful calibration of the amount of punishment necessary to meet this end, beyond which any punishment was unjust. Bentham also advocated a standardized level of punishment to be imposed in all prisons, and somewhat immodestly offered his own model, the Panopticon, as the ideal institution.

Before Bentham could rally British intellectuals under the banner of prison reform, however, the main impetus for the birth of the modern penitentiary had already come from an unassuming Bedfordshire sheriff, John Howard, and his Quaker allies. Howard's main contribution to penology was his decision to honor the generally ignored duty of English sheriffs in the late 1700s to inspect their county's prisons. Howard's disgust at their conditions propelled him on a campaign to document the horrors of the jails and workhouses of Europe.[5] Howard's most enthusiastic supporters were the Quakers. Punishment per se, they maintained, would not reform the criminal. Society could make him fit for society only by helping him reconcile himself with God, whom he had obviously spurned as evidenced by his criminality. Crime was the natural manifestation of the criminal's separation from God, since only the fear and love of an omnipresent heavenly sovereign ensured order. The criminal justice system therefore should seek to heal this rift. That said, the Quakers and the other members of the humanitarian school of prison reform that they helped found held no illusions about the steps required for the reformation of criminals. Once this spiritual divorce between God and man had occurred, no artificial, man-made constraints, such as positive laws enforced as part of Bentham's scheme of deterrence, could prevent the offender from reverting to what even the materialist Hobbes recognized as the "sin" of crime. A spiritual malady required a stern but caring sculpturing of the soul which they termed "rehabilitation."

The modern connotations attached to the term "rehabilitation" are misleading when applied to the original aspirations of the Quakers. The Christian conception of rehabilitation was the polar opposite of the theory of the same name supported by many modern criminologists, who often view criminality as a disease beyond the control of the offender. Early humanitarians held that the criminal's self-inflicted spiritual suffering could be rehabilitated only through the offender's voluntary reconciliation with his Creator. The prison minister could broker this reunion to some degree. But this renaissance of the soul mostly depended on the restoration of the criminal's faith in God. After faith, fear—or awe—of the Almighty would soon follow. Fear of the divine Leviathan would keep in check the criminal's wayward tendencies should he be tempted to fall into sin again. Isolated from other inmates, left to converse only with his own guilty conscience, the prisoner would rediscover God, repent his sins and, it was hoped, eventually rejoin society as an honest and productive member. The prisoner's social burial, by compelling him to probe his spiritual malaise and find God, could produce a real resurrection, first of the spirit and subsequently of citizenship.

This fusion of intellectual enthusiasm and religious zeal to do God's bidding led the English to become the first society to make incarceration its chief method of criminal punishment. In 1792, under the leadership of a Quaker justice of the peace, George Onesiphorrus Paul, England's Gloucestershire County established the first modern prison. It featured separate sections for those awaiting trial and for those convicted of both minor and major offenses. The creation of this new, long-term incarceration facility beat out by only a matter of months the christening of the Walnut Street Jail in America. Quakers in Philadelphia converted the jail into a penitentiary with thirty-six solitary confinement cells. Bentham subsequently endorsed and expanded the Quakers' solitary-confinement model.[6] He hoped, however, to replace the humanitarian vision of solitary spiritual rehabilitation with a secular, psychological conception, based on the isolated offender's extended opportunity to recalculate the pros and cons of a life of crime.

Yet even under the gentle care of the Quakers, this constant, total solitude proved too much for even the toughest offenders to bear. Criminals placed in solitary confinement, of course, soon discover that they have very poor company. Among the foreign visitors inspecting the new prison and disturbed by what they observed were two Frenchmen, Gustave de Beaumont and Alexis de Tocqueville. They noted the tragic effects of the Quakers' dabbling with complete isolation. The two mourned the fact that at one prison, "[t]he unfortunates, on whom this experiment was made, fell into a state of depression, so manifest . . . one of them had become insane; another, in a fit of despair, had embraced the opportunity when the keeper brought him something, to precipitate himself from his cell, running the almost certain chance of a mortal fall."[7]

The ever-compassionate Quakers eventually reassessed their methods, in part because of the additional incentives that came from competition. Humanitarian reformers had established a rival penal system in Auburn, New York. Like Philadelphia's Quakers, the Calvinists who developed the Auburn penitentiary wanted spiritual rehabilitation from their inmates, but they differed in their method of bringing this about. The founders of Auburn Prison had a theologically rooted preference for a harsh group-work regimen during the day. Solitary confinement was to be limited to nighttime. By centering their prison system around work, the Auburn officials happened upon a competitive advantage over the Philadelphia model in the eyes of prison-system architects throughout the young Republic— profit. The prospect of cheap labor and resulting revenues appealed to a populace unwilling to give their society's offenders a free ride. Beaumont and Tocqueville picked up on this selling point in noting the Auburn system's popularity. The two ultimately credited the Pennsylvania system with producing "more honest men," and the Auburn system with turning out "more obedient citizens."[8] Auburn's combination of prison labor and nocturnal solitude prevailed in America for a century, with chain gangs and prison industries becoming settled practices.

What eventually replaced the Auburn system is the present-day regime of rehabilitation-based "correctional facilities." The current system mirrors the predominant philosophy of modern criminologists and conforms to recent court rulings forbidding government entanglement with religion. The result is a penal system that incorporates the secular psychology of Bentham and Beccaria, but without the deterrence rationale that animated them. Accordingly, the system now lacks any methodical attempt to deter inmates from committing future offenses. Instead, the present prison regime often tries to rehabilitate offenders under the assumption that crime is caused by social forces. The feasibility of this effort is undermined by its lack of reference to religion, which could formerly be counted on to soften the hearts and stiffen the discipline of its inmates. And thus, gone too is any genuine hope of spiritual recovery, or rehabilitation properly defined.

Just as unknown to the early humanitarian prison reformers are the regimen and lifestyle of today's prisoners. The popularity of imprisonment as a means of punishment has far exceeded the willingness of Americans to adequately fund new prisons. The ensuing crowded environment mocks the original goal of at least semisolitary confinement, resulting in living conditions that are hazardous and all too often fatal for inmates. There are now close to one million prisoners in America,[9] who, because of political failures to allocate sufficient funding to prison construction and maintenance, are packed into prisons with shrinking (albeit still adequate) living space and—still worse—increasingly hardened cutthroats for roommates.

The dangers that early reformers recognized in throwing so many criminals together in tight quarters have once again materialized, this time probably beyond their worst apprehensions.

While the present free mingling of prisoners presumably should have at least produced an us-against-them inmate unity, and thus enough cohesion to begin to instill some basic common ties of citizenship, this has not come to pass. Instead, to the extent that these most atomized members of an atomized society unite at all in today's prisons, it is along fractured racial lines. Race had become one of the dominant social forces in American prisons well before Leo Carroll's 1974 study of a Rhode Island penitentiary, which documented the state of America's polarized prisons.[10] Inmates who refuse to accept such segregation risk violence and even death. White prisoners often join white supremacist and neo-Nazi groups, largely for purposes of self-protection.[11] To the extent that clergymen are permitted to proselytize in today's prisons, they find the going rough.

This violent fragmentation, combined with the other hazards of housing so many offenders together in close quarters, has created a prison environment so chaotic that prison administrators are today reluctant even to claim that rehabilitation is the penal goal. Surely nothing would have confounded Beaumont and Tocqueville more than this: some residents of maximum security prisons today *request* solitary confinement to avoid inmate aggression. Homosexual rape is now a standard occurrence; few offenders leave a maximum security facility without being sexually assaulted in some manner. To escape threats from other prisoners, weaker inmates often "marry" a bigger inmate, exchanging sexual privileges for protection.[12] Such practices might well have so mortified early prison reformers that they would have abandoned penology altogether as unfit for decent souls.

On top of these institutional failures is the tragedy of enforced idleness among prisoners. Federal laws today essentially *forbid* inmates to work. Incarcerated criminals are left to spend their time writing appeals of their convictions, bullying fellow inmates and planning their next offenses. No better evidence has ever been adduced to support the platitude that "idle time is the devil's workshop" than the brutality in U.S. prisons today. Indeed, we must wonder what a curious John Howard would say upon peering into our nation's prisons, and whether he would consider them an improvement over the houses of horror he frequented over two centuries ago.

CHOOSING AN EPITAPH

Why do we have prisons? Usually when a program of social engineering is implemented, the officials charged with its enforcement at
least inherit a clear reason for its existence. Not so for the administrators of American prisons. These caretakers of the socially
interred, to the extent they are given policy guidance at all, generally
receive conflicting directives on the simple matter of their job's *raison d'être*. Is it their duty to determine and inflict the amount of
punishment required to deter the rational, calculating criminal of
Bentham's depiction? Or should they try to rehabilitate prisoners in
the tradition of John Howard and the Quakers, except this time
through secular practices such as nonjudgmental counseling and
often orgiastic conjugal visits? How about some good old-fashioned
retribution, the kind that would have gladdened the hearts of
Calvinists and that is increasingly cheered on by a crime-hardened
nation seemingly turning nasty? Legislators rarely manage to tell
them. Judges sometimes do, but they must exceed their constitutional mandate to do so, and this is therefore exceptional. As a rule,
prison officials are left to themselves to define their mission, trying
out their own theories in a social experiment lacking even an accepted hypothesis.

This is not for lack of available philosophies of punishment. Most
of the penal aims vying for adoption by America's prison system are
as old as criminal justice itself. All are at least as old as the penitentiary. None is older than mankind's first justification for criminal justice, the philosophy that in our age is called retribution. For almost
every other known society, its synonym is justice, popularly defined.
Retribution is founded on the principle that the State is obliged to
punish the criminal in proportion to the harm and suffering he
inflicts on members of society. When applied to imprisonment, this
principle holds that the worse the crime, the longer the time.
Retribution is a notion as old as man himself, which is probably why
its earliest formulation, capturing the deposited wisdom of many
thousands of years, has not been improved upon. The oldest existing
codification of retribution, the *lex talionis,* is in the Sumerian Codes,
the laws of one of the earliest recorded human communities.
Hammurabi's Code, usually dated around 2000 B.C., reiterated the
principle for the Babylonian nation that succeeded Sumer. The most
famous expression of the *lex talionis* is found in the Mosaic Code of
the Old Testament. Exodus 21:23-25 provides that "thou shalt give

life for life, eye for eye, tooth for tooth, hand for hand, foot for foot, burning for burning, wound for wound, stripe for stripe."

As divinely codified in Exodus, the *lex talionis* was at the very least specific: equal justice under law means equal suffering by all offenders, down to the last limb. This conception of retribution views society as a moral order with essential, permanent laws, violation of which constitutes an assault on the nation's collective duty of self-preservation. Underlying this penal philosophy is a notion of retaliation-as-justice that treats an attack on one as an attack on all. This demands that society rally around the beleaguered individual to defend him and to punish, with the most precise equity possible, the citizen who has violated his community's moral order. By affirming the rights of its citizens through the administration of penalties that correspond in severity to the breaches of those rights, retribution honors this universal human vision of justice—the perfect fusion of retaliation and equality given the sanction and enforcement of the State. Retributive punishment also lends the masses a salutary sense of anti-criminal solidarity, a unity that functions as the social equivalent of patriotism as applied to internal enemies. No other philosophy of punishment can similarly affirm this devotion to the venerable, basic ties of human community.

Retribution strikes many modern Western ears as barbaric because it mirrors this most primeval thirst for justice. Many intellectuals, particularly criminologists, have expressed regret that society has not progressed to the point where it no longer has to require suffering from the citizens who violate its laws. It seems mean. This view is especially compelling if one accepts *a priori* the belief that society itself has led the offender into a life of crime. The more famous modern critiques of prison-centered retribution range from Karl Menninger's wonderfully titled *The Crime of Punishment* to Michel Foucault's *Discipline and Punish*, a Marxist history of prisons.[13] This is a remarkable, and somewhat puzzling, trend. James Q. Wilson and Richard Herrnstein observed of retribution's intellectual decline, "One should be curious, if not suspicious, [when] . . . an idea that has endured for thousands of years and through all the cultural changes of those millennia, has suddenly, in our time, fallen into disrepute."[14]

This tension between our national self-image as a criminologically progressive society and public demands for a tried-and-true theory of criminal punishment has proved long-lasting. This same clash convulsed an industrializing Great Britain in the nineteenth century.

Bentham responded with a utilitarianism that legitimized punishment only when done for the purpose of deterring criminals. Others, particularly Sir James Fitzjames Stephen, came forth with an uninhibited defense of the retributionist position and its belief that the law is an appropriate instrument for organized revenge. He noted dryly that "[t]he unqualified manner" in which intellectuals such as Bentham had denounced retribution "is in itself a proof that it is deeply rooted in human nature." Stephen minced no words in his endorsement of the philosophy: "I think it highly desirable that criminals should be hated, that the punishments inflicted upon them should be so contrived as to give expression to that hatred, and to justify it so far as the public provision of means for expressing and gratifying a healthy natural sentiment can justify and encourage it."[15]

Stephen elaborated his defense of retribution by offering an analogy. He argued that by harnessing the "deliberate anger and righteous disapprobation" of a victimized society, the criminal law has the same relationship to revenge as marriage does to sexual passions. Both social institutions channel primitive and, by implication, unseemly desires into less destructive methods of self-expression.[16] But Stephen's analogy, while insightful, was nonetheless an insult to marriage. And to revenge. Marriage stands for much more than the restraining of sexual passions. And revenge, when embodied in a retribution-based criminal law, is not an atavism on the order of slavery or human sacrifice. Correctly constituted, retribution is to society what a marriage vow is to marriage: a public affirmation of the intention to preserve a necessary and moral institution.

Immanuel Kant, writing only a few decades before Stephen to much greater acclaim, also saw retribution's popularity as due to the constitution of the human mind. He believed that all people innately hold certain core beliefs about how human beings should treat one another. These natural laws are chiseled indelibly into the conscience of man as "categorical imperatives." Categorical imperatives form a built-in code of conduct that no amount of social engineering or intellectual disdain can eliminate, short of eliminating the person himself (which, as this century has proved, is certainly not beyond the designs of determined men). Retribution, Kant contended, is the unavoidable, universal extension of this internal moral code. To the human mind, retribution is justice, pure and simple: "Only the law of retribution (*lex talionis*) can determine exactly the kind and degree of punishment appropriate." Moreover, retribution represents society's essential means of self-preservation, and the community's self-affirmation as a moral entity; "any undeserved evil you inflict on someone else among the people is one that you do to yourself."[17] A failure to uphold this natural moral code, manifested in the community's laws, means that society, as a collection of moral agents, technically ceases to exist.

For all of retribution's psychological and practical necessity, however, there is still something about it that gnaws at the conscience, or at least the national vanity, of the citizens of this American Republic. Some of these pangs of remorse radiate from the same nagging sense of moral inadequacy that begs the common thought "Why can't a great nation overcome the harsh business of having to inflict pain on violators of its common order?" Some have resigned themselves to this fact of life. Scholar Herbert Packer, for instance, concedes that "punishment is a necessary but lamentable form of social control."[18] Perhaps this discomfort is simply due to our general modern squeamishness about discipline in all its forms. Or, indeed, maybe the desire for order is itself selfish.

But punishment and the order it secures are not merely the products of self-interest. Order allows people to do wonderful things with the time they would otherwise spend dead or enslaved. This humanitarian aspect of order makes the ultraindividualist assault on the community all the more disheartening. While the Christian brand of determinism has prevailed in only a few isolated pockets of modern society, by contrast, this century has witnessed the triumph of radical-individualist determinism in criminology. The secular determinism that has gained ascendancy among modern Western scholars has little in common with the earlier, Judeo-Christian determinism of, for instance, the Protestant leader John Calvin. His doctrine held simply that certain souls are predestined to go to heaven, God having tagged them ahead of time to alert them of their promised admission to the Pearly Gates. These chosen people's ranks happened to joyfully correspond to Calvin's congregation. Man was still believed to have free will, to be able to choose his own actions. The new secular determinism thought the opposite. It broke with Judeo-Christian notions of individual accountability, placing the responsibility for crime not in a benevolent Lord who allows His sheep to wander astray in wrongful directions, but instead in the forces of a fundamentally unjust society.

This new determinism first appeared in the writings of the *philosophes* of the French Enlightenment. They provided the atheism and determinism that served as the intellectual blasting caps for the French Revolution. In the eighteenth century Julien Offroy de La Mettrie placed the blame for criminality on heredity and environment, safely beyond the reach of the individual. He described crime as a sickness requiring the cure of rehabilitation. La Mettrie also saw therapy as the solution: "it would be desirable to have for judges none but the most skillful physicians."[19] The "amiable atheist" Baron d'Holbach built on this foundation. He borrowed from British empiricism only its materialism and, in a theory that adumbrated the current criminological consensus, concluded that crime is merely the product of environmental factors.[20] Neither savant could answer the same criticism that dogged Rousseau, that is, how exactly do originally pure humans create impure social institutions—institutions which, by La Mettrie's and d'Holbach's reckoning, render them violent and socially suicidal? The ecological school of criminology that resulted took root and flourished in France throughout the 1800s.[21]

This French philosophy provided modernity with a determinism that lacked the literally awe-inspiring element of Judeo-Christian thought, and that offered an intellectual defense of offenders. At least the nonselected soul in Calvin's world did not know he was doomed, and had some incentive to behave himself. But as he emerged from the Parisian salons, the criminal was a noble savage, to be excused for poor manners. A servant of forces beyond his control, the offender deserved pity and rehabilitation. Sometimes specific social forces were named as the responsible parties; poverty, racism and other factors were often listed as some of crime's causes. In any case, it was unjust to punish the individual criminal for his transgressions. Crime by this theory was a disease spread by a society that should point to itself when assigning blame.

By the middle of the twentieth century, this new rehabilitationism became more or less the working ideology of American prisons. Some impetus in this direction came from the judiciary. In 1949 Supreme Court Justice Hugo Black declared in *dicta*, "Retribution is no longer the dominant objective of the criminal law." Instead, "Reformation and rehabilitation of offenders have become important goals of criminal jurisprudence."[22] Justice Thurgood Marshall later repeated Black's sentiments. In 1972 he argued that "punishment has been almost totally rejected by contemporary society."[23] But even with its notable success among these and other important intellectuals, rehabilitationism was eventually rejected both by many academics and by the American public. It did receive a fair hearing.

Prior to the late 1960s prison officials widely sought to implement the advice of criminologists and the apparent wishes of legislators by instituting the recommended means of rehabilitation: arts and crafts classes, group "rap sessions," plenty of recreation time and so on. Psychiatrists were also retained to facilitate the offender's return to an honest life. Virtually no prison in the nation failed to adopt at least some of the rehabilitationist agenda.

By the end of the 1960s, however, it had become clear to the public and a growing number of scholars that things were not going as planned. Crime was rising to unprecedented levels, and rehabilitationism had brought about no observable reduction in recidivism. The end of rehabilitationism as a serious penal philosophy ultimately came not in a single *coup de grâce,* but rather after three successive blows, beginning with the prison riots that began in the 1950s. Soon after secular rehabilitationism became America's predominant theory of punishment, a series of prison uprisings, culminating in the Attica Riot in New York, made prison officials wary of the philosophy, especially given the ingratitude of the inmates.[24] The event that almost single-handedly took away empirical support for rehabilitation and eroded its ranks among social scientists was the 1973 publication of Robert Martinson's exhaustive study of rehabilitationism in practice. Martinson's self-described "massive task" studied every available report on rehabilitation techniques in the English language published from 1945 to 1967, drawing from them a total of 231 studies. Martinson found that *none* of the rehabilitative efforts had an "appreciable effect on recidivism."[25] And although he later qualified his otherwise categorical rejection of rehabilitationism[26] (and then, before explaining his revised position, died), his earlier conclusions were stated with such apparent statistical firmness that his central finding—"nothing works"[27]—was accepted by many in academia. No comparable research refuting Martinson's analysis has yet materialized.[28]

The final major critique of rehabilitationism came from the far Left. Certain scholars began to criticize rehabilitationists in the 1960s for departing from French Enlightenment thought. The rehabilitationist treatment of criminals as such, rather than as tragic figures led into violence by an abusive society, was thought faulty and unjust. If anything cried out for rehabilitation, these theorists felt, it was society, not offenders. Jessica Mitford's *Kind and Usual Punishment,* published in 1973, argued that, far from aiding offenders with treatment and tender loving care, rehabilitation was insidious behavior modification imposed by the oppressing dominant class. In one passage she finds all criminal law to be an arbitrary sham: "When is conduct a crime, and when is a crime not a crime? Whenever Somebody Up There—a monarch, a dictator, a pope, a legislature—so decrees."[29] Being called naive is one thing, but being branded a collaborator with monarchs and popes? That was too much for many rehabilitationists. Some submitted to Ms. Mitford's forces. Others looked for ideologically acceptable principles in other penal philosophies.

Rehabilitationists might have been spared this disappointment if they had consulted Beaumont and Tocqueville. The theories of the *philosophes* in their native land did not interfere in Beaumont and Tocqueville's sober assessment of rehabilitationism's prospects in early American prisons. Even with the benefit of a rigorous religion that provided few excuses for offenders, Christian rehabilitationists had experienced little success. The two Frenchmen concluded that if rehabilitation does take place, it "must be very rare." Society's apologies for the criminal do him little good: "It is in vain that society pardons him; his conscience does not."[30]

What, then, will take rehabilitationism's place as the preferred penal philosophy of academia and policymakers? One candidate is deterrence, the classical liberal brainchild of Cesare Beccaria and Bentham. Deterrence, the consensus theory of the first criminologists, holds that society should hone the criminal law so that it inflicts on the offender the precise amount of pain necessary to persuade him (specific deterrence) and like-minded citizens (general deterrence) to avoid criminal activity. Bentham's was the most influential exposition of deterrence, and meshed with his overall philosophy of utilitarianism. "Nature," said Bentham, "has placed mankind under the governance of two sovereign masters, *pain* and *pleasure*. It is for them alone to point out what we ought to do, as well as to detemine what we shall do."[31] A society seeking to deter crime must carefully calculate the amount of pain needed to outweigh the pleasure gained from a criminal act. The criminal law is, to use the parlance of modern psychology, an instrument of operant-conditioning. Through this, society links the individual's reflexive desire to avoid pain to a healthy respect for the law, normally through the jolting experience of criminal punishment or the threat thereof. Among the more prominent advocates of deterrence today is Ernest van den Haag. He argues that society can deter crimes of violence by using the same swift and certain punishment that routinely deters parking violations.[32] James Q. Wilson also makes the case for deterrence with a thorough and convincing analysis of the relevant data.[33]

Deterrence's greatest shortcoming in the eyes of ex-rehabilitationists is that it is currently regarded as a conservative penal philosophy—a label that might well have repelled the proudly iconoclastic Bentham and Beccaria. That modern criminologists locate deterrence on the right of the ideological spectrum indicates the distance that criminology has traveled in its two centuries of existence. Deterrence has come to be viewed as a "get tough," conservative philosophy of punishment because, unlike rehabilitationism, its central principles require a belief in free will. Whatever else one may say about it, deterrence is profoundly egalitarian. All except the insane are believed to have an equal ability to calculate the costs and benefits of criminal activity and to act accordingly. Few of us, of course, would quibble with this. Even a child learns not to stick his hand onto a hot stove, usually after only one bad experience. But deterrence parts ways with rehabilitationism by treating the criminal as not socially predestined for a life of crime. One scholar, John Conrad, has argued this central article of rehabilitationism with brave frankness. In his debate over capital punishment with van den Haag, Conrad contended that an offender's rationality may vary depending on the crime committed. Murderers, as he sees it, are the least rational of all offenders; hence the injustice of the death penalty for homicide.[34] Insane acts presuppose insane actors. Thus, by this logic, the more awful the crime, the less justifiable the criminal punishment.

The founders of criminology did not similarly view reason as varying inversely with the severity of the crime, and they found deterrence more palatable because of their belief in individual free will. Beccaria, Bentham and many of the other first criminologists saw deterrence as an alternative to retribution, which they, like modern rehabilitationists, thought cruel and outmoded. Beccaria felt that criminal punishment was defensible only when "the evil it inflicts . . . exceed[s] the advantage derivable from the crime. . . . All beyond this is superfluous and for that reason tyrannical."[35] Bentham, whose utilitarianism was a liberal tendril of British empiricism, proclaimed that "all punishment is mischief: all punishment in itself is evil . . . it ought only be admitted in as far as it promises to exclude some greater evil."[36] They were also avid foes of the death penalty because they believed it to have no deterrent value.

Although both are seen today as hard-nosed penal philosophies, retribution and deterrence do eventually come to cross-purposes. Both retribution and deterrence assume the criminal to be a rational actor, and call for increased punishment to make their principles feasible. There they both bicker with rehabilitationism. But the two philosophies inevitably lock horns over the amount of punishment to be imposed. This is because some criminals may be deterred from committing future crimes with punishment that is greater or less than the amount popularly judged necessary for justice. For example, a mass murderer might well be deterred from further crimes by a few months in a maximum security lockup, with all the unspeakable modern terrors that would await him. Such a sentence would scarcely quench the inveterate demand for equal suffering that swells up in the retributionist—or, indeed, in most of mankind. To them, anything less than the death penalty—or, as a last resort, life in prison without parole—offends their natural sense of justice. By taking the life of another, the murderer has amassed a "debt" to society that he can repay only through relinquishing his own life, through either death or lifelong incarceration. But for those who believe that criminal punishment should rise above revenge and other related emotions, deterrence will remain an important, appealing alternative to retribution and its traditional global dominance.

Empirical studies into the practicability of deterrence are a recent development. The first factual examination of the criminal law's deterrent effect was not published until 1950.[37] Not until 1973 did a more comprehensive inquiry arrive in the publication of Isaac Ehrlich's study of "participation in illegitimate activities."[38] Using national data from the years 1940, 1950 and 1960, Ehrlich sought to determine the criminal law's ability to deter potential offenders. He developed a model of behavior in which the crime rate was a function of variables such as the probability of incarceration, the average length of prison sentence, the percentage of nonwhites and males in the subject population, income, unemployment and others. Ehrlich found that for seven selected violent offenses, the greater the probability of incarceration and the average length of prison sentence, the lower the crime rate. In other words, the threat of punishment, on the whole, appeared to deter potential criminals.

While Ehrlich's pioneer study, like all social "science," has some questionable methodological premises,[39] interest in his thesis spread. James Q. Wilson offered an analysis of the deterrence hypothesis several years later that came to much the same conclusions. He found that despite differences in individual internal restraints against criminal behavior, offenders were generally less likely to commit crimes when the costs for misconduct were made sufficiently severe. Greater criminal punishment can therefore in most cases suppress the crime rate.[40] Law-and-economics legal scholars have also seen evidence of the feasibility of deterrence in the current stew of data.[41]

While all these studies have trouble distinguishing the effects of deterrence from those of mere incapacitation, others have turned up a more straightforward finding: Longer incarceration generally means less crime, and an overall monetary savings to society. In 1987 economist Edwin Zedlewski calculated that the typical incarcerated offender is responsible for $430,100 in social costs per year (committing an average of 187 crimes per year at the average cost of $2,300). Since a year's imprisonment at that time cost an average of $25,000, Zedlewski estimated that the benefit-cost ratio of imprisonment was on the order of seventeen to one.[42] Although Zedlewski's figures have been soundly criticized as inflated,[43] others have found similar financial dividends to imprisonment based on more modest projections. In 1989 Assistant Attorney General Richard B. Abell affirmed the essence of Zedlewski's findings with more realistic numbers.[44] His analysis, however, was considered "sensationalistic" by many in academia because it appeared in a popular periodical. Professor John J. DiIulio of Princeton offered a spirited defense of Abell, stating that the reason why the "so-called experts" have such an "easy time lambasting an essay like Abell's is that the field's respected academic and quasi-academic journals seem to have placed a virtual embargo against any work, regardless of its quality, that supports strong incarceration policies. . . ."[45] DiIulio's own study also concluded that stingy incarceration policies are penny-wise and pound-foolish. His research regarding drug offenders estimated that the imputed monetary cost of releasing criminals was demonstrably higher than the cost of imprisonment, making incarceration "a positive social investment."[46]

Other studies that have roved beyond merely examining the remunerative wisdom of incarceration have run into more serious objections. Analysis that seeks to draw causal conclusions regarding incarceration and crime rates suffers from the flaws that plague all attempts to place human beings under the yoke of science and causation. Eugene Methvin, writing for Reader's Digest, compared the sentencing practices of several states in the latter half of the 1980s and inferred that incarceration rates had a significant effect on the crime rate. He concluded that longer incarceration policies, backed by the construction of new prisons, were responsible for reducing California's crime rate during the 1980s. The inmate population nearly quadrupled during that decade. These policies, Methvin felt, netted a reduction in the murder, rape and burglary rates of 24, 29 and 37 percent. Illinois during the same period released prisoners early, saving the state government $60 million but costing Illinois crime victims an estimated $304 million.[47] Marring these conclusions, of course, is the fact that many other things were also going on in California and Illinois at the same time. A state's penal policy by itself cannot take the credit or blame for something as multifaceted as crime rates. Professor Morgan O. Reynolds of Texas A&M University has even gone a step beyond Methvin, arguing that the Great Havoc is due almost entirely to the decreased likelihood of imprisonment.[48] Although such research cannot support the broad causal conclusions that its authors come to, common sense will continue to be a potent ally of the narrower thesis that effective punishment deters crime.

For those who still do not cotton to deterrence yet seek an alternative penal philosophy to rehabilitation, there are discouragingly few alternatives. Moral education, the fourth of the five most commonly identified penal philosophies, usually holds little appeal to itinerant ex-rehabilitationists. This theory represents an intersection of retribution and deterrence. Moral education is designed both to administer just deserts and to deter like-minded offenders by holding criminals out for public scorn from the community. Moral education squares best with retribution. The two working in concert provide society with a penal combination that both metes out equitable punishment and uses the offender's sentence as an opportunity to affirm the community's code of core values. Recent attempts to revive this dormant doctrine include proposals to publish the names of solicitors of prostitution in newspapers, identify the cars of drunk drivers with bumper stickers and post signs at the homes of convicted child molesters.

Community values, individual responsibility, punishment rather than treatment—none of this sounds promising to the ultraindividualist criminologist in search of a new philosophical home. The main problem with moral education, it seems, is its recalcitrant use of the word "moral." This runs counter to the current relativism. When Professor Etzioni, for instance, applied the term "moral" to his theory of communitarianism, many of his friends on the academic Left "expressed concern," saying that "it sounds like preaching."[49] There is also the modern presumption against "legislating morality," although honest students of legal history will acknowledge that every law ever enacted has reflected normative concerns to some degree. Finally, many of us would simply prefer to leave to the criminal justice system, and to the government generally, the task of teaching lessons in good citizenship to our community's more troublesome members. If community-based penalties must be enforced, it is thought, we must at least leave the "moral" out of it. The head of one of Kansas City's anticrime citizens' groups tersely acknowledged this understanding when asked to defend the publicizing of prostitution customers' names. "We are not making a moral statement on prostitution," he insisted. ". . . What we're saying is: We don't want prostitution on the streets where we live."[50]

The search for a new, post-rehabilitation theory of punishment finds a happier ending with the philosophy of incapacitation. Incapacitation's lone promise to a crime-weary society is that prisons will serve as warehouses for dangerous criminals. This policy of long-term storage is designed to remove them from society and prevent them from doing further harm to law-abiding citizens. There the promises stop. No more hope of rehabilitation or even justice; the sole purpose of the prison system is to keep criminals from committing further offenses against society. A wan substitute for the vibrant hopes held out by the penal philosophies of old, the trendy theory of incapacitation has nevertheless emerged as something of a crowd-pleaser. It now supplies the moral baseline of modern penology, the common ground where all penal philosophies converge because of their agreement on the need to segregate offenders from the rest of society.

The most attractive feature of incapacitation is that it spares us from having to make hard choices about human nature. Under this theory, the reasons people commit crimes—that is, free will versus the determinism of socioeconomic forces—are irrelevant. At least we can all agree that criminals should be prevented from committing further crimes. This consensus is mainly compliments of Mill, in that the libertarianism he authored did not extend to a legitimation of criminality and violence. Except for some on the far Left such as Mitford, incapacitation unites criminologists and public alike under the common mission of defending life, liberty and property with as few value judgments as possible.

Research on incapacitation has gone in two directions. Some scholars have sought to confirm that incapacitation can reduce the crime rate. Jacqueline Cohen's studies of incapacitation during the past two decades are foremost in this school, proving this assumption empirically.[51] Cohen and other scholars have also sought to help society fight crime more economically through the selective incapacitation of career criminals. The concept of career criminals, or lifelong chronic offenders, originated in the work of Wolfgang, Figlio and Sellin at the University of Pennsylvania. They examined the delinquency records of boys born in 1945 who lived in Philadelphia between the ages of ten and eleven.[52] They found that 6.3 percent of the boys committed five or more crimes. They termed them "chronic offenders." Since then, both criminologists and the public have aspired to target these offenders for especially lengthy sentences, sentences that would thus have a greater marginal effect on the crime rate. A RAND Corporation study by Joan Petersilia and Peter Greenwood concluded that incarcerating high-rate offenders was the only economically viable means of thoroughly instituting a policy of incapacitation.[53] Selective incapacitation appeals to different people for different reasons. Undoubtedly some criminologists like the idea because it seems to promise less punishment overall. For those who view punishment as "lamentable," as Herbert Packer put it, this would give the theory a compelling attractiveness. The public, on the other hand, supports selective incapacitation because it promises to cost less than other, farther-reaching policies.

Selective incarceration of society's worst offenders would certainly have a significant marginal effect on the crime rate. Wilson was confident that at least low-rate, occasional offenders could be identified, permitting shorter sentences for them so that greater prison space could be freed up for hard-core recidivists.[54] Recent experiments in various local jurisdictions are also commonly pointed to as proof of selective incapacitation's effectiveness. In the 1980s Oxnard, California, targeted its most serious habitual offenders with longer prison terms. The city's murder rate subsequently dropped 60 percent, robberies 41 percent and burglaries 29 percent. Proponents of selective incapacitation attributed the drop to their policy.[55] Recently President Clinton and many members of Congress have endorsed the selective-incapacitation policy of "three strikes and you're out"—three serious crimes and the malefactor is incarcerated for life. Incapacitation as a penal philosophy has finally come of age.

There are a few smudges on this otherwise wholesome new theory. First, under a "three strikes" system, offenders who already have two strikes will have an increased incentive to murder their victims. Since they will be imprisoned for life anyhow, two-time offenders can reduce the risk of getting caught by liquidating witnesses and face no additional penalty. This policy thus requires that capital punishment once again be enforced with vigor, which would be difficult because of recent unwieldy court rulings. Second, a "three strikes" program will require substantial increases in prison outlays. This will necessitate tax levies that are much greater than the public has been asked to bear in the past, and possibly more than we are even currently able to predict. The increase in expenses will be even vaster if the policy is broadened to include lifelong incarceration not simply of thrice-convicted offenders, but also of the entire sliver of the overall population that commits the overwhelming majority of the research of offenses. Frequently heard from advocates of tougher incarceration policies is the assertion that 6 percent of criminals commit 70 percent of crimes. But this is in error. This is simply a misconstrual of the research of Wolfgang *et al.*, which found that 6 percent of the *entire population* perpetrate the vast majority of crimes. Since only about 0.004 percent of the U.S. population is incarcerated at present, an attempt to confine the additional rambunctious 5.996 percent would mean an enormous increase in prison expenditures. We are a wealthy nation, and can certainly afford such worthwhile expenditures; but we should at least consult our bankers and spouses first.

Finally, a thorough policy of selective incapacitation also suffers from a certain intellectual dishonesty. The *sine qua non* of workable selective incapacitation, and the central focus of inquiry for incapacitation supporters, is the ability to single out classes of individuals who either are currently high-rate offenders or are likely to be in the future. If limited to individuals with a sufficiently long "rap sheet," such a policy could be applied fairly and equally. But some scholars and policymakers, seeking to economize further, propose something more. They recommend identifying *future* high-rate offenders based on noncriminal characteristics. Several criteria have been offered to enable accurate predictions of this sort. Cohen, for example, recommends taking into account not only one's prior criminal record, but also drug or alcohol abuse, age and even unemployment.[56] Similarly, Charleston, South Carolina, police chief Reuben Greenberg has offered as an intriguing rule of thumb that prisoners be released at the age of thirty-five, when the recidivism rate drops to near zero.[57] Van den Haag would raise the age to forty-five for three-strikes offenders.[58] Both appear to believe that the same policy should not apply to female offenders, and thus that men would receive longer sentences than women.

Harsher punishment based on alcoholism, unemployment and sex seems incredible enough, but might race be included as well? So it would seem. And here we see the beastly potential of selective incapacitation, at least when its most cost-efficient variation, "predictive" incapacitation, is pursued to its logical conclusion. Cohen justifies purging race from the list with a bit of circular reasoning. She says, "From a legal perspective, race is a 'suspect classification,' and an inappropriate criterion on moral grounds."[59] But this merely dances around the relativist's dilemma. Predictive incapacitation, as it now stands, is a nonjudgmental approach to crime control that denies the moral absolutes underlying other theories of punishment. This theory's relativism, coupled with the currently high crime rate of young black men, has the potential to lead to a genuinely neo-segregationist policy of sterner punishment for blacks, if its adherents are fully intellectually consistent. Jim Crow lives on as a modern, statistically educated Judge Roy Bean.

Therefore, at least when penal resources are rationed and the theory is applied selectively, even incapacitation is not as morally harmless as it first appears. Once society decides to punish criminals based on who they are instead of on the severity or quantity of the crimes they commit, there are all kinds of unintended consequences. The enthronement of predictive criteria as the determinant of punishment sets selective incapacitation into unavoidable conflict with traditional notions of justice embodied in retribution. Retribution, alone among penal philosophies, demands that the length of incarceration and amount of punishment be based on the seriousness of the crime rather than on who committed it. Under all other systems, punishment varies for each offender depending on how much is necessary for a given individual to be deterred, rehabilitated or incapacitated for the period in which he personally is a menace to society. All other philosophies of punishment treat people as a means to an end, which is what sent Kant into the retributionist camp. Even if we find its premises harsh, only retribution can be consistently counted on to provide equal justice under law. Thus, the wandering criminologist still cannot be entirely satisfied with this final destination of incapacitation. He ends his journey from the anti-retributionist utopia of rehabilitationism by arriving at a penal theory with hidden and remote, yet potentially monstrous, amorality.

This weary nomad can at least cheer himself with the knowledge that the masses seem as confused as he is. A 1981 national poll found that when asked which purpose the prison system should serve, 49 percent favored rehabilitation, compared to 17 percent for retribution and 31 percent for protecting society. In a 1982 Illinois study, over 80 percent of those surveyed agreed with the ostensible contradiction "While I believe that criminals deserve to be punished and sent to jail, I also believe that criminals should be given the chance to be rehabilitated during their prison term."[60] A 1991 survey found that Americans were still split down the middle. When asked to choose between rehabilitation and punishment, 48 percent favored the former and 38 percent the latter (14 percent were undecided).[61]

It is not at all clear what accounts for this confused jumble of attitudes. Part of the problem, undoubtedly, is that rehabilitation's inclusion in such a list of prison apologias implicitly portrays it as a viable option, even though it has now proved misconceived and impractical. Nevertheless, Americans seem to be genuinely befuddled. Perhaps the contradictory impulses of the Judeo-Christian tradition are to blame—"an eye for an eye" versus "turn the other cheek," and so forth. Regardless, when asked to choose a rationale for their prison system, people want to answer: all of the above.

Yet, as we have seen, these philosophies of punishment are not reconcilable. Or are they?

THE POLITICS OF RESURRECTION

From the birth of the prison, all five penal philosophies have, in one form or another, jockeyed for the attention and fidelity of legislators and prison officials. And while the intellectual team of retribution and moral education, harnessed together by centuries of social convention, has attracted more fans through the ages than any other rationale of punishment, the other justifications for the prison system have run a good race. American penal history is a pageantry featuring, first, the dominance of the Puritan Calvinist fusion of retribution and moral education; the Christian rehabilitationism of the Quakers in the late 1700s; a resurgent Calvinism touting profitable prison labor in the mid-1800s; and the rise and fall of secular rehabilitationism in the twentieth century, with deterrence elbowing its way in when it could. All of these philosophies remained attractive because all of them seemed to contain at least some small nugget of truth. They certainly all had their own appealing qualities, which played on a people alternately energized by outrage, compassion, economic calculation and relativistic libertarianism.

For all their incurable differences, these philosophies shared one common element: a belief in the therapeutic value of work. This was a very old view. Western societies had recognized idleness as the criminal's root vice long before the English and Dutch based their sixteenth-century bridewells and workhouses on that assumption. Ancient Athens' prohibition of idleness was undoubtedly typical of the attitudes of its day. Furthermore, the Judeo-Christian tradition had long warned about what happened when people had too much time on their hands. Adam, underemployed in his profession as a gardener, joined Eve in sampling forbidden fruit; the Israelites forged an idolatrous golden calf while awaiting Moses' delayed descent from Mount Sinai; the prodigal son in Luke and other parables in the New Testament—all warned of the perils of indolence. Laziness was a sin; it represented a failure to invest the ten talents of Christ's depiction, to contribute to society by cultivating one's God-given abilities. Worse still from society's standpoint, idleness permitted man to entertain himself in his excessive free time by preying on his neighbors, particularly those who obeyed the law and were blessed with riches. Idleness did not "cause" crime, but it provided the opportunities for man to be tempted into other misdeeds.

Work is thus vital to society and the individual, since it consumes opportunities for mischief. Even the Calvinist founders of the Auburn Prison encouraged work less out of greed than benevolence. Work gave the inmate direction and discipline, eating up otherwise idle time and showing him the fruits of productive, properly channeled labors. Inmate work also provided a handy system of funding the new, expensive institutions by requiring prisoners to pay for their keep. And just as important, prison labor occupied prisoners' time so that career criminals could not corrupt new inmates. The present-day concern that prisons are "schools of crime" where younger inmates learn the tools of a predatory trade was also expressed by John Howard, the Bedfordshire sheriff who helped establish modern prisons in the 1700s. He recognized the dangers of allowing older and younger prisoners to mix, and believed that work was crucial for blocking this transfer of illicit knowledge.[62]

Prison labor was one thing on which everyone could agree. Beaumont and Tocqueville were impressed by the results of this consensus. In their interviews of prisoners they noted, "There was not a single one among them who did not speak of labor with a kind of gratitude, and who did not express the idea that without the relief of constant occupation, life would be insufferable." In one striking observation, the two scholars noted how the conflicting rationales of the predominant penal philosophies seemed to dissolve in their shared endorsement of prison labor, coalescing into a practical philosophical synthesis. "But if it be true that the radical reformation of a depraved person is only an accidental instead of being a natural consequence of the penitentiary system, it is nevertheless true that there is another kind of reformation, less thorough than the former, but yet useful for society, and which the system we treat of seems to produce in a natural way." This "less thorough" reformation came from work. Work not only punished and deterred the offender; it helped to reform him spiritually. These "habits of order . . . influence very considerably his moral conduct after his return to society."[63]

Although Beaumont and Tocqueville did not retreat from their overall pessimism as to the prospects for rehabilitation—spiritual, psychological or otherwise—to the extent that rehabilitation was a feasible penal aim, this "useful" kind of reformation was based on prison labor that inculcated "habits of order." Work in prison might fulfill all the essential aspirations of the contending penal philosophies, at least in a practical sense. Prison labor was the common ingredient in this mélange of philosophies. And it still presents a practicable, consensus rationale for modern prisons.

Early American legislators saw the obvious merits of this system. They recognized in the Auburn system the opportunity to satisfy worthwhile penal aspirations with a self-sustaining revenue mechanism. From Auburn's policy of requiring prison labor within the penitentiary itself emerged the notion of leasing convicts out to private contractors and allowing them to work outside the prison. This second arrangement, the so-called lease system, made inmates much more profitable by providing a pool of available, reliable labor for almost any low-skilled job. In 1825 Kentucky became the first state to adopt the lease system. States from Illinois to California soon instituted the practice. It was popularly judged a success in all but two states.[64] Texas boasted a particularly successful program, with net proceeds reaching almost $187,000 over the two-year period of 1878-1880.[65]

It was not until the twentieth century that America finally departed from this ideological unity. Like so many other defects in the country's criminal justice system, the disbandment of prison labor resulted from the common delusion that effective crime control could be had without paying for it. In the case of prison labor, the price was marginal economic sacrifice by select categories of politically influential workers in free society. It did not take long for prison labor to become a powerful competitor with private labor in the lower-skilled industries. Not only were inmates' wages lower; employers also had in prisoners a captive, readily available workforce that was always on time and could neither complain nor quit. But unlike inmates, free laborers could vote. Politicians were soon forced to respond to free laborers who saw their wage levels threatened. The grumbling from those in the lesser-skilled classes wishing to keep their wages artificially high was clearly audible by at least 1853, when Andrew Johnson, then governor of Tennessee, complained that the state prison had been converted into a "State Mechanic Institute" competing with free laborers.[66]

The labor movement made other politicians take notice. Union leaders rightly saw prison labor as a threat to the earnings and job security of their lower-skilled members. Between 1895 and 1923 state legislatures, responding to labor's growing political clout, enacted laws prohibiting the sale of convict-made goods. During this period the percentage of employed prisoners dropped from 72 percent to 61 percent.[67] Some states compromised. Many adopted New York's state-use system, which permitted convicts to manufacture goods to be sold solely to the state government (such as license plates). But this invariably meant inmate underemployment, since the public sector provided a very limited market. By the end of the 1920s New York, the state where prison labor began, employed only about one-fifth of its inmates.[68]

The few states that resisted this economic self-interest had their prison-labor laws overridden by Congress. In 1929 Congress passed the Hawes-Cooper Act, which authorized states to ban commerce in prison-made goods within their borders. The Walsh-Healy Act of 1936 banned convict labor on government contracts exceeding $10,000. Most important, the Sumners-Ashurst Act of 1940 made it a federal crime to transport prison-made goods within a state for private use. Lenient judicial interpretations of the Constitution's interstate commerce clause ensured that such federal legislation was constitutional. Congress loosened these requirements only slightly in 1979 with the passage of the Percy Amendment, which allowed the interstate sale of prison-made goods provided that prisoners were paid the prevailing wage (i.e., the union scale), labor union officials were consulted, free labor was not affected and the goods were produced in an industry without local unemployment. Since businesses could get free laborers for the same price and without the bad press associated with employing criminals, prisoners have found few employers. Prison labor remains prohibited *de facto* by federal statute.

The original conception of the penitentiary was thus turned on its head. Prison labor, once viewed as indispensable for restoring a healthy relationship between the criminal and society, was made literally a federal offense. Instead of ceding certain jobs to prisoners to aid in their reformation, or simply allowing reductions in free laborers' wages to reflect the incentives of the market, Americans sought crime control on the cheap. As it turned out, these jobs were eventually lost anyhow to lower-paid foreigners. Yet prison labor remains illegal. Ninety percent of American inmates are currently unemployed.[69]

The emerging empirical proof of prison labor's regenerative benefits has made the current state of affairs even less defensible. A recent, extensive study of prison labor's effect on recidivism suggests that the early prison reformers knew what they were talking about. Research by the U.S. Bureau of Prisons released in 1991 showed that only 6.6 percent of federal inmates employed in prison industries violated their parole or were rearrested within a year of their release. This was in contrast to a 20 percent recidivism rate for non-employed prison inmates.[70]

If a growing crime rate cannot make prison labor politically acceptable again, maybe patriotism can. Prison labor today represents America's brightest, and perhaps final, opportunity to rebuild its industrial base. America stands to recover the low-wage jobs lost overseas to cheap foreign labor by involving its growing criminal class in productive employment. Prison labor would make available a pool of low-wage workers to the American capital that today is being sent to foreign markets. Entire industries could return to the United States. Who knows—maybe a few inmates would get caught up in the nationalist spirit and learn to think about someone besides themselves. Prison labor thus stands to do much more than engage prisoners in activities that are more ennobling than weight lifting and sodomy. Prisoners can be the workforce for revitalized industries, bringing jobs back to America.

Prison labor could also provide a safety valve that would alleviate prison overcrowding, and thus improve prison conditions. Of course, the term "overcrowding" is relative, and a notorious question-begger. Prison officials, with their own unique perspective, have complained of overcrowding since Philadelphia's Walnut Street Jail became unable to provide solitary confinement.[71] Prison labor could help free up more living space for inmates, to the general satisfaction of all. By employing prisoners in round-the-clock shifts, a prison labor regime would permit cells to be used only for sleeping, and thus two prisoners could share the same sleeping quarters. Crewmembers on U.S. Navy submarines must rotate and share beds because of limited space; surely inmates can make do with the same conditions expected of American sailors. This system could, in many cases, literally double the amount of available prison space. Inmate work shifts would allow more criminals to be incarcerated, or for criminals to be incarcerated longer. And all the while they will learn the virtues of industriousness.

The opportunity for discipline and introspection uniquely offered by labor, especially hard labor, is still lost on too many of us. Many Americans, especially in academia, are still inclined to think of labor, the practical synthesis of our civilization's warring penal philosophies, as too severe and mean-spirited. These scholars would do well to follow the example of their fellow intellectuals from the same France that conceived the crime-as-disease philosophy. First, like Beaumont and Tocqueville, they might ask inmates for their thoughts on the matter. They will likely find that a slothful lifestyle, for all its obvious delights in the short run, now seems crushing to many inmates. Second, they should consult a fellow salon-mate of their fathers in the French Enlightenment, Voltaire. Candide's apt horticultural reply to Pangloss serves well in response to such well-intentioned sympathy: "That is well put, but we must cultivate our garden."[72]

That, of course, means uprooting a few weeds here and there. In particular, it means deracinating America's true "black flowers," as Hawthorne would have it—the penal philosophies and their intellectual seed that give incentive to criminality by excusing it as a disease or as otherwise caused by forces beyond the individual's control. If America's prisoners are given work and discipline and required to confront their transgressions as sins against their neighbors, sins for which they are individually responsible, prisons could actually prove beneficial for a change. The thing-in-bloom that remains might just be a resurrection.

PART TWO

UNNATURAL LAW: SCIENCE AND THE "CAUSES" OF CRIME

CHAPTER FIVE

The New Noble Savage

Deign on the passing world to turn thine eyes,
And pause a while from learning to be wise,
There mark what ills the scholar's life assail—
Toil, envy, want, the patron, and the jail.

—Samuel Johnson

Jeremy Bentham was, it is true, a bit self-centered. History remembers him for other reasons, but Bentham must forgive us if we, for present purposes, highlight one of his less renowned, and less flattering, qualities. The founder of utilitarianism and the most influential of criminologists, he was the most happily eccentric of men. This was by self-design. As he grew older, Bentham sought to recapture his youth by liberating himself from settled habits and routine through a personal revolution of sorts. He did this by devising new idiosyncrasies. Through this self-change Bentham hoped to shed what he viewed as the gloomy orthodoxy of his childhood, and to become, in the words of one historian, M. P. Mack, a "gaily radical patriarch."[1] In doing so he would also give us insight into the traits that, to one degree or another, define most intellectuals and practitioners of the criminology he fathered up to our own day.

127

Many of Bentham's oddities were harmless and childlike. His daily costume included a broad-brimmed yellow straw hat and embroidered carpet slippers. Once suitably dressed, Bentham would enjoy leisurely strolls with his walking stick, which he christened "Dapple," as well as his constant companion "Dick," a favorite teapot. At night he would retire to his bed only after each of his secretaries—or, as he called them, "reprobates"—would "swear fealty" to something called a "*trinoda necessitas*—the asportation of the window—the transtration of the window,—idem of the trap window." His bemused amanuenses holding court, Bentham would then drift off to sleep, into a world where his droll manners and preciosity might seem less peculiar.[2]

Bentham's intellectual colleagues and perceived competitors at times saw something less endearing in his self-absorption. He often complained that his life was an "unrecognized existence. I feel like a cat or a dog that is used to be [sic] beaten by everybody it meets." But Bentham at least forthrightly acknowledged the quirky self-interest that drove him. Like all intellectuals, Bentham had spent years in solitary research experimenting with ideas and acquiring the knowledge necessary to master his area of interest. Both the personality traits that led him to this lonely profession and that profession's requirements once a member made a certain amount of self-centeredness inevitable. These factors also made Bentham, like most academics, inclined to favor philosophies that exalted the individual over the community, and self-interested rights over responsibilities. A man alone with his thoughts views society as an unwelcome intruder. Like most philosophers through the ages, Bentham concentrated on himself, and on theories that would justify his way of living.

Toward this end, Bentham hoped to attract what Mack described as an "army of disciples," distributing the "sacred literature" that he produced and going forth into the world to convert his previously isolated thoughts into a "great religion." In Bentham's entreaty to one potential recruit, Edmund Burke, he bared his soul. "I am a self-conceited man," Bentham acknowledged, "as all system-mongers who converse much with themselves and little with the rest of the world are apt to be, and as a system-monger must be." Burke, himself a conservative "system-monger" of some stature, did not enlist.[3]

But Bentham's efforts eventually bore fruit. He succeeded in bequeathing to future generations a philosophy of utilitarianism that would ensure him a seat in the pantheon of great Western thinkers.

Certain projects, such as the Panopticon and his exhaustive critique of the English common law, were brilliant and sufficiently practical to endure to the present as influential monuments to his genius. Bentham's estate also included another donation. In his will he decreed that his body should be presented to the public once he had expired. Bentham left instructions that his corpse, which he termed an "autoicon," be dissected in the presence of his friends and then suitably preserved to inspire future generations of "system-mongers." Upon Bentham's death his head was covered and filled with wax, and his skeleton dressed in his daily attire. His remains were then set upright in a glass case at Oxford's University College, topped by his favorite straw hat, his face smirking slightly. Bentham's mummy remains there to this day.

Bentham provides an easy target for critics of the intelligentsia, and it is easy to overgeneralize based on his example. But in certain respects, Bentham was not a mere caricature of the modern ultraindividualist intellectual. He merely revealed plainly and happily the energies and peculiarities that, to some extent, propel all academics. His unusual, bohemian lifestyle, the end product of a financial independence that shielded him from real-life preoccupations, has a parallel in campus life today for the most prominent of American intellectuals: college professors. He made no effort to hide his desire—common for intellectuals, and for that matter people in general—to be accepted and admired by his colleagues. But to the end, Bentham did not compromise his principles for professional approval. His egotism, if at times overbearing, was earned.

In criminology today this pride remains, but there is less to be proud of. The volumes of criminological literature generated by the American academy today endanger far more trees than Bentham did in full tilt, yet lend much less insight into the reasons for social conflict in general and crime in particular. There is, for instance, an unfortunate uniformity of thought throughout much of the discipline. Some of this is not by choice. As Princeton professor John DiIulio noted, those who disagree with the prevailing consensus in criminology, which inclines toward ultraindividualism, face a virtual "embargo" of their works in the social science journals that determine the success of academic careers.[4] Isaac Ehrlich has received stronger sanctions for his nonconformity. After applying his deterrence formula to the death penalty, he concluded that capital punishment "may" save several lives for every life it takes by deterring future offenders.[5] Although Ehrlich's conclusion was highly tentative, and he himself remained personally opposed to the death penalty, one prominent opponent of the death penalty, Professor Hugo Adam Bedau of Tufts University, exclaimed that Ehrlich's research was "utter garbage." He also warned that "the abolitionists are getting their hired guns out, too, to torpedo Ehrlich."[6]

In one narrow sense, most criminologists benefit from these standards, which are at once relaxed and rigid. Free to research and write with each other in mind as a future audience, they can focus on efforts that will gain them acceptance from the most esteemed figures in their field, whose approval is often necessary for their success. Since most theories are ultimately dressing for private biases, the "self-conceited," ultraindividualist inclinations that Bentham cheerfully conceded tend to work their way into criminological findings. Usually this is not premeditated. These values are simply impressed unconsciously on research and data during scholarly interpretation. This ideological content, in fact, is almost unavoidable for human-based studies, especially studies that offer causal analysis. The philosophy that often imbues modern criminology has, at its center, an ironic alloy: an emphasis on individualism and individual rights, with a simultaneous belief that the individual should not be held responsible or punished for his crimes.

Criminological energy is, as a result, currently concentrated on cataloguing and explaining the different social forces that are thought to compel the individual into a life of crime. Drugs, poverty and, most recently, biology are some of the prime subjects of inquiry; other objects and entities believed to cause crime range from guns to unemployment to racism. Some criminologists have even gone tit-for-tat with Ehrlich, claiming that by encouraging violence, the death penalty causes more deaths than it deters.[7] All of this has brought about profound and relatively sudden changes in criminology and its view of the individual. The belief in individual free will shared by Bentham and the other founders of criminology has become in this century the minority position, and its faithful are sometimes subject to professional penalty.

It is a good thing that mummies do not change their expression. The current situation might well be enough to bring a sad frown to the face of even the whimsical Bentham.

THE "CAUSATION" CHIMERA

Causation is arguably the essential principle of science. It is certainly important. If science is the compilation of facts and principles based on objective observation and experimentation, then the concept of causation is what makes science thus defined understandable and practical. Scientific principles are induced from repeated, before-and-after factual observations. Gravity causes apples to fall to the ground; setting fire to gunpowder causes explosions; and so forth. Experience tells us that certain events invariably follow other events; we use the term "cause" to explain the apparent force that the first event exerts on the second. By systematizing and enumerating these helpful rules of everyday prediction, science allows us to avoid harm and productively harness the forces of nature. When limited to formulating these empirical rules, rules inferred from human experience with tangible objects and natural forces, the concept of causation is both sensible and scientific, rightly defined.

When, however, causation is applied to human beings, we must bracket the term with quotation marks. Causation makes sense conceptually only when applied to objects that lack free will, such as falling apples and exploding gunpowder. Imbedded in the term is the assumption that the object being acted upon cannot choose its own fate, cannot overcome the contrary pressure applied by the external stimuli. This distinction is crucial, yet often not observed in current criminological research. An apple falling from a tree, for example, does not choose to fall. A person jumping from a building, on the other hand, chooses both to fall and to hit the ground below. That his jump followed a series of personal tragedies and anguish may help to explain why he *chose* to jump. But to argue that these problems caused him to fall, like gravity affecting the apple, is a semantic sleight of hand that denies his fundamental nature, that of a free agent capable of choosing his own destiny. Thus applied, causation becomes "causation," and any "science" derived therefrom must always be approached skeptically.

It is a revealing indication of the state of Bentham's discipline that criminology has now been redesigned as a science dedicated almost exclusively to ascertaining the causes of crime. Criminology is today devoted mainly to identifying the social forces that conscript criminals to do what they do. Implicit in this is the premise that criminals lack free will, the ability to choose responsible conduct. They are soldiers of nature and socioeconomic inequity, at the service of Caesars they can neither see nor understand.

We have yet to learn the lessons of a contemporary of Bentham's who saw the potential for such grave error in the concept and term "causation." In the late eighteenth century David Hume put forth a critique of causation so penetrating and uncompromising that his conclusions have hardened into truisms of Western philosophy. His central thesis was, and remains, a bombshell: the very concept of causation is, as commonly understood, nonsensical. Hume believed that human knowledge is limited to impressions, or mental images received from experience (for instance, the red color and shape that one associates with an apple), and ideas, the various combinations of stored impressions mixed and matched by the brain (such as those that led to the invention of applesauce). Impressions and ideas stemming from impressions provide our only source of knowledge, the units of daily know-how that we call facts. Anything else, Hume held, is either superstition or arbitrary personal preferences unmoored to a lodestar of experience, ideas that he termed values.

Hume's analysis spoke to more than narrow questions of epistemology, the philosophy of knowledge. His main point was that since there is no impression for causation, determining causes is a tricky business. To prove this, he went to the extreme of arguing that causation is merely a mental abstraction learned from habit, a handy name applied to the concept that people invented to explain the predictable interactions of forces.[8] Hume, who joked of taking off his philosopher's hat when leaving his study so that he could go about the real world equipped with common sense, believed that causation should be accepted for both its obvious benefits and its less obvious traps. While causation is a helpful rule of thumb for predicting the way objects will respond when mingling with each other, its main hazard was the temptation to enlist it in areas of inquiry that allow for the dishonest molding of empirical data, findings deformed by values. Lacking a direct connection to reality, causation under such circumstances could be colored by subjective preferences. In other words, the researcher could see what he wanted to see, projecting all sorts of personal views into pseudoscientific analysis. If incorrectly applied to free agents such as humans and ideologically filtered in its application, causation becomes "causation," an outright impediment to knowledge.

No discipline has better illustrated the misconceptions behind the term "social sciences," and the potential for abusing the principle of causation, than modern criminology. In its application to criminology, causation has been utilized in an academic province devoted solely to the study of people. Most folks assume that they control their own actions, and thus find the basis for this endeavor a bit silly. But our use of causation in a human-based study like criminology has important implications. It suggests that man is not individually responsible for his actions. This assumption grew out of French Enlightenment determinism, as we have seen. If fully implemented, this view would carry some very disruptive consequences, starting with large-scale unemployment for policemen, prosecutors and prison guards. For why should they be hired to harass offenders who know not what they do?

The use of causation in criminology, as Hume foretold, has allowed an interplay of research and the scholar's own views to produce creative science; and this allows us an ostensibly scientific basis for granting amnesty to offenders. It also allows us some fun, at least those of us who enjoy committing crimes (as most of us do, at least for a while). Modern criminology has generally proved generous in denominating a wide variety of social factors as causes of crime. Those who can successfully lay claim to abuse from such factors thus receive an excuse for not observing the law. The applicability of these causes depends on which group of victims thus defined the criminal belongs to. Individuals are deterministically pigeonholed according to these various categories, and are, with some exaggeration, essentially the following. Poor folks? Poverty made them do it—even for non-property-related crimes. Black crime? A tragic but understandable vestige of racism. Black-on-black crime? More tragic, but the same excuse applies. Wives who murder their abusive husbands rather than simply leaving them? Justifiable self-defense; the pigs deserved it. There are double standards to this general rule. Those who resist violent crimes with like violence are sometimes judged more harshly than their assailants. But otherwise this practice is followed consistently. In the end, of course, nothing is free; society must pay for these new liberties. Criminality predictably abounds among these privileged social classes once the news of these rights spreads.

Given the amount of criminological attention paid recently to the causes of crime in modern America, a review of the most commonly offered causes promises to be an exhausting trek through terrain with plenty of mirages and possible pitfalls. Yet it is a necessary excursion if we are to understand the intellectual origins of the Great Havoc. Occasionally we will stumble across studies that draw conclusions at odds with the current consensus. These deserve serious scrutiny, since at the very least such risky departures from orthodoxy make their authors presumptively honest. Other studies will also be examined, if only to reveal the hidden dynamics of causal analysis that Hume detected, and against which we must be on guard. Throughout the rest of this section of the book, the main causes of crime will be examined in proper Aristotelian order, starting with the individual. Later chapters will discuss the family, gangs and drugs, race and, finally, nationality—to wit, American citizenship. Just remember to remove your criminologist's hat when the tour is completed.

CREATIVE SCIENCE AND THE LUXURY OF POVERTY

American social science's extraordinary transformation of Rousseau's noble savage from happy camper to glorious outlaw does not trace its roots directly to the French Enlightenment. This theory became caught up in other movements that have concurrently been seeking the attention of Western academics. One influence was Marxism. Marx, like Rousseau, saw man as corrupted by unjust social institutions. But the two differed in their solutions. Rousseau's remedy for this seduction was a rejection of society through a mass back-to-nature movement. His proposal earned Voltaire's famous contemptuous retort, "On reading your book one feels tempted to go on all fours."[9] Marx, in contrast, proposed revolution. He urged the poor, or proletariat, to fulfill History's mandate by sacking the upper classes. Of course, by assuming that his readers could choose to instigate this final struggle ("Workers of the world, unite!"), Marx's call to class warfare was, if not contradictory, certainly a bit redundant. But Marx seemed at times less interested in consistency than in begetting a famous movement that would bear his name. Thus, in setting a standard followed by too many other theorists, Marx went to some highly questionable lengths to validate his thesis of historical causation, including falsifying data.[10] The present conception of criminals as lacking individual culpability reflects the coalition of Marxism, French Enlightenment philosophy and radical individualism that predominates in American academia today.

This conception has taken hold, also, because of the fuzzy modern conception of science. As the late Allan Bloom noted, the relativism of our era has managed to dominate not merely philosophy, but even science.[11] Criminology's popular status as a science, of course, allows it to benefit from the impression that its principles are arrived at objectively and without collusion with values. But sometimes, as Hume noted, the analytical mix is more complex than that. There remains the potential that he recognized for using causation as a vehicle for values-smuggling in scientific analysis. Science indeed is now not the study of someone else's centuries-old observations, or the tedious, time-consuming stuff of the laboratory. The new, liberated science allows for creativity. It also permits social scientists to be, in the words Paul Johnson used to describe intellectuals in general, "free spirits, adventurers of the mind."[12] And, in fairness, we cannot realistically expect anything less of the heirs of the freethinking Bentham, especially given the relativism of our popular culture.

Professor Bloom was off base in attributing this creativity fetish to Nietzsche. It is as old as intellectuals, and a result, as Bentham suggested, of their almost inevitable self-centeredness and desire to flex their inventive genius. Plato was perhaps the first to display these tendencies brashly, mentally tinkering with the Greek society of his day on a broad scale. Mill devoted one-fifth of *On Liberty* to a defense of intellectual originality for its own sake. In praising "individual spontaneity," Mill criticized the "despotism of custom," the accepted patterns of life that, for most people, preclude wild intellectual flings: "It is for him [each individual] to find out what part of recorded experience is properly applicable to his own circumstances and character." Mill believed that "[o]riginality is the one thing which unoriginal minds cannot feel the use of"; these minds belonging to the "mass" of "collective mediocrity." Libertarian intellectuals, he felt, must "commence new practices and set the example of more enlightened conduct and better taste and sense in human life."[13]

There is, however, a stubborn truism that intrudes upon this new intellectual bliss: most original ideas are wrong. Ideas that are at odds with the inherited collective wisdom of antiquity are always, on their face, suspect. They merit great scrutiny before being thrust on society through the brute force of law or armed revolution. It is a postulate of democracy, first identified and defended by Aristotle, that two heads are better than one—the more people who take part in the formation of law or custom, the more likely it is that that law or custom is just and helpful. There are egregious exceptions to this rule, of course, exceptions we do well to acknowledge. But if the twentieth century has taught us anything, it is that, as a general proposition, someone who seeks to remake society in his own image has a lot of explaining to do.

There are other complications as well. Creativity requires targets for its effective display. The most obvious and inviting target, as Mill saw, is custom. But custom, we must realize, usually exists for good reason. It represents the stored wisdom of thousands of years of preceding generations; history teaches that societies that cast off traditions for transient thrills invite chaos and conquest. Thus, ideas that rebel against the prescriptive common judgment of the masses, the values and cultural habits unassumingly accumulated and treasured over centuries of social development, must be viewed warily by any society that wishes to avoid becoming a laboratory for potentially hazardous theories. Will Durant put the same proposition nicely when he observed that "our ancestors were not all fools."[14]

We as a society have recently overlooked these truths, and it should not surprise us when criminologists, under the new creative ground rules, do the same. Americans' traditional understanding of crime has, as a result, come in for some strong academic opposition. The earliest steps toward this new science were tentative. In 1942 criminologists Clifford Shaw and Henry McKay published a seminal study of crime-ridden neighborhoods whose debt to Marxism probably was unconscious. Their research was the acorn of the American ecological school of criminology that grew from their efforts. Shaw and McKay surveyed and contrasted several Chicago neighborhoods and the extent of criminality that each appeared to incubate. Unexceptional by the standards of today's criminology, which has by and large adopted Shaw and McKay's central thesis, the duo departed substantially from the presumptions of the day in arguing that neighborhoods, or one's environment, cause crime.[15] Previously it was assumed to be the other way around. Criminals cluster in certain neighborhoods because the same personality traits that lead them to a life of crime, such as lack of self-discipline and what would later be called short "time horizons," necessarily mean that they end up in the poorest section of town. There they often prey upon one another. Shaw and McKay turned these suppositions on their head by suggesting that criminals were pawns of society, moved to and fro by environmental forces including but not limited to their neighborhoods. It would take several subsequent decades before this new theory of criminal causation was accepted to the point that its implicit core law would be confidently extracted and argued: poverty causes crime.

The poverty-causes-crime theory developed further with the work of Robert K. Merton. In 1957 he published a book that introduced an original variation of this view, "strain theory." It held that crime was caused by a criminal's frustration at being unable to legally obtain property and other desirable goods from other members of society. The criminal experiences a strain between his goal and his means of permissibly fulfilling it.[16] This strain, in turn, is essentially a result of society's teasing the criminal by dangling the fruits of other people's industry before him, especially via the media, knowing that he has placed himself in a position where he is unable to acquire them rightfully.

While strain theory made a great deal of sense absent any causal assumptions, other scholars took Merton's thesis several steps further. Richard A. Cloward and Lloyd E. Ohlin published an influential elaboration of Merton's strain theory three years later. Like Merton, they agreed that the relationship between a person's desires and his ability to indulge them legally dictates civil obedience. Cloward and Ohlin applied this theory specifically to adolescents. They concluded that teenage boys steal to obtain the material goods that they cannot otherwise afford, usually status symbols essential for acceptance by their peer groups. All of this seems true and insightful. But then Cloward and Ohlin went on to propose a then-innovative solution to such criminality: "They [delinquents] must be taught that better worlds exist and that these worlds are populated with flesh and blood people with whom they may interact. Persons such as detached workers and school teachers fit the bill quite nicely."[17] While this prescription may be easy to smirk at with today's hindsight, their work was of crucial importance to later scholars and policymakers. It set a standard for the many subsequent criminological solutions offered for the crime surge of the sixties, one which taught that criminals are victims to be pitied rather than punished. By endorsing social workers and teachers as qualified to massage miscreants and remove their strain, Cloward and Ohlin and the criminologists they influenced helped to lay the intellectual foundations for the Great Society agenda.

Cloward and Ohlin's proposals, while obviously well-intentioned, did not lend themselves to simple, effective implementation. The government programs that resulted were rooted in a defective materialistic conception of criminals as a class whose strain could be appeased only through redistributed money and goods. The federal programs pursuing these hopes, in turn, were haphazardly conceived. Charles Murray, surveying the progress two decades later, found that the War on Poverty was not only a "war" waged against an elusive enemy; the anti-poverty programs had actually *increased* poverty among their recipients.[18] By then, however, the only serious intellectual competition for the poverty-causes-crime thesis was its parent, the Marxism that had finally come out of the criminological closet. Both theories shared a core materialism, viewing as life's primary mission the quest for superior possessions.

The poverty-causes-crime theory, which was eventually endorsed by the Kerner Commission's report in 1968, took issue directly with the teachings of the founders of criminology. The classical liberal scholars who had created and raised criminology from its infancy (Beccaria, Bentham, Sutherland) had believed almost exactly the opposite. They agreed that crime—or, more precisely, the lack of self-discipline and other predispositions that incline a man toward a life of crime—in a sense "causes" poverty. The same traits that make someone unwilling to abstain from short-term criminal gains typically lead that person to prefer instant gratification over the tiresome education and self-denial that are usually necessary for lawfully securing material success. In short, criminals are generally poor because unindustrious, antisocial people do not, as a rule, prosper. The theory that poverty causes crime is thus almost a classic *non causa, pro causa* fallacy, a confusion of cause and effect. Voltaire, Rousseau's nemesis, would have relished the opportunity to skewer criminology's new noble savage. He would have recognized the poverty-causes-crime paralogism as similar to Pangloss's happy observations in *Candide;* for instance, our good fortune that "noses were made to support spectacles, hence we have spectacles."[19]

Although America can boast of a greater degree of upward mobility for motivated citizens than any other nation, we have paradoxically become the most fertile ground for modern criminology's central project. We have generally accepted the poverty-causes-crime theory uncritically. Rather than a natural result of shortsighted, often egoistic conduct, poverty is presumed to be a cruel twist of fate. In response to these benevolent assumptions—which constitute, in effect, public charity—criminals have responded with almost poetic ingratitude. Never before has poverty been such a luxury.

It is, in fact, so widely accepted that poverty causes crime that even to question this premise strikes many of us as profoundly unfair and hardhearted. But submerged beneath these beliefs are some simple truths that must be retrieved if we are serious about understanding crime. Let us start with the first commonplace that deserves rehabilitation: most prosperous people, at least in free, egalitarian societies like America, deserve to be prosperous. Although there are certainly exceptions, the well-to-do in the United States are generally so because they have sacrificed, often greatly, to achieve a goal in the distant future. Frequently they have deferred gratifications, forfeited all income for many years while studying in college and graduate schools, worked extremely long hours and risked their entire life savings to gamble on an idea. For every well-off American who inherited his wealth, there are many more who invented or perfected goods and services that make life more convenient and pleasant for the rest of us. We, as consumers, compensate them accordingly. The prosperous, and by the same token those comfortably within the middle class, must be recognized as people who generally deserve to be where they are in life, no matter how distasteful the greed and egocentrism that often propel them to the top.

An accompanying truism is harder, but even more necessary, for us to accept. Most poor people in America are poor for just reasons. That is to say, poverty is usually not a harsh, arbitrary turn of events that strikes the otherwise deserving. Instead, it is mostly the result of bad decisions. The decision to conceive a child out of wedlock, to forgo education, to quit work before obtaining alternative employment or most often a combination thereof: poverty is a capitalist society's rough but fair punishment for a series of major economic mistakes. Obviously the poor are not, by nature of their income bracket, immoral people or lousy citizens. Indeed, often their simple religiosity and contempt for middle-class yuppie self-centeredness make them far better souls than those who succeed in the business jungle. The materialism in which the wealthy wallow is surely no cure-all for this crime-plagued Republic. But the sincere Christians who are disproportionately among the lower class understand Christ's teachings that, while it is easier for a camel to go through the eye of a needle than for a rich man to enter heaven, it is equally true that the poor will always be among us—by definition, since poverty is relative. There are many factors that help to frame behavior and lead to the bad decisions that result in a life of poverty: anti-education peer pressure, a subculture of predatory sex, etc. One especially important factor is short time horizons, an unwillingness to defer present gain for possibly greater income in the future.[20] The same short time horizons that often condemn the relative poor to their status mean that, at the margin, these Americans will generally not fare as well as others in any economic competition. Poverty, then, often serves as a reliable indicator of who is most likely to give in to criminal temptation, since the same qualities that predispose one to bad economic decisions often make crime attractive. Thus it is that, for instance, homicide, a non-property crime seemingly unrelated to low income, is disproportionately concentrated in areas of poverty, *regardless of race and other oft-cited explanations.*[21]

Those who would, based on these facts, pat themselves on the back and feel no sense of duty toward their lower-income fellow citizens should not be so hasty. Any humane civilization must actively assist those who have landed in poverty and wish to improve their status. On the other hand, scholars such as Charles Murray have demonstrated empirically what Aristotle had intuited millennia before—simple justice and sheer practicality limit the scope of such schemes. Eschewing the classical liberal Adam Smith in favor of Marx, excessively egalitarian politicians have recently overlooked these restraints. In furthering their conception of justice while at the same time seeking to calm the lower classes producing much of America's crime, policymakers have sought to reduce or soften class distinctions through taxation. This has too often amounted to taking the property of those who made better decisions in life and redistributing the proceeds to the less wise. The result, at times, has been the subsidizing of unproductive and even criminal behavior. In denying the inevitability of class distinctions in a dynamic, capitalist society, we ignore some essential truths, which seem harsh only because we have become so forgetful of them. Poor people are usually poor for the same reasons that they tend to smoke, eat the wrong foods, drink alcohol too frequently, drop out of school and make other ill-considered choices. They are poor not because they are moral wretches, but because their judgment is too often clouded by a background and culture that encourage shortsighted behavior.

So it is with crime. One of the main reasons that crime is concentrated among the lower classes is that that is where the citizens with predisposing short time horizons are the most numerous. The lowest class is also the most vulnerable to our popular culture of egoism. The short time horizons that often effectively assign the relative poor their economic status also make instant gratification in pursuit of life's material goods especially alluring, goods that are increasingly flaunted in this libertarian age. The poor are, in addition, less likely to appreciate the esoteric distinctions in libertarianism that mandate living the epicurean good life in a solitary war against the community, yet without interfering in others' quest for the same. Finally, by marginalizing religion, the historically necessary constraint on lower-class materialistic envy, libertarianism removes the poor man's last inhibitions against ransacking the community until he gets what he wants, be it loot, sexual gratification or power.

When put under the social science equivalent of a microscope, the poverty-causes-crime thesis simply does not withstand scrutiny. The causation component of the thesis sneaks in a validation of criminality that is contrary to any genuinely scientific undertaking. Perhaps poverty might *explain,* as the classic example goes, a starving man's stealing bread to feed his family. But poverty cannot *excuse* such criminality, unless, of course, normative considerations are included in the analysis. In any event, poverty can credibly explain only property crimes. How can rape or arson, for instance, possibly be written off to the understandable misconduct of a pauper? How are these predations rooted in economics, other than a quasi-economic cost/benefit analysis of the likelihood of getting caught? What sort of economic reasoning would precede such behavior? "Well, I'm broke—time to go get my mind off things by raping Betty Sue or torching old man Louie's grocery store"—are these the likely calculations of even the most down-and-out offenders?

The very definition of poverty is hard to pin down. For example, 40 percent of all households identified as poor by the U.S. Census Bureau own their own homes.[22] While poor by American standards, the American poor appear almost well heeled to most of the rest of the world; indeed, people in destitute, undeveloped nations are, by virtually *any* measure, much more law-abiding than citizens of industrialized, "advanced" countries. Much of what is defined as poverty is also a very temporary condition. The turnover in the nonelderly poor is almost 45 percent a year.[23] Professor Edward Banfield has noted that the definition of poverty is both ambiguous and subject to dispute. He concludes that the definition of poverty that "will serve rather well today" is that offered by the British economist Alfred Marshall. Marshall defined poverty as lacking the "necessaries" of life, such as

> a well-drained dwelling with several rooms, warm clothing, with some changes of underclothing, pure water, a plentiful supply of cereal food, with a moderate allowance of meat and milk, and a little tea, etc., some education, and some recreation, and lastly sufficient freedom for his wife from other work to enable her to perform properly her maternal and household duties.[24]

"Measured by this standard," Banfield concludes, there is little if any poverty in America today. The current American conception of poverty "is not so much one of income *level* as one of income *distribution.*" In short, poverty in modern America is simply "lack of *status.*"[25] Poor Americans are labeled as such because they lack certain status symbols owned and, regrettably, often thoughtlessly shown off by the wealthy—large homes, expensive cars, designer apparel. Thus, while poverty is a transparently inadequate explanation for crimes not involving property, even property crimes by poor Americans cannot be excused. These offenses amount to the plundering of the (usually) justly prosperous by members of the less-well-off social strata jealous and covetous of their frivolous status symbols and luxuries. As George F. Will once said of criminologists' claims that looting during a New York blackout was a "cry for help," "the 'cry for help' seems to be a cry for a free color TV."[26]

Banfield predicted the failure of the Great Society when he noted the futility of such income redistribution programs. If, as the available research suggested to him in the late 1960s, lower-income Americans consider themselves poor because of their inferior income status, then "nothing can help."[27] Charles Murray simply confirmed what Banfield had augured. To some extent, welfare and related social programs have simply served to prove the old adage that if the wealthy's income were taken and given to the rest of society, they would earn it back in due course. Indeed, Murray's analysis indicates that the poor unintentionally have been made even worse off than before, with government transfer payments reinforcing their least advantageous qualities and predispositions.

If anything, as we have seen, to the extent that causation applies at all to criminological analysis, crime "causes" poverty. Crime depresses property values, raises insurance premiums (which are passed on to consumers) and requires costly gadgets for self-protection. It is in this light that we must analyze the anticrime solution often pointed to by modern criminology: the further subsidizing of both poverty and crime, through increased government transfer payments and reduced penalties and vituperation for criminals. The impoverished, chaotic end result of these policies is accomplished through force, either implied (taxation) or express (violent crime). That, of course, is not much of a way to instruct would-be offenders on the virtues of nonviolence. Nor, for that matter, is it truly likely to make life among the poor any more pleasant.

MEAN GENES

The recent construction of theories explaining the "causes" of crime has drawn many spectators and fellow workers to the job site. One is a hardy band of intellectual archaeologists working to preserve some of the important lessons of criminology's past. A busy group of independent scholars, spearheaded by James Q. Wilson, has sought to reexamine the old notions of individual accountability accepted by earlier generations of criminologists. They have good news to report. Wilson and company have concluded, based on these efforts, that individuals are in fact personally responsible for their crimes after all. Sort of.

The product of these labors is neodeterminism. The "neo" represents a bow to the founders of the school. They introduced the notion that criminality is determined, but not by external entities. The determinant is biology. Thanks largely to Wilson's perseverance, the hottest trend in criminology today is the attempt to explain crime as the result of genetic composition, the natural extension of wrongful impulses present since birth. Heredity, alas, is the culprit. The original determinists, who conceived their theories around the turn of the century, could not draw upon the recent explosion of information on genetics. They were forced to focus on more obvious physical traits. In their attempts to objectively prove the link between criminality and innate characteristics, they managed to fasten the scientific method, despite its obvious limitations, to criminology, making their findings at least independently testable by other scholars. We should bear this in mind if, when reviewing their works, we enjoy a few giggles at their expense.

Since the most eye-catching human traits are facial, they were naturally the focus of the first branch of determinism, physiognomy. Cesare Lombroso, its founder, asserted in the late nineteenth century that certain men were born criminals. Fortunately for society, they could be identified without too much effort—in fact, just by looking at them. Sloping foreheads, bushy eyebrows, long arms and other resemblances to cavemen were supposed to reflect a physical "atavism," or genetic throwback to prehistoric or subhuman man. For instance, Lombroso thought he saw an atavism in what he believed was the general obesity of prostitutes, which he linked to the supposedly immutable plumpness of Hottentots. He looked over photos of French and Russian trollops and female criminals and invariably found suspicious features: "deep-set eyes wide apart, and wild in expression," "gigantic canine teeth," neck muscles "exaggerated as in oxen," and so on.[28] Lombroso felt that since biology caused crime, retributive theories of punishment should be rejected in favor of rehabilitationism. Despite the appeal of this last conclusion, modern criminologists have generally dismissed Lombroso's writings as irredeemably confused. His reputation was certainly not helped when French anthropologist Paul Topinard, who gave criminology its name, remarked after viewing a collection of photographs of Lombroso's allegedly atavistic criminals that they looked like some of his friends. Still, the determinist school survived its Lombrosian intemperance and even sprouted other now-amusing disciplines such as phrenology, or the determination of latent criminality from head bumps.

Other determinists' work strengthened criminology's emerging mastery of crime-related public policy. In 1914 Henry Goddard claimed that a lack of intelligence, or feeblemindedness, predisposed individuals toward criminality. He broadly concluded that between one-fourth and one-half of prisoners were "mentally defective."[29] Goddard invented the term "moron" as the English translation of Albert Binet's *débiles*, or "weak ones," applying it with broad brush to people from southern and eastern Europe and advocating immigration restrictions based on his worrisome findings. Determinism took a more tolerant route in the studies of physician William Sheldon. Sheldon stretched an entire theory of criminality from the banality that criminals tend to be stocky. He coined the word "somatotype" as the umbrella term for three subtypes of physique: endomorphy, mesomorphy and ectomorphy, or fat, medium and skinny builds, respectively. Sheldon discovered, rather unamazingly, that criminals tended to be mesomorphs, or more muscular than most.[30] Sheldon's somatotype theory was, strictly speaking, on the borderline of determinism. People can, of course, change their somatotype; for instance, those ectomorphs, or skinny men, who embark on a life of crime surely see the utility of beefing up to protect themselves from their colleagues. Even so, this rather unexceptional theory still commands broad respect, earning a rather extraordinary amount of attention from Wilson and Herrnstein, who, not surprisingly, confirm his conclusions.[31]

Some of the first evidence genuinely suggesting a genetic basis for criminal propensities was found in a revolutionary study released in 1965. A brief scientific report published by the research team of Patricia A. Jacobs, Muriel Brunton and Marie M. Melville suggested that an extra Y chromosome might indicate a predisposition to criminality. In their survey of a maximum security prison in Scotland, the group found a disproportionately high number of inmates with an XYY chromosome configuration.[32] The frequency of XYY males in the general population is approximately one per one thousand; Jacobs (and others subsequently) found the extra Y present ten to twenty times more often among the inmates. Since a male normally receives an X chromosome from his mother and a single Y from his father, the additional Y chromosome suggested to some that the genetic abnormality could make the affected men supermales with presumably greater aggressiveness. The extra Y's actual effect on the male recipient has yet to be determined. Moreover, since as many as 98 percent of XYY men are never criminally incarcerated, the XYY configuration tells us little about the overall causes of crime.[33] The study is intriguing, however, in suggesting at least tentative support for a possible biological link to criminal behavior.

Drawing on the Jacobs study and the rich tradition of criminological determinism, Wilson and Herrnstein had a treasure trove of intellectual artifacts from which to choose in conceiving their own neodeterministic theory of criminality. The title of their resulting treatise showed that they were confident they had found the answers: *Crime and Human Nature: The Definitive Study of the Causes of Crime*. For all the natural Humean chuckling that might accompany such certitude, the publication of Wilson and Herrnstein's book was one of the landmark events in the history of criminology. Wilson and Herrnstein almost single-handedly revived the determinist school of criminology in their massive and engrossing review of the available criminological research.

Their book is not a mere collection of available criminological data, although some of their critics have suggested that it should have been.[34] It is instead an important synthesis of neodeterminist studies. Wilson and Herrnstein's debts to their intellectual forebears are clear. "Criminals are more likely than noncriminals to have mesomorphic body types [Sheldon], to have fathers who were criminals even in the case of adopted sons who could not have known their fathers [classical determinism generally], to be of somewhat lower intelligence [Goddard]"and so forth.[35] To support these findings, the two scholars weave through both the classical studies of Lombroso and his intellectual successors, and the newly deposited piles of data that have lent credence to the determinist position. And although their critics have accused Wilson and Herrnstein of selectively adopting evidence like "a clever lawyer building a case,"[36] in fact they qualify their conclusions carefully, frequently and consistently with the data.[37]

In all, Wilson and Herrnstein make a strong, balanced case that criminal tendencies are inherited or acquired at a very early age. These qualities therefore may be observed in early childhood. Hyperactivity is an especially strong predisposition observable in young children. Delinquents are notable even in infancy for being "assertive, unafraid, aggressive, unconventional, extroverted, and poorly socialized." Wilson and Herrnstein discuss an early study by Lee Robins, whose survey of St. Louis guidance clinics found no case of adult sociopathy that did not manifest itself as antisocial behavior before the age of eighteen. Failure in school, the two add, helps both to presage and to determine general failure in life, which often ends in the individual's resorting to crime. Still, while at-risk children may be nudged by innate antisocial inclinations of varying intensity, crime may be deterred through appropriate sanctions. "The larger the ratio of the rewards (material and nonmaterial) of noncrime to the rewards (material and nonmaterial) of crime, the weaker the tendency to commit crimes."[38]

At least one subsequent study seemed to bear out Wilson and Herrnstein's main conclusions. A U.S. Department of Justice survey headed by Allen Beck analyzed long-term juvenile correctional institutions across the country in 1987. The researchers found that more than half of all the juvenile delinquents questioned reported a family member who had served time in jail or prison. Nearly a fifth had two or more family members who had been criminally incarcerated. Most important from Wilson and Herrnstein's standpoint, one-fourth of the delinquents had fathers who had been imprisoned.[39] The Beck study suffered from a handicap common to other social science analyses, that is, the difficulty of unraveling the interconnected data and determining the supposed causal factor—in this case, whether the familial influence was biological or environmental. All the same, the report suggested that Wilson and Herrnstein were onto something.

While Wilson and Herrnstein are still mavericks bucking the social science establishment, in the decade since *Crime and Human Nature*'s publication many criminologists have come to accept its central findings. Indeed, their sudden interest in neodeterminism might fairly raise some eyebrows—even large bushy ones of Lombrosian suspicion—given the recent tendency of many social scientists to seek excuses for criminality rather than explanations. The emerging neodeterminist consensus was clear in an extensive report published in 1993 by the National Research Council of the National Academy of Sciences. The panel that wrote the report included some of the leading scholars and crime experts in the country, including Albert J. Reiss, Franklin E. Zimring and Jerome Skolnick. Their report did contain a few obeisances to governing criminological assumptions. Refurbished Marxist excuses for criminality appear, as does the poverty-causes-crime thesis.[40] Otherwise the report reveals a signal shift toward determinism from the poverty-based theories of criminality of the past half century. Frankly acknowledging that "ethically charged beliefs" have previously been injected into theories of crime causation, the panel criticized its colleagues for being "less innovative and effective" than they should have been. The shift then begins in earnest. The panel adopts wholesale many of the deterministic views that were once widely dismissed. These include the findings that violent criminals tend to have lower intelligence and a more aggressive temperament than the average person.[41]

This new, vigorous search for genetic markers of criminal predisposition led the panel to examine other possible links. There was some evidence that levels of the neurotransmitter serotonin are higher among violent offenders, but not enough for it to qualify as a marker. Excessive testosterone was considered a possible cause, but the panel concluded that the ostensible "correlation is probably confounded by alcohol abuse," which affects testosterone levels. The panel even considered the effects of hypoglycemia and diet.[42]

Some of the panel's other recommendations were even more noteworthy. They urged society to address the "breakdown of social capital—the capacity to transmit positive values to younger generations." The panel also noted the detrimental "psychosocial influences" of pregnancy "complications" and low birth weight. To combat this, they advocated "intervening in the biological and psychosocial development of individuals' potentials for violent behavior."[43]

The last of these policy suggestions would appear to reveal something of an ideological implosion among the panel's members. They acknowledged the unanimity among researchers studying the subject that prenatal damage to children is a very serious social hazard. Such abuse results in a broad variety of mental and physiological disorders that predispose children toward antisocial behavior. Prenatal damage is most prevalent among the poor, particularly single mothers, who give birth to the children already the most at risk of delinquency. Nicholas Eberstadt's research, for instance, has shown that regardless of a mother's race or age, her child is more likely to suffer from low birth weight if born out of wedlock. Infant mortality, in turn, is much higher for out-of-wedlock births.[44] Single parents are also more likely to expose their unborn children to drug, alcohol and tobacco abuse. A 1992 study by the U.S. Department of Health and Human Services found that 20 percent of all pregnant women still smoke, and a full 25 percent of teenage mothers.[45]

Such prenatal child abuse is perhaps the most conspicuous instance of determinism—innate tendencies toward antisocial behavior demonstrably inflicted on certain children before birth. The result is something on the order of self-fulfilling poverty. Yet the panel's commendable concern for these infants, and their instinctive recommendation of social intervention, run into barriers erected by their own philosophy. The extreme individualism they uphold usually maintains that society may not prohibit such prenatal child abuse because of the mother's "rights" over "her" body— including the right to use drugs, if one is to be theoretically consistent. The community is powerless to prevent both this prenatal child abuse and the resulting postnatal costs and crimes attributable to the affected children. This freedom, we are learning, is not free. Financially, we pay for it by providing postnatal intensive care for the battered infants and incarcerating the victims of this mistreatment when they mature.

While neodeterminism is a useful heresy that has helped to locate a likely biological tendency toward criminality, the theory has a less promising potential. This potential may well explain its recent, growing appeal. Criminologists have long rejected determinism because of the racial connotations thought connected to it. As Edwin Sutherland remarked, determinism suggests the "necessity of selective breeding."[46] The reason for determinism's current attractiveness is not immediately apparent. Indeed, determinism initially appears to be the ultimate theory of individual responsibility, invalidating the various external entities thought to cause crime.

Determinism, however, also provides the basis for an individual-based theory of criminal apology. If crime is the result of biological composition, then the real malefactors are the offender's preprogrammed antisocial impulses, not the out-of-control humans who serve as the mere vehicles for committing predestined criminal acts. Offenders, it follows, lack individual responsibility because biology has given them criminal inclinations that make it harder for them than for most to resist temptation. Thus construed, determinism seemingly substantiates Enlightenment crime-as-disease thought. And, if crime is committed by malfunctioning organisms, this carries significant implications for criminal justice. Justice requires that criminals be punished lightly, if at all.

But of course, genes do not "cause" crime. An inherited proneness toward criminality does not make crime either inevitable or forgivable. People must resist daily all kinds of natural but destructive impulses. Just as those born with other physical disabilities are rightly expected to fight to overcome them, rather than languishing in indolence and self-pity, so too criminals with possible built-in antisocial inclinations must be held to a standard necessary for social stability. Wilson and Herrnstein offer a truth that puts determinism into perspective: "crime is ultimately behavior."[47] When normative insertions are guarded against, determinism can claim its proper place as a valuable explanation for why certain people are more likely to commit crimes. But no scientific theory is a substitute for an open discussion of the ethics of criminal punishment, no matter how consoling the "causation" chimera.

Nonetheless, determinism appears to have only begun its new career in the service of modern criminologists. Their creative excesses in its employment are legitimate cause for concern, given their hand in the intellectual architecture of the Great Havoc. They, like the objects of their research, must be held accountable for their misdeeds; as Dr. Johnson said of Rousseau, "a man who talks nonsense so well, must know that he is talking nonsense."[48] But let us not turn our evaluation of their work in subsequent chapters into a punitive expedition. We must seek solutions. Only a fair and honest assessment of our crisis's intellectual origins will permit us to draw back from the abyss. And only an evenhanded analysis of the other alleged causes of crime can ensure that the scholars who have resisted the recent trends in Jeremy Bentham's troubled discipline receive the laurels that they have earned.

CHAPTER SIX

The Flight from Parenthood

Why, then, was this forbid? Why but to awe,
Why but to keep you low and ignorant,
His worshipers? He knows that in the day
You eat thereof, your eyes, that seem so clear,
Yet are but dim, shall perfectly be then
Open'd and clear'd, and ye shall be as gods.

—John Milton

If we are to understand why men do the evil that they do, with increasing frequency and ferocity in this bedeviled Republic, we must look to the source of their earliest ideas of right and wrong. We know that the clusters of moral principles that mold character and help to determine our actions, often unconsciously and almost magically, are a result of childhood. And a child learns these moral precepts, his social etiquette, from his family. The family is the manufacturer of the bundles of values we call people. In the cozy nest of familiar faces where the child spends his most impressionable years, he absorbs the principles that will largely dictate his conduct for the rest of his life. While it is no "cause" of crime, contrary to the suggestions of some commentators and, in a recent poll, a plurality of Americans,[1] the family is the necessary starting point for fathoming the attitudes that, with parental nurture, harden into antisocial behavior and violence when a child becomes an adult.

Such analysis is no enviable task. We cannot delve into the family and parenthood without giving offense and pain. Few things hurt as much as the realization that we are not as wholesome as we perceive ourselves; and since the way we raise our children is tied to our innermost beliefs and most heartfelt rationalizations, an exploration of this topic means crossing a veritable minefield of emotionally charged issues. But if we love our children as much as we say we do, we must brace ourselves for an honest inquiry. Some age-old assumptions, which have only recently lain fallow, must be dusted off and reinspected, including the previous blandishment that where there is a bad child, there is often a bad parent to share the blame. Before we project our own sins onto America's youngsters and march them off, in growing numbers, to prisons and the gallows, let us first consider whether we, as parents and as a society, have done right by them.

Although many criminologists have only recently resumed studying the family's importance in shaping behavior, our knowledge of the family's central role in this process is not a modern insight into an ancient riddle. The legal systems of every known human community, from Sumer to St. Louis, have presupposed that the values which the family teaches, often with little thought or effort, are the primary determinant of a person's capacity for good citizenship. Aristotle, writing some 2,300 years ago, stated what was by then already a commonplace when he noted the family's power to shape character for good or ill. The family, he held, supplies the child with a crucial interpersonal bond that cements his ties to the rest of the community. The family is where the child first learns loyalty to a cause beyond himself. In learning to love and obey his parents, the child acquires his first building block of fidelity to other human beings, and recognition of an authority larger than his own inherently selfish appetites. Children who do not receive this instruction from their parents are often overwhelmed by their innate self-absorption later in life. Ultimately they become detached from other people and their society, shriveling into an all-consuming narcissism that makes compliance with the law impossible, if not incomprehensible.

More and more scholars are attempting to test empirically Aristotle's belief that strong families are the best crime prevention policy. The first major inquiry into the family's influence on delinquency appeared in 1950 and seemed to back up this conclusion. That year Sheldon and Eleanor Glueck released the results of a ten-year study of delinquent boys in the Boston area. Their report concluded that delinquency appeared to result from the relationship between two key groups of variables: constitutional (and possibly biological) predispositions, such as impatience or aggressiveness, and family environment. The Gluecks found delinquency to flourish among families in which one or both parents were indifferent or antagonistic to the child, or in which the child was disciplined rarely or erratically.[2] Parental neglect and abuse of the child both encouraged violence and reinforced the child's inherited inclinations toward criminality. These were predispositions that, even under the best of circumstances, would have been difficult to restrain and channel productively.

Despite the Gluecks' intriguing findings, for years most criminologists concentrated on other subjects. Assessing the state of criminological research three decades after the Gluecks' study, Wilson and Herrnstein observed that the link identified by the Gluecks between "individual predispositions" and "family experiences" in criminals was "perhaps the best documented (though, of late, least-repeated) generalization in all of criminology."[3] The family's reemergence as a common subject of criminological research has actually been quite recent. Indeed, the family is now a vibrant field of criminological study, at least in part because the number of available research subjects—that is, dysfunctional families—has risen exponentially. The nation now teems with such families, making for plentiful subjects and analysis. Most of the researchers probing this old subject have found that the Gluecks, and Aristotle before them, were right.

Various theories have been enlisted to explain and flesh out these hoary assumptions. Travis Hirschi, investigating whether a poor parent-child relationship retards the child's social skills, conceived his "social control" theory. It maintains that the probability of delinquency increases as an individual's feelings of attachment to family, and subsequently to society, weaken.[4] Wilson and Herrnstein's analysis of the limited studies available in the early 1980s supported Hirschi's findings. They saw some tentative support for the link between crime and both genetic makeup (biology) and parents (environment). The main factor in curbing deliquency, Wilson and Herrnstein concluded, was the parents' ability to instill three qualities. They were attachment, meaning the child's "desire to win and hold the approval of others and the belief that, given certain conditions, he can count on having that approval" (a concept very similar to Hirschi's social control theory); a time horizon (a rough synonym for patience); and conscience, "an internalized constraint against certain actions, the violation of which causes feelings of anxiety."[5]

Another primeval presumption—that two parents are better than one—has also become controversial, and then demonstrated persuasively, in recent years. Since families, like other subjects of the social sciences, cannot be placed in a petri dish and monitored for their reaction to controlled stimuli, partisans of all persuasions are free to read into family-based studies the causes of their choice. Even these occasionally obscurantist efforts, however, have been unable to forestall the emerging consensus on the social dangers of single-parent families. Building on the Gluecks' conclusions, a longitudinal study of more than five thousand British children conducted over a thirty-year period concluded that children with only one parent were more prone to delinquency.[6] A later Yale study of forty-eight preliterate societies further strengthened the theory that fatherless families are literal breeding grounds for problem children. The study found crime to be markedly higher in cultures centered around polygynous mother-child families, in which husbands usually had several wives who were expected to raise the children in residences separate from the father's.[7] Henry B. Biller analyzed over a thousand such studies in concluding that children growing up in single-parent homes consistently do worse on any social health criterion, including delinquency. Biller observed, "Directly or indirectly, paternal deprivation is a factor in the great majority of incidents of child maltreatment, both within and outside the family."[8]

One of the more important recent examinations of this dysfunctional dynamic was a 1991 essay by Urie Bronfenbrenner. Bronfenbrenner is a Cornell professor known as the founding father of Head Start. He has concluded, based on his analysis, that the single parent's greatest disadvantage is the inability to provide enough intellectual and emotional stimulation for the child. This stimulation comes from an extended period of interaction. This interaction should be mutual, regular and increasingly complex, similar to a game played between familiar partners. The second parent is needed not only to free up more time for the other parent to interact with the child; he also "assists, encourages, spells off, gives status to, and expresses admiration and affection" for the interacting parent.[9] In short, the interacting parent needs help, both financially, to allow one parent to devote more time to the child, and emotionally. While Bronfenbrenner recognizes that others, such as the extended family and churches, can sometimes assume this crucial supporting role, such second-string parents are increasingly hard to find, and are generally a poor substitute for the child's second parent.

While the analysis itself was not revolutionary, Bronfenbrenner's study has been instrumental for helping to make the broken family a legitimate topic of research for his fellow social scientists. His departure from the social science consensus, which held that it was improper to criticize single-parent families, served notice to other academics that it was appropriate to assess the damage done by recent changes in family and sexual mores. The culmination of this academic revival came in April 1993, with *The Atlantic*'s publication of Barbara Dafoe Whitehead's controversial article "Dan Quayle Was Right."[10] Her audacious and dispassionate analysis of single-parent families' shortcomings, as shown by mounting data and everyday experience, helped to solidify an emerging bipartisan consensus on the subject.

This new academic understanding is of vital importance. The scholarship currently undertaken to document the perils of single-parenting is performed before the essential backdrop of philosophical justification. Empirical examinations of, for instance, claims of Aryan racial supremacy and, increasingly, Marxist economics no longer take place because these topics no longer seem like reasonable objects of research. Fascism and communism have lost most of their intellectual admirers and returned to the fringe of public policy. The current political preferences in American academia similarly narrow the scope of "valid" research. When the topic of interest is the family, the resulting research can suffer from all the distortions that naturally occur when a philosophical tug-of-war takes away the scientific method and replaces it with an expectation that the scholar will defend a given position. In the case of the family, the accepted hypothesis in recent years has been that broken families and the revolution in sexual values that preceded them are institutions beyond rightful reproach.

This struggle for the hearts and minds of America's intelligentsia, and therefore the political and media figures who rely on them, is merely the latest skirmish in a philosophical dispute that is one of the oldest in Western thought. Alfred North Whitehead once observed that Western philosophy is nothing more than a series of footnotes to Plato and Aristotle. True enough of modern philosophy as a whole, this statement is unassailably true of the current debate over the family. Indeed, the present-day argument over the family and its proper role in American society is but a poor, modern English translation of the far more eloquent exchange that occurred between these two citizens of ancient Greece. The acceptable scope of scientific inquiry regarding the family, as with so many other areas of research, depends on which of these philosophers is ascendant, or who happens to be up and who down in the continuing see-saw struggle between these two titans of Western thought.

Today, it is Plato who reigns supreme, as he has for most of this century. It is not at all clear that the modern theorists in his debt understand this. Plato's *Republic* was the first work to address the relationship between the family and social justice. The ultraindividualist's conception of the family relies heavily on the vision of society he articulated in that work four centuries before Christ. Plato's greatness lies not simply in his sheer brilliance, but in the uncompromising boldness of what remains, even now, a radical conception of justice. Plato's most basic and marked departure from prior thought was his very conception of societal institutions. He looked upon them almost as intellectual playthings, although he was obviously far too serious a thinker to offer social criticism that was not in complete earnest. One institution in particular caught his fancy. But not for long. The family, Plato argued, should be expeditiously abolished for society's upper class. He looked upon the traditional family as a quaint but unnecessary inheritance from precivilized man. In Plato's more advanced era, the family blocked humanity's march toward an improved society engineered by the State. The two-parent family and the institution of marriage that preserved it were incompatible with mankind's pursuit of justice. Justice, as he envisioned it, entailed the proper ordering of social classes and duties. Plato proposed an alternative. Adults should meet at specified times with predetermined mates for the purpose of conceiving children. Then, following supervised procreation, the momentary family unit would simply and unceremoniously disband. The State would subsequently assume responsibility for raising its future leaders, or "guardians," produced by these liaisons. This arrangement would permit men to get on with the business of creating literature, training in the art of war and other, more important pursuits.

However socially destabilizing his philosophy might appear, Plato felt that he had society's best interests at heart. He believed that his new regime would unify the citizenry and especially the leadership class by banishing the concept of "'mine' and 'not mine'" inherent to parenthood.[11] The guardians of his ideal *polis* would be allowed to supervise the community without the parochialism that often stems from paternity. He explained, "They will not rend the community asunder by each applying that word 'mine' to different things and dragging off whatever he can get for himself into a private home, where he will have his separate family, forming a centre of exclusive joys and sorrows." This should sound familiar. In this, as in other respects, Plato's views foreshadowed Marxism. America's social atomists are equally direct descendants of this philosophical line.

It was left to Plato's wisest student to take his master to task for this troubling, if creative, scheme. Aristotle thought it a bit presumptuous to treat the family as an arbitrary collection of Lego toys to be pulled apart and joined together at the whim of the State. The family, after all, had been around for quite a long time. He offered a contrasting view. The individual, he observed, is inseparable from his family for purposes of social analysis. Aristotle defined the family as "the association established *by nature* for the supply of men's everyday wants," among which he included men's "natural desire to leave behind them an image of themselves."[12] "Mine" and "not mine" are endemic to parenthood. Parents have children in large measure to procreate a miniature version of themselves. Moreover, it is in the family where a human being breathes his first breaths, learns his first words and thinks his first thoughts. A human life is, to continue Whitehead's metaphor, a series of footnotes to one's childhood. The family is where a person learns the loyalties and concern for others on which all his duties to society, particularly obedience to the law, are based.

Aristotle warned that Plato's social setup would undermine order by making parental love "watery." Under Plato's system, "there is no reason why the so-called father should care about the son, or the son about the father. . . . [H]ow much better is it to be the real cousin of somebody than to be a son after Plato's fashion!"[13] Those who would chisel away at the family would strike at the only known means of converting members of a naturally self-centered species into beings devoted to maintaining a common order. Instead of ushering in an era of selfless leaders no longer preoccupied with parenting, Plato's utopia threatened to do the opposite. It would destroy the essential method of making people dedicated to a cause beyond themselves, and thus of ensuring the State's survival.

The most fundamental difference between Plato's and Aristotle's theories was their approach to social analysis. Plato thought that society was fair game for a complete restructuring, including the repeal of its basic institutions, if presented with a sufficiently compelling master plan. The problem with this optimism, of course, was that Plato's social inventions, while ingeniously creative, had been tried nowhere other than the cramped quarters of one person's mind. Aristotle, while not remembered as a notably modest man, at least had a more realistic grasp of his abilities. His approach to analyzing social institutions, as a result, was very different. If, he noted, the family has been a feature of human existence since the dawn of man, this is probably for good reason. Intellectuals, acting through their alter ego, the State, should be reluctant to toy with this inherited, proven pattern of life. The family reflects the common judgment of prior generations and the collective wisdom of many more people than those currently debating the proposition. Such inherited arrangements represent the accumulation of far more knowledge than any one citizen of Athens is capable of, however brilliant he or his students might be.

Aristotle's most significant contribution to the debate over the family, then, was to place the burden of proof squarely on the family's intellectual critics. Since such thinkers are taking on the stored knowledge of every preceding human society, it is only fair that before the family is dismembered, they must first candidly make their case. They must do so not through murky appeals to justice, rights or other indefinite concepts, but by reference to concrete facts. And so it should be for the modern debate. Those who argue that the two-parent family is a relic of less sophisticated times must do better. They must address the misgivings that many Americans feel, justifiably, over this prehistoric institution's abandonment. At the very least, they must show that the disruptions that their plan entails will not result in chaos. Plato could not satisfy Aristotle's demand. Let us see how we have fared.

AMERICANS KARAMAZOV

Nowhere is justification for the family's disappearance more in need, or more lamentably lacking, than in America's dying black community. Much of the recent attention paid to the relationship between broken homes and criminality has focused on black Americans, mainly because of the concern over high black crime rates. By now the statistics are so frequently repeated that their familiarity blunts the shock that they deserve. At present more than two-thirds of all black American children are born out of wedlock. Half of all black children are born to teenagers. There is also a sharp trend among blacks away from early marriages—and, indeed, from marriage at every age level. In 1975, 63 percent of black women aged twenty to twenty-four were or had been married; in 1990 the number plunged to 39 percent. Even more disturbing is the indication that about 25 percent of today's young African-American women will *never* marry, compared to less than 10 percent of young white women.[14] The end result is that a black child born today has only a one-in-five chance of growing up with two parents until the age of sixteen.[15]

This, in turn, is a prime ingredient of black poverty. While the black poverty rate for two-parent families is 15 percent, the rate rises to 55 percent for single-parent families. Similarly, illegitimacy spurs young mothers to seek welfare, indeed, regardless of race. About half of all unwed teen mothers go on welfare within a year after their child's birth, 77 percent within five years.[16]

The disintegration of the black family was hardly a culturally inevitable event, as some have suggested. From 1890 to 1950 black women were more likely to be married than white women.[17] Even prior to emancipation most black children were born to two-parent families.[18] Only by the mid-1960s had the African-American illegitimacy rate begun to rise significantly above that of whites. The disbandment of the black family is not, of course, commonly taken as a sign of social progression; Plato is not *that* popular. Both the NAACP and the Urban League have consistently decried the disappearance of the married black father. Yet many white Americans have assumed these trends to be unique to blacks, and thus a problem that, except for black crime, affects them little.

The warnings issuing from America's ghettos for the past three decades have not been heeded, and we must confront the consequences. The upswing in white illegitimacy that is currently spurring the white juvenile crime rate was visible over twenty years ago. In 1970 Charles Murray observed that among certain communities of lower-class whites, the illegitimacy rate was already over 60 percent.[19] The seriousness of this broader social acceptance of illegitimacy was not fully known until 1993. The U.S. Department of Health and Human Services reported that year that white illegitimacy rates during the 1980s had doubled, so that more than one out of five white children is now born to an unmarried mother.[20] By contrast the black illegitimacy rate rose only 43 percent during the decade, or less than half the rate of growth among whites. Thus, the white rate for both juvenile crime and unwed motherhood grew at slightly more than double the black rate during the 1980s, the two pathologies rising almost in lockstep. Currently almost one out of four white children is raised by a single, never-married parent, a number that continues to climb steadily.[21] Charles Murray updated his figures in 1993 and found that 44 percent of all births for white mothers below the poverty line are now illegitimate.[22] But the growth of out-of-wedlock births is not confined to the white lower class. Eleven percent of all single women with some college education have had children out of wedlock, up from 5 percent in 1982.[23] Recently groups such as Single Moms by Choice have even organized to defend the growing number of middle-class white women who deliberately deny their babies fathers. No longer a "black thing," illegitimacy is becoming as American as apple pie and motherhood itself.

With illegitimacy expanding beyond the black community, now would seem the obvious time to reassess the theories of sexuality that precipitated these events. White illegitimacy is far more ominous than black illegitimacy in more than one respect. A number of studies, for instance, have shown that single black mothers tend to do better than their single white counterparts at raising emotionally stable and responsible children.[24] Yet the rise of white illegitimacy has, until very recently, escaped everyone's attention, and has still not prompted serious corrective action. Perhaps this is because whites already have enough sexually rooted family problems to worry about. For while African-American children are being born in increasing numbers to mothers who have never been married, a trend now expanding to lower-class whites, middle-class white children are born in similarly high numbers to mothers who are married only temporarily.

White divorce rates have increased at a rate comparable to the rise in black illegitimacy rates over the past several decades. During the 1970s, as "free love" and sexual self-expression advanced from the relatively innocuous hippie counterculture to become a fixture of American society, state legislatures began to repeal the laws that required a finding of fault such as adultery or spousal abuse before a divorce could be granted. While these requirements sometimes encouraged perjury by spouses intent on parting, they did at least restrict the number of frivolous divorces and encourage couples to try to resolve their problems. In 1969 California adopted the nation's first no-fault divorce statute. By 1985 all 49 other states had followed suit.[25] America's divorce rate, consequently, has quadrupled since 1960.[26] Currently half of all American marriages end in divorce. Demographers now predict that by the beginning of the next decade, the majority of Americans under eighteen will spend part of their childhood in single-parent families, many of them created by divorce.[27] White children are more than twice as likely as black children to have stepparents.[28] Although the celebrities associated with the TV show *Murphy Brown* have taken justifiable flak for making light of another type of single-parenthood, other, predominantly male entertainers such as Johnny Carson have escaped their fair share of criticism for helping to make divorce not simply acceptable, but positively humorous.

Divorce is especially complicated when children are involved. Since over half of divorcing couples have children below the age of eighteen,[29] the new regime of no-fault divorce has meant a major and often wrenching change in the lives of American children. Throughout the 1970s and 1980s a million children a year watched their parents divorce.[30] The likelihood that white children would live with both parents fell from 81 percent in the early 1950s to 30 percent for those born in 1980.[31] Many of these children rarely or never saw their fathers again. Only about one-third of divorced fathers see their children at least once a week, a number that drops further with time.[32]

Any nation should find these developments baneful; all the more so one with a soaring adolescent crime problem. Although there are intrinsic impediments to empirically determining the correlation between delinquency and divorce,[33] other results of divorce are easier to identify. Princeton sociologist Sara McLanahan observes, "Almost anything you can imagine not wanting to happen to your children is a consequence of divorce."[34] Divorce is, for instance, the most common reason for childhood depression.[35] Children of divorce are disproportionately likely to suffer mental disturbances and headaches and other related physiological afflictions, including cardiac disorders. Over one-third of all children of divorced parents are still "troubled and depressed" a full five years after the divorce.[36] Boys from divorced families are more likely to be "hostile" and "withdrawn" than those from intact families.[37]

There is also an increasingly well documented link to juvenile criminality. Single parents in general are far more likely, by the mere fact of that status, to raise children who have trouble obeying the law. Seventy percent of juvenile offenders come from single-parent homes.[38] Even after controlling for income and race, boys from single-parent homes are significantly more likely to become criminals than their two-parent cohorts.[39] These patterns apply to children of divorce in particular. In their groundbreaking investigation of the recent assumption that divorce is a "liberating experience,"[40] Judith Wallerstein and Sandra Blakeslee instead found that one-third and one-tenth of the boys and girls in their longitudinal study of divorce children became delinquents engaged in serious crimes. They also noticed a "surprisingly high incidence of alcoholism," with 20 percent of divorce children drinking heavily. One-third of these children came from homes in which neither parents nor stepparents ever abused alcohol.[41] The antisocial differences between illegitimate and divorce children are negligible in additional respects. For example, while 17 percent of children raised by never-married mothers are suspended or expelled from school, 11 percent of children from divorced families draw the same sanctions.[42]

Children of divorce also frequently find themselves destined, along with their mothers, for a life of poverty. Approximately 75 percent of single-parent children must endure a period of poverty before reaching eighteen. This compares to 20 percent of children from two-parent families.[43] Feminist Lenore Weitzman, initially a supporter of no-fault divorce laws, reexamined her position after documenting the extent to which no-fault divorce condemns women and children to penury. She found this to be the case despite determined efforts to collect child support payments. She concluded that the very attempt to equitably distribute property that was originally of one household meant that women were "unequally disadvantaged by divorce."[44] In discussing the "tragic victims" of divorce, Weitzman recounted in detail the many cases of "older homemakers who not only lost their residence of twenty-five or thirty-five years, but also lost their whole social structure in a forced move to the other side of town."[45] But since women receive custody of the children in 90 percent of divorce cases, such upheavals invariably affect the kids as well. Based on these somber facts, Weitzman concluded that the current divorce laws "only serve to enlarge the gap between men and women and create even greater inequalities."[46] Professor Mary Ann Glendon of the Harvard Law School drew much the same conclusions in her analysis of modern divorce law. She likewise found no-fault divorce statutes to be a corrosive element in American marriages and an inherent bacillus of poverty.[47]

By the time parents go their separate ways, they often find that their children are not as well equipped to cope with these changes as they are. In far too many cases, as the above statistics suggest, they discover that their babies have become nothing less than self-indulgent little terrors. That the engine behind parental schisms is usually, at its core, self-interest on the part of at least one parent does not help matters. In one of the few polls published on the subject, parental self-interest was shown to be the overwhelming reason cited for divorce by ex-spouses. The most common justification was "communication problems," at 64 percent. This could probably be fairly translated as "My spouse won't listen to *me* and *my problems*." Tied at second with 58 percent each were infidelity (a by-product of today's sexual self-absorption) and "constant fighting"; these were followed by "emotional abuse" (52 percent), "falling out of love" (49 percent) and "unsatisfactory sex" (45 percent). Physical abuse was cited as a contributing factor by only 28 percent (more than one factor could be named).[48]

Of course, many couples divorce for sound reasons. And, in any event, one spouse is often far more responsible for the breakup. For their part, many social scientists, psychiatrists and lawyers aggravate the situation. Often they counsel feuding couples that it is worse to expose a child to squabbling parents than to eliminate one of them, an empirical claim that is clearly false in view of the emerging evidence. But few children even attempt to sort out these distinctions. They see only the parental dissolution of their family, with the duties for their upbringing settled by lawyers. Children of divorce witness firsthand the ultimate proof of their society's willing disintegration— to wit, the one unit of society on which all preceding generations could rely, the family, is now, like everything else in the modern United States, up for grabs. As a result, we have joined other Western countries as part of the first major civilization in which children are generally raised by only one parent, and in which fathers are relieved of their traditional duty to discipline boys.

It can be no enigma, in view of this, that the West, and America in particular, has produced an unprecedented number of unruly, dangerous children. But Americans do not need criminological confirmation of these repercussions. The West has been warned of these dangers since at least Aristotle. Reiterating the point was a later expert on the family, Christ. His firm position on marriage and divorce, in particular, was arguably Christianity's greatest contribution to the stability of Western civilization. He taught that marriage was more than a Jewish cultural convention; upon marrying, a man and a woman "cleave" together to become an indissoluble "one flesh."[49] Those who today automatically disparage these traditions seem tragically ignorant of several pressing sociological truths. For the past two millennia the only thing that has kept women's lives from being much worse than they were, and still are in the world's non-Christian cultures, was this social disapproval of illegitimacy and divorce. This rule was basic to the protection of European women from the sort of male exploitation that every society has experienced, but that is far more pandemic in non-Christian societies. The Judeo-Christian vision of marriage treated husband and wife as spiritual equals. The wife was fully one-half of the "one flesh" that could not be torn asunder during a man's midlife crisis. If a man impregnated a woman, he was obliged to marry her; and once married, they were married for good, divinely ordered to love each other and raise their children together. It was a very challenging doctrine, and it did not always satisfy the parents. But it was a doctrine that, among other dividends, was instrumental in raising many generations of law-abiding children.

The Roman/barbaric view of marriage that competed with Christianity's, that of a contract to be opted out of at will, has reemerged in new, more persuasive form in the twentieth century. Its modern messenger was Freud. He joined the idea of marriage-as-contract with new theories of sexuality that made greater sexual exploitation of women inevitable. Fundamentally, as Freud recognized, no-fault divorce is an instrument of male sexual liberation. Easy divorce meant the freeing of the man from the socially productive yoke of monogamous marriage and family life, and the commencement of a sexual competition in which men are bound to fare better than women. Biology has prudently endowed men with a stronger sex drive to ensure the survival of the race; it has also made men more individualistic and aggressive—more pushy—in everyday relations, which accounts for the male domination of every known, extant society. Nowhere is this essential pushiness more glaring than in sex: the male preferences for power, egoism and sexual variety combine to make promiscuity for men a uniquely pleasurable enterprise.

Women did not receive the same package of traits from Mother Nature. And while, for women unwarrantably seeking to be more like men, this disparity may seem like nothing short of an epic injustice, our knowledge of genetics and human history suggests that this primal slight had a method to its madness. As the half of humanity entrusted with childbearing, and as the more social of the two sexes, women are civilization's first line of defense to the egoistic barbarism that skulks within humankind's darker nature. Women face biological punishment for random sex because a child requires two parents for maximum intellectual and emotional growth. By forcing women to bear the human offspring of casual sexual encounters and by giving women the compassion that makes them less comfortable than men with abandoning this offspring once born, nature hands women the incentives that, combined with courage and social convention, make society viable.

The flip side of this arrangement is just as stark. Life in the sexual jungle makes exploitation of women as inevitable as it is wide-ranging under the current "liberated" regime ushered in by Freud. Because divorce is the form of paternal desertion preferred by men of the white middle class, it is today the seemliest method of abetting this male desire for serial, individualistic sexuality. There are obviously important reasons for the modern rise in illegitimacy and divorce rates other than Freud's teachings; the economic emancipation of women, industrialization and the declension of religion also stake a large claim for our attention here. But Freud and later, less inventive scholars provided something else, something essential and intangible—the intellectual ratification for these trends. They supplied for sexual narcissism the theoretical respectability that is almost always necessary for a successful mass rebellion against custom.

While the basis of Freud's popularity among men is clear, the appeal of sexual liberation among many American women today is much harder to explain. Feminism, as currently defined, has played an important role in the development of today's Freudian consensus. It was not always so. Amid the social atomism of the present and the extremes to which some advocates of feminism have gone, it is easy to lose sight of feminism's contributions to Western thought and policy. The fight for basic legal and economic equality for women was one that required zealous participants. Because of such ardor, this struggle was almost completely successful—to society's great betterment. But as with all revolutions, some leaders of this movement are not anxious to admit that the battle is over, perhaps because they enjoyed the fight a bit too much. Thus it is that feminism today has largely gone from being a commendable catalyst of national progress to a social atomism of the sexes; even, at times, the spark for genuine sexual combat.

If this criticism seems hard, consider, if you will, the following witnesses for the prosecution—the defendants themselves. Prominent feminist theorists today frame sexual relations in terms of outright warfare. Their *casus belli* is the many indignities and occasional cruelties that women through the ages have suffered at men's hands, with some gross exaggerations thrown in to get women on a full wartime footing. Theorist Andrea Dworkin best summed up this line of thought when she remarked, "Romance . . . is rape embellished with meaningful looks."[50] Better known is Catharine MacKinnon, a University of Michigan law professor who was a TV network commentator during the Clarence Thomas hearings. Regarding women in general, she writes, "You grow up with your father holding you down and covering your mouth so another man can make a horrible searing pain between your legs. . . . Your doctor will not give you drugs he has addicted you to unless you suck his penis." These truths have, "for hundreds of years," been Western woman's lot in life;[51] and now, we infer, it is payback time.

There are important ironies in these developments, as well as crucial implications for our Republic's sexual disintegration. For example, this same, recent feminism that views men per se as adversaries at the same time exalts perceived male virtues, such as men's promiscuous sexual instinct and lesser concern for children. Traditional, stabilizing female qualities such as compassion and mother love are either overlooked or disparaged. This ideology's impact on crime and criminal justice is sometimes direct; mostly it leads to long-term fraying of the community that only later flares up into criminality and strife. Sometimes, as with burning-bed cases, when wives murder abusive husbands rather than leave them, this feminism seems to seek for women a general criminal pardon. More generally this philosophy joins in implementing Freud's theory of sexuality, with deliquescent results for American families.

These changes in sexual values, with their manifold theoretical origins, have meant in practice that many American children must do without fathers. Although the growing acceptance of illegitimacy has allowed many men to escape the responsibilities of fatherhood, divorced fathers have been able to do so only after courts overturned the centuries-old practice of giving fathers custody of the children after divorce.[52] While many of America's single mothers have shown inspiring courage in the face of indifferent former lovers and ex-husbands, it is now undeniable that many of these mothers are simply unable to control their children. Much of this maternal deficiency is less biological than mathematical. As Wilson and Herrnstein observed, "if one parent must do the work of two, then, at the margin, less of that work will get done."[53]

Yet there is more to this disparity. It is a bromide that both men and women have something special to offer children. For boys, one of the most important things that fathers supply is awe, in the Hobbesian sense. Teenage boys today are often ungovernable because they lack one of the basic and crucial deterrents to juvenile misconduct—fear of answering to an angry father. Anyone who questions paternal awe's unique capacity to deter naughtiness in young males should enter an inner-city school and compare the behavior of boys in classrooms headed by male and female teachers. One member of a black gang in Los Angeles described the difference:

> Most of the time your momma knows what's going on, but Momma's not going to be the one to tell the kid to stop it. . . . Moms are too gentle. When I started gangbanging, my mother tried to get me to stop. I wouldn't; she saw that's what I wanted.[54]

One of the eternal reasons for the two-parent family was making fathers available to discipline their sons when they misbehaved. This task, like most other social duties, has now been given to mothers. They cope as best they can, often heroically. But the rising juvenile crime rate from fatherless homes can no longer be construed as unrelated to the lack of a second, awe-inspiring parent. Indeed, often the only male role model in the house for many of these children is a violent live-in boyfriend who abuses them because he lacks any familial "bond."[55]

There is still another family-related concern tied to our soaring crime rates, one that has escaped public apprehension even more effectively. It is today's cultural expectation that both parents will join the workforce, and that somebody else, another laborer, will be compensated to tend their children. The rise of day care in modern America says some painful things about us as parents and as a nation and culture, things that are easier for adults to leave unsaid. But the truth is always worth telling, and it is this: many American parents today simply do not wish to raise their own children. Indeed, never before in history have a people become so intensely individualistic that their love for their children can be purchased so cheaply. It is as if Fyodor Karamazov's fatal relationship with his children has materialized in the majority of American homes in a single generation. Parents in the United States today spend less time with their children than parents in any other nation in the world, 40 percent less time than even a generation ago.[56] American teenagers spend an average of five minutes a day alone with their fathers, and twenty minutes with their mothers. This compares to three hours a day spent watching television. Even most of the few minutes spent with parents consists of eating and watching television together.[57]

These new mores owe to several particulars, all rooted to various degrees in the shadowy side of human nature. One reason for these developments is the change in the way we view parenthood, and motherhood in particular, compared to generations past. Our new child-rearing arrangements are based on a view of motherhood unknown, mercifully, to the women of all previous societies. American women today are commonly thought to be shiftless or, at best, behind the times if they do not hand over their babies to the anonymous arms of a stranger, so that they can then work outside the home. Day care, the institution reflecting and accommodating these changes, is often defended philosophically as essential for female equality in the workforce. In reality, though, day care's biggest supporters are often men, whose compassion for children is generally, probably biologically, less than women's, and who prefer the extra income made possible by places to deposit children during the day.

The materialism and egoism in which America has recently been awash naturally play a role as well. We have almost come to view children as satellites to our self-concept, rather than as precious beings for which, previous generations tell us, parents once were expected to sacrifice all. As a result, we increasingly have children to feel well rounded and good about ourselves—like complete people "having it all"—without letting them come between us and self-fulfillment. American parenthood no longer implies the surrender of self traditionally expected of those charged with raising the young. We have, in fact, come to think of it as just the opposite: parenthood as keeping up with the Joneses.

The relatively sparse research into the effects of day care on infants has revealed that such children, and the society that later sustains them, eventually suffer from their parents' shortsightedness. As one might expect, most of the social scientists investigating the topic, consistent with the ultraindividualism dominant in their profession, have concluded that day care is "benign" or even "good for children." However, as one researcher pointed out, "A notable exception to this trend is the research relating day care to a somewhat loose constellation of child behaviors that might be called 'aggression,' 'assertiveness,' or 'negative behavior.'"[58] Or, in other words, the ingredients of future violent criminality. Although there has yet been no study of day care's relationship to delinquency per se, the available related evidence indicates that day care psychologically impairs many of the children most at risk of delinquency. A seminal 1974 effort headed by J. Conrad Schwarz showed that children who entered day care before they were twelve months old were "significantly more aggressive" than non-day-care children. They were also more physically and verbally abusive toward adults, less cooperative with grown-ups and less tolerant of frustration than their parentally raised counterparts.[59] Another longitudinal study by Ron Haskins compared two groups of day-care children and found that those who had spent more time in day care suffered from proportionately greater ill effects, regardless of the quality of day care provided. These early-care children were found "more likely to . . . hit, kick, and push than children in the control group." They were also more likely to "threaten, swear, and argue"; "teachers were more likely to rate these children as having aggressiveness as a serious deficit of social behavior."[60] Michael Rutter, Christopher Bagley and Urie Bronfenbrenner reported similar findings in separate studies.[61]

The reason for this behavior is clear enough, and presses to the fore no matter how hard we try to evade it. Even Darwin, no blind acolyte of custom, observed that the "social instinct," or man's allegiance to society and its laws, "seems to be developed by the young remaining for a long time with their parents. . . ."[62] Of the more recent explanations for the effects of such child-rearing, Bronfenbrenner's is as good as any. A child's mental development, he notes, is severely impaired if he lacks someone who can play increasingly complex and regular "games" with him. What other researchers have shown is that, for the infants whose parents want dual incomes for the household or become disenchanted with parenthood, such games are almost always absent in the impersonal places that provide most day care. The workers at such centers lack the extra, essential personal bond with the children, described by Bronfenbrenner as an "irrational emotional attachment."[63] That is, they do not love them.

America's multibillion-dollar day-care industry represents the delayed triumph of Plato and his modern medium for the social sciences, Marx. Formerly confined to small (and since abandoned) social experiments, such as the Israeli kibbutzim, day care has now become part of the average American childhood. As Dr. Brenda Hunter has observed of what she termed a "massive human experiment," "never before in American history have so many children been raised by strangers."[64] Such children spend most of their waking hours during their earliest, most impressionable years in these centers, where they learn the Platonic communal spirit as best they can. There is indeed no "mine" and "not mine" here, as Plato would have it, since there is no love. On the infrequent occasions when individual attention is shown these children, it is very rarely the sort required to constrain the harmful predispositions in some infants. These children are denied the self-restraint that can only be cultivated one-on-one by a loving but strict parent who, at the end of the day, must still live with the child. For all of Plato's and Marx's valiant egalitarian efforts, no stranger, no matter how well paid, is psychologically capable of providing the same affection. Parental love is discriminatory.

There are several misimpressions that underlie the debate over day care and inflate our appraisal of that institution. One, as noted before, is the belief that day care is necessary for both parents to have careers. Yet the idea that most members of the workforce have anything resembling a career is itself untenable. It is a notion invented by the intellectual elite who provide the exception to the rule. The overwhelming majority of people work at rote, rather dull jobs. Moreover, the common belief that both parents must work to maintain a "decent" standard of living is both erroneous and irrelevant. Per capita disposable income in constant dollars is more than twice as high as it was in 1950, and three times as high as in 1930.[65] Parents then sacrificed for their children and made do with what they had. Today, on the other hand, we never seem to have enough. The same materialism that leads to today's high crime rates mandates that even children are to be neglected so that the more powerful members of society, adults, may have more material luxuries (bigger houses, newer cars). All of this contributes to a crime rate among white children that, it bears repeating, is now growing at more than double the rate of growth among black juveniles.

To their infinite credit, most mothers, quite unlike many of today's fathers, seem to sense and regret their children's situation.

Fathers, of course, can stay home and take care of their children too. It is generally only women, however, who feel the tug of conscience. It takes some doing to persuade them to ignore their maternal instincts and hire someone, usually a stranger, to nurture their children. They must be spurred by forces inside and outside the home: acquisitive liberated husbands who, utilizing the pressures in the materialistic popular culture, drive their wives into the workplace more like pack mules than anything approaching equal partners; and the common, media-recited insistence that there are no more *Leave It to Beaver* families—usually with just enough derision to make their assessment self-fulfilling. Judges have also exacerbated things by formally writing these values into law. In a growing number of jurisdictions courts are reducing men's child support payments based on their wives' potential income; this makes divorce more financially attractive to men, further worsens women's economic status and effectively requires mothers to place the children in day care.[66] Eventually most young mothers submit, often somberly. Ironically, the guilt that often follows, that despised gadfly of conscience, generally descends only upon the women, who in most cases are far less to blame for such decisions. Children, it is true, are resilient, and many of them persevere. But overall, society pays a price. The children emerge from this upbringing, much too often, emotionally malajusted and unmanageable.

Other familial disorders have lately befallen the American family, and similarly conspire against long-term civil unity. For instance, America's estimated 3.4 million latchkey children are a bigger immediate threat to society than day care because they are not infants; the hours that they spend at home alone at the end of the day, waiting for parents to return from work, give them far more opportunities for antisocial activities than their smaller siblings have. We might place the other various familial shortcomings on a continuum of parental selfishness. They would range from what is arguably the least objectionable, day care (two parents in the evening), to divorce (weekend parenting, at best, for the man), to illegitimacy (no second parent at all), to child abuse, to abortion/infanticide. Children see a powerful moral to this story. They learn from these early civics lessons that the real sovereign in this arrangement is not their parents or society, but the self. They are taught, literally from the cradle, that life is looking out for number one. If, as their parents unwittingly instruct them, money and sex are life's supreme goals—superior even to family, where the basic loyalties are learned—children conclude that they must themselves acquire these goodies, by hook or by crook. They must become gods unto themselves. And so it is that children who might otherwise be raised to be considerate, loving adults withdraw to a life of self-absorption, where they can no longer be hurt by those who say they love them; and, in time, the society that sanctions this mind-set collapses from the resulting murderous solipsism.

In the end, women will decide whether these trends continue, and whether this society survives or perishes. It is ultimately women who determine the viability of the family, by convincing men to submit to their longer time horizons and by channeling male energies into providing for a wife and children.[67] Because they are generally more sociable and religious than men and have a greater pity toward infants, women will always be the chief defenders of the family and the social values that keep two parents in the home. Men are only as good as women make them.

Men will never relinquish the current arrangement, however, without a good deal of encouragement from their mates. They have far too much to lose, in the short run, from a truce to the War between the Sexes. The family unit will be preserved, and future delinquents tamed, only when women resolve to tolerate the current sexual order no longer. The distress and genuine misery of millions of deserted American women have provided the staggering repudiation of promises made at the onset of these changes, promises that spoke of an enlightened new order that would better the lot of women. The repeal of our former cultural standards on marriage and family—which, as Irving Kristol has noted, were instituted precisely to ensure better treatment of women by making their abuse by men considered dishonorable[68]—has actually made life considerably worse for the average American woman in many important respects, and for the children she is left to tend to. Today's woman must not simply contend with the men of the modern era, whom she often finds boorish and self-absorbed. She must also deal with men's increasingly predatory sexual behavior. And, in the dwindling spare time she has left, she must do her best to raise her children—alone.

PARENS MATRIAE: GOVERNMENT AS OVEREXTENDED PARENT

"The central problem of every society," Margaret Mead observed, "is to define appropriate roles for the men."[69] Women, she saw, instinctively sense their most basic, genetically ordained social role to be the bearing and raising of children. Men are harder to figure out. They can, for instance, be self-destructive and dangerous when denied a mate to focus their energies productively. Some ultraindividualist intellectuals have gamely sought a fanciful escape from these dictates of chromosomes. To those who argue for tying men to productive, time-consuming labors, if only to keep them out of trouble, these theorists have responded, Let my people go! Men have been shackled long enough to family responsibilities, sometimes toiling for women who still will not get a job themselves. It all seems unnecessary, given that the State, that Platonic panacea, stands ready to discharge men of these duties. Government can provide the support for women and children that will allow men to pursue more egoistic interests, which many intellectuals, based on their own experiences, assume to be more rewarding. The State can assume all these old chores and become the Big Single Mother, overloaded with duties that should belong to men.

Perhaps more than any other government policy, welfare propels this illusion. A financial incentive for procreation as recreation, welfare provides an explicit monetary reward for bringing children into the world without fathers. The prospect of free, if rather limited, income for the small price of a jolly time in this age of sexual relativism has not gone unnoticed. By rewarding both indolence and illegitimacy, the surest and second-surest guarantors of poverty, welfare policies have greatly eroded the black community, as is now well documented and of bipartisan concern. But as with recent trends in illegitimacy rates, which are tightly related to welfare, welfare is today a magnet wresting apart white families as well. While 30 percent of American women who go on welfare do so because of the birth of an illegitimate child, the main reason for welfare dependency, at 45 percent, is divorce or separation—overwhelmingly a white phenomenon. In turn, the most common cause of cessation of welfare is marriage.[70] Welfare's popularity has grown steadily since its creation, with thirteen million people currently receiving Aid to Families with Dependent Children (AFDC) benefits. The program was expanded significantly in the 1980s, as part of a bill that President Reagan optimistically predicted would ensure "lasting emancipation from welfare dependency."[71] President Clinton's recent proposed welfare reform would remove fewer than 3 percent of adult recipients from the rolls.[72]

Another institution newly dedicated to assuming parental responsibilities is the public schools. No longer merely centers of learning, schools now provide a myriad of services formerly expected of the family: school lunches and increasingly even breakfasts, counseling, sex and values education. Yet even as school systems have been assigned these additional tasks, they have been concurrently limited in their ability to maintain order in the classroom and thereby fulfill the same.

Central to this has been the removal of corporal punishment, schools' ultimate, sometimes sole means of ensuring students' safety and inculcating respect for others. Corporal punishment has been practiced and publicly demanded in schools since the first public schools were opened in America two centuries before Horace Mann's famous efforts. The judges who addressed the legality of corporal punishment applied an old English maxim to shore up these school powers. The doctrine of *in loco parentis,* meaning "in the place of the parent," permitted broad discretion in disciplinary measures to the school officials charged by the rest of society with molding young people's character. This principle shielded schools from lawsuits except in cases of egregious abuse. Parents and teachers alike recognized that to correct misbehavior, schools must be at liberty to use the same disciplinary method that parents themselves used, a young boy's Leviathan—a spanking.

In loco parentis was, in turn, a supplement to the more expansive legal doctrine of *parens patriae. Parens patriae* emerged in the English courts as a principle giving the State wider authority to intervene in the otherwise inviolable realm of family life. The precept was invoked to rationalize governmental protection of children from parental abuse, and society from that abuse's human products. The doctrine, which Blackstone believed appointed the State "the general and supreme guardian of all infants,"[73] formed the legal basis both for the community's custody over mistreated and neglected youths as wards of the State and for the juvenile justice system. Although this judicial contrivance, like any government policy, was subject to misuse, *parens patriae* at least gave government a practical means of fulfilling its multiplying responsibilities toward rebellious children. The State was expected to rescue children from parents who either victimized them or declined to honor their civic obligation to discipline them properly.

These dual Latin principles from the English common law provided the legal foundation for extrafamilial child discipline until recent decades, when the same courts that once handed down these rulings turned against them. State and federal judges diluted the twin policies in the 1960s and 1970s. A series of court decisions greatly restricted corporal punishment in some cases, and abolished it by judicial ruling in others. In 1977 the Supreme Court in *Ingraham v. Wright*[74] came within one vote of declaring corporal punishment in the public schools unconstitutional as violative of the Eighth Amendment's cruel and unusual punishment clause. A majority of justices in *Ingraham* did decree that the Fourteenth Amendment endowed schoolchildren with a right of procedural due process before corporal punishment could be administered. Schools were subsequently required to conduct a mini-trial before punishing disobedient students. The Supreme Court went on to explicitly repudiate the doctrine of *in loco parentis* in 1985 in *New Jersey v. T.L.O.*,[75] greatly limiting schools' powers of search and seizure. Since then the Court has held that schoolchildren can sue violators of these rulings for treble damages.[76]

The Supreme Court has not been very far ahead of the American people in these decisions. By the time *Ingraham* was handed down, corporal punishment was already going out of fashion. In the year that *Ingraham* was decided, California and New York banned corporal punishment in their public schools on their own initiative. Corporal punishment is now prohibited in the public schools of twenty-seven states. Its unpopularity grows at an accelerating rate; nine banned the practice between 1987 and 1990.[77] Some of this reappraisal stems from liability exposure and shows financial prudence. Corporal punishment suits are a growing area of the law, usually settling for between $15,000 and $85,000.[78] But these political prohibitions of corporal punishment also reveal a major shift in public opinion. The expulsion of corporal punishment from our schools was made possible only after parents themselves concluded that corporal punishment—and increasingly punishment of any sort—was something to which reasonable adults should not subject children. In 1962, 59 percent of American parents reported using spanking for disciplining their children. Thirty years later that number had dropped to 19 percent. Rising to take the place of corporal punishment were lecturing, at 24 percent, and "time-outs," at 38 percent.[79] The latter is essentially a parental demand for the child to sit in a corner and think over his conduct; it is reasonably effective for many children if administered consistently, but frequently it seems to degenerate into negotiation with children, or, worse, a mere facade of punishment.

None of this would appear auspicious for a society coping with a record number of troublesome adolescent boys, children who seem frightened of nothing. The roots of this shift in child-rearing practices stretch back well beyond recent decades. There were two important watersheds, the first coming in the mid-1800s, when a Congregationalist minister named Horace Bushnell published a book titled *Christian Nurture*. Bushnell did not poke fun at traditional parenting, but did recommend a moderate reevaluation of the child-rearing practices of his day. He mutinied against the extravagant emphasis then placed on iron-fisted paternity by previous American authorities on child-rearing. One such figure was the famous Puritan leader Cotton Mather. Mather taught that children were born with original sin. Parents must therefore break their children's wills to overcome this natural, selfish tendency to revolt against God. "Look to it," Mather urged, "that you keep up a *Fear* of you, in the hearts of your children, and make them tremble to *Refuse* any fit thing that you shall *Enjoyn* upon them."[80] He recognized that parents were often ambivalent about corporal punishment, but he encouraged them with a quintessential Puritan epigram: "Better whip't than damned."

Bushnell believed in gentler methods, but agreed with some of these basic premises. He was no less convinced that a child's obedience and rejection of self-motivated desires depended on the instillation of a fear of God. The notion of the "radical goodness of human nature," Bushnell felt, was contrary to both Scripture and the "familiar laws of physiology." But Bushnell preached that this essential fear of the divine sovereign was better achieved if the child was merely "touched with some gentle emotions toward what is right," rather than ruled with undue fatherly fury.[81]

Bushnell's welcome proposed softening of parents' benevolent dictatorship, it is true, bears little similarity to our current general distaste for corporal punishment. This is because in the century and a half since Bushnell's influential writings, parents seeking guidance on child-rearing have come to rely on other figures. Easily the most influential has been Dr. Benjamin Spock. His *Common Sense Book of Baby and Child Care*, published in 1946 just in time for a generation of baby boomers, became the most widely read American book on child-rearing of this century. Spock built on the intellectual structure erected by Rousseau in *Emile*. Rousseau instructed parents and society not to punish children for perceived misbehavior. Children must be permitted to pursue their own individualistic ways even if at times they test our patience and property, lest these little noble savages be corrupted by civilization like their parents. Spock, in this vein, maintained that parents should not seek to mold the child's will. He also counseled moral relativism. He suggested that parents permit their children to lie on occasion without punishment, and recommended parental self-criticism as the proper response to a child's stealing.[82] Rather than being cute little anarchists whose innate egoism threatened to bring society down around them, children deserve liberation from our crass enforcement of arbitrary conventions.

Although Spock later amended his instructions, his relativism remained unchanged; and other, less gifted scholars sought to copy his success. Spock's writings appealed to a generation of young parents who disliked the literal preaching of earlier scholars. As couples had fewer children and families shrank in size or decomposed, parents had fewer teachers of child-rearing around them. A market for parental counseling ensued, as parents sought guidance and, in some cases, reassurance about the propriety of the parental self-interest that today pervades the home. These latter parents were often, understandably, the most uncomfortable with corporal punishment. It is no fun to mete out the penalties that make our children frown or curse at us. This is especially true if punishment is complicated by guilt over our neglect of them in other contexts. The last thing we want is to ruin our "quality time" with our kids with discipline, even though that may well be just what a child needs, for instance, after a long, unruly day at a day-care center. Thus, not simply corporal punishment but punishment in all its forms is no longer enforced in many American homes. Appeasement is easier in the short run, and the shortsightedness common to our age makes this the normal course. So we tolerate juvenile pathologies that earlier, simpler-minded generations would not have brooked, and resort instead to trying to befriend our children rather than scolding or judging them; for how can we discipline our children if we cannot discipline ourselves? And we forget, in the process, that we can be a real friend to our children only by being a parent.

The growth of matriarchal families, integral to these trends, reinforced this aversion to discipline. Punishing children has always been the preserve of the father. This is because mothers often shrink from spanking children, and because maternal discipline often does not frighten adolescent boys. As fathers fell out of favor or out of the marriage, interest in corporal punishment waned. More and more school boards recognized the inevitable, disbanding the practice and other effective forms of discipline and accepting school disorder as a consequence.

One especially insightful study of this link between school discipline and delinquency came from British professor Michael Rutter.[83] Rutter found that the schools most effective at discouraging delinquency were those with an "ethos" that combined a caring, learning atmosphere with firm disciplinary practices. Rutter found that by maintaining a system of clear rules and consistent rewards, and by punishing children who disregard them, schools can encourage self-restraint among all students and prevent the gifted students from sliding into delinquency themselves. Without such order in the classroom, Wilson and Herrnstein add, "deficits [leading to delinquency] that had a constitutional or familial origin accumulate and, possibly, worsen."[84] Rutter's findings were consistent with a report by the National Institute of Education, which found higher rates of student violence in schools lacking effective disciplinary or order-maintenance procedures. Schools where rules of conduct were rarely or weakly enforced were the most likely to produce chaotic classrooms incapable of repelling the disorder in surrounding society.[85]

It will not be easy to restore this ethos of order to America's schools, with or without corporal punishment. Schools will always reflect, to some degree, the values and manners of the society that sustains them. But schools can be an agent of order if they, like the government as a whole, put first things first. Respect for the law and school rules must be taught as an absolute principle to American schoolchildren. Like the society they are drawn from, too many of today's teachers would probably take exception to this. We have come to believe that children should be allowed to "find themselves" individually without adult meddling and discipline, even at an age when few children know their own address. As if to illustrate the point, recently the ACLU filed suit against a New Jersey high school for requiring students wishing to join sports or extracurricular activities to agree not to become involved in any enterprises that violate the criminal code.[86] Occasionally parents resist this complacency. Such was the case recently in Michigan, where a state panel provoked a parental backlash against a model curriculum in which 347 of the 863 learning objectives for elementary and secondary schoolchildren dealt with emotions rather than academics. Teachers were to instruct young children to decide right and wrong for themselves without consulting their parents, even on matters such as premarital sex and substance abuse.[87]

Many teachers, like many Americans, see a certain amount of classroom disorder as necessary so that young Americans can express their individuality. And so they do. Young children prone to impatience, aggressiveness and worse are allowed to hone these traits for later use against society, rather than being taught and obliged to observe permissible limits of human interaction. This educational regime ultimately reflects the lack of an overarching system of absolute moral principles to teach—under Rutter's theory, the "goals" enforced by rewards and punishment to maintain this "ethos." Rutter's terminology is revealing, probably unconsciously so. For the Greek term *ethos,* as used by Aristotle, meant far more than a rough synonym for environment, the sense in which Rutter uses it. *Ethos* is the term from which "ethics" is derived. And to the ancient Greeks who invented the word, *ethos* meant "habit." To them, proper behavior was the result of society's vigilant efforts to ingrain in its citizens a common nucleus of absolute laws of proper conduct. These laws bind the community together physically and spiritually. They are to be taught by the family, the schools and any other likely source of children's habits. Because of the limitations of his language, Aristotle found it unfathomable that children should be left to their own devices to learn right from wrong. As he saw it, ethics and habit were linguistically, and thus practically, indistinguishable.

Currently, the only such course of instruction that would appear to command enough support to enable its implementation in public schools is so-called values education. These classes deliver general lessons of orderly conduct modeled loosely—but never explicitly, and hence never effectively—after the Ten Commandments. Such lessons in ethics and basic social etiquette, of course, are a step in the right direction, but an unacceptably small one. They are rather like teaching table manners to cannibals. And even these attenuated appeals to basic social values are the exception in today's schools. Children are, as a rule, left to express their ethical individuality. They meander through their own value systems, free to pick and choose from the cafeteria of contending principles whose chaos inevitably reinforces the latent delinquent inclinations in certain children. America's public school teachers were probably not surprised by an extraordinary 1992 survey of high school students, in which one-third said they would lie to get a job, 61 percent admitted cheating on an exam and 77 percent said that their most important goal in life was "getting a job you enjoy."[88]

In one of his assaults on religion and other things sensible, Bertrand Russell leveled what he thought was a lethal blast at organized worship of the divine when he said, "Fear is the basis of all religious dogma."[89] For the frustrated citizens of a crime-battered American Republic, the response to this should be: So what? Fear works. Much more than redistributed money or rights, fear is the commodity that children at risk of delinquency so desperately need. Fear will do the job that this dissolving society requires. And while the threat of the principal's paddle is frequently all that can keep pupils with short time horizons obedient, the sort of children most prone to criminality, only the fear of an Almighty Power who holds misbehaving youngsters accountable for their wrongdoing can lay the foundation for a lifetime of good behavior once the threat of immediate corporal punishment is withdrawn. Today, however, America's public schools are legally barred from providing religion-based values education. Courts have prohibited such instruction in the public schools for almost four decades,[90] based on a "separation of Church and State" that, in fact, is nowhere to be found in the Constitution, and that would have surprised the Constitution's Framers.

We must, at a bare minimum, teach our children in absolute terms that it is wrong to break the law. Devotion to the rule of law is the most basic principle that a free people must impart to its children. It is the moral baseline for any society that is even remotely serious about self-preservation. No one better articulated this necessity than the American who was probably the most acutely aware of America's inherent tendencies toward disunity. Abraham Lincoln first rose to national prominence not from his views on slavery, but by lecturing on teachers' most fundamental lesson in a tough-on-crime speech delivered to a receptive crowd in Springfield, Illinois, in 1838. He saw domestic discord as the Achilles' heel of the still-young Republic:

> At what point then is the approach of danger to be expected? I answer, if it ever reach us, it must spring up amongst us. It cannot come from abroad. If destruction be our lot, we must ourselves be its author and finisher. As a nation of freemen, we must live through all time, or die by suicide.[91]

In response to the rise in lawlessness at the time (an increase that, in comparison to today's rates, now seems humorously low), Lincoln urged his fellow countrymen to teach obedience to the law as "the political religion of the nation." "Let reverence for the laws, be breathed by every American mother, to the lisping babe. . . . Let it be taught in schools . . . written in Primmers, spelling books, and in Almanacs."[92]

Such classes would be both inspiring and highly educational. Among other benefits, they offer the prospect of requiring American children to read some of the world's greatest literature, from Plato's *Crito* to Confucius's *Analects*. Only such rule-of-law education, inserted as a moral component to civics classes and backed up by school disciplinary practices, can provide the ethos in which obedience to the law can become second nature, an internal command ingrained by habit. Americans must once again be taught that the law, rather than inviting self-interested rebellion, is their protector and something worthy of obedience. Such an education, in the beautiful analogy of the Chinese philosopher Han Fei Tzu, enables the law to be like morning dew, pure and uncomplicated, effortlessly absorbed by those thirsting for it beneath.[93]

Recognizing that the public schools are no longer the traditional prop for social order that they once were, Americans have recently experimented with other ideas. Some states have begun restoring parental duties to the family through legislation. Implicit in these reforms is the acknowledgment of Blackstone's adage that it is inconceivable "that a parent has conferred any considerable benefit upon his child, by bringing him into the world; if he afterwards entirely neglects his culture and education, and suffers him to grow up like a mere beast, to lead a life useless to others, and shameful to himself."[94] These recent efforts have created a patchwork of innovative laws, often suggesting local concerns but all returning certain limited duties to the family. California's Street Terrorism Enforcement and Prevention Act holds parents criminally liable if they knowingly fail to supervise or control delinquent children, a law targeting Los Angeles's exploding gang population. A Florida law, passed after a rash of accidental shootings by children, subjects parents to a five-year prison term if a child uses a gun left around the house. In response to growing illegitimacy rates, a Wisconsin statute makes grandparents support the babies of teenage mothers. South Carolina prosecutes for criminal negligence mothers of babies born drug-dependent.

The resistance to these laws has been disconcertingly strong. California's Street Terrorism Enforcement and Prevention Act, for instance, has already been essentially nullified. Prosecutors now decline to enforce the law because of the public controversy over the 1989 arrest of the mother of a fifteen-year-old accused rapist in Los

Angeles. She had posed with him and other overt gang members in several photographs displayed in the family photo album. Two months later prosecutors dropped the case after learning that she had already taken a mandatory parenting course.[95] The law itself is now of interest only to legal historians and wistful crime control advocates.

Crime cannot be halted by an overextended government accumulating power at the expense of the family. A society under its care seems headed in another, rather haunting direction. The Romanian Revolution in 1989 offered a glimpse of how such a State treats its citizens' children when given responsibility for their upbringing. As Westerners began rooting around in the communist institutions left behind after Ceauşescu's execution, many were shocked at how babies born with birth defects had been carted off to huge, anonymous facilities. There some children lived their entire lives in urine and squalor, never to receive parental affection. Surely, it was assumed in the West, their parents could not have chosen to surrender them to such institutions. Communism must have somehow caused them to do this. Interviews of Romanians revealed otherwise. They seemed, in fact, satisfied with the arrangement. Inconvenient, bothersome children could be discarded with minimum fuss, all at public expense. Westerners, for a while at least, promoted adoption of the abandoned children. For Americans, however, it struck an ominous chord. We have not yet reached Romania's harsh culmination of parental egoism, which was promoted and accelerated by the former regime. But our emerging popular culture of radical individualism is philosophically kindred (extending back to Plato and Marx), and has made our nation seem not nearly as remote from this scenario as it once was. And, most important for crime control purposes, such children were not in a position to retaliate against their parents and society, unlike the many millions of neglected but otherwise healthy youths in America.

American children, indeed, have already witnessed comparable, foreboding happenings in their own land. They see their parents leave more troublesome family members at often government-supported institutions, such as nursing homes and day-care centers. They see that all the material, sensual good things in life that adults seek may actually be had at little cost, if only the frail bonds of conscience applied by a morally desiccated society can be snapped, and law enforcement authorities dodged. Their self-centeredness, inculcated so diligently by so many, makes the choice rather simple.

Abused and neglected from the cradle through adolescence, American children watch and learn. And if their parents finally realize the error of their ways, it is often not until they are living their twilight years in solitude because their children are too busy to visit them. There, alone, they spend their idle final days gazing out at their surroundings through the iron bars on their windows, welded on to prevent the next generation of children from blowing their brains out.

CHAPTER SEVEN

Gangs, Drugs and Plato's Other Children

Entities should not be multiplied beyond need.

—William of Ockham

"Enough is enough."[1] With that, President Bush's wavering ended in December 1989 with a final, firm order to invade Panama, and a resolution to carry the War on Drugs to its logical conclusion. Operation Just Cause dispatched 11,500 American troops to join the 12,700 already stationed in Panama to perform what amounted to an international drug bust: decapitating the Panamanian government and its base of operations for funneling cocaine into the *coloso del norte*. Unlike the law enforcement officials back home enlisted for combat against domestic drug dealers, U.S. soldiers had a meaner, and yet in some ways simpler, task. They were given broad, extraconstitutional latitude to bring to justice a single drug kingpin—"Maximum Leader" Manuel Noriega.

To get to Noriega, whom grand juries in Miami and Tampa had indicted for drug trafficking, America had to pierce the defenses of several thousand troops under Noriega's command, as well as 1,800 hard-core bodyguards in his "dignity battalions." Harassed by 3,000 paratroopers and American forces pushing out of their Canal Zone base en masse, Noriega's Panamanian Defense Forces were soon overwhelmed. His men put to flight, General Noriega himself went on the lam, and eventually holed up at the Vatican embassy. Inspecting Noriega's abandoned office and hideaways, U.S. soldiers found some decidedly un-Catholic novelties: remnants of odd voodoo rituals (a bucket of blood and talismans), 50 pounds of cocaine, a stack of pornography, a photo of Hitler.[2]

Other American troops laid siege to the general's new abode. They even made him the guinea pig for one of the weirdest offensives in the history of combat. U.S. troops ringed the compound with loudspeakers and unleashed an earsplitting barrage of . . . rock music. Few Americans caught the unflattering implication of this audio attack. It did not speak well of modern American culture that its most popular genre of music was commonly judged a brutal implement of war, one that, even at decibels fairly normal for its predominantly adolescent customers, would force the unconditional surrender of this hardened strongman. One favorite tune at the siege was the 1965 Motown classic "Nowhere to Run."[3] U.S. forces later turned up the heat, blasting the fallen general with the unofficial theme song of the occasion, Guns N' Roses' heavy metal classic "Welcome to the Jungle."

By January 4 Noriega had had enough of inhospitable priests and electric guitars. He surrendered to U.S. forces, apparently coaxed in part by the American criminal justice system's promise of an institutionally pro-defendant trial. Once again, however, Noriega seemingly miscalculated. On April 10, 1992, a Miami jury convicted the deposed general of eight counts of cocaine trafficking, racketeering and money laundering. He was sentenced to forty years in prison, at no less than the federal big house for incorrigible offenders in Marion, Illinois. Yet by year's end signs of potential judicial relief had already taken shape. A federal judge ruled Noriega a prisoner of war, and found it "open to serious question" whether his incarceration was legal under the Geneva Conventions.[4]

The invasion itself vividly captured America's line of attack against its drug problem. The nation sought to subdue the menace with a minimum of sacrifice, opting for the consensus choice of an aggressive single strike: round up a posse, administer a healthy dose of rock and roll and wait for the barbarian to yield to the forces of civilization. But this approach failed to achieve any discernible drop in the drug trade. Three years after the invasion U.S. officials found no measurable reduction in Panamanian drug trafficking.[5]

All the same, the invasion was popular with Mr. Bush's constituents. A *Newsweek* poll found that 80 percent of Americans thought the invasion "justified."[6] This support for America's latest sacrifice to Mars seemed to owe at least in part to the belief that at last something was being done about America's drug problem. The popular unwillingness to make the personal sacrifices necessary to reduce the domestic drug demand added to the appeal. No more artificial war on these crime-generating substances with policemen and prisons; we had finally gotten down to business. And surely, it was thought, fewer drugs meant less crime, since by the late 1980s many Americans had come to think of drugs as a prime "cause" of crime. The people in commerce with these substances, their buyers and sellers, often did not encounter similar criminal blame, even though crime occurred by definition when such business transactions occurred. Drugs seemed at the root of our problems, as did gangs, the predominant purveyors of drugs. The United States' successful assault on Panama's drug lords, it was assumed, entitled us to a less crime-ridden society. We had killed the beast.

Americans have since had to reevaluate matters. Crime has proved much more resilient than anticipated. Celebrations over our victory in Panama were short-lived; the foes we thought we had slain have proved elusive and, as we shall see, intellectually spirited—in more ways than one.

CHILD'S PLAY

Children are laboratories of parental vices. Given the popular culture preferred by adults, it would be not only unusual but historically unprecedented if America's children became selfless defenders of the common order. Too often it is all they can do to find someone who sincerely sympathizes with them. As young Americans go forth into this proudly dog-eat-dog society, they have come to rely on each other for mutual sympathy. Delinquency and gangs are not far behind. Such juvenile support groups frequently adopt the lifestyle of the only male role models around in the post-family inner city, criminals. Organized into criminal cells by a semipaternal figure, these aggregations of bruised souls revel in the male camaraderie they find in jointly getting the better of society.

The cliques of young offenders that have taken root in America's ghettos and *barrios* are the result of both innate and distinctly American influences. The urge to band together to do battle with others, given free reign today in the inner city, is natural, a propensity recognized by the Italian philosopher Gaetano Mosca as man's "instinct for herding together and fighting with other herds."[7] Young Americans' political culture also encourages these clashes to some degree. It exhorts them to unite with one another to affect their country for good or ill, just as adults join civic groups or lobbies to secure either national goals or, more commonly, their own self-interests. Tocqueville called the more respectable products of this civil right "political associations," and judged them a defining characteristic of American society.[8] He would recognize these same jostling forces in their most common, disfigured manifestation among young Americans today: delinquent youth gangs.

Legitimating the antisocial instinct latent in all adolescent boys, these cultural tendencies also help to determine peer pressure, the gang's method of self-perpetuation and arguably the single greatest direct stimulant of juvenile crime. For a period in a teenage American's life coextensive with his most high-crime years, adolescence, peer pressure is the most powerful external influence on his life. More than fidelity to family, church and community, especially in an age in which such ties are highly relaxed, peer pressure, or the desire to look "cool" in front of and be accepted by one's friends, is the prime mover behind a teenage social animal's conduct. Teenagers, of course, are usually not smart enough to define cool for themselves. Just as most of us wear what a small cabal of designers say is acceptable, purchase goods hawked by celebrities and aspire to careers popularly considered glamorous, children accept uncritically the definition of cool bestowed by the popular culture. And currently, crime is cool. For young men, the people who define the values enforced by peer pressure are typically the most rebellious; in American society, these are generally young black males, the arbiters of cool. To earn this vital badge of peer honor in the inner city and to gain the friendship and acceptance that fill the emotional void of children lacking family, one must join a gang.[9]

From the inception of their discipline, criminologists have documented the inherent tendency of male adolescents to unite and jointly commit crimes. The first thorough examination of gang behavior came in Frederic Thrasher's *The Gang,* published in 1927. Thrasher defined the gang as "an interstitial group originally formed spontaneously, and then integrated through conflict," the "interstitial areas" where gangs were generally abundant being the city's slums. He concluded, based on a study of 1,313 gangs in Chicago, that gangs were training grounds for adult criminal activity. Thrasher also believed—optimistically, it turns out—that there is "little permanence" in gang membership.[10] In addition, Thrasher accepted the emerging belief that the gang member's criminality was caused by social conditions in his interstitial area.

Albert Cohen and Edwin Sutherland contributed works that achieved similar influence in American criminology. Cohen's *Delinquent Boys*, published in 1957, applied strain theory specifically to adolescents. He observed that most gang members are from the lowest socioeconomic class, and he recognized the materialistic origins of much of their delinquency. Young gangsters espied the possibility of getting with a single well-executed crime what they would otherwise have to spend years working for to obtain legally.[11] Sutherland's theory of differential association saw criminality as learned rather than genetically inherited or acquired against the offender's will. The young delinquent picks up how to be a criminal from the people with whom he voluntarily associates. By interacting with delinquents one learns not merely the techniques of committing offenses, but also the attitudes, motives and rationalizations that form the necessary foundation of a life of crime. Sutherland saw the gang as "a means of disseminating techniques of delinquencies, of training in delinquency, of protecting its members engaged in delinquency, and of maintaining continuity in delinquency."[12] The lack of alternative values taught by the family makes easier this process of criminal assimilation.

These theories established two easy, observable explanations for how delinquency happens. First, antisocial values are learned from gangs and enforced by peer pressure. Second, the crimes perpetrated once one joins a gang often reflect the strain between the expensive possessions glamorized by a materialistic culture and one's limited means of legally acquiring them. A recent empirical examination of strain theory found "moderate" evidence of its applicability to drug abuse among adolescents, but "relatively substantial" evidence as to delinquency in general.[13] Still, quite a few contemporary criminologists reject these classical views. Some even deny a recent surge in juvenile delinquency. One example was the 1989 work of Ira M.

Schwartz, *(In)justice for Juveniles.* Schwartz, with the help of some selective statistics, concludes flatly that "we are not in the midst of a juvenile crime wave."[14]

In fact, of course, we are in the midst of an unprecedented and daunting juvenile crime wave, just as we are in the midst of a Great Havoc generally. Reflecting the incentives of a lucrative illegal drug trade and a criminal justice system that rewards adults who enlist young people for illegal enterprises, the violent-crime rate among juveniles has soared. Since 1965 the juvenile violent-crime arrest rate has more than tripled. Despite leveling off somewhat during the mid-1980s, the overall crime rate for children between ten and seventeen years of age rose 27 percent from 1980 to 1990. Although many scholars had assured the nation that it would enjoy a reprieve from teenage crime during the 1980s, when the at-risk population— the number of teenagers—would ebb to its lowest level in decades, instead the juvenile violent-crime rate has rebelliously skyrocketed. While the eighteen-to-twenty-four-year-old age group dropped to 10.3 percent of the population by mid-1991, the lowest since 1965, the nation's murder rate, driven largely by teenage homicide, jumped to 9.8 per 100,000 population, the highest in a decade.[15] Most striking was a phenomenon confirmed by other multiracial crime studies. As noted earlier, the FBI found in its 1991 juvenile crime statistics that the increase in teenage crime involved not only "minority youth in urban areas" but "all races, all social classes and lifestyles."[16]

The extent and sheer viciousness of today's juvenile crime are simply mind-boggling, unfathomable to even the most callous mafiosi of a few decades ago. This methodical savagery would seem to belie the assurances of the Scottish moral sense philosophers, from Hume to Adam Smith, that all people have an instinctive "sympathy" for one another. Smith, for instance, contended that "[e]ven the greatest ruffian, the most hardened violator of the laws of society, is not altogether without" this quality.[17] This sympathy, it was presumed, would balance and lessen the messy materialism that their philosophies fostered. Such hopefulness quivers in the face of recent statistics. From 1985 to 1991 the homicide arrest rate for fifteen-year-olds rose 217 percent. Arrest rates for thirteen- and fourteen-year-olds more than doubled during the same period.[18] In 1991 more than 2,200 murder victims were under eighteen; nearly a million young people between twelve and nineteen are raped, robbed or assaulted each year, frequently by their peers.[19] Even schools, formerly a child's oasis of order and protection in high-crime areas, have absorbed this chaos. In 1992 one student in five reported carrying a weapon to school, with one in twenty carrying a gun.[20] African-Americans suffered the most. As gangs responded to the economic stimuli of the drug market, the number of black males murdered between the ages of fifteen and nineteen more than doubled from 1984 to 1988.[21] The *New York Times* recently gave this sobering synopsis of three juvenile atrocities that occurred within a few days of one another, all committed by New York's young drug gangs:

> As a woman starts across the street, a van roars up. Strong arms wrest her purse from her grasp. As the van lurches away, she falls beneath the wheels and is crushed to death. . . . Members of a drug gang kidnap an enemy's 12-year-old brother, hack off the boy's finger and enclose it with a ransom request. . . . A group of teen-age boys blame a 12-year-old girl for stealing $45. They take out their anger by raping her and torturing her with a heated knife and an ice pick.[22]

Studies have long revealed the unique dangers posed by teenage crime. The recent dramatic rise in juvenile crime is doubly discouraging because youths who become enmeshed in delinquency tend to become criminals for life. Lee Robins's study of St. Louis psychiatric patients was the first to note that sociopathy among children was a prime indicator of adult criminality.[23] The research team of Wolfgang, Figlio and Sellin, in their classic 1945 Philadelphia Birth Cohort Study, likewise reported a relationship between delinquency and adult criminality among violent offenders. Joan Petersilia's RAND study of California inmates showed that offenders who committed a serious crime before age sixteen "tended to report more adult crime, commit more types of crimes, commit violent crimes at a higher rate, and hold professional criminal attitudes." Petersilia also found that "the earlier the first arrest, the likelier it is that sustained criminal behavior will follow."[24] It is probable that the juvenile crime rate is actually higher than officially estimated, since, as Barbara Boland and James Q. Wilson have noted, the chances of being arrested for a crime are lower for juveniles than for adults.[25]

Woe to the citizens and communities that present blocs of potential market share to these delinquent conglomerates. The most ravaged of these war zones is Los Angeles. It is not a random somersault of history that has selected southern California for such rough treatment.

There are reasons for this special status rooted in the area's political and social culture. Libertarianism has saturated the popular culture of California and, more generally, the western United States more than any other region of the country. This mindset is nourished by the West's historic individualism, and today it realizes itself in everything from insignificant matters, such as the nation's highest percentage of individualized license plates, to more pressing concerns, such as extreme materialism, rampant litigiousness, low church attendance and, especially unfortunate in this crime-beset age, a general disrespect for government. This trait seems to provide the only credible explanation for the West's enormous crime rates—the highest in the country, and well out of proportion to the region's ethnic makeup or any of the other pat explanations for widespread crime.[26]

Gangs in the L.A. Basin have thus found a uniquely vulnerable habitat. They have lost little time in setting up shop in what was once the nation's promised land, sending its incredulous residents fleeing to other states in a reversal of California's proud traditions. Federal officials have estimated that gangs from the Los Angeles metropolitan area control almost one-third of the nation's crack trade. Approximately 90,000 youngsters are affiliated with the gangs in Los Angeles County. In only five years, between 1985 and 1990, the number of young gangsters doubled, from approximately 400 with 45,000 members in 1985 to 800 with 90,000 five years later. Of these, 25,000 belong to African-American gangs. Forty-five thousand are members of Latino, largely Mexican-American, gangs, which differ in both history and purpose from black gangs.[27] The distinctions derive from different pathologies.

Black gangs are a relatively recent phenomenon. They reflect both the breakdown of social controls in the inner city and a Pavlovian response to the economic incentives of the drug trade. Most of the upswing in gang membership during the 1980s was due to increased enrollment in black gangs. The bulk of L.A.'s African-American gang members are, in turn, members or affiliates of the two criminal superpowers of the South-Central ghetto, the megagangs known as the Bloods and the Crips. These two gangs enjoy a network believed to extend to 32 states and 113 cities. Police estimate that 25 percent of Los Angeles County's black males between the ages of fifteen and twenty-four are either members or "associates" of these two gangs.[28] Their well-publicized wars illustrate less the inimical nature of the two groups' motives than the highly atomized constitution of their members. This "defiant individualist character" of today's adoles-

cent gangsters, as criminologists have described it, leads these otherwise like-minded fellow offenders to lock horns on occasion.
Indeed, *intra*gang fighting is more common than either intergang or
extragang violence.[29] Their gang wars, in turn, represent the sparks
and friction to be expected of a highly egoistic society and subculture. The Bloods and the Crips operate a more or less joint oligop-
oly over the drug trade in Los Angeles County, and, given these circumstances, run it reasonably well.

Latino gangs, particularly Mexican gangs, provide a striking and
intriguing contrast: violent, individualistic groups dedicated to
upholding quasi-communitarian values. The ranks of these gangs are
thinner; only about 10 to 15 percent of L.A. County's Mexican
teenagers belong to them. But while some of the earliest black gang
members proudly call themselves "O.G.s" for "original gangsters," it
is the Mexican "gangbangers" who are the real originals in this criminal enterprise. The Mexican *cholo,* or gang member, lays claim to a
far older group history of delinquency. It is composed of a web of
rivalries and inveterate sense of honor that trace back to the
Spanish.[30] The founders of the modern Mexican-American gangs,
who remain the models for the contemporary *cholo,* were known as
los pachucos, or "the mischief makers." The Mexican gang subculture originated from the language and mores of these groups of
Mexican-American teenagers in the 1930s. They developed a taste
for baggy zoot suits and speaking *calo,* an English-Spanish slang.
The main impetus for their evolution from an informal social network to an association of delinquents was the 1943 Zoot Suit Riots.
That year gangs of white servicemen on leave from World War II
roved the streets of East Los Angeles and savaged the flamboyant
pachucos, apparently for amusement. Coming on the heels of a
questionable murder prosecution of several Mexican teenagers one
year before, this pogrom drove a firm wedge between Los Angeles's
Mexican community and the Anglo majority, especially the city's
predominantly white law enforcement authorities. In the half century since these events, Mexican gangs in East Los Angeles have
become "quasi-institutionalized."[31]

Mexican-Americans thus view their juvenile gang culture as primarily social rather than criminal in origin. Mexican gangs are still
clannish neighborhood self-defense networks for heirs to a recent
history of segregation and racial abuse. This does not mean, of
course, that Latino gangs are above delinquency. The peer pressure
that today makes crime cool has corrupted these cooperatives as

well, although not quite to the degree of the black gang. The defining prerequisite for Latino gang membership remains not a strong profit motive but, in most cases, an old code of honor like the zoot-suiters'. One of the main features of this code is that violence is not random. If one must *sacar* a rival gangster, this axiom holds, one must do so without brutalizing his family members or bystanders. This rule contrasts with the general attitude of gangs in the black inner city, whom Mexican gang members often regard as haphazardly violent newcomers to the gang culture. Latinos also believe blacks to be more likely to turn each other in to the authorities when subjected to police questioning, which arouses no small contempt.[32]

This *Lord of the Flies*-type regime that today characterizes much of southern California has generally withstood greater law enforcement efforts. A few successes have been netted, mainly those centered on community involvement. In the Los Angeles Police Department's South Bureau, gang-related crime plunged 36 percent from January to March 1990 over the same period of the prior year. Murders involving gang members fell 45 percent during the same period, this despite the rise in drive-by shootings in other parts of the city. Police credited the drop to community involvement organized by black neighborhood activists.[33] Elsewhere, there was a 67 percent cut in the crime rate when police erected barricades to cordon off high-crime neighborhoods, complete with signs that read NARCOTICS ENFORCEMENT AREA: OPEN TO RESIDENTS ONLY. The Community Resources Against Street Hoodlums (CRASH) program, a reactive patrol-car strike force organized specifically to combat gangs, has enjoyed some limited success in its strategy of deploying rapidly to eliminate targeted gang nests.[34]

Overall, though, Los Angeles' gangs have proved tenacious, mainly because of the collapse of the court system. Gangs have multiplied so exuberantly of late because their members realize that they are unlikely to encounter criminal punishment, less likely even than today's adult offenders. An encapsulation of this street knowledge may be heard in the slang term "minutemen," used to describe young ghetto kids enlisted for their criminal services by older gang members because they know they will be in jail only for a short time before being released.[35] This incentive for juvenile crime is the result of relatively recent changes in the court system. They are the product of a penal philosophy that states that juveniles are to be punished on the basis of age rather than their ability to distinguish right from wrong. The recent growth of militant juvenile gangs and violent crime among young people must make us reevaluate these assumptions.

The same nineteenth-century Progressive movement that produced probation and parole, the indeterminate sentence and the notion of rehabilitating offenders sponsored this system of juvenile justice, based in turn on the view of child-rearing then budding conceptually in America. In 1899 these efforts led to the establishment of the first juvenile court in Chicago. Progressives envisioned the juvenile court as providing individualized care by professionals devoted to the child's best interests. To eliminate any suggestion of a criminal proceeding, courtroom procedures were altered, a euphemistic vocabulary was created and a separate court building was used to avoid the stigma of adult prosecutions. Juries and lawyers were excluded and formal rules of evidence disregarded, since the important issues were not the circumstances of the offense but the child's background and welfare. Stretching the old English doctrine of *parens patriae* to justify active government intervention in dysfunctional families, American judges upheld the juvenile court as a narrow, legally acceptable divergence from the adversary system's trial by battle. As one observer stated, "Principles of psychology and social work, rather than formal decisional rules, guided decision-makers" under this new regime.[36]

Of course, any system of justice founded on such shaky science was hampered from the start. Worse still was the nomination of the judge—who was, after all, simply a lawyer—as the chief psychiatrist and fortune-teller under the new system. Although a judge-centered model was, as we have seen, in many ways an important improvement over the adversary system, far too much was expected of the juvenile-justice judge. He was charged with divining through unspecified means a delinquent's chances of reformation, and prescribing ad hoc treatment for his illness. Indeed, the judge was expected to render decisions "without any reference to rules or norms but in what appears to be a completely free evaluation of the particular merits of every single case."[37] Deterrence of juvenile offenders, which requires predictable punishment, thus became impossible. Later court decisions confused things further. In the 1967 case of *In re Gault*,[38] the Supreme Court grafted onto the juvenile justice system a broad array of constitutional rights that the child could use against his governmental substitute parent. Although intended to ensure fair play for accused young citizens, these rights were simply not feasible as a matter of consistent legal theory when imposed on such an explicitly nonadversarial system. The culmination of these theoretical developments became evident in 1990, when Atlanta officials attempted to crack down on mounting juvenile crime by imposing a late-night curfew for children under seventeen. An Associated Press headline noted the possibilities beckoning to aspiring young delinquent-litigators: "Atlanta Police to Begin Enforcing Youth Curfew; ACLU Awaiting Plantiffs."[39]

Juvenile justice is further complicated by the continuing disagreement over how to determine whether youthful offenders qualify as adults. Two systems are currently used for this segregation process, neither of which works effectively: the waiver system and the legislative-offense system. The waiver system is the more common. It seeks to blend the retributive aspects of adult courts with the rehabilitative impulse of the juvenile justice regime. The waiver system allows the judge to remove the accused from juvenile court jurisdiction and try him as an adult on a discretionary, case-by-case basis. The judge decides this after holding a hearing on the youth's amenability to treatment and threat to public safety. This system, accordingly, represents piecemeal Progressivism, a middle ground in which neither justice nor rehabilitation is consistently served. Deterrence is also thwarted, since there is little predictability to the system. Moreover, the waiver system requires the judge to predict the youth's likelihood of recidivism, a power of prophecy that few members of any profession have been able to demonstrate convincingly.

The legislative-offense system is little better. It is explicitly retributive in design, excluding all youths from the juvenile courts for certain offenses specified by the legislature. Usually these are the more serious crimes, offenses seemingly too dangerous to be adjudicated by judges impersonating counselors. The legislative-offense system is inherently arbitrary. Why, for example, should an offender be treated as a child if accused of shoplifting but as an adult if accused of burglary? The seriousness of the crime does not determine the maturity and judgment of the offender. The selection of crimes for such adult treatment is, in addition, often the result of political pressure rather than anything intrinsic to the mentality of teenage offenders.

As usual, Blackstone, formulating the long-standing customs ensconced in the common law, had a better idea. Following his advice and traditional jurisprudence, the pre-Progressive system determined, on an individualized basis, what Blackstone called the youngster's "capacity for doing ill, or contracting guilt," which had been the law in Great Britain since the reign of Edward III.[40] This "capacity" was not a matter of clairvoyance or politics. The jury had to determine whether the accused was able to comprehend the nature and seriousness of his conduct at the time he committed the crime. Blackstone noted that this capacity "is not so much measured by years and days as by the strength of the delinquent's understanding and judgment." American juries prior to the Progressive era decided guilt in this case-by-case manner for all accused youngsters between seven and fourteen years of age; those above fourteen were tried as adults. A modified system today could raise the presumption of adulthood to a later age if popularly desired. The essential reform is the elimination of the judge-as-prophet, allowing for greater deterrence and consistent justice in an age that cries out for both.

Another urgent reform required of the juvenile justice system is making juvenile convictions part of the offender's permanent criminal record. The Progressives who designed the juvenile justice system believed that a young offender's records should be sealed from public knowledge and destroyed once he reached adulthood. The reasoning was that the youth should not be stigmatized—or, as later criminologists put it, "labeled"—as a criminal in a way that proves self-fulfilling. Thus, a repeat juvenile criminal today usually has his entire rap sheet eliminated when he becomes an adult, and enjoys what one observer called a "virgin record" when prosecuted for an adult offense.[41] If juvenile convictions are made part of an offender's lifelong record, career criminals can be better identified and punished; and adulthood will once again carry with it responsibilities as well as the promise of a new dawn.

We must not shrink from these reforms. The preference for juvenile rehabilitation is understandable and well-intentioned, and pity for today's children can never be totally misplaced given the modern travails that confront them. But optimism over the chances for such reformation melts before the realization that recidivism rates run as high as 88 percent for juvenile offenders.[42] Even juvenile boot camps, the short-term, military-style disciplinary programs sprouting up across the country, have failed to reverse these trends. Roughly half of boot camp graduates are convicted of new crimes and returned to prison.[43] More effective, longer-term punishment is called for. The current system of "two-track justice"[44] often serves only to send today's minutemen scurrying to their weapons and delinquent comrades.

For all the mistreatment that many of them have endured, both from inattentive parents and from a narcissistic society, the last thing that ungovernable boys need is greater lenience from the government as a belated substitute for love. The only proven method of steering boys away from the delinquency abetted by today's peer pressure is a strong paternal hand, provided artificially, as a last resort, by the State. Recent events have shown that governmental kindness cannot hope to tame an unfettered adolescent ego, especially one that sees the world as his for the taking if only he can summon enough companions.

CLOUDED JUDGMENT

When we hear drugs confidently termed a distinct cause of crime, we have good reason for puzzlement. Many of those who would identify drugs as such, after all, are the same academic and political figures who have expressed skepticism at labeling other crime-related factors—single-parent families, extreme individualism and the like—as fellow causes of crime. They explain, persuasively, that it is generally too hard to separate the effects of such social forces from others to be able to confidently assign them causal blame. That drugs represent an all-culpable departure from this rule is a position that is freighted with ambiguities, and that deserves our careful attention.

Indeed, if there is any social phenomenon that seems impossible to disentangle from the rest of America's pathologies, it would be the drug problem. The prevalence of drugs in society is, it would seem, actually the handmaiden of other crime-inducing social shortcomings. To wit, the drug plague is not an unforeseeable thunderbolt from Mount Olympus, but a direct outgrowth of the same sybaritic popular tendencies that we see behind the Great Havoc in general. Our drug-related crime surge is simply one of the more unamiable realizations to date of the logical climax to which Mill's libertarianism inevitably leads. If, as he taught and we increasingly believe, we may do whatever we want with our own bodies as long as external violence is not the immediate result, then I'm OK, you're OK and drugs are OK. The substances that one inhales or pumps into one's bloodstream are beyond rightful societal meddling. While the crime that drugs do ultimately engender is troubling, it is usually sufficiently remote from drug use to preclude proper governmental intervention. The State should tend to roads and treaties, and leave us to our own business.

Yet we encounter here some inconsistencies. It is indeed telling that thorough drug legalization has not come to pass, mainly because the gloomier effects of such extreme individualism—crack zombies littering the streets, drive-by shootings and other violent market forces of the drug trade—have proved too unsettling. Libertarian, middle-class America has lately taken a dim view of laissez-faire drug statutes because too many participants in the drug trade have begun pillaging the suburbs, seeking valuables to sustain their "habit." Residents of the inner city have agreed with this assessment, as they have seen many of the same inquisitive faces in their windows over the years. The price that drug legalization demanded of society was more than most of us were willing to pay.

Although the history of America's entanglement with drugs tracks the nation's overall trajectory following the 1960s, America's initial involvement with drugs began well before that fateful, somewhat maligned decade. Drugs had been dissolved in potions and peddled by companies and hucksters since before the turn of the century. Coca-Cola contained cocaine until 1903. Even Freud prescribed various narcotics as both a general tonic and, curiously, a cure for addiction.[45] The only restriction on opium smoking prior to 1909 was a federal tariff. In December 1914 Congress passed the nation's first major antinarcotics legislation, the Harrison Act. The act imposed stiff taxes on a wide range of formerly acceptable narcotics.[46]

The drug trade eventually stirred up stauncher resistance. By 1918, during World War I, Americans began to view addiction as a threat to the war effort. Also important was the growing popular identification of drugs with racial minorities. Opium was always linked symbolically with the Chinese. For similar cultural reasons, marijuana came to be considered a Mexican drug. Its false reputation as a violence-inciting stimulant made marijuana a legislation magnet in the 1930s. This disrepute also resulted in some hysterical films during the 1950s, such as the current cult classic *Reefer Madness*. A true stimulant, cocaine had demonstrably violent effects that frightened white Southerners, who feared that black cocaine users might forget their place in society. The fear of the cocaine-addicted Negro coincided with the peak of lynchings, legal segregation and discriminatory voting laws in the early twentieth century. Myths surfaced about the superhuman behavior of blacks on cocaine. One held that users were unaffected by mere .32 caliber bullets, which apparently prompted some Southern police departments to switch to .38 caliber revolvers.[47]

By the 1920s public opposition to the nonmedical use of drugs solidified. This public pressure heightened during World War II, when narcotic use dropped to its lowest levels since the beginning of America's drug trade. In the 1950s it was highly unusual to personally know a user, or "dope fiend," as he was by then commonly branded. The federal government endorsed this trend with the passage in 1956 of the Little Boggs Act, which authorized the death penalty for the sale of heroin to minors.

From this apogee of drug intolerance America has, in recent years, swiftly returned to its pre-twentieth-century laissez-faire passivity. Many young Americans in the 1960s forged a counterculture that viewed drugs as essentially harmless; college students sampled traditionally forbidden narcotics as well as newer stimulants such as LSD. Adult social scientists ratified these attitudes in 1972, when the federal Commission on Marihuana and Drug Abuse advocated reduced penalties for drug use, and in the case of marijuana their elimination. The acme of official tolerance of drug use was reached when the Carter administration embraced the commission's findings several years later. President Carter explained, "Penalties against possession of a drug should not be more damaging to an individual than the use of the drug itself."[48] In 1977 his administration also interpreted the Rehabilitation Act of 1973 as providing civil rights benefits to drug addicts, viewing them as "handicapped" based on the "medical and legal consensus that alcoholism and drug addiction are diseases."[49]

A latecomer to the ensuing illegal drug market, but one that made its presence known in a hurry, was crack. Crack's emergence as the staple of the inner-city drug addict was sudden and violent. In 1985 the National Institute on Drug Abuse could find no regular crack users. As the volume of cocaine smuggling grew, the price for a vial of crack eventually dropped to $3. Crack's high addictiveness earned it a captive market fast, as three-fourths of crack users become addicted to the drug after only three uses. With an inelastic demand and plenty of customers, crack was a businessman's delight. By 1990 there were at least eight million casual users of cocaine, including 2.2 million frequent or heavy users, many of them addicted to crack.[50]

Crack's aggressive marketing campaign is perhaps the closest, most valid approximation to the external causes that most criminologists blame for crime; but America's drug problem begs further analysis. Drugs do not, and cannot, "cause" crime. For all of crack's and other drugs' addictiveness, it is axiomatic that almost all of their consumers freely choose to take at least the first puff, snort or injection. Although such choices cannot be made in a vacuum harbored from the forces of persuasion that impinge on all human decisions, in the end addiction results from voluntary conduct. As with gangs, peer pressure is an enormously important contributing factor. Elijah Anderson examined its effects in his study of ghetto subculture:

> The roles of drug pusher, pimp, and [illegal] hustler have become more and more attractive. . . . Among young people there is sometimes a strong desire, induced partly by peer pressure, to try a certain type of "high" just one time. But in such peer groups there are individuals, users and nonusers, who have an interest in "beaming up" or "hooking other people up." In the crowded situation of camaraderie and sociability, one dealer's approach to prospective users is, "Everybody else is doing it, why not you?" There may be mental coercion bordering on strong-arming, and when mixed with peer pressure it can be deadly.[51]

While it is, of course, no consolation to the people who manage to get "hooked" on drugs, for purposes of criminological discussion it is important to acknowledge that drug addicts are, in the final analysis, individually responsible for their plight. The great majority of people, even in the impoverished inner city, overcome peer pressure and other social influences to avoid drug dependency. Drug abuse, then, is a matter of choice—a choice made much harder to resist by peer pressure and the cultural values that mold it, but a choice nonetheless. The scourge of drugs is, in the end, the scourge of free will.

These truths give rise to other questions and concerns. Why, given these facts, is there so much media and criminological attention paid to drugs, as distinct from the crime on which their use is predicated? Drugs are commonly treated by our government and the media as an almost comic-book-style archvillain, the Lex Luthor of this otherwise Platonic paradise. Representative of this tendency was the practice of NBC Nightly News in the late 1980s of using "Guns & Drugs" as a heading for its feature stories on crime. The users of these items, as a result, escaped responsibility for their commerce in them and were denied their rightful minutes of national fame. Similarly, Ramsey Clark's reflections on crime include a chapter titled "Drugs: When Chemistry and Anxiety Meet," the implication being that crime is a product of this apparently uncontrollable synergism.[52] At times this determination to view drugs as our root evil has been even more heated. In 1991 federal drug czar Robert Martinez appeared before the Senate Judiciary Committee to deliver a progress report on the War on Drugs. He informed its members that, while arrests for drug abuse crimes had dropped 14 percent between 1989 and 1990 and the number of Americans using cocaine had fallen 45 percent since 1988, the overall crime rate still had risen 2 percent from 1989 to 1990. This, he felt, presented "solid evidence that the percentage of violent crimes that are drug related is declining, yet violent crime overall is not." Maybe, it seemed, drugs were less cause than effect. The committee's chairman, Joseph Biden, was not persuaded. Instead he insisted, with visible irritation, that the administration recommit itself to curing the "new epidemics" of drugs "appearing on the horizon"—apparently with or without supporting evidence of such policies' effectiveness.[53]

Biden's reaction to such statistics is hardly unusual, and for that reason it deserves our attention. Presumably a certain consensus can be reached over drugs' effects on American life. There is, first of all, an undeniable relationship between crime and drugs. Drug addiction can both lower inhibitions among offenders and spur them on to other crimes to finance their dependency. For example, 56.6 percent of all convicted jail inmates are under the influence of drugs or alcohol at the time of their current offense. Twenty-nine percent are on alcohol only; 15 percent are on drugs only; and 12 percent are on both.[54] Yet this synergism of crime and drugs cannot compel the conclusion that drugs cause crime. Drugs do not ingest themselves. Unlike viruses or other living parasites, drugs reach their human hosts only after being invited, almost always by the same person using them. The user is typically someone who has broken other laws; by definition he has violated at least one by consuming illegal narcotics.

The common assumption that many crimes are committed to underwrite a drug habit is also in error. The Bureau of Justice Statistics reports that only 13.3 percent of jail inmates in 1989 committed their offense "for money to buy drugs."[55] While obviously not an inconsequential amount of crime, this falls well short of a full explanation for the Great Havoc. In criticizing the "presumption [that] . . . using psychoactive drugs causes violent offending," the National Academy of Sciences cited research showing that "only small fractions of adolescent and adult drug users ever commit a 'predatory' offense (i.e., robbery or other crime for gain)."[56] Yet we as a society have come to think of drugs as a primary cause of crime, and their vanquishing as the best route out of the current crime wave. Americans, in fact, now cite "cutting the drug supply" as the "most important thing that can be done to help reduce crime."[57]

The popularity of this vivacious view of drugs seems to owe in roughly equal parts to human nature and the recent course of Western philosophy. It is much easier for us to regard crime as a parasite than as due national punishment for ill-considered living, especially when the latter opinion implies the need for changes in our preferred lifestyle. Supplementing such basic psychology is a venerable philosophy that reflects it. Providing the platform for drugs' current causal reputation is an intellectual conception of drugs as one of several nonhuman entities believed at fault for crime today. To understand these theories, which assign criminal responsibility to a number of seemingly inanimate objects such as drugs, we must once again return to the fecund philosophical disagreements of the ages.

Ancient Athens is not recorded as having much of a drug problem; its citizens, of course, had other, nonnarcotic mental stimulants. One was the animated metaphysical controversy over the distinction between concepts and their real-life representatives. In ancient Greek philosophy, there was a major dispute over a basic idea called a "universal." All parties agreed that a universal was a general concept, a label for describing a category of actions (crime, justice), objects (prisons, firearms) or qualities (truth, courage). For example, the word "drugs" was a universal, describing all the various substances used as medicine or for artificially arousing the senses. But these Athenians and later philosophers parted ways, as usual, over one of Plato's ideas, this time his concept of the universal. Plato's analysis of universals became arguably his most influential contribution to Western philosophy: his theory of Forms or Ideas.

Plato observed the impermanence of individual things and creatures on earth, and from that concluded, a bit queerly, that the universals that described such things were more lasting and real than any member of the classes they encompassed. He believed that universals actually exist; they have a life of their own. More than merely names, universals are actual, real-life entities that exist apart from the things they describe. They are denizens of an airy netherworld somewhere "out there," in an unspecified location, perhaps above the clouds. In his famous Allegory of the Cave, Plato portrayed the world as composed of merely dim, transitory reflections of universals, which he called Forms or Ideas. The wise man of Plato's depiction did not strive to learn about and identify merely beasts and flora here on earth. That he left for Aristotle, the first biologist. Rather, he searched for knowledge of the Forms, of which life on earth was but an inferior image. By Plato's reckoning the Form of Man was more real than Socrates, Leadership more real than Pericles and Water more real than the Aegean Sea. In our society Plato would surely argue that the Form of drugs is more real than the kind sold in pharmacies and on street corners.

Once again, Aristotle had to take issue with his master's hyperbole. He observed that the universal is not an autonomous entity inhabiting the heavens, but is instead simply a human-created idea to describe a class of like objects. As Aristotle saw it, universals are names, nothing more. The class or concept thus defined exists only as its constituent members. Thus, for instance, the Platonic Idea of Man is only a useful, humanly invented label to describe people, or the class of species *Homo sapiens*. It has no separate existence in a heavenly domain, and cannot be blamed for the mischief committed by man with a lowercase *m*.

Although Aristotle's refutation of Plato's extreme rationalism guided Rome for many centuries, Europeans of the Middle Ages were denied the same valuable inheritance. Aristotle's works were not generally known and available during most of medieval times; Arab scholars reintroduced his writings to Europe in the twelfth century. Plato, as a result, enjoyed centuries of unquestioned dominance. By the time Aristotle's critique of Plato's theory of Forms was discovered, Plato's views dominated the most powerful institution in Europe, the Catholic Church. Defenders of the Church's prerogatives claimed, based on Plato's investigations, that the Church was a genuine spiritual entity, distinct and additional to the sum of her human associates. Moreover, as the repository of the Holy Spirit, the Church was endowed with superhuman qualities and powers beyond those of her constituent adherents. Interpreting as literal Saint Paul's description of the Church as the flesh-and-bones bride of Christ, the Church's advocates rejected the more straightforward conception of the Church as merely a divinely guided human institution, one with all the potential frailties of its members. Martin Luther and others would find out that the Platonic defense of the Church had more than theological motivations. The Church's Form supplied a rug under which the sins committed by its human agents could be swept, thus helping them and their employer avoid criticism and reforms.[58]

An alternative philosophy sprang up within the Church to salvage its unique divine status while still making sense of planet Earth, a theory called nominalism. In the fourteenth century a nominalist English priest named William of Ockham questioned the layers of abstractions and theoretical devices used to justify the Church's broad powers, powers that seemed excessive even to one who had been well educated and housed because of them. He scrutinized this intellectual state of affairs with a theory that he boiled down to one famous maxim: "Entities should not be multiplied beyond need." Ockham meant that, as a general rule, the simplest explanation is to be preferred to more complex ones. In particular, a universal was but a "sign of several things,"[59] a name for describing classes of real, concrete objects. These were the only entities whose existence one could know of without the valuable but separate assistance of faith. One must seek the simplest analysis of objects. The simplest description of the Church, for example, was that of an institution of men rather than an abstraction, although faith allowed one to assume additionally that God guided the Church even despite the overexuberance of some of its proponents. Thus forged, this principle, posthumously called Ockham's Razor, cut down to size the misconceptions that the Church inherited from Plato.

Today, Father William's lessons forgotten, we Americans have relapsed into Plato's beguiling theories in our analysis of the nation's drug problem. Just as the medieval Church was intellectually dependent on a Platonic conception to excuse its (sometimes literal) indulgences, we too are inclined to call forth the Platonic Form of Drugs to explain away things that we would prefer not to confront. Thus the talk of drugs as having the same sort of separate, sentient existence, able to happen upon certain individuals and cause the antisocial behavior that results. The same Platonic use is made of the concept of poverty, with much the same, if often unconscious, motivation.

This illusion endangers society because such theories create an amnesty for offenders. This view of drugs allows us, for a time at least, to avoid the nettlesome business of determining criminal blame. But ultimately crime in America cannot be seriously remedied until we cut through these misperceptions. Let us reiterate: drug *usage* is directly related to crime, both by financially encouraging criminality and by reducing internal inhibitions. But drugs do not themselves cause people to murder, rape and steal from one another. For example, in Great Britain, where most heroin addicts are registered with state methadone programs, a large number of drug addicts still live a life of crime.[60] We must also reprove those who would use drugs and other Forms as scapegoats for criminal activity under the wrongful assumption that drugs hurt no one but their users. The harmfulness of this delusion is exposed by its fruits. As James Q. Wilson observes, "crack-dependent people are, like heroin addicts, individuals who regularly victimize their children by neglect, their spouses by improvidence, their employers by lethargy, and their coworkers by carelessness."[61] Certainly the thirty thousand to fifty thousand crack babies born annually would not regard their physical deformities and neurological damage as a tolerable consequence of "self-regarding" conduct, to use Mill's increasingly familiar terminology.

While some on the Left and Center have been using drugs as a rhetorical aegis against intellectual candor, the Right has, at the same time, been confronting an equally significant identity crisis in its response to rising drug-related crime rates. When the full dimensions of the drug crisis began to register in the late 1960s, it had been almost a full century since a branch of rights-based liberalism succeeded in what Clinton Rossiter has called the "Great Train Robbery of our intellectual history."[62] In the nineteenth century, as wealthy Americans worked to consolidate their gains from the Industrial Revolution, they sought to solidify their natural influence on the American Right—which has traditionally been concerned with preserving the spoils of economic victory—by infusing America's rightist ideology with an intellectual defense of their privileged status. The result, as explained previously, was American libertarianism. This has become the radical individualism of the Right, and the one that appeals to the American public today because, unlike ultraindividualism, it omits an apology for criminals. With its distaste for an imperious government, libertarianism is naturally attractive to American conservatives, who seek to conserve the Founders' legacy of limited government. Less noticed today is the fact that limited government, as understood by the Founders, bears little resemblance to the State envisioned by modern libertarians. Libertarianism managed to attach the concept of limited government to a materialistic theory of economic rights. Today the heirs of this theory seek to extend the rubric of limited government even further, to safeguard certain values and lifestyles such as sexual liberation. Matters that were formerly subject to community control are now, by the modern libertarian's reckoning, matters of private decision-making beyond the rightful reach of the society that may be adversely affected by them.

Libertarianism was unable to rise above suspicions on the Right until the late twentieth century. The materialism of our day, largely a result of the unprecedented American prosperity of the post-World War II era, has required a philosophy to validate it. Modern rights-based liberalism has not been equal to this task. This is because rights-based liberalism ambivalently sets the capitalist economy's atomistic forces in motion, yet expects the winners to relinquish a large part of their earnings for community purposes, even though the community that remains is unable to accomplish much. In addition to filling this philosophical niche, libertarianism, the antigovernment philosophy, has also benefited from the current widespread perception of corruption in all levels of government.

Among libertarianism's most celebrated recent ventures is its intellectual defense of the individual's right to use drugs. And do libertarians not, based on the current clichés, have a valid point? If "limited government," as applied to private personal behavior, means anything, does it not encompass the right to use substances that do not directly cause violent harm to others? Mill thought so. He provided the explicit theoretical basis for this position by urging the repeal of the nineteenth-century prohibitions on the importation of opium into China. He contended that these drug laws, or "interferences" in "self-regarding" conduct, "are objectionable, not as infringements of the liberty of the producer or seller, but on that of the buyer."[63] Modern libertarians fairly interpreted that to mean that drug dealers in the ghetto could and should be imprisoned, but suburbanites had an absolute right to consume their products.

The libertarian position on drug laws, in fact, lays threadbare the brutish core of the underlying philosophy. The growth of drug-related crime in the ghetto, detonated by the market forces servicing a mostly white demand for drugs, has imposed the worst suffering and brutality suffered by Americans since slavery. Yet libertarians, in sincere but sobering fashion, do not relent in their call for abolishing drug statutes in the name of limited government. Undoubtedly the only reason why this view does not hold far greater currency today is the fear of criminal invasion from the addicted lower class; there is little else in the popular culture today that would countenance such community curbs on private behavior. In contrast, and to their great credit, many on the Left seem to regret the disorder issuing from the implementation of this philosophy, even though, for social atomists, libertarianism is a kindred line of thought. Sometimes social atomists try to make amends, in effect, by redistributing money to the victims through government spending. By comparison libertarianism, an offshoot of Hobbes's classical liberalism, sheds what has historically been the Left's most appealing quality, concern for the less fortunate, in favor of a social Darwinist ethic that holds that compassion is for the faint of heart. If the poor can't handle drugs or the other pleasures of modern, liberated life, that's their problem. My body and my rights come first. This, then, is the dishonorable soul of the libertarian philosophy. Libertarianism is politically rationalized selfishness; it is liberalism without the guilt.

Many of the chief intellectual defenders of libertarian drug laws offer nonlibertarian arguments, but alongside an ethic of radical individualism. The most renowned member of this school is Nobel Prize-winning economist Milton Friedman. In an article published in *Newsweek* in 1972, Friedman based his case for legalizing heroin on two grounds, one of which was explicitly libertarian. Economically, he said, the costs of today's drug prohibitions far outweigh their benefits; and philosophically, government is obliged to stay out of a person's personal choice about whether to use drugs. In support of his latter contention, Friedman offered a paraphrasing of Mill:

> On ethical grounds, do we have the right to use the machinery of government to prevent an individual from becoming an alcoholic or a drug addict? . . . [F]or responsible adults, I, for one, would answer no. Reason with the potential addict, yes. Tell him the consequences, yes. Pray for and with him, yes. But I believe that we have no right to use force, directly or indirectly, to prevent a fellow man from committing suicide, let alone from drinking alcohol or taking drugs.[64]

Friedman even suggested that legalizing drugs might not increase the number of addicts, since "forbidden fruit is attractive, particularly to the young." James Q. Wilson noted that Friedman's "uncharacteristic lapse from the obvious implications of price theory" also overlooked the fact that peer pressure, rather than the drug's price, is the main creator of addicts.[65] Other notables on the Right urging drug legalization include William F. Buckley and former Secretary of State George Shultz, pillars of the American political scene who support legalization for various reasons.

With the Right embroiled in a civil war and the Left searching the Platonic clouds for criminal pardons, the nation's drug enforcement efforts would seem a tragic waste of life and taxes. We find unexpected encouragement in the fact that America actually significantly reduced heroin use in the mid-1970s, and marijuana and cocaine use by the late 1980s. The number of heroin addicts has essentially held steady for two decades, as the pool of heroin addicts is contained and grows older.[66] Marijuana and cocaine abuse peaked in the mid-1980s, immediately following the pivotal, long-overdue event in the War on Drugs: the decision of many Hollywood celebrities to join the "just say no" antidrug abstinence movement. As these role models of cool among American youth produced commercials discouraging drug use, the rate of usage instantly plummeted. There were some limitations to this enterprise, to be sure. Children were urged to forswear drugs not because they were immoral or antisocial, but because they were unhealthy—"they threaten *you* and *your body*." Overall, the relativistic approach has worked. By 1986 polls of high school and college students revealed a substantial drop in use and tolerance of drugs, one which more or less continues to the present.[67] It remains uncertain, however, whether the celebrity-dictated peer pressure that now considers it uncool to take drugs will hold fast; relativism is not known for its absolute assurances. And indeed juvenile drug usage appears to be on the rise again, even as the current optimism has led to an 80 percent staff reduction for the Office of National Drug Control Policy.[68]

Other recent antidrug successes have come from improved law enforcement. Wilson noted that heroin use dropped in inner cities because of an increase in legal penalties and heightened knowledge of physiological sanctions. When these were combined with the interruption of the opiate supply from foreign countries, the recruitment of new heroin addicts was made much more difficult. Wilson discounts the role of treatment, observing that it could not explain the drop in the number of *new* users. He notes that while some drug-dependent people genuinely want treatment and should receive it, "there are far more who want only short-term help after a bad crash; once stabilized and bathed, they are back on the streets again, hustling."[69] Even many addicts who genuinely solicit treatment drop out soon after enrollment, since they often have short time horizons and limited patience, which work against such long-term commitment.

Until the modern self-obsession that makes drugs irresistible dissipates, society will have to rely on stiffer law enforcement and penalties to reduce drug-related violence. Increased border patrols have puny marginal returns. A study by the RAND Corporation has estimated that more than doubling the interdiction rate would increase the street price of most illegal drugs by only 10 percent.[70] But the salutary effects of legal sanctions on drug use are clear, both from what we know of human nature generally and from the way people have responded to libertarian drug policies. The harsh end result of legalizing drugs has been documented in libertarianism's homeland, Great Britain. There, liberalized drug laws have allowed drug addiction to skyrocket, an increase of thirtyfold during the 1960s alone.[71] Rather than weakening drug laws, America must make its criminal justice system more efficient in processing and punishing drug offenders. Toward that end, the elimination of the Fourth Amendment's exclusionary rule would be a special boon to prosecutors of these crimes, since drug charges are highly subject to dismissal under this rather draconian rule of evidence.[72]

Drug legalization represents perhaps the ultimate surrender to the suicide of libertarianism. Such a policy would only marginally reduce crime, since few offenses are committed to maintain a drug dependency. The pathologies in the ghetto that the drug market has reinforced, and that provide the true link between drugs and crime, cannot be bottled up through such legislation. Legalization would sentence millions of unborn children to hideous birth defects, and society to an accelerated undoing. Even with the current prohibitions, the number of young foster children who were exposed to cocaine while in the womb grew from 17 percent to 55 percent in just five years, from 1986 to 1991.[73] Contrary to libertarian claims, the lure of the drug trade is not irresistible to lower-income people; they rebuffed it and comparable vices for centuries. The role of religion in this should also not be discounted. Religion has persistently proved successful at deterring amoral entrepreneurship when given the appropriate social imprimatur and amplified by society's elite. The drug trade is one market that must, and can, be largely shut down.

This, of course, will take more than stepped-up law enforcement. It means changing people's minds, about what they are willing to buy and the role they want for their government. This war cannot be won by a clash of arms. It will be won individual by individual, in the lonely heights of each person's conscience—not by accepting as inevitable something that is not, nor by searching the skies for a "cause" that, at least at last report, is not to be found.

CHAPTER EIGHT

The Rough Justice of Black Crime

Yes, I will pull off that liberal's halo that he spends such efforts cultivating!

—Malcolm X

Black Americans are a wonderfully contradictory people. In this, as in perhaps most other respects, they are the most American of Americans. Our popular culture, disproportionately a product of black folkways and artistry, abounds with examples. The United States, and thus the world, pulsate to the rhythms of black-inspired popular music, or rock and roll, music that inspires the globe's masses to lofty hymns of love, brotherhood and freedom, but that, in its paeans to predatory sex and violence, sometimes makes parents quake as much as dictators. The same African-American entertainers author some of the most profane lyrics in contemporary music, yet, unlike most white performers, reverently thank God for their success at music awards programs. Other, more important paradoxes present themselves. The same generation of black Americans offered the world one of its greatest peacemakers,

Dr. King, and, simultaneously, history's highest levels of violent crime. Blacks, the most tenaciously spiritual of Americans, have today given in in large numbers to the worst of what they, as devout Christians, readily recognize as sins. Drugs, promiscuity, materialism and, most alarming to whites, belligerent selfishness in the form of street crime all have reached unprecedented heights in a community seemingly overwhelmed by the terrible, and occasionally bloody, charms of extreme individualism.

We are all uncomfortable talking about the plague of African-American crime, and nowhere is this sensitivity more understandable than among African-Americans themselves. None of us enjoys hearing about our faults, either personally or as a people when, like blacks, we retain a strong group identity. Matters are not helped, of course, when politicians and celebrities manipulate these racial sensitivities to further their careers or to inoculate themselves from criticism. That the reasons for America's high black crime rates have only rarely been discussed forthrightly in recent years is only to be expected, given the emotional whirlpool in which such debate takes place.

Yet this silence must be shattered if black Americans are to regain their former, undisputed status as the moral paragons of a stable Judeo-Christian society. For what the politicians and prominent intelligentsia of all races are afraid to admit, perhaps in part because of their culpability in its creation, is this singular social fact: black Americans are fast becoming a feared race. This is due almost entirely to the rise in black criminality, and whites' inability to confront the real origins of this growth. Black Americans have always suffered a uniquely intransigent bigotry from whites throughout our history, a brand of racism different in kind from that visited upon America's other minorities. Things have not changed much in this regard. Today, the newest excuse for this unique racial bias is whites' growing fear of black crime. Whites, themselves enchanted with materialism and radical individualism, fear for their lives and property from the gathering storm of black anarchy. Thus emerges the white stereotype of the African-American criminal, which serves as a convenient scapegoat for whites' sensible fear of the crime fomented by libertarian, Anglo-Saxon ideas. Stereotypes, we must note, do not materialize out of thin air. They always have a kernel of truth, which, when it grows, is selfishly twisted into a tangled mass onto which its cultivators project their own most unbearable sins. At present the fact of rampant black crime is used for stereotypically viewing blacks as a uniquely lawless population. This makes them nicely severable from white folk for crime control purposes, both theoretically and physically.

There is no denying that black Americans have yielded to the current radical individualism and accompanying anomie and violence at a rate far exceeding that of whites. Homicide has become the main cause of death for black Americans between the ages of fifteen and twenty-five. Black men of that age are more likely to die from homicide than were U.S. soldiers in the Vietnam War.[1] An African-American male between the ages of fifteen and nineteen is now three times more likely to die from a shooting than from an illness. Black men in inner-city neighborhoods are less likely to reach the age of sixty-five than men in Bangladesh, one of the world's poorest nations.[2] In 1990 a study by the Sentencing Project did much to unwittingly promote these stereotypes despite the stated aims of its sponsors. The study found that 23 percent, or almost one out of four, black males aged twenty through twenty-nine are currently being punished in some fashion by the criminal justice system—in prison, in jail or on probation or parole.[3] This percentage was almost a third higher than the number of black males enrolled in college. The researchers despaired that young black men are "an imprisoned generation," and hoped that their findings would spur government officials to soften penal policies.[4] Instead, their figures merely confirmed long-standing suspicions and, it is true, prejudices among many whites. A poll of white Americans a year later found that 56 percent *admitted* that they thought African-Americans to be more "violence-prone" than whites,[5] a figure that does not include the undoubtedly large number of whites who would not confide such thoughts to a pollster.

The crime disparity between the races becomes more pronounced when given a broader statistical context. Blacks, who constitute 12 percent of the U.S. population, account for 55 percent of all murders; and, lest we forget, an almost equal percentage of murder victims.[6] Even taking into account blacks' lower average age and other mitigating factors, blacks are overrepresented, based on their percentage of the overall population, by a factor of nearly three to one among those arrested for property crimes and four to one for violent crimes.[7] More telling still was a 1970 study by the California Finance Department. Using a regression analysis that measured the crime rate in California's fifty-eight counties, while controlling for variables such as poverty, education and unemployment, the study found that the most reliable predictor of high crime rates was the number of black Americans living in the area. The correlation factor for this variable was .7, meaning that 70 percent of the crime difference between any two areas could be predicted by the size of the local African-American population. Factors such as poverty and unemployment correlated weakly or even negatively.[8]

These statistics, however, give a very selective view of things, and we must guard against substituting a rash "Aha!" for a more searching analysis. Racism endures in America because far too many Americans are unwilling to look beneath the surface, both of a person's skin and of the above numbers. Race is merely the most physically obvious correlative between crime in America and its agents. Our confusion is compounded when social scientists, instead of looking beyond such superficial explanations, simply attribute black crime to white racism, and accuse those who depart from this assumption of being guilty of racism themselves. The high point of this mind-set was the Kerner Commission's report in 1968, which averred that poverty and racism were the chief "causes" of the sixties ghetto riots, and that "[w]hite racism is essentially responsible" for the turmoil.[9] Scholars who dispute this dogma and examine the hypothetical link between crime and racial characteristics too often find such research censured and construed as per se proof of racial bad faith. This is a great pity. For, by ignoring the stark disproof of a genetic racial relationship to crime, social scientists have passed up a chance to slay a stereotype.

To the extent that this inquiry is restricted to the standard dichotomy of genes versus environment, the evidence zealously supports the latter. The case for a black genetic tendency toward criminality falls apart when one considers the crime rate among black Africans. There, the homicide rate is roughly the same as in western Europe, and well below the rate among either white or black Americans. The black American homicide rate is three to five times that of black Africans.[10]

An intriguing alternative hypothesis about the causes of black crime comes from renowned social scientist Charles Silberman. Silberman tenders this view in *Criminal Violence, Criminal Justice,* a book that, Wilson and Herrnstein noted, "received much attention" from many in academia and the press.[11] Silberman infers from the high level of African-American crime a racial motivation, one flowing from blacks' unique desire to retaliate against whites for the racial evils inflicted against earlier generations of blacks. "Beware the Day They Change Their Minds," Silberman titles the chapter expounding this view; and as Silberman sees it, "blacks *have* changed their minds" from one of silent submission to genuine racial warfare. Silberman bases much of his analysis on black folk tales such as the Br'er Rabbit stories of the hitherto kindly Uncle Remus, which he interprets as allegories of criminal vengeance against whites. But while he elucidates this thesis at length, Silberman omits any practical recommendations for dealing with this rage, even assuming its causal underpinnings. His only suggestion is for white society to effectively try to pay off black Americans so that they will behave themselves, which is to be accomplished through more money (government spending) and rights: "If we are to reduce the level of criminal violence, we will have to pay the price."[12] If that does not work, the best advice he can give to crime-battered Americans is, in essence, to duck.

Like most of his writings, Silberman's thesis is intelligent food for thought; but its creativity gets the better of him. Even if his proposed Great White Bribe in the form of expanded social programs and rights could reduce black criminality, it no longer seems politically feasible. Despite today's high crime rates, white Americans would likely respond to this proposed reparation as the first generation of Americans did to similar demands by the Barbary pirates, that is, by resolving to spend millions for defense but not one cent for tribute. Moreover, Silberman's conception of black crime as racial retribution is incinerated at the approach of one stubbornly searing fact: most crimes committed by blacks are committed against other blacks. Ninety-three percent of all black murder victims, for instance, are murdered by other blacks. African-American criminals in 1991 murdered 691 whites and 5,035 members of their own race.[13] If blacks are in fact collectively trying to revenge their ancestors, their aim is unbelievably terrible.

Silberman's essential mistake was systematizing and stating explicitly what many other scholars and criminologists had previously hidden in cluttered dogma—namely, that racism causes black crime. His honest theorizing exposes this assumption to factual scrutiny. Interestingly, despite the discernible defects in Silberman's approach, the core of his theory has recently become bipartisan. An important critique of modern race relations from a right-wing, social Darwinist perspective also adopts, and seeks to prove, Silberman's view. In *Paved with Good Intentions*, published in 1993, Jared Taylor quotes Silberman in support of his scathing thesis that black crime against whites is racially motivated.[14]

But this consensus conceals some refractory facts, facts that demand their moment in the limelight. For instance, we find that the correlation between black crime and racism—at least its most powerful and empirically identifiable form, lawful or *de jure* racism—is, if anything, precisely the opposite of the outcome anticipated by Silberman. The great rise in black crime, it will be recalled, occurred in the early 1960s, contemporaneous with the civil rights movement. The repeal of legally institutionalized racism culminated in the Voting Rights Act of 1965. Although laws can never eradicate sin, one would expect that the federal prohibition of the most glaring legal prop to racism, and society's formal condemnation of such attitudes through law, would have reduced racism at least a fraction during the 1960s. That being the case, under the racism-causes-crime thesis, black crime rates should have dropped perceptibly. Instead, they soared. Indeed, if one were to apply social science's conventional modes of analysis to these data, one would have to extrapolate that a reduction in open racism actually "caused" an *increase* in black crime. Even under the most generous interpretation of the data, black crime's rise has been entirely independent of racism, the Platonic form that, like drugs and poverty, can be no excuse for crime despite the able efforts of its intellectual handlers.

All the same, in attempting to pinpoint the reasons for the unique extent of crime among African-Americans, we must investigate whether there is at least some unique explanatory trait or cluster of traits to distinguish blacks as especially susceptible to criminality. Again, racism will not suffice, since we know that other minorities have suffered at least comparable intolerance at times. Though never slaves, Mexican-Americans were virtual peons for over a century; Japanese immigrants were subject to housing and school segregation, not to mention forced relocation during World War II; Chinese immigrants were *de facto* indentured servants of railroads and similar industries; American Indians did not have it so good. But one thing that blacks did suffer from, as distinct from other minorities, was a unique Southern subculture that patronized black-on-black crime. In his classic 1937 study of Southern society, John Dollard noted how the white supremacist establishment did not punish black intraracial crime as severely as black-on-white or white-on-white offenses. He observed that "Negroes are not nearly so severely punished as whites would be for the same crimes." Southern authorities seemed to believe that it was a "merit of southern white persons" that they were "lenient and indulgent" toward black-on-black criminals. "The result is that the individual Negro is, to a considerable degree, outside the protection of white law . . . [which] leads to the frontier psychology . . . and to its consequent idealization of violence." This "immunity" bestowed on black criminals had an invidious motive: "the value of Negro disunity from the standpoint of the master caste."[15]

Southern white supremacy thus reduced generations of blacks to the State of Nature, with all the legacy of criminality that that entails. That black Americans have survived this regime, which in important respects is worse than the oppression endured by their enslaved ancestors, is powerful testimony to their strength as a race. If Southern blacks migrating to Northern industrial cities after World War II took these criminal attitudes with them, such is at least understandable, if still not pardonable. And it is, if nothing else, a fascinating irony that this repugnant, unconstitutional Southern regime has found admirers among ultraindividualist intellectuals.[16] Today, far too many criminologists and judges view black Americans as still, in a sense, unworthy of equal enforcement of the law. Their racism-causes-crime thesis means in practice that the worst members of the black race must be intellectually pardoned and spared punishment, and quietly returned to the black community when public outrage has subsided. The grievous end result is a black American society that, after surviving 350 years of racist cruelty, is now literally dying.

This ghetto environment is, of course, reported on and fretted over by the white middle class. But the emerging majority of whites who accept the philosophical roots of these conditions, often out of shortsighted egoism, are now watching the same phenomena take hold over their own children. It remains to be seen if they respond more effectively to these latter events, although, judging from current trends, there is not much reason to hope for a better outcome in the suburbs. In the meantime the criminal monsters of the inner city are taking aim at the white libertarian authors of their predicament. To date, they have not been easily appeased.

THE TROUBLE WITH MR. CHARLIE

Given this array of ill-informed intellectual analysts, black Americans would do well to consult prominent thinkers of their own race in seeking to better understand the reasons for the crisis of the inner city. The best place to look for a coherent explanation of black crime is, it turns out, a black criminal—that is, a reformed one, who is therefore committed to preserving the free society in which he lives. No one appears better suited for this task than Malcolm X. Malcolm was a self-described "hustler" in his youth, and his conviction for a string of burglaries eventually landed him in prison. There he converted to Islam. His experience as both a black American ex-con and a Muslim gave him an unusually insightful vantage point for inspecting the ills of the black community, and for offering a compelling explanation of African-American crime. Like the formulations of all serious thinkers, Malcolm's philosophy— and his was a philosophy—is complex and open to different interpretations. And, like all revolutionaries, he is sometimes inclined to sweeping execration of his opponents. There is nonetheless much wisdom to be gleaned here.

Malcolm X saw two primary, home-grown foes of the black community: the black "leadership" and the street hustler. He saved most of his criticism for the former, assuming that the latter, although morally responsible for their actions, largely reflect the values determined by society's elite. Malcolm believed the then-emerging black "leadership" (he embraced the term with derisive quotation marks) to reflect what he regarded as the dishonorable tendency among many blacks to imitate whites, particularly upper-class whites, and adopt their values. He told of how blacks who worked around whites in upscale environs "considered themselves superior" to other blacks, "prid[ing] themselves on being incomparably more 'cultured,' 'cultivated,' 'dignified,' and better off than their black brethren down in the ghetto. . . . Under the pitiful misapprehension that it would make them 'better,' these . . . Negroes were breaking their backs trying to imitate white people." Malcolm recounted how he, like other African-Americans following the example of these neighbors, was captive to this mentality for a time. He even "joined that multitude of Negro men and women in America who . . . violate and mutilate their God-given bodies to try to look 'pretty' by white standards," "conking" his hair with harsh chemicals and "literally burning my flesh to have it look like a white man's hair."[17]

When black political figures rose to the forefront of the civil rights movement, Malcolm X believed most of them to be the same people who, prior to this racial awakening, had imitated whites and implicitly belittled their own people. He even felt their relationship to the black masses to be essentially the same as that between the "house" and "yard" slaves on white plantations. "[I]f you make a list of the biggest Negro 'leaders,' so-called," Malcolm insisted, "then you've named the ones who began to attack us 'field' Negroes who were sounding *insane,* talking that way about 'good massa.'" He saw this new "Uncle Tom" as a *"professional* Negro . . . by that I mean his profession is being a Negro for the white man." (Emphasis in original.) "Black 'leaders' were out in the public eye—to be seen by the Negroes for whom they were supposed to be fighting the white man. But obscurely, behind the scenes, was a white boss—a president, or board chairman, or some other title, pulling the real strings."[18]

These whites, in turn, were typically "domineering, ego-ridden whites." Their "characteristic design permitted the white man to feel 'noble' about throwing crumbs to the black man, instead of feeling guilty about the local community's system of cruelly exploiting Negroes." Malcolm tarred these whites with too broad a brush, calling them "liberals" rather than the more narrow, correct term "libertarians"; but he made his point all the same. He encouraged these "liberals" and the black "leaders" they influenced to concentrate instead on improving the lives of blacks in the inner city, to "remove so many of them from the relief and welfare rolls, which created laziness, and which deteriorated the ghettoes into steadily worse places for humans to live."[19]

What Malcolm X seemed to identify was white libertarianism's corrosion of the ghetto with the help of black "'leaders,' so-called." He, like most blacks to that time, rejected the white libertarian lifestyle and values, and he urged black society's upper echelon to do the same. Malcolm believed upper-class blacks guilty of forsaking the distinct African-American culture, one developed during their three and a half centuries of tortured but morally exemplary existence as a people. Since the lower classes of any race usually esteem the lifestyle of their upper crust, it was natural that ghetto blacks would both mirror the self-obsessed values of their upper class and adopt the white values that this elite promoted. The black community's subsequent pathologies arose, then, from the imposition of an alien white radical individualism on a communal, deeply spiritual people. Eventually, lower-income black Americans yielded in large numbers to this aggressive egocentrism. In essence, the higher level of black crime that resulted was due to blacks' overcompensation in their attempt to imitate whites, much as the unpopular kid in school tries too hard to get the attention and admiration of his more popular classmates by cutting up in class. At the implicit suggestion of upper-class blacks and well-off white libertarians, blacks were putting into effect chaotic, radical-individualist theories that whites had not had the courage to fully execute themselves. Black crime, by Malcolm's theory, was a result of blacks trying too hard to be white.

Another distinctly white phenomenon exacerbated these social problems. Malcolm noted one white vice that especially repulsed him as a devout Muslim—sexual liberation. As a hustler he had received firsthand "schooling about the cesspool morals of the white man," mainly through his mingling with prostitutes. "And then as I got deeper into my own life of evil, I saw the white man's morals with my own eyes." What Malcolm saw was a debauchery that far exceeded anything practiced by even the most wretched members of his race. "This hypocritical white man will talk about the Negro's 'low morals.' But who has the world's lowest morals if not whites?" He added, pointedly: "And not only that, but the 'upper-class' whites?" He illustrated his point by recounting a recent newspaper story about a group of "suburban New York City white housewives and mothers operating as a professional call-girl ring." He also noted the furtive institution of sexual wife-swapping among white men. Malcolm concluded, "I have never heard of anything like that being done by Negroes, even Negroes who live in the worst ghettoes and alleys and gutters."[20]

Is this stinging indictment fair? To determine this, we must place Malcolm's beliefs in a broader philosophical landscape. While not an expert in British political philosophy, Malcolm X seems to have sensed that what we recognize as Anglo-Saxon libertarianism was consuming the black ghetto. The "cesspool morals" he deplored were the essence of sexual liberation, the theories popularized by Freud that have resonated among Europeans and European-Americans more than among any of the world's other peoples. These values are also prominent in America's white-dominated mass media, whose programming often promotes radical individualism if only because explicit violence and sex generate higher revenue. Black Muslims' denunciations today of "low-down Hollywood producers" are echoes of Malcolm's contumely. In contrast, white Americans have resisted the encroachment of these values with much less ardor—which is only to be expected, since these attitudes issue from the philosophies of white European theorists. Black Americans' retention of traditional views on social issues and religion bears witness to this growing racial divide, even though, as with

American society as a whole, many African-Americans fall short of these ideals. There are many specific examples and evidence of these trends. One was the ouster in 1993 of the head of the New York City schools, Joseph Fernandez, because of his support of libertarian sex instruction for schoolchildren of all ages. Although it was Mary Cummins, a white woman, who led the opposition, it was inner-city blacks who provided much if not most of the manpower and votes in the school board elections.[21]

In view of these developments, the average African-American, contrary to popular stereotypes, would actually appear spiritually superior to the average white American. Blacks, that is, still look upon crime and the behavior that fosters it as the socially ruinous sins that they are, rather than morally neutral personal decisions beyond the proper scope of community action or concern. This recognition allows them a way out of their condition. Whites, on the other hand, have invested centuries of intellectual effort in declaring God dead, and in explaining antisocial behavior as either the result of psychological disorders or a means to a more personally fulfilling life. Thus, to oversimplify, blacks have guilty consciences; whites, increasingly, have no conscience at all. This distinction is very much like the one Dostoevsky drew between the Russian peasant and the aristocracy of his time:

> . . . though the peasants are corrupted and cannot renounce their filthy sin, yet they know it is cursed by God and that they do wrong in sinning. So that our people still believe in righteousness, have faith in God and weep tears of devotion.
>
> It is different with the upper classes. They, following science [i.e., materialism], want to base justice on reason alone, but not with Christ, as before, and they have already proclaimed that there is no crime, that there is no sin. And that's consistent, for if you have no God what is the meaning of crime?[22]

Blacks' social faux pas, then, is merely pursuing these shared libertarian ideals with more gusto than whites. Whites err in viewing the ensuing crime as racially motivated. It's nothing personal; in the war of all against all, that's life. By the same token, although it is not intended as such by the pathetic inner-city criminals who act out the tenets of European philosophies by brutalizing blacks and whites alike, black-on-white crime does embody a certain amount of rough justice. Black crime is chickens coming home to roost for white libertarian America.

Malcolm X's insights are seemingly seconded by another pro-found source, the brilliant allegory of black crime underlying Richard Wright's classic novel *Native Son*. Wright describes how Bigger Thomas, a young ghetto black man living in Chicago before World War II, becomes a subject of sociological research for two young Marxists from the white upper class. The two insist that Bigger accompany them as they tour his neighborhood, mainly so that they can show their sympathy with the lower class. Bigger finds the treatment patronizing. One of the two whites, Mary Dalton, is the daughter of the slumlord who owns Bigger's tenement. Wright depicts Bigger's feelings toward his new, tenacious companions: "He felt naked, transparent; he felt that this white man, having helped to put him down, having helped to deform him, held him up now to look at him and be amused. At that moment he felt toward Mary and Jan a dumb, cold, and inarticulate hate."[23]

The novel's denouement occurs one night when Bigger has to help a drunk Mary to her bedroom. As he lifts her into her bed, he panics on hearing what he thinks is someone approaching her room. The fear of being found alone in a white girl's bedroom paralyzes him. To keep her quiet and avoid being caught, Bigger stuffs a pillow in her face, accidentally suffocating her. After his offense is discovered, he is eventually apprehended. In the end, Bigger is sentenced to death. Although Wright's powerful story is, again, subtle and subject to different interpretations, one of them is an evident metaphor for the pathologies of the ghetto—by implication a laboratory for social-atomist intellectuals.

Often worsening this state of affairs are the black officials whom Malcolm X held up for special criticism. There are indeed far too many black politicians and celebrities who have adopted the radical individualism denounced by Malcolm and, traditionally, by African-Americans. In doing so these figures generally have accepted the standard principles of libertarianism as decreed by white intellectuals, but with a handful of explosive additions. Under this philosophy, what W.E.B. Du Bois correctly called the "ancient African chastity" of blacks[24] has yielded to sexual liberation, with the result of high black illegitimacy rates, overwhelmed single mothers and pandemic juvenile crime. The welfare system, as Malcolm saw, also hastens this process. Many prominent black figures have, for their part, taken Mill's libertarianism to a new dimension. They sometimes omit his proscription of crime per se in favor of theories that excuse black offenders on racial grounds, even those who impudently sack the neighborhoods of their white tutors.

There has even, at times, been something of a merger of black leaders and criminal offenders. This union, in fact, has yielded the most powerful African-American criminal syndicate in America. Some of the most prominent black political figures of the 1960s founded Los Angeles's two most powerful gangs, the Bloods and the Crips. Prior to the Watts Riots of 1965, the gangs that operated in L.A.'s black neighborhoods had been satisfied with small-scale, uncoordinated criminality, such as random thefts of lunch money and other petty offenses. With the riots came a new generation of offenders who saw, like Clausewitz, that their actions ultimately carried political ramifications. These figures appealed to racial solidarity in assembling the smaller, scattered black gangs into two larger units, uniting them through calls to resist the predominantly white law enforcement authorities. From these arose two principal groups, which, because of the atomism of their business, inevitably became enemies: the Black Panthers and US. One former Black Panther functionary, Earl Anthony, observed that both cliques "had been gang fighters long before they were nationalists," making armed conflict only a matter of time.[25] By 1967 members of the two gang superpowers were frequently engaged in shoot-outs in Southeast Los Angeles as they battled to broaden their power base. In 1969 two US members shot and killed two Black Panther members on the UCLA campus, as they fought for control of the university's Afro-American Studies Center. The breach between the two gangs erupted into open warfare.

So began the Bloods and the Crips, which are the direct descendants of these two Black Power cells.[26] They quickly earned a reputation for being more brutal than their competitors, and thus flourished in the power vacuum they created. By the mid-1980s this sanguinary investment paid off, as these gangs became the chief drug suppliers to Los Angeles's ghettos. The only time since that they have reunited was following the Rodney King Riots, when they temporarily joined forces to declare "open season on LAPD."[27] The founders of these gangs have gone on to various futures. Huey Newton, one of the more famous Black Panthers, was shot to death in August 1989 in Oakland while selling crack. His murder came at the hands of a "small-time drug dealer" hoping to solidify his position in a drug-running syndicate,[28] an intriguing coda to a life that included, among Newton's various crimes, manslaughter of a policeman and embezzlement. Other such figures have diversified, and some are still commonly referred to as black "leaders." Bobby Seale is a professional speaker in frequent demand for sensitivity training against racism. At one Washington seminar he told the student audience that he was available to plan strategy, secure bail money or "when you need some guns."[29] Sonny Carson, out of prison after serving a sentence for kidnapping, is now a Brooklyn "community organizer" leading the boycott of Korean grocery stores. Carson has pledged that "in the future, there'll be funerals, not boycotts."[30]

In the tradition of Malcolm X, Professor Walter Williams of George Mason University has disputed the very use of the term "black leadership" to describe such people—for which he has incurred, rather remarkably, charges of racial disloyalty from these same figures. He asks where the so-called leaders are for the Chinese and Irish, and wonders about the attitudes of those who employ the term "black 'leaders'": "What kind of assumptions are you making about black people? That we are too damn dumb to go on our way without someone pointing out which direction?" Williams also notes how far many of America's black politicians have strayed from the traditional spirituality of the black community. "Black people," he observes, "have more in common with Jerry Falwell than with Jesse Jackson. If you look at opinion surveys, black leaders have more in common with white hippies."[31]

Crime control has suffered significantly from the election of these figures. Many of these leaders practice, with honest consistency, the ultraindividualism that they espouse, which means that far too many black elected officials are either involved in questionable practices themselves or lack serious commitment to strong law enforcement. There are certainly plenty of white politicians guilty of the same shortcomings, since, of course, white theorists were the ones who thought up the ideas being effected. But the besieged residents of the black inner city are entitled to hold their politicians to a higher standard. Their community is literally confronting anarchy; they can rightly demand that government leaders respond to this emergency effectively. At the very least their elected officials should not worsen things by participating in crime personally, thus implicitly encouraging youngsters in their constituency to do the same.

But while most black elected officials serve honorably and pursue what they sincerely believe to be best for their people and society, there is nonetheless a substantial, prominent minority of black political leaders who take radical individualism to its practical extreme.

Marion Barry is but the most famous example. Equally flamboyant and noteworthy in his abuse of power was former congressman Gus Savage of Chicago. Among his offenses was his alleged harassment of a black Peace Corps volunteer in Zaire in March 1989, while she rode in a limousine during one of Savage's African trips. He reportedly questioned her fidelity to their race for resisting his advances. He eventually lost his seat in 1992 to Melvin Reynolds, a young African-American liberal aided by the inclusion of suburban areas in Savage's new, reapportioned congressional district. Reynolds had to accept the Democratic nomination in bandages. He had been injured several days before the election in a mysterious drive-by shooting that blew out the window of his car.[32]

Although, to repeat, many black mayors have served with distinction, a depressingly high number of black mayors have implemented anticrime agendas in many of America's largest cities that are at once ineffectual and counterproductive. David Dinkins, the first black American mayor of New York City, was elected in 1989 by promising to be "the toughest mayor on crime this city has ever seen," and to bring about racial healing.[33] Upon entering office he instead tacitly condoned an avowedly racist, predominantly black boycott of two Korean-American grocery stores in Brooklyn, to the point of opposing the enforcement of a court order requiring protestors to stand fifty feet from the stores. A state report commissioned by Governor Mario Cuomo that explored Dinkins's response to the anti-Semitic violence in Crown Heights presented what The New York Times called a "scathing portrait of ineptitude and miscommunication."[34] Prior to Dinkins's election it was also revealed that like a surprising number of other black elected officials, he had failed to pay his income taxes for several years.[35] Other mayors have fallen well short of legitimate expectations. Tom Bradley and Coleman Young, the recently retired mayors of Los Angeles and Detroit, were confronted with questions about financial ethics and corruption scandals through almost their entire tenure in office.[36] Even Kurt Schmoke, the young mayor of Baltimore, has endorsed drug legalization policies, which would seal the death of the inner city. Other such examples are in tragic abundance, and would, in any case, merely verify the obvious.

The most influential black political leader remains the Reverend Jesse Jackson, and only recently has he made anticrime efforts a top priority. Indeed, Jackson's current campaign against criminal violence began only after his own home in Washington, D.C., was burglarized and menaced by neighborhood offenders in 1992.[37] While Jackson's recent efforts are encouraging, they are overdue by many years, and undermined by the example he has set in his rise to the top rung of American politics. Indeed, his background suggests that he lacks the credibility and tenacity to successfully lead the fight against criminal violence and its intellectual roots, and that his current campaign may therefore be only a temporary enterprise. Jackson came to prominence because of his services in the racial struggles of the 1960s. However, he accomplished this through some well-documented falsehoods, including his story of cradling Dr. King's head in his arms as he lay dying. The late Reverend Ralph Abernathy, who did hold Dr. King during his final seconds of life, described Jackson's problem as one of "character" that "began right at the start." Abernathy recalled, "Jesse was ambitious, overly ambitious. He wanted to be Martin." These tensions eventually led King, in a fit of exasperation, to almost disown Jackson five days before his assassination.[38] Despite the doubts about Jackson's motives among many black Americans—as the saying in the ghetto goes, Martin had a dream, Jesse has a scheme—his high visibility has helped him keep a large following among those who are forgetful of his past, or who sincerely hope that he has turned over a new leaf. We should all hope the same.

There is more bad news to be confronted. Other prominent black Americans commonly treated as leaders seem to sympathize more with offenders than with law-abiding citizens. In the Central Park "wilding" case, New York's black political establishment almost uniformly criticized the prosecution of the mainly black offenders. Mayor Dinkins argued that the trials showed a racial "double standard of justice."[39] The moral nadir of these trends thus far came in the 1992 Mike Tyson rape trial. After being convicted of raping Desiree Washington, a teenage participant in a black beauty pageant in Indianapolis, Tyson attracted a protective phalanx of celebrities and political officials. Miss Washington reported that certain officials had privately offered her $1 million not to press charges. They suggested that she explain her withdrawal of charges by telling the media "that I was afraid because of what happened to Patricia Bowman, that I was afraid because of how Anita Hill was exploited." Even leading black church figures participated in this obstruction of justice. The head of the nation's largest black religious group, the Reverend T. J. Jemison, president of the National Baptist Convention U.S.A., acknowledged that he called Washington and urged her to drop the charges. "I asked her why she was going through with this," said Jemison. He was "hoping she would not use the trial to hurt this fellow."[40] It later came to light that Tyson had been a substantial donor to Jemison's network of churches. One of the National Baptist Convention's member pastors explained, "It was a dollars-and-cents proposition—Tyson can't give money when he's in jail."[41]

Lest we find in these events aid and comfort for today's stereotypes, we must also observe that the notoriety of black Americans engaged in crimes and questionable practices is often due less to their misdeeds than to other factors. Although the scrutiny attendant to big-city mayorships and the Tyson rape trial is inevitable, many of the least appealing members of the black community become household names because of a white-dominated media interested in reporting on strife and sensationalism. Malcolm X pointed out thirty years ago the media's partisanship in framing the national debate on public issues, often to the detriment of blacks.[42] Today, the mass media have become much more powerful. And frequently, in the quest for profits and consistent with a social-atomist worldview, they promote a painfully distorted set of values and view of black life. In such cases they emit into black and white homes alike programs that glamorize gratuitous violence and sex, portray common offenders as black leaders and inflame racial hostilities.

The Rodney King Riots were a stunning example of this inclination. Professor Williams has observed that most television stations used a selectively edited videotape of Rodney King's beating to provide "snippets" making King appear more sympathetic. These tapes cut out "portions where Mr. King is seen lunging at the cops." Williams enumerated some facts which, it would appear, were deliberately left out of the media's accounts of the King beating and trial:

> Did you know that Rodney King, who the media described as simply a "black motorist," was clocked traveling at 115 mph by Officer Melanie Singer? Did you know that his two passengers, Bryant Allen and Freddie Helms, who complied with police orders, were handcuffed, later released and not beaten? Did you know that Rodney King, at 6 foot 4 inches, 240 pounds, knocked Officers Theodore Briseno and Lawrence Powell down while resisting arrest? . . . Did you know that Mr. King was hit with a Taser stun gun which shoots darts with wires attached that give 50,000 volts per hit? Rodney King was hit

twice and got up twice, leading the police to believe he was drugged with PCP, which they later found out not to be the case, but his blood alcohol level was 0.19, about twice the legal limit.[43]

These facts are probably news to the reader presently because of these apparent deceptions. Certain key facts were not reported, and evidently held back, to give an unbalanced version of the story. Never was it reported, for example, that King at one point admitted that race was not a factor in his beating.[44] After watching the footage of the entire trial, Williams even endorsed the jury's verdict. And although a federal jury, probably fearing a second riot, subsequently disagreed, Williams termed the news media the riots' "agents provocateurs" because of their coverage.

Hobbes wryly observed that the best proof of the inherent equality of men is that everyone is equally convinced that he is superior to everyone else.[45] The rise of black criminality is striking proof that blacks are equal or superior to whites in every respect, including their response to the economic and social incentives that society has placed before them. The Havoc that has sprouted unintentionally from Hobbes's individualistic efforts found its weakest resistance in the black community. Because of their inherent limitations, the social sciences will never be able to determine scientifically why African-Americans were less resistant to this trend, at least initially, than other Americans. We must instead rely on empirical common sense, which takes note of the dynamic identified by Malcolm X. Lower-class blacks, at the urging of the black upper class, essentially compete with one another to be, in an oversimplified sense, "whiter-than-thou." And what better way to out-libertarian white folks than by outdoing them in the crime and sex that the libertarian white media glorify? When we consider the fact that America is a uniquely conducive habitat for raw individualism, it is not hard to grasp why black Americans, more than any other people, have brought libertarianism to its criminal consummation.

Many black Americans, unbreakable to the end, are fighting to burnish their heritage as the moral pillar of American society, a heritage tarnished when their Christlike humility born of slavery and subjugation gave way to the present crime and violence. The first step, many are realizing, is to replace the leaders of the civil rights movement with new figures. Many of these older leaders have resisted, even though it is now clear that many of them are unable to deal effectively with the current problems of the inner city. In 1992, as one of the most famous figures of the civil rights movement, Benjamin Hooks, prepared to step down as head of the NAACP, a poll showed that 94 percent of African-Americans wanted civil rights groups to concentrate more on problems such as crime, poor schools, teen pregnancy and drug abuse. By nearly two to one, they said the groups' crime-fighting efforts were poor or mediocre.[46] Civil rights groups had already sensed this dissatisfaction. Hooks acknowledged as he left office that he and his group were having trouble meeting these demands and maintaining their influence. He compared the civil rights establishment to "a man treading water." "We're just holding our own," he lamented.[47]

Explanations of these changes are, like most conjectures as to mass motives, complex and uncertain. The fissures between African-Americans and these officials probably widened to some degree during the Supreme Court nomination proceedings of traditionalist Judge Clarence Thomas, whom a majority of blacks wanted to see on the Court but whose nomination these groups opposed.[48] In all likelihood the eruption of violent crime has exhausted their patience most of all. After watching their neighborhoods taken over by crack users and former Black Panther units, many residents of Southeast Los Angeles in the late 1980s joined together to chart a new course. There was a common theme to their complaints about the status quo. R. Masada, chairman of an L.A. chapter of Daughters of Zion, a black women's civic association, wrote one local newspaper: "Black leaders jump on every bandwagon to accuse white police of brutality when a black man has his toes stepped on and call conferences and councils together if a cop fails to read a black man his rights. These same black leaders have yet to call a town meeting on the number of black females who are raped, robbed, beaten and murdered . . . by violent black predators in a continuous and ongoing holocaust that no one [has] dared speak out against."[49]

Spontaneous demonstrations for greater police protection have become more frequent. One mother, Pat Moore, organized an impromptu march of a hundred people through the streets of Compton after a two-year-old boy was shot and killed nearby. "I don't care if I see a soldier on every corner as long as I know my child will be able to get to school and back home safely," she stated. When, during an anti-gang raid, police mistakenly burst into Anthony Spears's apartment, fired a shot through the floor and briefly held him in arrest, Spears told a reporter that the raid was "great" and that more would be appreciated. Eventually even the local NAACP started to give in, conceding, "We've got to apply the same pressure to civil wrongs that we applied in seeking our civil rights."[50]

The mangled souls of black Americans are rising from the dead. They are returning, in steady, perceptible numbers, to the only proven antidote to the current chaos: tradition and religion. Theirs is a lesson still lost on most whites, whose emerging, and ultimately fatal, culture of middle-class yuppieism is doomed to end in the same disorder currently gripping the ghettos. Despite the best efforts of many libertarian scholars and celebrities, African-Americans remain probably the most socially traditional of all American ethnic groups. Polls show them to overwhelmingly support the death penalty, school prayer and other traditional institutions. There are other intriguing and related indications of such attitudes. Forty-eight percent of blacks are against abortion under *any* circumstances; the *Boston Globe* article discussing this poll delicately described "abortion rights" as a "tangled issue for minorities."[51] According to the Batelle Human Affairs Research Centers, white Americans are six and a half times more likely to describe themselves as homosexual than black Americans.[52] Blacks have also retained a great reverence for military duty, reflecting their roots in the South. In the Gulf War one out of four servicemen was black, twice the proportion of blacks in the overall U.S. population. African-Americans, indeed, have seen their young men enjoy extraordinary success in the military. There they receive the discipline they often lacked in childhood, and are otherwise tucked away in an institution that honors tradition and duty, thus placing them safely out of libertarian harm's way. One study found that the homicide death rate for black servicemen was only 9 percent of the civilian rate for the same age category;[53] black males today are safer as soldiers than in the ghetto. African-American politicians nevertheless are often among the most steadfast advocates of reduced military spending. This is so even though this amounts to cutting the sole government jobs program that has clearly worked for black Americans, precisely because it reinforces their strengths as a people.

Just as their Savior promised that one day the last will be first, blacks may very well lead the rest of America out of its moral dead end. For they, more than any other group, have been impervious to the growing disdain for traditional religion in America, and it is religion that is uniquely capable of instilling the internal moral imperatives that can deter crime when the policeman goes around the corner. While James Q. Wilson and Jared Taylor argue that black crime can be remedied only by blacks' adoption of white "middle-class" values,[54] in view of the materialistic and almost pagan culture taking shape in the white suburbs, these prescriptions, it would seem, would merely make things much worse. Indeed, Taylor's startling suggestion that our society encourage abortions of unborn black children as a crime control measure[55] amounts to merely combating one form of violent selfishness with another. The logical focus of our efforts, and of black self-help, is the black church.

W.E.B. Du Bois presciently remarked a century ago that the black man's problems in America could not be solved by material self-advancement. This belief set him at odds with Booker T. Washington, then the most famous African-American. Washington saw black progress as essentially a matter of economic development, and his *Up from Slavery* is an inspiring testimony to the powers of black self-help. All the same, while they disagreed over government's proper role in improving the black man's financial status, both saw religious faith as essential to his betterment. Du Bois conceded the need for economic improvement, but feared that it would lead to a betrayal of their African roots. In particular, he believed that an undue emphasis on money would encourage among blacks the greed and individualism that even then was a noticeable, historical characteristic of European-Americans. He remarked, ". . . we black men seem the sole oasis of simple faith and reverence in a dusty desert of dollars and smartness." Du Bois indirectly took issue with libertarianism by criticizing the "deification of Bread" and "lust for gold" that in his time were rapidly overtaking blacks as well as whites. Although he applauded gainful work—which, in an eloquent swipe at Adam Smith, he termed the "saner selfishness"—Du Bois wondered what would befall blacks who succumbed to libertarianism: "What if the Negro people be wooed from a strife for righteousness, from a love of knowing, to regard dollars as the be-all and end-all of life?"[56] The tragic answer to this question is the ghetto, the enthronement of the self in an all-consuming, brutish quest for possessions and pleasures at the lowest possible price.

Du Bois saw hope, as we should, in the black church. The black man is a "religious animal," he advised. "The Negro church of to-day is the social centre of Negro life in the United States, and the most characteristic expression of African character." The black church evolved from the fervently spiritual constitution of black Africans, "being[s] of that deep emotional nature which turns

instinctively toward the supernatural. . . . Endowed with a rich trop-
ical imagination and a keen, delicate appreciation of Nature, the
transplanted African lived in a world animate with gods and devils,
elves and witches; full of strange influences,—of Good to be
implored, of Evil to be propitiated. Slavery, then, was to him the
dark triumph of Evil over him." Today, the uniquely religious
essence of blacks can be seen in their frequent appeal to Christian
beliefs to make sense of the evils that have lately overtaken them.
This great religiosity among blacks largely transcends class lines,
quite unlike the growing spiritual divide between middle- and lower-
class whites. "Sprung from the African forests, where its counterpart
can still be heard," the music of the black church became the hall-
mark of this religion,[57] music that still inspires the hope that we may
yet be saved from the present Havoc.

The black church has not survived the twentieth century unmarred,
of course. African-American churches, like their Caucasian counterparts, have also fallen away from their mission of late, especially
when they have been dominated by leaders who prefer to use their
pulpits for political purposes. The Reverend Bruce H. Wall is one
heartening exception. After interviewing inner-city Boston teens, Wall
concluded flatly, "I fault the churches in general for the plight of the
African-American community today." He noted that on one drug-
dealing corner nearby there were six churches, none of which
appeared to exert any moral influence over the youngsters congregating around them. Remarking on modern children's disrespect for
authority, Wall observed, "They have become gods unto themselves.
They have no God-conscience. They have no values which clearly
show right from wrong." He ventured a solution: "It's time these
churches on this block went to [that] corner and put our hands of
love on the shoulders of these kids. . . . No social worker, no psychol-
ogist or police officer can do what a hand of love on a kid's shoulder
will do."[58]

Words of wisdom from a minister trained in them. In the end, the
resurrection of black America must come, as Du Bois put it, from
the souls of black folk. Du Bois had faith that African-Americans
could overcome the misery of his own time, the late 1800s, by drawing from their deep well of spirituality. "But back of this still broods
silently the deep religious feeling of the real Negro heart, the stirring, unguided might of powerful human souls who have lost the
guiding star of the past and seek in the great night a new religious
ideal."[59] Although recent signs are encouraging, it remains to be

seen if this abiding black faith can perform another miracle of this magnitude during our own century. This time the miracle will have to be big enough to revitalize the rest of American society as well, since the radical individualism that has reduced black Americans to this state originated and is today popular with America's white majority. The white captives of this moral decline await just such a deliverer themselves. Since black Americans have always been forced to bear this nation's worst sins on their backs, perhaps it is fitting that they should be chosen to lead our society back from the edge. It would indeed be the most divine of ironies, and the ultimate act of Christian love, if the only race to arrive on this continent in chains were to lead the descendants of their masters back to freedom from the self-imposed slavery that now shackles them.

CHAPTER NINE

Atom Bomb, or America's Culture of Chaos

Violence is as American as cherry pie.

—H. Rap Brown

Although Americans are often comfortably igno-
rant of things demanding a global perspective, one fact that has generally not escaped our attention is that the United States is a uniquely
crime-troubled society. We are much less knowledgeable about the
reasons for this status. While shelves sag from the weight of works
written about America's high crime rates, many of the forests felled
for these purposes deserved a better fate, or at least a more imagina-
tive one. Most of these commentaries are satisfied with fixing the
responsibility for America's unparalled crime problem to our history
of social injustice. It is thought that crime in the United States is especially high because we as a people have always been especially brutal
toward one another, particularly toward disfavored ethnic groups;
and, by implication, we get what we deserve. "Men murdered themselves into this democracy," goes the line from D. H. Lawrence

quoted by Charles Silberman,[1] and apparently by their standards, we did.

Silberman's is one of the most influential analyses of the reasons behind America's unsurpassed crime rates. His thesis is commendably straightforward. In a chapter titled "As American as Jesse James," Silberman contends that Americans are, and have always been, the most violent people on earth. He leads the reader past a procession of American outlaws, riots and more commonplace crimes in winding up at his conclusion. In offering the thoughtful theory that American culture is laced with various unique stimulants to crime, Silberman ascribes these not to the more obvious source, Americans' historically turbulent individualism, but to past Anglo-American transgressions (racial injustices, the rough self-help of the frontier, etc.). America's high crime rates, he believes, are the natural social residue of our prior abuses of one another.

Likewise, Silberman's discourse on the origins of the Great Havoc is both thought-provoking and ultimately lacking in empirical support. He explains the crime explosion of the 1960s as the result of a generation gap between overabundant baby boomers and their parents. A "youth culture," which he seems to regard as inherently criminal, emerged in that decade when "the traditional channels for the transmission of culture from one generation to another broke down from demographic overload." Yet Silberman fails to explain why this failed "transmission of culture" to the next generation resulted in a record crime wave, given that, by his assessment, the culture to be transmitted was already uniquely violent. We are left to wonder whether this omission permits one of his later, improbable conclusions—that is, that the rampant crime of the sixties grew from a supposedly distinct "youth culture," rather than from the extreme individualism in the broader popular culture in which this subculture incubated. The sixties, as Silberman sees it, produced a new, original culture among America's young people that resulted in record crime rates.[2]

While Silberman's theory is valuable grist for debate, it has several major pitfalls. First, as we have seen, the "youth culture" that sprang up on college campuses in the sixties was not the intellectual product of its participants. It is, of course, almost inconceivable that any generation of young people could coin and adopt a wholly new set of cultural values in a matter of one decade without substantial reference to existing ideas. In any case, the social atomism featured in the sixties was centuries in the making, rather than the concoction of a lone, unruly Me Generation. This theory was thought up by Anglo-Saxon intellectuals with a good amount of gray hair among them.

Second, for all of Silberman's extensive, if somewhat selective, discussion of American history offered in support of his thesis, it neglects to take into account trends in other countries over the same period. His theory, in short, suffers from a certain amount of ethnocentrism. For while Silberman documents in great detail America's past social wrongs, he does not consult other societies to see if they have suffered from or inflicted the same evils, and what they have to teach us. What Silberman would discover is that (1) crime rates were simultaneously lurching upward throughout other Western societies during the period he scrutinized, and clearly not because of the same, unique American youth culture; and (2) the atrocities that white Americans have perpetrated against America's racial minorities, while terrible stains on our national honor, have been committed by peoples in all other parts of the globe—and with even greater viciousness and duration. As to the latter point, America's relative purity in matters of ethnic brutality is mainly due to youth. Had we existed for several thousand years like some cultures, we would undoubtedly have compiled a similarly extensive record of mistreatment of each other. But the fact remains that countries such as China, Egypt and Greece have been in the business of slavery and genocide far longer than we, yet suffer a tiny fraction of our crime rate. The evils that have shamed America are almost universal in commission, but the Great Havoc is not.

When it comes to crime, America is simply in a class by itself. Violent crime is four to nine times more common in the United States than in, for instance, Europe. Even in the mid-1980s, before the recent paroxysm of teenage gang violence, the American homicide rate was four to five times higher than Europe's. The U.S. crime rates for rape and robbery are seven and four times greater than the European rates. Burglary is the only street crime for which American rates are not at least double those of European countries. When the U.S. crime rate is compared to those of non-Western countries such as Egypt, the Philippines and Thailand, the U.S. rate towers even more over its international competitor's. The American rate for robbery, for example, is over six times the Philippines' rate, twenty times Thailand's and five hundred times Egypt's.[3]

The volume of lawlessness in America, coupled with historically unprecedented crime rates in Europe (though they are still much smaller than U.S. rates), has led some to conclude that we are in the throes of a worldwide crime wave. An important book proffering this view is *The Growth of Crime: The International Experience*, published in 1977 by Sir Leon Radzinowicz and Joan King. Their book based the thesis implicit in its title on the large rise in American and European crime rates over the latter half of the twentieth century. At one point the authors offer the following distillation of their argument: "The one thing that hits you in the eye when you look at crime on the world scale is a pervasive and persistent increase everywhere."[4]

Again, such analysis reveals a certain Western bias. A global crime wave cannot be extrapolated from merely American and European crime statistics. The remaining roughly 85 percent of the world's population, newly emancipated from Western colonialism and its crime problem, beg to differ. The vast majority of people around the world continue to live as they have for centuries, with very low crime rates by modern Western standards. A narrower generalization than that offered by Radzinowicz and King would note that the countries currently convulsing from high crime rates have several traits in common: all are rich, "free," Western societies, and all are following, to varying degrees, the latest fashions in Western ideas. All have given in to some extent to the criminal-as-noble-savage mind-set, as well as the culture of narcissism in which this ignoble fellow flourishes.

While the West's unique crime problem is presumably due to the West's doing something uniquely wrong, in one respect, at least, Western crime may be a result of our doing something too well. The growth in Western crime may partly reflect the bare fact that there are more opportunities to commit profitable crimes in affluent industrialized societies. There is more stuff to steal here than anywhere else. Wilson and Herrnstein conclude that the larger Western economies present criminals with comparatively more opportunities to get rich quickly by illicit means. This phenomenon explains why underdeveloped countries experience increases in their crime rates during industrialization. Wilson and Herrnstein rightly limit this explanation to property crimes, the category of offenses most obviously driven by greed and materialism.[5]

This theory has its merits, but cannot provide a comprehensive explanation for America's current crime wave. In addition to considering the goods to be gained, inchoate offenders also calculate the severity and certainty of the possible penalties they face—the

demand side of the equation. The lower the penalties or the likelihood of their imposition, the greater the incentive for breaking the
law. On the demand side, America is clearly one of a kind. The
American criminal justice system is, one might say, *sui gener*ous: no
other nation punishes criminals as ineffectively as the United States.
The judicial expansion of offenders' rights, in particular, has made
the prosecution and punishment of American criminals uniquely difficult, and thus American justice random and fleeting. The political
neglect of the criminal justice system has also contributed significantly to this breakdown. A Japanese criminal, by comparison, is
three times as likely to be arrested and convicted as an American
offender.[6] America's status as the world's most crime-plagued nation
is consistent with this unique combination of plentiful goods and
ineffectual criminal justice.

An additional dose of criminal incentive would appear to flow
from today's racial antagonisms. America's prosperity and moral
goodness derive in no small part from its openness to immigrants
and people of all ethnic origins. But when the leadership of a society's minorities suggests to its followers that it is acceptable to commit offenses against their better-off or differently colored neighbors,
the balkanization that ensues can be among the most virulent of
social problems. Under these circumstances, America, which Paul
Johnson has described as "the largest and most varied multinational
society the world has ever seen,"[7] finds what would otherwise be a
national strength converted into yet another national predisposition
toward crime. Indeed, upon examining other cultures for suggestions as to how to repair these ethnic fractures, we discover that one
of the few truly universal beliefs is that societies should not be universal. Asian nations in particular view racial and ethnic diversity as
a recipe for social disorder. They discount the charges of bigotry
that this assessment, with some justification, attracts; to them, ethnic
unity is simply a requirement for national survival.

While criminologists have generally declined to research the possible links between ethnic diversity and crime, the few investigations
of this thesis have found no correlation between immigration per se
and crime rates. Walter Reckless's study of German, Dutch and
Scandinavian immigrants concluded that they suffered no greater
tendency toward criminality than Americans of old-line Yankee
stock.[8] The Wickersham Commission found in 1931 that even in the
heyday of Al Capone and Prohibition-related crime, immigrants'
crime rates were no higher than natives'.[9]

The problem, it seems, is rooted not in immigration or a multi-hued population, but in how society deals with these sometimes disruptive social changes. Historically, the perception of immigrant-generated crime has had much less to do with law than with order. Disorder is, to some degree, endemic to immigration. Communities that are absorbing a wave of immigration and that have carefully adorned themselves with laws and practices that reflect the ethnic preferences of the dominant group often feel threatened by the strange babble of ill-clad foreigners who by their very presence challenge the settled regime. Sometimes Americans have confused this temporary, innocuous disorder with lawlessness, although the two are distinct. Thus, throughout American history the biggest waves of immigration have coincided with the greatest levels of public preoccupation with law enforcement. This cycle began when rising immigration in the early 1800s prompted Northeastern city-dwellers to demand the first American police departments. That one of the larger groups of later immigrants, Italians, came from a society afflicted by an unusually tenacious organized crime network only deepened these fears. This cycle continues to the high-immigration present.

For all its historically proven virtues, immigration does have its downside. While America receives from its immigrants a vital, continuous influx of industrious workers and taxpayers, the nation also incurs certain social costs, in addition to the obvious increased governmental expenditures required for schools and such. A sudden infusion of generally young, male, individualistic immigrants to a rapidly aging society cannot help but drive up the crime rate. The reason is simple and applicable to all races and nationalities: young people are much more likely to commit crimes than their elders. Fifteen-to-nineteen-year-olds, for instance, are about sixteen times more likely to be arrested for property crimes than fifty-to-fifty-four-year-olds.[10] A large, steady increase in young males, as occurs today under our liberalized immigration laws, swells the pool of young males, who are the bulk of potential offenders.

The combined effects of age, sex and a generally pro-defendant criminal justice system make immigrants, disproportionately young and male, prime candidates for criminality. It is remarkable, in view of this, that so *few* of them take America up on this offer. Those who would seal the borders to ward off this perceived danger would do well to remember that our crime epidemic originated here because of distinctly American traits. Still, these fears of immigration's relationship to crime at least deserve to be addressed.

Although the government has not yet taken the politically sensitive step of collecting data on the crime rate among immigrants, one confirmation of these suspicions came from the Rodney King Riots. U.S. Attorney General William Barr noted at the time that nearly one-third of the first 6,000 rioters arrested were illegal aliens.[11]

The influx of Southeast Asian refugees into southern California has accelerated these trends somewhat, as we might expect. The rise of so-called Asian gangs in the past few years has significantly boosted the level of violence in an already crime-plagued metropolis. These gangs earn income primarily by extorting their own fellow immigrants, and secondarily by competing with other youth gangs for a share of the organized-crime market. As open gang warfare broke out in Los Angeles in the late 1980s, a *Los Angeles Times* poll showed that for 41 percent of the Vietnamese immigrants interviewed, crime and gangs were their top concerns. Eighty-seven percent thought they were serious problems.[12] Southeast Asian immigrants' cultural hesitancy to cooperate with the police has worsened their predicament. The Vietnamese expression *vo phuc dao tung dinh*, literally translated as "no happiness in going to court," is a frequently heard reason for not assisting law enforcement authorities. Many also cite their distrust of the U.S. criminal justice system and its ability to curtail crime, concluding that they should not expose themselves to possible retaliation from youth gangs when the chances of criminal punishment are slight.[13] Long Beach is today a stronghold of Cambodian gangs, which, according to one police officer, have battles with other gangs, often racial in origin, "almost every other day."[14] Similar shoot-outs are more and more common in South-Central Los Angeles between Southeast Asian and black gangs.[15]

Even more alarming is the looming conflict between African-American and Mexican-American gangs in southern California. Racial hatreds have existed as long as races themselves, and Americans are at last learning that Caucasians are not the genetically determined targets of this seething. As black and Latino gangs have begun to compete for turf and drug profits, a power struggle has been set off that, "if it explodes, won't compare to anything we've seen before," warns one L.A. gang specialist. Black residents of housing projects have been fire-bombed and had racist threats emblazoned on their doors as part of this conflict. Last year there were fifty-three racial brawls in Los Angeles County jails between blacks and Mexicans, some of which involved as many as eight hundred inmates. In South-Central Los

Angeles, an ongoing battle between an established Crip gang and a fast-growing Latino gang has claimed more than twenty lives since a prison clash sparked the feud some three years before. Mexican offenders seem to have grasped the advantages that their superior numbers entail, and that sheer demographics favor their criminal enterprises if they are united against rival black gangs. Police officers who have infiltrated meetings of the Mexican Mafia have determined that the group is seeking to organize L.A.'s Latino gangs in order to dominate narcotics trafficking along the West Coast. A confidential memorandum summarizing these findings stated that the "information received was there will be an upcoming race war between blacks and Hispanics."[16]

While the melting down of the melting pot has surely figured prominently in rising U.S. crime rates, white Americans should guard against assuming this to reflect a unique disrespect for the law among racial minorities. Indeed, the social fraying that America is now experiencing, as we have seen, is the result not of inherently antisocial tendencies among minorities, but of their predictable response to the intellectual defense of such practices by primarily white intellectuals and policymakers. This has brought about a state of affairs very much like the unintended homicidal effects of Ivan Karamazov's lectures to Smerdyakov. By the same measure, the high crime rate of America's minorities cannot be excused as a painful remnant of racism. America's history of slavery and bigoted brutality, as we have seen, is not an especially ruthless entry in the annals of man's hatred for man. For instance, Japan, which today is often touted as a crime-free sociological miracle, has been something less than a model of pacifism through most of its history; the militant, male-dominated samurai culture of old is surely not something that most criminologists would be comfortable teaching to inner-city youth. How quickly we forget that only a few decades ago, Japan conquered and annexed many of its neighbors to the Greater East Asian Co-Prosperity Sphere, committing far worse bloodshed in a single decade than Americans have in over twenty.

The comparison with Japan entices other questions as well. Why, in view of its recent national transgressions, does Japan lack the sort of racially motivated criminals predicted in the theories of Silberman and other criminologists? Why have Japanese racial minorities, such as laborers from Korea and other East Asian nations, not criminally retaliated for the abuses suffered at Japanese hands, both in their homelands and in Japan proper, over the years? Why don't the Japanese produce crime as they do cars?

If the explanation for the first two questions is clear—racism does not "cause" crime—the answer to the last question is not as easy for most Americans to accept. Today the Japanese not only frequently make better products than we do; they also, overall, practice self-government better. Unlike Americans, the Japanese have not abandoned their traditional, informal means of law enforcement because of their material success. Indeed, the level of Japanese prosperity cannot account for the difference in crime rates. That Japan is only half as rich in terms of gross domestic product as America might explain some of the difference in property-crime rates, but cannot account for Japan's "deficit" in non-property crimes. The answer seems to lie less in what Japanese culture has done well than in what ours has done poorly of late. Unlike American children, who today are often taught by the popular culture to dispute even their parents' authority and judgment, Japanese children still learn to revere the rule of law. When Japanese children become adults, they file a tiny fraction of the number of complaints lodged against policemen on this side of the Pacific.[17] And Japanese police can count on more than just token courtesy from the citizens they protect. While America has generally forgotten the system of citizens' law enforcement inherited from the British, Japanese neighborhoods are still organized into such units. These provide a Neighborhood Watch program every bit as good as the frankpledge at its zenith. The Japanese *chokai* supplements government with a private organization that collects dues from neighbors, keeps residents apprised of local concerns, and provides a natural structure for community self-defense. Since many Japanese children these days are more familiar with Jefferson's writings than Americans are, it is perhaps not too surprising that they have better institutionalized the Jeffersonian virtues of small-town life in a highly urbanized setting, taking the time to get to know their neighbors and care about their well-being. The Japanese remember their roots, and the difference shows.

The Japanese also have a different conception of government that makes law enforcement much simpler. Americans in this libertarian age too often seem to view government as almost akin to an occupying power, something that must be tolerated only to keep individualism from getting too messy. The Japanese, in contrast, view their government as bestowing on the public their greatest aspiration:

order. The Japanese government buttresses the traditional family and is active in promoting children's respect for their parents and the law. Also, like the people it serves, the Japanese government is less concerned with rights than with responsibilities. This contrasting conception of government is evident in the differences between American and Japanese criminal defendants. Americans accused of a crime see as their first imperative the retaining of an attorney to uphold their rights *against* the State and the community it represents. The Japanese, on the other hand, look upon arrest as a humiliating experience warranting submission and public repentance. Although Japan has outlawed plea bargaining, 95 percent of all Japanese prosecutions end in guilty pleas, pleas made with no strings attached. As David Bayley has observed, "In the United States, arrest marks the beginning of the criminal justice process; in Japan, the end."[18]

Mired in self-generated violence, Americans naturally look to others to blame. But the villains are right here at home. Our criminal justice infrastructure creaks and shudders from the strains of a mounting crime rate, producing widespread injustice due at least partly to political, and thus ultimately public, neglect. Our children are raised in a relativistic, self-concerned culture and have seen and acted on the incentives favoring a life of crime. America's open immigration policies also somewhat help to explain the jump in the crime rate, as does the racial unraveling of the nation.

There is surely not much to be proud of in these developments. We are rightly surprised, therefore, when we see libertarian scholars defending the current situation as almost a point of national pride. A recent book by Professor Lawrence Friedman of Stanford provides a timely example of this tendency. Friedman criticizes what he calls the "law-and-order crowd" for advocating increased criminal penalties alone as a solution for America's rising crime rates. But his own proposed solution to the Great Havoc is no less apathetic. As he sees it, "the siege of crime may be the price we pay for a brash, self-loving, relatively free and open society. . . . for now, at least, there may be nothing to do but grit our teeth and pay the price."[19] This is a puzzling, distressing conception of nationalism, to say the least. That this pride in country is sponsored by some of the same theorists whose ideas have helped bring about the current crisis suggests that though their patriotism should not be questioned, their judgment manifestly should be. After all, love of country is possible only as long as there is a country left to love.

THE TYRANNY OF THE SELF

Maybe we had it coming.

A nation that subjects itself to the abrupt overhaul of institutions and customs that America has recently endured must wonder whether it is entitled to an orderly existence. To put it simply, we have not been very well behaved of late. Through either acquiescence to decisions by elites or active participation, Americans have, as a partial list of our recent vices, permitted the malfunctioning of the criminal justice system; followed the crime control suggestions of criminologists and theorists who view crime as a disease and criminals as patients without free will; egoistically severed the families that provide the sole means of making society more than the sum total of aggressively self-centered individuals; and treated as spokesmen for their communities racial leaders whose social-atomist values are at odds with those of the people they are said to represent. Maybe, given Americans' recent track record, justice in the higher sense has been served by the erosion of justice in the national sense. Maybe.

Or perhaps we were, in an important sense, doomed to inherit such lawlessness as our birthright. We must remember that the American Republic was explicitly founded as an experiment, a benign form of social engineering. Participants in this continuing trial in self-government have inherited a political system that, at its inception, was fundamentally untested and, by the admission of all its Founders, potentially dangerous. The failure of the Articles of Confederation had proved this to everyone's satisfaction. Indeed, the Founders' second blueprint for the nation, the Constitution, was still a novel concept. Except for the state constitutions and the Articles of Confederation that preceded it, the Constitution was arguably the first attempt in history to design and implement an entire political system from scratch. Prior to 1787, the year of the Constitution's adoption, a handful of societies sprinkled throughout world history had sought to bind their otherwise all-powerful rulers with written impediments to despotism, a system that Aristotle recognized as the rule of law. But these select political regimes had all evolved over many centuries, as certain peoples slowly weaned their rulers from absolute power. Although Americans had cautiously tested certain newfangled political ideas before the Revolution, they knew that they remained under the restricted and reasonably safe auspices of the British Empire. Never before had an entire people suddenly assumed political authority and imposed on itself a new, largely untried form of self-government. Never, that is, until a small band of British expatriates along the Atlantic seaboard sought to instantly transform the excogitations of political intellectuals into a working system of government.

We are at least fortunate that when the Founders turned to philosophers for guidance, they selected the predominant British thinkers of their time. Unlike the intellectuals relied upon following other revolutions, the theorists whom American leaders consulted in crafting the new regime recognized the benefits of the rule of law and the wrongfulness of tyranny. In the late eighteenth century, the snapshot in time in which the Founders erected the American constitutional scheme, the political authorities who seemed best qualified to advise them on how to satisfy their main preoccupation—securing the blessings of liberty—were two servants of the Crown who, for all their other incendiary beliefs, knew the value of stability.

What Hobbes and Locke were less capable of providing was a sense of history. As we have seen in regard to the notion of the social contract, their theories, while commonly viewed as ideologically right-of-center in this era of extreme individualism, represented a sharp departure from the political assumptions of the past. This was especially true of their concept of individual rights. Previous societies, such as the ancient Greece of Plato and Aristotle, thought those who put forth theories of individual rights to be at best queer, at worst certifiably mad. This is not to say, of course, that earlier Western societies rejected the concept of the individual as distinct from society. The idea of man as an independent being with a personality and soul of his own, originating in Judaism, has always been the West's core distinction from other civilizations. But like every other recorded society up to then, the West in Hobbes's time held to the still-universal belief that man, while a political animal, is ultimately a social animal whose political attachments must be analyzed as such. It defied common sense and seemingly invited chaos, pre-Hobbesian folks thought, to theorize that the individual could socially detach himself from the State and, for purposes of theoretical analysis, go off into a State of Nature as a solitary political animal hurling rights against his fellow humans.

Medieval philosophers assembled a host of arguments to uphold this unified vision of society, some of which were rather fatuous. One of the odder intellectual currencies of the Middle Ages was the common analogy between society and the human body. Such scholars predictably placed the king at the head of the body, the priests and intellectuals in a suitable place, and the peasants in the feet, or worse. These philosophers were at least conscious of their social mission. They knew that ideas matter, regardless of how uneducated and seemingly insignificant the idea's host. And for all the well-documented abuses of this theory of national community, it worked—at least in regard to crime control. The conception of society as a great extended family, the only living relative of both the present generation and their ancestors, bound people together into a compact of self-preservation that, among other welcome by-products, kept Western crime rates comparable to those of the rest of the world for many centuries. The laws of society deserved obedience, it was thought, because a crime against one's neighbor was a crime against the community and, in a sense, a crime against oneself.

As noted in the earlier discussion of the social-contract theory, the most reluctant of revolutionaries led the rebellion against this idea. But Hobbes's fatal error, which deserves separate treatment presently, was basing the social contract and the authoritarian State on an appeal to the dark side of human nature: selfishness. He argued that his countrymen owed obedience to their king not because he served society justly, but because, and only so long as, he served *their* individual interests. The monarch did so by honoring their right to self-preservation, terminating the war of all against all through effective law enforcement. That this arrangement might promote justice was only an incidental concern. Thus, the modern conception of rights treats rights as inherently selfish. Locke multiplied Hobbes's sole right of self-preservation by three, tying together the rights of life, liberty and property into a bundle of God-given entitlements held against the State and society. Locke took his counterrevolutionary mentor to his logical extreme, using Hobbes's theory of rights to assert the morality of revolution against the leaders who failed to uphold these liberties. The American Revolution transmuted Locke's bundle into a bayonet; modern America has turned it into a machine gun, and pointed it at society as a whole.

This theory of rights was risky, and the American Founders knew it. If limited to tempering the excesses of the prevailing communitarianism administered by the Crown, Hobbes's and Locke's theories could have had fewer ill effects. By restricting the conception of rights to that of ramparts of human freedom, necessary but limited concessions to man's selfishness designed to defend ordered liberty against a high-handed government, these philosophers could have secured the free life without unduly glamorizing potentially destructive rights. Recognizing that society would suffer if rights became too attractive and extended, the Founders candidly addressed the shortcomings of this rights-based individualism. One of the greatest fears of the Framers of the Constitution, and the one that provoked their most profound writings, was the vision of rights-armed citizens coalescing into groups dedicated solely to self-promotion at the expense of the community. The Framers especially feared the appearance of such blocs of self-serving individuals in the political arena. They termed such groups "factions," and questioned whether the new system could avoid the paralysis that they predicted would occur once individualism was codified in the Constitution and Bill of Rights.

Probably the greatest accomplishment of James Madison, the author of the Bill of Rights and the finest mind to fill the White House until Lincoln, was his defense of the new Constitution against charges that it would rip the nation apart. His brilliance was a function of his audacity. Madison responded to the main criticism of the proposed Republic by turning it on its head. He argued that the new nation's vastness, which most thought to be an impediment to self-government, was actually a guarantor of civil cohesion. In essence, Madison's flippant response to critics of the constitutional order was "the more, the merrier." That is, the bigger the country, the more factions it would spawn, and the less likely it was that one single faction would grow large enough to cow the nation into submission to its egoistic ends. In any case, the potential dangers of factions would have to be tolerated lest liberty itself be snuffed out. Madison described factions as "a number of citizens . . . united and actuated by some common impulse of passion, or of interest, adverse to the rights of other citizens, or the permanent and aggregate interests of the community";[20] he viewed them as squatters in the new Republic that could not be safely ejected. Of course, this entailed risks. Government-sponsored individualism predicated on self-centered rights could all too easily degenerate into atomism, and an institutionalization of the war of all against all. But that risk, Madison insisted, was the price the nation had to pay to secure basic freedoms. He and his supporters were also confident that later generations would be wise enough to avoid uncorking these latent tendencies.

Big things were bound to happen when atoms collided. The constitutional order the Framers left us was established with the known potential to come apart, possibly violently. With the assistance of all the previously discussed agents of criminality, this theory of rights-based self-centeredness was taken to its inherent, rough-and-tumble culmination in the late twentieth century. At first, factions used rights as weapons to secure lawful goals. Later, when the nation's law enforcement regime began to break down, the worst form of factions filled the breach, using both rights and even sturdier implements to divide up society. Armed clusters of egocentric citizens have emerged in this era to promote the aims of either a faction of many (such as a racially balkanized section of the populace) or, most commonly, a faction of one. The enormous crime rates of our time have thus largely vindicated the original opponents of the Republic. The Great Havoc has demonstrated the hazards of enacting a fresh, untested political system, especially one based on an individualism at great odds with the lessons of antiquity. While the Founders were correct in viewing rights as an essential bulwark against tyranny, the particular philosophy of rights they selected had defects that, in time, have proved lethal. The community is no match for self-interested factions who know their rights.

Of course, to be fair, the Founders could not possibly have predicted the strains that Americans have today placed on their system. The factions they envisioned were primarily political. The Framers' careful erection of institutional checks and balances helped to guard against this astutely predicted phenomenon, although modern political factions, or lobbies, continue to try the nation's patience. What the Founders failed to contemplate was the rise of radical individualism in the twentieth century, contemporaneous with the decline of Judeo-Christian religious values in favor of secular relativism. As to the former development, perhaps they should have known better. In the same year that the Declaration of Independence was signed, Adam Smith published his *Wealth of Nations*. It defended economic self-interest as the main, tumultuous ingredient of national prosperity. His theory accorded with, and was undoubtedly a reflection of, the innate materialism of the Anglo-American race,[21] a mercurial trait that bestowed upon them science and industrial prowess, but at the recent expense of shallow souls and a growingly unstable society. While Smith was certainly no anarchist (chaos is not conducive to commerce), his lenient view of selfishness, combined with this inherent Anglo-Saxon materialism, provided an intellectual basis for the roots of the current crisis. A decade before the Constitution's adoption, factions received the moral support that in our times has become the popular mind-set.

Although ideas are always important, they have had uniquely momentous consequences in America. The United States is virtually alone among nations in having been founded expressly on abstract philosophical ideas, ideas that, as it turns out, were not entirely sound. The flaw was not, as James Q. Wilson has contended, that "we grafted a Lockean (and in part, Hobbesian) national government onto a communal life that was explained and defended in the language of Rousseau."[22] Heaven knows, reliance on Rousseau would not do wonders for any nation's cohesion. However, the communitarianism that Wilson recognizes was due to Judeo-Christian influences, not to the writings of an eccentric French-man.[23] Rather, the Framers relied upon homemade English philosophy from the giants of their time. They were thinkers whose only, yet mortal, sin was ignoring the lessons of the past. Like a gifted child born with a dangerous tendency to devote his talents to self-destructive pursuits, America, by virtue of its political system, is in constant risk of indulging such propensities if its political leaders and citizens do not cling to a shared regime of family, community and religion.

Crime in modern America, then, is the resounding refutation of libertarianism. The violent selfishness across our land is but the most forceful manifestation of this rights-based philosophy's internal miscalculations. Our nation's savage solipsism is traceable not so much to Rousseau and the German nihilists, as Bloom argued,[24] although their system provided an extra layer of respectability to made-in-America relativism that has certainly not helped the underlying egoism. The seed of American self-centeredness did not need to be imported. It was right here inside all of us, as Hobbes recognized. Man is naturally, predominantly selfish, and will act on these instincts unless society goes to great lengths to restrain them. With the decline of the social penalties to brazen narcissism, accomplished through homespun, Anglo-Saxon libertarianism, the primordial "solitary" life of plunder and strife that Hobbes feared has flowed to the surface, well rested and eager to please.

Libertarianism's confusion arises from two main misconceptions. The theory's disregard for tradition and custom, the stored common judgment inherited from millennia of human civilization, was its most fundamental error. This project was begun tentatively by Hobbes and Locke themselves and taken to a new dimension by

Mill. By treating individuals as islands of absolute sovereignty and religion as wearisome and dispensable, libertarianism eroded the prescriptive, internal ties of selflessness that had previously kept society intact. Compounding this mistake was Mill's subsequent elaboration and endorsement of rights-based individualism's innately self-interested premises. Mill's belief that all human conduct that does not result in immediate harm to others should be socially permitted, while currently popular in America with its inconsistent, self-motivated exceptions (e.g., drug policies), is the nub of libertarianism's, and thus modern America's, predicament. For a while at least, many of us were judicious enough not to overextend Mill's offer. We would, for example, smoke dope and cheat on our taxes, but not commit violence. Others, particularly Americans who were less disciplined or less enchanted with libertarianism's arcane distinctions, were not as restrained. The wedge that Mill's philosophy had driven between them and the community was far more important than a strained academic distinction between "self-regarding" conduct and civic ties. They were on their own. Crime, the most extreme form of selfishness, seemed much less extreme in this environment of rights-solitude and doing your own thing. Criminals were just getting their own pieces of the community, a natural entitlement in the breakup that followed.

The reason for modern America's unprecedented crime rates is thus clear enough. Our crime rates have become the highest in the world—indeed, in history—because America offers the most fertile ground for a freedom-seeking, individualistic, Anglo-Saxon libertarianism.

RIGHT TO THE EXTREME

Although radical individualism has lately become popular with Americans of all social strata, its popularity has largely trickled down from an unelected elite. The lawyer-theorists on the U.S. Supreme Court have hastened the rise of libertarianism at times through the sheer force of law. They have done so mainly by expanding the liberties listed in the Bill of Rights. Although, as we have seen, the broadening of certain criminals' rights in the Fourth and Fifth Amendments has necessarily aided offenders directly, it is the growth of another right, one in the First Amendment, that merits special attention: freedom of expression. This right's growth has been both symptomatic of and essential to the rise of radical individualism in modern America, and, in some instances, it is responsible for the direct outgrowth of crime and violence. Certain citizens, out of diverse motives, have taken this right to an extreme unforeseen by its creators. Since such expression is often injurious to the community, popular exercise of the right has thus helped to prod the nation's innate, slumbering atomism into the current upsurge in crime. The unsettling consequences of this right's overnight ascent from obscurity to center stage in American jurisprudence have made freedom of expression uniquely important among rights in shaping America's current disorderly culture.

The constitutional existence of freedom of expression is not apparent from the language of the First Amendment. That amendment provides in relevant part, "Congress shall make no law . . . abridging the freedom of speech . . ." Originally, as the text of the amendment suggests, this prohibition applied only to Congress, or the federal government. "*Congress* shall make no law" seems to mean exactly that. Also, only "speech" was protected, not expression, which implies actions. But starting in the 1966 case of *Memoirs v. Massachusetts*,[25] the Supreme Court offered a markedly different interpretation. In *Memoirs* the Court held that communities could restrict sexually related material only if the legislation satisfied a number of rigorous tests to determine if it was "obscene." Since the Court took a relatively lenient view of what constituted obscenity, including a requirement that the material be "utterly without redeeming social value," *Memoirs* effectively marked the end of pornography controls in America. More fundamentally, the decision has been built upon to judicially preclude almost *all* community controls on violent and obscene programming and material by the mass media.

The new freedom of expression framed by this jurisprudence profoundly affected both the way Americans communicate with one another and the values thereby transmitted. By barring community restrictions on the mass dissemination of programs and material that threaten the integrity of society, the judicially created right has transformed the First Amendment into a social acid unanticipated by its Framers—or, for that matter, by the creators of the new freedom itself. These events have given rise to two important concerns that relate directly to crime: (1) has the ensuing increase of sexually explicit material caused a higher incidence of rape? and (2) does the increased violent and sexual content of media programming foster either greater crime and violence, or greater predatory sex and illegitimacy, the long-term ingredients of crime?

As to the first concern, the link between pornography and rape is tenuous and empirically unconvincing. There have been many intriguing studies in this area. Most of them (perhaps not surprisingly, given the views of most social scientists) find no relationship between the two. Even the Meese Commission on Pornography found no demonstrable link between soft pornography and rape, although media reports of the commission's findings often strangely suggested otherwise.[26] Research that purports to show a causal relationship between the two phenomena suffers from problems that plague any venture into social science. One notable study demonstrating these flaws was performed by Laron Baron of Yale University and Murray A. Straus of the University of New Hampshire. They found that states with the most pornography per capita had the highest rape rates. Western states, with their culture of rugged libertarianism, were the most conducive to both pathologies. Alaska had the highest pornography circulation rates and the highest rape rate; Nevada was second in both categories. Arizona, California and Colorado were also in the top ten for both social blights.[27] However, the relationship that Baron and Straus identify is less cause than effect, much like the supposed causal link between poverty and crime. Crime *in general* is higher in the West. As explained earlier, this is not because of "sexual liberalism," as Baron and Straus allege, but because of the hardy individualism native to the region, which has lately been aggravated by a host of social stimuli. All other things being equal, pornography sales are more likely in individualistic cultures. The same is true of crimes of all descriptions, including but not limited to rape. Active commerce in pornography is especially likely in the western United States and anywhere else when, as now, sexually explicit material is constitutionally protected, and when defended by libertarian theorists as a legitimate market, the "invisible hand" being frisky.

Nevertheless, while pornography does not cause rape, rape is unquestionably related to sex as well as violence, contrary to recent misconceptions. There is very little in history or biology to support the modern belief, circulating in many libertarian and feminist circles, that rape is a crime of violence, but not of sex. Too many questions hound this assumption. For instance, if rape is merely a crime of violence, why do rapes generally terminate only after the rapist ejaculates? Has he not made his point and enjoyed himself enough without this purely sexual climax? Rape, in fact, would appear a crime of both sex and violence. For some men, namely psychotics, rape uniquely quenches a desire for violent domination and humiliation that normal people cannot fully understand. However, the history of rape in war and peace offers a more balanced conclusion than that urged by current dogma. When the penalties for rape are taken away, some men will act on natural, egoistic urges that, for them, make rape enjoyable if it can be gotten away with. For these men, rape is an amoral way of getting sexual gratification at a powerless woman's expense.

Two important 1985 studies supported the age-old assumption that rape can be both psychotic aggression and sexual predation. In a study cited favorably in the National Academy of Sciences' report on violence in 1993,[28] a team headed by Ron Langevin studied a group of 40 rapists, 40 nonviolent sex offenders, 40 normal controls and 25 nonsexual assaultive offenders. The rapists were found to be most similar to the sexually anomalous men. Both groups had a history of exposing, peeping, making obscene calls and frottaging (rubbing against women in crowds). "Contrary to expectation," the rapists were not "ultra-masculine"; "If anything, they were feminine and even engaged in transvestism."[29] In a second study headed by Langevin, twenty sexually aggressive offenders were tested with a phallometric device to determine arousal to audiotaped acts of rape and consenting intercourse. The group reported, "In *no* case did any group react differentially to rape and consenting intercourse." (Emphasis in original.) Rapists were thus no more aroused by rape scenes than by consenting sex. Langevin and his colleagues concluded that a possible reason was that many rapists found "nothing inherently attractive about rape." Rather than a pleasurable act of violence, rape is simply "stolen sex."[30]

Robert Martinson's yeoman study of criminal rehabilitation was equally, albeit more indirectly, informative in the study of rape. His review of sex-offender studies found that the recidivism rates for rapists who were castrated were only 3.5 percent. That is, 96.5 percent of all rapists whose sex drive was eliminated did not rape again. Those treated with therapy and hormones had recidivism rates just under 30 percent. While the 3.5 percent who managed to rape again are an intriguing group (Martinson's explanation: "where there's a will, apparently there's a way"),[31] the fact remains that the removal of the rapist's sex drive almost completely eliminated the problem. For these rapists, it seems, rape was more about sex than violence.

Lessened criminal punishment for rape plays an essential role here also. The reductions in both the probability of apprehension and the severity of penalties once convicted have conspired to make rape rise more or less in lockstep with other violent crimes. Currently only 52 percent of rapes even result in an *arrest*, much less properly strong punishment.[32] Those convicted face at worst a few years in prison, rather than capital punishment or castration, the traditional and rightful retribution for such acts. While pornography and media programming are not the cause of this state of affairs, a people whose popular culture emphasizes self-centeredness and sexual gratification, and yet who claims to have been ambushed by unforeseen higher rape rates, does more than try a reasonable person's patience. Such a people take liberties, literally, with what we know of human nature's darker half.

Yet while their connection to America's rising rape rates is questionable, the judicial expansions of the First Amendment have had much less nebulous effects on overall American culture. In particular, the greatly increased amount of random violence and sex in media programming today has demonstrably coarsened society, altered our conception of community and, in some cases, made celebrities out of genuine criminals. A series of court rulings has effected this, permitting broadcasters to determine the content of their programming with almost complete discretion.[33] The result, as William J. Bennett has observed, is "a culture that at times seems almost dedicated to the corruption of the young, to ensuring the loss of their innocence before their time."[34]

Freedom of expression is today employed by the twin megaphones of mass communication in modern America, music and television, to foster, either directly or indirectly, both crime and violence and its social antecedents, illegitimacy and male-motivated predatory sex. Music's profound effects on the young are sometimes overlooked in our evaluation of the state of the culture. Earlier analysts would not have been so remiss. Plato, for one, worried enough about music's misuse to devote much of his *Republic* to discussing the possible consequences of antisocial music. He advocated strict censorship of music, noting the corrupting effects of certain music on the young and its resulting capacity to undermine the social order. Plato's conclusions have never been seriously challenged, probably because their truth is so evident: martial music can stiffen the tired back of an old soldier; patriotic tunes can bring tears to the eyes of a nation; religious hymns can create hysteria in entire congregations. Moreover, unlike literature or theater, music demonstrably compels a spiritual assent from its listener. It digs down deep into the soul, stirring and throbbing man's inner nature with sounds that demand loyalty to their message.

There has been, overall, an odd lack of popular concern over the effects of American popular music on our children. Bloom was mystified by this remarkable disinterest, since he saw music as one of the main cultural influences on the nation's young people.[35] And although he somewhat rashly dismissed all rock and roll as music of cultural cretins, his critique remains one of the few serious reflections vouchsafed by serious scholars of any field on music's relationship to our current decline.

A few social science studies have looked into music's connection to violence. In a study of almost 200 young people, Jeffrey Arnett of the University of Chicago used a regression analysis that controlled for family relationships, drug abuse and other factors. He found that fans of both sexes of heavy metal music, which frequently features themes of violence and crime, were significantly more likely to engage in "reckless behavior." "Liking heavy metal music remained significantly related" to recklessness "even when sensation seeking and family relationships" were controlled for.[36] In 1991 a trio of researchers at the University of Florida interviewed 120 adolescent offenders in two youth detention centers in the South. They also turned up a "strong relationship" between heavy metal music and antisocial or destructive behavior.[37]

Although these studies, like all social science, can never convincingly disentangle the many factors that affect human decisions, a consensus of sorts has nonetheless emerged regarding music's influence over modern lives. If, as libertarians insist in other contexts, truth is best discovered in the marketplace, where people are forced to put their money where their mouth is, then the media's ability to shape the thoughts and decisions of their audience is undeniable. Wilson and Herrnstein point out that "if so many commercial and political interests invest so much money in media advertising, it would seem absurd to believe that the media have no effect on our behavior, including, perhaps, our criminal behavior."[38] Advertisers spend huge sums peddling their wares via the media, knowing that a favorable portrayal of their product will invigorate sales. When, for example, California recently financed a high-profile television advertising campaign to discourage smoking, it was widely credited with cutting the number of smokers in California by 28 percent in five years. If the present trend continues, California will fulfill its goal of reducing the number of smokers by 75 percent by the year 2000, thanks to media cooperation.[39]

While only a small percentage of popular music today openly praises criminality, that percentage is growing, and is often from the genres that are highly influential among the young men who make up the bulk of potential delinquents. Rap and heavy metal music are the preferred music of the biggest blocs of crime-prone citizens, young black and white males, respectively. This music is often filled with lyrics that, prior to recent court rulings, could have been legally banned as leading to imminent violence. Aside from relying heavily on sexually explicit lyrics, rap songs also routinely encourage listeners to commit violent crimes; or, more generally, just to give the police a hard time. The rap group Public Enemy's breakthrough hit was "Fight the Power," which urges mass racial revolt. Groups such as 2 Live Crew tell their fans to violently jam various instruments into female orifices, with or without consent. In 1992 rapper Ice-T released a song, and originally an album of the same name, titled "Cop Killer," which policemen picketed nationwide. Three years before, the Fraternal Order of Police had tried the same tactic against Public Enemy and N.W.A., or Niggas with Attitude, because of similar lyrics, but again met with little success.[40]

N.W.A. has been an especially engaging and influential rap group. Before the band's breakup, its most famous song was "F**k the Police," with verse exhorting listeners to armed confrontation. Since N.W.A.'s disbandment, its members have taken their bitter contractual disputes public by filling the airwaves with threats to murder one another. Dr. Dre sings of sodomizing the band's former lead singer, Eazy-E; Eazy-E has countered with an album and title song that threaten his former bandmate with homicide. One song by former N.W.A. star Ice Cube proved prophetic, at least in a self-fulfilling vein. His song "Black Korea," released a year before the Rodney King Riots, warned Korean grocers back in his South-Central ghetto that they had better "pay your respects to the black fist / or we'll burn your store right down to a crisp." His paean to the ensuing riots, released in 1992, was titled "We Had to Tear This Motherf****r Up."

So-called gangsta rap has become so popular, in fact, that today the roster of American Top 40 performers almost reads like a Most

Wanted list: Dr. Dre (real name: Andre Young), arrested for breaking his producer's jaw and for armed assault; Tupac Shakur, costar with Janet Jackson of the popular movie *Poetic Justice,* charged with shooting two off-duty policemen in Atlanta; Flavor Flav (William Drayton) of Public Enemy, arrested for attempted murder and criminal possession of a weapon after allegedly shooting at a neighbor in New York; and Snoop Doggy Dogg (Calvin Broadus), with the highest-selling debut album in history, *Doggystyle,* arrested for murder after allegedly driving the getaway car following a drive-by shooting in southern California.[41] Rap concerts often erupt into riots because of this message. Many insurance companies will not insure rap concerts, or will do so only for an inflated premium.[42]

Such music is scarcely confined to minorities. Heavy metal groups, which market their trade to young white males, also rely on such lyrics. Unlike rap stars, many heavy metal acts glorify Satanism, occasionally encouraging ghastly Satanic crimes by tragically confused young fans. Others sing about more pedestrian offenses. Guns N' Roses, America's most popular heavy metal band, has sold tour shirts depicting a scantily clad rape victim collapsed beneath the spray-painted message "Guns N' Roses was here." The group was prosecuted for inciting a riot in July 1991 in a St. Louis suburb, in which 40 concertgoers and 25 policemen were injured and which caused $200,000 in damage.[43] Inherently macho and occasionally belligerent elevator sex is a strangely recurring theme, present in Mötley Crüe's "Ten Seconds to Love," Aerosmith's "Love in an Elevator" ("Livin' it up when I'm goin' down") and Judas Priest's "Eat Me Alive," an ode to sodomy at gunpoint.

It is now also typical for a majority of the songs on the American Top 40 to contain explicit references to or graphic simulations of sex. Indeed, it is now so common that some of music's greatest celebrities are men and women of notoriously questionable virtue. Madonna's commercial ventures in pornography, including her 1992 book *Sex,* a compilation of explicit photographs of sexual encounters, are only the most brazen and famous of these efforts. Sexually explicit lyrics are now so common that their reiteration here would require a second volume, and in any case would not faze the children whose ears are filled with them daily.

Television is at least subject to some organized, sustained public pressure. While most parents do not listen to the popular music recruiting their children for various antisocial projects, almost all watch the same television shows, where judicial rulings have allowed the same sort of message. Sex and violence are now frequently used for higher ratings. One study tallied over 10,000 sexual encounters during prime time by the three major TV networks in 1991; the ratio of extramarital to marital sex was fourteen to one.[44] Today the prospect of 500 television channels, children's video games such as "Mortal Kombat" (which graphically simulates bloody decapitations of its characters) and the current explosion in telecommunications and entertainment technology all stand to make further use of these gimmicks—and, inevitably, to add to the country's crime rates.

The TV violence transmitted to U.S. homes and its relationship to crime rates have come in for much more empirical scrutiny than TV sex. The available research reflects this imbalance. Wilson and Herrnstein note that, as with these social scientists' other preferred areas of research, their "ideological predispositions" dispose them to proving a relationship between TV violence and crime.[45] Still, common sense also suggests this relationship. Celebrities in the media define the popular culture and peer pressure, sometimes to society's detriment, especially when, as now, criminal violence is portrayed glamorously. In the mid-1970s David Phillips documented the now-accepted phenomenon of copycat acts that follow well-publicized suicides and infamous crime sprees.[46] Other studies, such as the so-called Rip Van Winkle study begun in 1960, delved more deeply into a possibly broader causal relationship between TV violence and violent crime. Conducted by the research team of Eron, Huesmann, Lefkowitz and Walder, the Rip Van Winkle study compared children exposed to violent and nonviolent programming during childhood and monitored their aggression over the next twenty years at ten-year intervals. They concluded that a causal relationship existed independent of the individual traits inclining such children toward a life of crime.[47] Huesmann and Eron found in their international survey of television violence that "more aggressive children watch more violence in the media in almost every country," inferring from this a causal effect.[48] Citing Eron's and other research findings, the National Academy of Sciences study in 1993 noted that the mass media, through such programming, may teach children that aggressive or violent behavior is a proper response to frustration.[49]

Independent government commissions have come to the same conclusions. The 1972 report by the Surgeon General's Scientific Advisory Committee on Television and Social Behavior, and subsequent reports by the National Institute of Mental Health and the U.S. Attorney General's Task Force on Family Violence released in the 1980s, found a correlation between violent TV programming and greater violence in society. The NIMH study stated that "the consensus among most of the research community is that violence on television does lead to aggressive behavior by children and teenagers who watch the programs. . . . In magnitude, television violence is as strongly correlated with aggressive behavior as any other behavioral variable that has been measured."[50] While rejecting much of the social science on the subject as too simplistic, Wilson and Herrnstein did find "a small amount of systematic, carefully done research that lends strong support to the view that prolonged viewing of televised violence will, independently of individual characteristics, produce a significant and lasting increase in the incidence or prevalence of serious violence."[51]

The amount of academic and public concern has not been equal in regard to the often male-dominated sexuality on TV and other media. While TV networks, under pressure from Congress and Attorney General Janet Reno, recently agreed to at least label televised violence, they made no such pledge regarding TV sex, even though it inevitably affects illegitimacy and long-term crime rates. The repeal of federal television guidelines in the 1980s has allowed the sexuality previously confined to late-night television to enter prime time. Dramas such as *L.A. Law* and *thirtysomething* were prominent pioneers in this regard, often labeled adult entertainment intended to bypass children—although broadcasting by definition cannot distinguish in its viewership. By the 1990s even that pretense of covering the children's eyes disappeared. Programming targeted specifically at children, such as the highly popular teen series *Beverly Hills 90210,* is currently filled with casual intercourse and frank sexual humor. Even comic-book heroes are often reduced to common playboys, and then marketed to child audiences. In the recent movies dedicated to them, Superman, Batman and Dick Tracy all sleep with their extramarital heroines.

Consider, then, the deleterious effects on the culture. Children see their role models in the media rollicking in antisocial behavior that we expect them to abstain from until they reach majority. They have smiled at our naiveté, and in due course pierced these unreasonable hopes one by one with a wave of juvenile pathologies. As teenage sex in particular has become more prevalent, we have, rather than reconsidering the wisdom of exposing children to such values, instead convinced ourselves that such behavior is normal and inevitable. But it is neither. We do a grave disservice to our children, especially girls, in assuming so. In Phoenix, for instance, two of the most common reasons that teenage mothers gave for having sex and getting pregnant were that there was "so much pressure from the guy" and that they were trying to "hold on to a boy."[52] Theirs was reasonable behavior, given the circumstances; today's girls know that the boys they like can readily go elsewhere for sexual favors, in large part because of the current popular culture. Nationally, a large majority of teenage girls who have had sexual intercourse report having done so involuntarily at times. Nearly three out of four girls who had sex before the age of fourteen say they were coerced by the boy, who is usually several years older.[53] Yet "boys will be boys" has become our exasperated, routine excuse for rising illegitimacy rates among adolescents, behavior that cannot help but lead to greater crime rates in the long run. Instead of risking unpleasantness with our children or accusations of puritanism from our neighbors, we have come to tolerate juvenile behavior that no other previous civilization would have accepted, or felt conducive to social stability. At present over half of American high school students have had sex. This number rises to over 70 percent by graduation time.[54] The cost of government aid to families of teen mothers is $21.6 billion annually.[55]

The chilling consummation of these trends was evident recently in Lakewood, California. Described by the press as a "conservative, middle-class Los Angeles suburb," Lakewood is the home of the Spur Posse. It was revealed in April 1993 that members of the Posse, a clique of popular high school boys, were engaged in a secret fraternal contest: seeing how many girls they could pressure into having sex, earning a point for each occasion. Local feminists were outraged at this exploitation, and at first they accused the boys of rape. When these accusations rang hollow (the girls were seen afterward still seeking the affection of the boys), the participants defended their actions on Freudian grounds. One boy attributed all the fuss to "penis envy." The boys' parents, true to the sexual attitudes common in California suburbs today, defended their predatory competition as, in the words of one mother, a "testosterone thing." One father insisted, "Nothing my boy did was anything any red-blooded American boy wouldn't do at his age." Another boy recalled his father bragging about his adventures to his friends.[56] The grim culmination of this mind-set appeared later that month, when it transpired that teenage girls in San Antonio, as part of a gang initiation ceremony, had consented to sex with HIV-positive gang members to prove, with perhaps perverse feminist machismo, that they were "tough enough."[57]

Except for the violence it portrays, which is philosophically less defensible, the entertainment industry has, in abetting this crisis, merely taken libertarianism up fully on its stated premises. The criminal violence ultimately generated by the growth of teenage, single-parent families is a direct but delayed result of libertarianism. Hence, Mill's relativistic instructions have been followed carefully, if not religiously; and since celebrities have usually not explicitly advocated violent crime, they can draw their income without moral regrets. Yet the results of this revolution are a terrifying reminder that Mill and his libertarianism are simply wrong as a matter of human nature. What we do to ourselves, or to each other consensually, ultimately affects everyone else. While it may take years for the offspring of such conduct to finally manifest the criminal violence that provokes libertarianism's sole, lame rebuke, the chaos will surely come in time. In the end, the community must atone for the sins of its members.

In response to this crisis, the issue for most Americans is not censorship versus no censorship. Almost everyone agrees that at least some curbs should be placed on what entertainers can encourage less responsible members of society to do, particularly children. Rather, it is a choice that was well demarcated by Judge José Gonzales in the Florida obscenity trial of the rap group 2 Live Crew in 1990: "a case between two ancient enemies: Anything Goes and Enough Already."[58] "Anything Goes" has, to date, been putting its worthy old opponent to rout. Although three-fourths of Americans believe that current television programming encourages violence, only 12 percent support legislation that would restrict TV violence.[59] Few prosecutors are willing to press charges against obscenity offenders, and even fewer juries appear willing to convict them. According to the jury in the 2 Live Crew obscenity trial, a group whose album was chock-full of four-letter words and sexually graphic lyrics, an acquittal was required because their lyrics were "just not obscene." "People in everyday society use those words," one juror explained.[60] And, of course, that juror was right. Yet the freedom that makes this possible is not free. We pay for this bloated, frivolous freedom, as recent events suggest, with the eventual destruction of all the rest.

The only practical route out of America's rights-created predicament is a return to the primacy of duty and responsibility over rights. An absolute freedom of expression may be jolly for a while, but if we wish to retain a functioning society, eventually we must recognize and honor our duty to defend the community from such socially disruptive conduct. Wesley Hohfeld was the first to recognize that all rights have corresponding duties.[61] Thus, when the Supreme Court discovers new liberties in the Constitution, the Court manufactures packages of both rights and accompanying duties. American government has become unable to enforce the law effectively because it has been saddled with virtually all of these simultaneously minted responsibilities. Government must now primarily serve other, subsidiary rights, and often those of criminals. Civic duties have always been rightly regarded as societal chores imposed to mitigate self-centeredness. Yet although we need duty's community-strengthening qualities today more than ever, we often find it difficult even to say the word. Before the Persian Gulf War showed that patriotism could still be a successful marketing tool, even the U.S. Army at one time replaced its categorical imperative "Duty, Honor, Country" with the hypothetical, self-serving imperative "Be All You Can Be."

America must revive the notions of duty and responsibility if our most fundamental rights are to have any chance of enduring. In Plato's *Crito*, Socrates gave a lesson about duty that we would do well to reexamine. Socrates was sentenced to death in 399 B.C., following his prosecution on trumped-up charges by powerful Athenians whom Socrates had humbled in public debates. *Crito* recounts how Crito and other friends of Socrates came to his prison cell to inform him that they had arranged for his escape. Socrates refused to go. They pleaded with him by arguing, essentially, that he had the right to flee an unjust society that wrongly imposed such punishment. But Socrates did not bend. He thanked them for their trouble, but explained that a good citizen must obey the laws of his State, down to the bitter end. Citizenship, he said, is a transaction between the State and its citizens. For many years the State had provided Socrates the protection of the law and all the benefits that came from that protection. His end of the bargain was to swallow the fatal hemlock that Athens, itself a dying organism, had sentenced him to drink. Such was his duty:

> Suppose the laws and the commonwealth were to come and appear to me as I was preparing to run away . . . and were to ask, "Tell us, Socrates, what have you in your mind to do? What do you mean by trying to escape but to destroy us, the

laws and the whole state, so far as you are able? Do you think that a state can exist and not be overthrown, in which the decisions of law are of no force, and are disregarded and undermined by private individuals? . . . Was that our agreement?"[62]

Many Americans today, consistent with our relativism, will marvel at Socrates' courage and beliefs, yet reject his example as old-fashioned. From Socrates' death, however, we may find our own means of survival. His parting lesson to his pupils is even more relevant in our day than in his own: a society that lives by rights dies by rights. So it is that a people preoccupied with its "right" to avoid family and community responsibilities, and enjoying the other temporary dividends of inflamed individualism, ends up drinking its own poison.

PART THREE

ILLUSIONS AND SOLUTIONS

CHAPTER TEN

Placebos

. . . for look there, friend Sancho Panza, where thirty or more monstrous giants present themselves, all of whom I mean to engage in battle and slay, and with whose spoils we shall begin to make our fortunes; for this is righteous warfare, and it is God's good service to sweep so evil a breed from off the face of the earth.

—Miguel de Cervantes

To deal convincingly with the crisis raging around us, let us first acknowledge the obvious. Any nation whose shortcomings arise from a penchant for instant gratification is unlikely to hurriedly embrace remedies that require protracted, sweeping change from everyone. Crime in America, in fact, has the peculiar tendency to always appear to be the fault of somebody else—minorities, our schools and neighbors, a negligent government, or especially other people's children. Sacrifice, it follows, is incumbent on others. This assumption and our resulting reluctance to alter the way we think about and treat one another have had many untoward effects, one of them being the creation of a thriving market for sociological snake-oil merchants. They fill the policy vacuum with panaceas designed to divert the blame for crime from its rightful, unhappy owners.

265

This impulse finds purchasers all along the ideological spectrum, and these proposed cure-alls are accordingly tailored to the consumer based on his political philosophy. All, however, share at least one common ingredient: a bustle of government activity, albeit superficial and sometimes costly, designed to demonstrate anticrime resolve. Since anything more fundamental will demand more than grudgingly given tax dollars and limitations of somebody else's rights, these initiatives are too often the extent of our crime control efforts.

Yet we sense that such placebos will do very little to improve our situation, and history provides a reliable basis for this intuition. "History," Will Durant reminds us, "is a process of rebarbarization." He explains in typical pithy fashion the process by which nations decline and, eventually, perish:

> It is almost a law of history that the same wealth that generates a civilization announces its decay. For wealth produces ease as well as art. . . . The surplus generates a leisure class, scornful of physical activity and adept in the arts of luxury. Leisure begets speculation; speculation dissolves dogma and corrodes custom, develops sensitivity of perception and destroys decision of action. Thought, adventuring in a labyrinth of analysis, discovers behind society the individual; divested of its normal function it turns inward and discovers the self. The sense of common interest, of commonwealth, fades; there are no citizens now, there are only individuals.[1]

Durant did not spare his own nation the same harsh diagnosis. He applied impartially to America history's "highest law," which "seems to be the schoolboy's rule that everything that goes up must come down":

> America comes, and builds a civilization broader-based than any that the world has ever seen before. . . . But if there is any validity in history, if the past has any light to shed upon the future, then this civilization too, which we raise with such feverish toil and care, will pass away; and where we labor today, thousands of years hence savages will roam once more.[2]

Seeing these very signs of decay befalling the American Republic in his twilight years, Durant repudiated the libertarian extremism that he and his wife had championed in their youth in a dual essay "Have

We Too Much Freedom?"[3] But in doing so, he suffered no illusions about the prospects of dissuading his countrymen. The savages that he thought to be thousands of years away had arrived early, and, it turns out, are from our own ranks.

America's Great Havoc finds plenty of historical precedents. The one most familiar to Americans, and therefore the most useful for present purposes, is the erosion and downfall of the Roman Empire. Rome, it will be recalled, did not collapse from economic want or error. The decline of the empire's *latifundia* and Diocletian's wage and price controls were only incidental signs of a more basic social undoing. Rome died from its citizens' self-indulgence. The prosperity and security earned from previous centuries of self-denial allowed later generations of Romans the leisure and antireligious skepticism that always mark the decline of a civilization. Sealing their fate was Romans' belief, in the empire's final days, that their homeland could be defended without public participation. Thus, when the barbarians, sensing the empire's lethargy and its people's egoism, threatened to pour into Rome, Romans entrusted their security to foreign mercenaries, continued with their luxuries and public games, and apathetically awaited word of the outcome of the battles surrounding them.

Gibbon's account of the typical Roman's lifestyle right before the city's sacking, one of materialism and extreme individualism, applies with some force to Americans fifteen centuries later—or for that matter to citizens of almost any dissolving civilization. He described them as people

> who loitered away whole days in the street or Forum to hear news and to hold disputes; who dissipated in extravagant gaming the miserable pittance of their wives and children; and spent the hours of the night in obscure taverns and brothels in the indulgence of gross and vulgar sensuality.[4]

In the end, Rome fell because too many of its citizens were unwilling to check their vices for the common good. Gibbon summed up these enfeeblements, in an unusual choice of words, as betraying a "selfish and unmanly delicacy," one that corroded the Roman soul and left them powerless before their enemies. An anonymous observer of Rome's unraveling added that the only thing that seemed able to shake off Roman complacency was the promise of "bread and circuses"—meaning in one sense food and entertainment, and more generally diversions from their crisis of the soul. An early Christian priest named Salvian offered the same assessment shortly after Rome's first sacking. Romans, he felt, were bogged down in a luxurious, self-centered lifestyle that took greed and hedonism to be the twin pillars of life, virtue and self-denial to be obstacles to pleasure, and conventions such as marriage and industriousness to be jests. Even at the height of its wealth and games, the Roman Empire was disintegrating. *Moritur et ridet,* said Salvian—"It laughs and dies."[5]

It is a truism, then, that civilizations rise and fall; and so we should not automatically snicker at comparisons between deceased nations such as Rome and ours. America is not above the fate that other noble nations have suffered. Indeed, one of history's iron lessons is that the speed of a nation's descent ultimately depends on its citizens' degree of willingness to forgo private pleasures for public duty. We have been through some tough times before, certainly. Shays' Rebellion and the War Between the States were no walk in the park. But Americans seem to rightly sense that the catastrophe looming before us this time is fundamentally different. It threatens a civil war of unprecedented proportions, in which violent, egocentric individuals menace not merely other sects or regions, but everyone who owns something they want—including members of their own family. We are right to be worried. The Great Havoc is different: arguably the first time, at least in recorded history, in which a nation has stared into the jaws of a complete, individualistic social meltdown.

Once a majority of people in a democratic society come to regard self-interest as more important than public obligations, and to view their laws as behavioral suggestions rather than moral imperatives, their government must, and will, collapse. No amount of economic growth and concomitant material goods can safeguard a society whose main enemy is its own citizens. Indeed, wealth makes criminal mischief all the more likely, both by providing expanded opportunities for profitable crimes and by making the economics of this life seem more important than answering to an angry Deity in the next. These are singular history lessons to bear in mind when reviewing the current policy prescriptions for America's social ills. They are produced for a people that would prefer to change the subject from its own historically suicidal lifestyle, to the point that we will accept almost any program that promises not to distract us from our self-interested pursuits. The situation confronting us is just as stern as Salvian would have it. We laugh and die.

GUN CONTROL: BROTHER, CAN YOU SPARE A RAZOR?

"It's just like war," observed Richard Rhee, owner of a supermarket at the corner of Fifth and Western in riot-torn Los Angeles.[6] Rhee's assessment was backed by the obstinate realism of experience. A survivor of the Korean War and the Watts Riots, Rhee knew a war when he saw one. And what he and his Korean-American neighbors saw in the Rodney King Riots in May 1992 was indeed an atmosphere of festive, atomistic violence that Hobbes would have recognized all too well as the war of all against all.

Or at least a war of all against Koreans. In Rhee's neighborhood, Koreatown, the violence assumed some cohesion along racial lines. The loosely united enemies of Koreatown typically attacked in waves. First, Orientals and other nonblacks were pulled from passing vehicles and stoned into unconsciousness. Then came the looters, who culled through neighborhood businesses divested of police protection by the magnitude of the uprising and the miscalculations of the L.A. police force. Arson seemed to serve as the crowning racial *auto-da-fé*. Watching their stores become the preferred targets of the mob, many Korean merchants sat on nearby sidewalks and broke into tears as their family-owned monuments to years of eighteen-hour workdays collapsed into heaps of charred rubble. At one point all of Koreatown appeared imperiled because of the systematic drive-by arson perpetrated by neighborhood street gangs. Eighty percent of Koreatown's businesses were damaged. In all, 1,839 Korean enterprises, many uninsured, were ransacked and/or burned.[7]

As the rest of the nation stared hard at the balkanized violence that seemingly awaited them given a similar spark, L.A.'s Korean immigrants essentially saw two options. Some chose to return to their homeland, as seven thousand had done the prior year.[8] Rhee, on the other hand, resolved to stay. He grasped intuitively what Hobbes had tried to explain to an often inattentive West 350 years before. The most fundamental natural right and corresponding duty of government are that of personal security. And when government can no longer do the job, that liberty gives rise to a second, essential right of self-defense.

"Burn this down after thirty-three years?" he rhetorically asked one reporter. "They don't know how hard I've worked. This is my market and I'm going to protect it."[9] With that, he and his neighbors resorted to the same traditional methods of self-protection used in like circumstances by the first settlers in southern California. They took up arms.

From the makeshift command post atop his supermarket, Rhee helped oversee a volunteer brigade of Korean-Americans. Bearing shotguns and semiautomatic weapons, Rhee and his lieutenants set up fields of fire to ward off the assaults on his property. Warning shots usually seemed to do the job, although more than a few bursts were required; one of Rhee's colleagues estimated that he and others had fired about 500 shots into the ground and air. But as the riots raged around them, quickly engulfing undefended establishments, any doubts as to the effectiveness of Rhee's strategy of raw deterrence were quickly erased. This store would stand.

Rhee's redoubt was far from unique. His was part of a string of Korean businesses audaciously resisting the riots, a line of defense running from small liquor stores in South-Central Los Angeles to upscale Korean-owned boutiques in Mid-Wilshire. Spearheading this resistance was a small cadre of Korean-American Marine veterans.[10] When a call went out on L.A.'s Korean-language radio stations for volunteers to defend Koreatown, they responded by hastily organizing an impressive improvised defense system to shield besieged Korean shops. They established defense perimeters at the edges of parking lots with strapped-together grocery carts, buttressing the line of parked automobiles to form a mini-DMZ. Other shopping carts were stacked in front of windows, and pallets of bagged rice and boxed cabbage barricaded the stores' entrances. Scores of other armed volunteers patrolled the darkened parking lots or crouched behind the automotive firewall. The leaders of the effort sought higher ground on store rooftops, coordinating the operations with binoculars and cellular phones.

"Vigilante" was the most common, anguished aspersion given Koreatown's defenders. But few Koreans desired confrontation. Some of the volunteers, for instance, were members of the same Presbyterian church, and, before assuming their posts, they gathered together and prayed for peace.[11] Rather, in the tradition of the minutemen and the pioneers, they appealed to the old American right to repel armed aggression by using like force. And as the revolutionaries who framed the Bill of Rights recognized, this necessarily implies a basic right to keep and bear arms, free of interference from a government which, in Rhee's case, was viewing almost passively the creation of a new tyranny.

As they watched the unprotected stores around them reduced to ashes, Koreatown's peacekeepers lost patience with their critics. "We have to stay here," explained Dong Hee Ku, a student at Los Angeles City College who responded to the call for volunteers and helped in the defense of Rhee's market. "All the victims are always Koreans."[12] Many black residents of South-Central concurred as to the anti-Korean animus behind the riots. According to members of the Eight-Tray Gangster Crips, the gang responsible for much of the initial rioting at the intersection of Florence and Normandie, the riots started as a flare-up from the smoldering racial tensions between neighborhood blacks and Koreans. By their recollection the riots originated from a dispute between several gang members and the son of the Korean owner of a neighborhood liquor store.[13] Once the riots began, however, L.A.'s Korean community did not need to know the reasons for the unrest to realize they faced a stark choice: either resort to self-defense or meekly submit to imminent violence.

Although Korean merchants had repeatedly asked police for protection, the groundswell of crime soon made that all but impossible. Their resentment of the government's failure to honor this duty did not dampen the spirits of Koreatown's guardians. From the rooftop of one establishment, a Korean flashed a thumbs-up over his automatic weapon to television cameras. One defender of a supermarket-turned-fortress summed up their entrepreneurial optimism by telling one reporter, with a wave: "No trouble. Come back tomorrow."[14]

If the rest of the country did not share this hopefulness, it was because America had seen its second-largest city fall off into the abyss, and with alarming alacrity. During the previous three decades of unprecedented violent crime, many of the nation's leading criminologists and policymakers had stated that the best means of preventing such displays was to limit or ban privately held firearms. The responsibility for armed community defense, which the Founders believed to rest ultimately with private citizens, was to be shifted to policemen, a paramilitary class thought to be capable of safeguarding order without the support of the community. But while polls prior to L.A.'s Korean War suggested that gun control appealed to a substantial number of Americans, many suburbanites previously disposed to leaving their deterrence duties with policemen were forced to reconsider things following the riots.

Some of L.A.'s government officials were slower to acknowledge these lessons. Their first response to the riots was to attempt to disarm legal gun owners of what rapidly became, for many of them, their sole means of self-protection. At the outbreak of the rioting the Los Angeles city council promptly voted to ban the sale of ammunition within the city limits. This decision supplemented the existing state law mandating a fifteen-day waiting period on the purchase of all firearms; this law, it was argued, provided for a "cooling-off" period during which precipitate inner-city youths were, in essence, to abandon their homicidal intentions after two weeks of embarrassed introspection. Thus, many lawful residents during the riots found that they could not obtain firearms before it was too late, and could not even purchase ammunition for the weapons they already legally owned. One poignant example of what followed involved Edward Valencia, owner of the Ace Gun Shop in Northridge. He was forced to turn away a man in his seventies "who looked like he could use a little comfort and said he wanted a box of ammo for his 30-year-old gun. He said he wanted to protect himself." He had to refuse to sell the man any because of the city ban.[15] Meanwhile the city's offenders by definition ignored the gun control strictures, stealing from gun shops and further contributing to the imbalance of forces.

Despite the hurdles placed before legal gun ownership, Californians in the wake of the rioting purchased firearms at a record rate. In the first eleven days after the riots, California residents bought 20,578 guns, a 50 percent increase over the same period the previous year. Other states that track gun sales reported a comparable rise immediately following the unrest.[16]

Although we might have reasonably thought gun control to have died in the embers of the Rodney King Riots, this policy has retained considerable, and increasingly bipartisan, appeal. The reasons for this widening support for gun control are not as self-evident as we often assume. On the one hand, many on the political Left in government and academia advocate a rights-based atomism based on the Bill of Rights and its modern judicial interpretations. Presumably the Second Amendment's right to keep and bear arms is a natural candidate for similar treatment. It is, after all, a freedom also enshrined in the Constitution, and if nothing else is helpful for coping with the instability attendant to the expansion of the Constitution's other rights. Indeed, the right to bear arms is, except for Locke's trinity of life, liberty and property, arguably the most hallowed individual right in the Western tradition, one that chiseled itself into the American Bill of Rights millennia after ancient Greeks similarly recognized its usefulness. But vying with this Second Amendment freedom for fidelity from the Left is an aversion to violence that sometimes reaches the unhealthy extreme of pacifism, and that makes gun control appealing.

There are other reasons for gun control's popularity. One is the old antagonist of William of Ockham, the British priest who used his theoretical razor to cut through the early Church's reliance on the Forms, or misleading abstractions, inspired by Plato. Like drugs, poverty and the other modern Forms in the criminal justice debate, gun control is a Platonic means of diverting criminal blame from offenders. Other aspects of gun control appeal to the American people as a whole, and further account for the policy's longevity in the national crime control debate. As a public policy in a relativistic age, gun control has the virtue of allowing us to avoid self-criticism in searching for answers to the crime crisis. Since most Americans today, unlike prior generations, do not own guns, gun control also does not require sacrifice from most of us. The majority may therefore merely use their superior numbers to enlist government in collecting the weapons of the armed minority, and convince themselves that more far-reaching steps can be forestalled. Many of us also feel that the rationale for firearms of old—that is taming a wilderness—has no modern counterpart.

These are explanations, rather than compelling reasons, for gun control's durable appeal. For guns do not cause crime any more than hemlock was morally responsible for causing the death of Plato's master. Rather, guns provide useful instruments for a variety of human endeavors—some good, some bad—in which people choose to invest them. Like the War on Drugs, the War on Guns cries out for a British priest's razor.

Father William would have his work cut out for him. There is a surprisingly large number of studies in the social sciences purporting to show that guns cause crime. Professor Franklin Zimring, now a law professor at the University of California-Berkeley, rose to national prominence with his theory that violent crime is a function of the number of firearms available. He and his colleague George Newton were appointed to the Eisenhower Commission's Task Force on Firearms in 1968, and succinctly offered their thesis as the title of one section of the commission's report: "More Firearms—More Firearms Violence."[17] Newton and Zimring, both gun control activists, found that more guns mean more violence; it is as simple as that. To reach this conclusion they relied on zero-order correlations between gun ownership and gun use in violence, analysis which discounts other, equally plausible factors that could also influence gun use. In addition, the study did not consider the possibility that more violence produces more gun ownership, rather than the reverse. Nevertheless, in their closing recommendation for a "nationwide restrictive licensing system for handguns," the two criticized the "partisan research" infecting the debate over gun control.[18]

To be fair, any scholar would be hard pressed to come up with scientific evidence of the utility of a private-gun ban. There is very little historical proof of its feasibility. While Charles Silberman and many others have argued that guns represent a frontier mentality that leads to greater violent crime, gun control is not a fresh, modern idea suggested by recent advances in civilization. Gun regulation of some sort has existed in the United States since colonial times, beginning with the Massachusetts Colony's prohibition of carrying firearms in public places. At present there are over 20,000 different laws of varying severity controlling the use of firearms. These range from municipal ordinances prohibiting the discharge of firearms within city limits to complete bans on handguns in New York and Massachusetts under the Sullivan and Bartley-Fox gun laws. Federal laws also control the interstate sale of firearms and prohibit the sale of certain firearms, such as fully automatic weapons. There is no nook or cranny in America that does not have at least one layer of firearm regulation, and usually many more.

Similarly, just as Americans have always sought to keep criminals and the insane from obtaining firearms, we have always viewed guns as an indispensable preserver of freedom and personal security. Florida State professor Gary Kleck's evaluation of polling data from nine independent polls concluded that between 27 and 34 percent of gun-owning households questioned reported possessing guns primarily for self-defense. Between 28 and 65 percent reported owning a firearm either primarily or secondarily for self-defense. When the same questions were asked of handgun owners, between 43 and 67 percent stated that self-defense was their primary reason for gun ownership. Over 73 percent responded that self-defense was a primary or secondary reason.[19] Alan Lizotte and David Bordua found the same correlation.[20] Kleck concluded: ". . . it is clear that defense or protection is a very common reason for owning guns in general, and that it is the *dominant* reason, although clearly not the only one, for owning handguns in the United States."[21]

Given that so many Americans own guns because they fear for their safety, it is hard to imagine a total gun ban being enforceable. How likely is a freedom-loving people embroiled in an unprecedented violent crime wave to voluntarily relinquish its firearms to a government that is clearly unable or unwilling to provide for its personal security in return? The dimensions of such an enforcement effort should also give us pause. The Bureau of Alcohol, Tobacco and Firearms has estimated the number of privately owned firearms in the United States to be 200 million, almost one gun for every American.[22] The demand for guns, moreover, is highly inelastic. It is determined by criminals who use them as valuable business assets and by citizens reacting to the criminal demand. Don Kates, Jr., a self-described antigun "liberal" who is nonetheless skeptical of gun control's merits, has drawn the obvious parallels between Prohibition and gun control. Kates notes that any attempt to eliminate guns would likely incite similarly widespread resistance because of its perceived illegitimacy. He believes it reasonable to "predict that the percentage of noncompliance [of a gun ban] will be approximately coterminous with the percentage of protection ownership," meaning that the only citizens who would comply are those who do not own weapons primarily for self-defense. That amounts to only one-half of the guns held by the *law-abiding* population.[23] This is not an inconsiderable number, to be sure, but it would still leave quite a few weapons in private, clenched hands.

If the ban were limited to handguns, as is often recommended, the effect on the violent crime rate would be minor at best. Kleck, another self-labeled "liberal" critic of gun control, estimates that rifles or shotguns, or "long guns," could "easily" be substituted for handguns in anywhere from 54 to 80 percent of all homicides.[24] Since long guns are much more lethal than handguns, a gun prohibition limited to handguns could actually increase the fatality rate from armed crimes. Moreover, whether or not such efforts are limited to handguns, government confiscation of the 200 million privately held firearms seems unworkable at any level of government. Kates notes that New York City, with its strict Sullivan Law, still has an estimated two million illegal handguns circulating.[25] Similarly, handgun bans have never been shown to yield lower violent crime rates. Since Massachusetts enacted the Bartley-Fox Law in 1975, which mandated a one-year jail sentence for persons carrying a handgun without a license, the state and its capital, Boston, rose from the nineteenth and fifth most violent state and city, respectively, to eleventh and first by 1983. During the same period gun-related assault jumped 20 percent in Massachusetts, while increasing only 6 percent nationwide.[26]

A federal prohibition of firearms seems just as impractical. Even if all 200 million or so private firearms could be rounded up, a society that cannot prevent illegal narcotics from seeping through its unavoidably porous borders despite a similar, complete embargo can hardly hope to keep out objects long considered a birthright of citizenship, and now seen as vital for personal security. A federal government incapable of halting the more than one million illegal immigrants currently believed to enter the country annually seems unequal to the task of blocking the importation of firearms, which, of course, these same immigrants could carry across the border with them. Kates estimates that if handguns were illegally imported at the same volume as marijuana, approximately twenty million of the size used to kill John Lennon would enter the nation annually.[27] Furthermore, a black market of do-it-yourself gunsmith guides, which are already widely available,[28] would likely combine with a cottage industry of underground gunsmiths to form a sizable, additional criminal enterprise.

All of this, of course, assumes that we are prepared to seek what very few policymakers thus far have had the courage to recommend publicly: the outlawing of all privately held firearms. It is not hard to see why elected officials seldom advocate this. Police officers under this system would be required to pursue law-abiding citizens worried about self-defense rather than concentrating on apprehending gun-toting criminals. Of course, if this ban were to extend only to the sale of *new* firearms, or expensive and relatively rare "assault weapons," there would be virtually no effect on the availability of guns. Far more sweeping steps would be necessary. There would be public resistance to a prohibition of private firearms, but not nearly as much as we might expect from a nation founded on armed self-defense. Forty-one percent of Americans in a 1991 poll approved of banning all private gun ownership.[29] In addition, 93 percent of Americans endorsed the concept of a seven-day waiting or cooling-off period on the sale of firearms,[30] as was recently enacted in the federal Brady Bill. Still, Americans seem drawn to gun control less out of a sober evaluation of its merits than because of its popularity among society's opinion leaders, and because many of us would prefer to believe the government still capable of defending us against offenders, when it increasingly is not.

If guns were more like drugs, gun control could make a greater claim for our loyalties. Just as drug prohibitions are successful at reducing the volume of drugs in America, so too gun control would reduce commerce in firearms, *if* guns were not already plentiful in society. To argue otherwise, as some gun enthusiasts do, means denying that people respond to incentives and are governed by uncontrollable urges, a notion which we have already seen to be faulty. The difference is that drugs, unlike firearms, have historically been subject to strict government regulation. In addition, certain kinds of narcotics, such as heroin and cocaine, are produced overwhelmingly in foreign countries. Thus, enforcement of drug laws primarily involves interdiction of foreign drug smuggling. This is a hard task, certainly, but much easier than commandeering 200 million birthrights from private, vigilant hands; if America truly desires thorough gun control, we are about four centuries too late. Gun control, furthermore, would affect only law-abiding folk. Criminals by definition would evade the ban; indeed, *only one firearm of every six used in a crime is obtained legally.*[31] In view of this, it would seem that a complete ban on private gun ownership would simply result in massive law violations by otherwise responsible citizens and a redistribution of firearms to the government and its criminal foes—neither of which needs them.

When the interim, and somewhat dishonest, steps such as cooling-off laws and mandatory registration are taken out of the picture, gun control ultimately comes down to this core belief, as phrased by Professor Kleck: ". . . we must deny guns to the 99 percent of the population who will never commit a serious act of violence in their lives in order to produce some marginal reduction in the ease of access to guns among the 1 percent who will commit such an act."[32] And the payoff from this would be slight. As Bordua and Lizzotte confirmed in their cross-sectional analysis, the levels of legal gun ownership have no discernible relationship to violent crime rates.[33] Their evidence and other statistics, in fact, "implied that where the rate of legal firearms is high, the crime rate is low," and it is therefore "implausible to assume that legal firearms ownership increases crime."[34] Even the National Academy of Sciences report in 1992 overruled Zimring, one of its panelists, in finding, "Available research does not demonstrate that greater gun availability is linked to greater numbers of violent events or injuries."[35] Their review of the literature revealed, "Even where positive correlations are found between measures of gun availability and nonfatal violent crime, the direction of this causal chain is unclear," as a result of regional disparities in gun use and other factors.[36]

There is still further reason for concern and skepticism over gun control. Except for a small group of unenterprising offenders at the margins, the only people who would be denied firearms under gun control would be lawful citizens, many of whom are poorer, more vulnerable people who adamantly believe these weapons necessary for their self-protection. Traditionally, gun control has meant denying a means of self-defense, and thus equal protection of the law, to the most powerless and preyed-upon echelon of society: racial minorities. Roy Innis, chairman of the Congress of Racial Equality, points out that gun control originated from the Supreme Court's *Dred Scott* decision of 1857. The Court's establishment of a *de facto* constitutional right to own slaves was based on Chief Justice Taney's fear that blacks would enjoy, among other freedoms, "the right . . . to keep and carry arms wherever they went," leading to "insubordination." Based on this Innis concludes, "Gun-control legislation of the late 19th and early 20th centuries, enacted at the state and local levels, was implicitly racist in conception."[37] Northern cities, for their part, imposed gun restrictions at the turn of the century to deprive new immigrants, particularly Italians and Jews, of guns.[38]

Certain gun control measures, such as permit requirements, would create a police monopoly over what is rapidly becoming the sole method of protection from violent offenders, a monopoly that is sometimes abused. Although one study of lower-income blacks arrested for carrying illegal weapons discovered that 70 percent were carrying them for self-protection,[39] Innis observes that fewer than 2 percent of the handgun permits currently issued in New York go to blacks. Of these, many go to the wealthier, better-connected blacks rather than residents of the inner city. One recipient of such special treatment in suburban Washington, D.C., was syndicated columnist and staunch supporter of gun control Carl Rowan. Having frequently endorsed in his column the confiscation of private firearms, many of which would be taken from his fellow African-Americans in the District, Rowan himself used an illegal handgun to shoot a suburban teenager who was swimming uninvited in his pool in June 1988. "I am for gun control," Rowan reiterated, but not "unilateral gun control, in which I leave my family naked to the druggies and the crooks out there."[40] Under a permit regime many permits go to the similarly well-to-do. In 1977 a list of New York residents holding these carry permits was leaked to the public. While official policy required that such licenses be granted only upon proof of a unique need for self-defense, the roll included names that were known less for the daily peril they faced than for their wealth and political connections, which they had dedicated to, among other things, advocating gun control. They included Arthur Ochs Sulzberger, publisher of *The New York Times* and frequent pro-gun control editorialist; Nelson, John Jay and other Rockefellers; former Republican mayor John Lindsay; and the husband of Dr. Joyce Brothers, she having claimed that firearm ownership was a sign of male sexual inadequacy.[41]

It is easy to make hay of such hypocrisy; but such hypocrisy is also, as La Rochefoucauld would have it, the tribute that vice pays to virtue. Many supporters of gun control implicitly recognize, even if they smile at it publicly, the wisdom of the hoary bumper sticker slogan "If guns are outlawed, only outlaws will have guns." One of the founders of criminology, Cesare Beccaria, spoke of this in the 1700s. He even foretold, quite remarkably, the later attempts of the discipline he helped found to deny this truth, in a passage that deserves to be quoted at length:

> False is the idea of utility that sacrifices a thousand real advantages for one imaginary or trifling inconvenience; that would take fire from men because it burns, and water because one may drown in it; that has no remedy for evils, except destruction. The laws that forbid the carrying of arms are laws of such a nature. They disarm those only who are neither inclined nor determined to commit crimes. Can it be supposed that those who have the courage to violate the most sacred laws of humanity, the most important of the code, will respect the less important and arbitrary ones, which can be violated with ease and impunity, and which, if strictly obeyed, would put an end to personal liberty—so dear to men, so dear to the enlightened legislator—and subject innocent persons to all the vexations that the guilty alone ought to suffer? Such laws make things worse for the assaulted and better for the assailants; they serve rather to encourage than to prevent homicides, for an unarmed man may be attacked with greater confidence than an armed man. They ought to be designated as laws not preventive but

fearful of crimes, produced by the tumultuous impression of a few isolated facts, and not by consideration of the incoveniences and advantages of a universal decree.[42]

Confronting a popular culture in which they are often seen as quarry for violent exploitation, women are also increasingly relying on firearms for self-defense. Paxton Quigley, herself a former gun control activist who now trains women shootists, cites studies showing gun ownership among women jumping 53 percent in three years, with 40 percent of female-headed households in one state, Louisiana, reporting owning a handgun.[43] Firearms, of course, are women's best means of defending themselves against physically overpowering men. Carol Ruth Silver and Kates argue that firearms are women's only practicable way of exercising their common-law right to resist rape with deadly force.[44] Gun control would thus disarm women of the great equalizer, one of the few things that can inspire awe in today's violent men.

Gun control, then, is precisely opposite the direction in which a nation that desires the rule of law should be moving. Such measures represent a literal laying-down-of-arms surrender to criminals. The wording and the history of the Second Amendment provide better suggestions. Notable is the amendment's use of the term "militia" to describe the class of people to enjoy the right to bear arms. Rather than an approximate synonym for the modern National Guard, as is often assumed, the word "militia," as then understood by Anglo-Saxons, meant the entire adult male citizenry. The term entered the English language during the national panic over the Spanish Armada in the late sixteenth century. Frequently the English at the time used "militia" interchangeably with phrases like "the whole body of the people." In contrast they referred to a more elite military force distinct from the militia as a "select militia," usually pejoratively.[45] The militia of the time, in fact, were not simply permitted but *required* to keep and bear arms as a civic duty, both under the frankpledge and in case of needed military service. The Founders shared this understanding. In 1792, three years after passing the Second Amendment, Congress enacted the federal Militia Act. The act defined the militia to include the nation's entire able-bodied male citizenry of military age and required every member of the same to own a firearm.[46]

A new federal law to that effect today would, of course, be enormously controversial and presumed absurd. Given the current popular mistrust of firearms and their common abuse by society's least responsible members, many Americans will shudder at this suggestion. The last thing we need, we have come to assume, is more guns in private hands. But is this true, or even relevant? As we have seen, the issue as a practical matter is not whether we can collect 200 million firearms (we cannot), but rather what can be done to deter their criminal use. American criminals will always be able to get firearms; the question is whether we are prepared to resist them with necessary force given that the police alone cannot do the job. The Founders of this Republic, it turns out, were well acquainted with these concerns, and they left us important lessons on the matter. We should hear them out.

A new federal Militia Act would be both constitutional and prudent. Of course, the Second Amendment, contrary to the claims of its overexuberant friends, was not intended to be absolute, any more than were the other freedoms in the Bill of Rights. Blackstone spoke of the right as "that of having arms for their defense, *suitable to their condition and degree, and such as are allowed by law*"(emphasis added). He discussed one statute that codified the right "under due restrictions," a law that, while not absolute, still protected "the natural right of resistance and self-preservation, when the sanctions of society and laws are found insufficient to restrain the violence of oppression." Blackstone also commended a statute that made it a breach of the peace to carry "dangerous or unusual weapons . . . apt to terrify the people."[47] Proposals to ban so-called assault weapons such as the AK-47, though occasionally demagogic and of very limited value given the scale of the crisis, are therefore constitutionally sound. So too are more thoughtful proposals for registration and licensing requirements. Under the militia laws of the colonies and, later, of both the state and federal governments, men and households subject to the laws were required to prove compliance by submitting their firearms for inspection periodically.[48] These statutes were predicated on a preexisting registration list.

A new statutory requirement that heads of household with noncriminal backgrounds keep a serviceable firearm in their households and that all private firearms therefore be registered with the government would likely provide one of the most efficacious means of deterring offenders. This law would clearly have to be wedded to mandatory training requirements, as well as properly strict penalties, as are now on the books in several states, for adults who failed to store them so that they were inaccessible to children. Also, conscientious objectors to the requirement would be exempt. Aside from reinforcing the historically vital conception of the community as ultimately responsible for crime control, such a law could have an immediate deterrent effect. Thirty-five percent of all rapes, for example, occur in the victim's home, making the home the most common place of occurrence for that crime.[49] Many other crimes, including murder, are disproportionately committed at or near the victim's home; all residential burglaries by definition take place in the home.

Private firearms possession would at least make most such offenders think twice. Kleck and Bordua have calculated that at present, the average burglar in the United States faces less chance of punishment from the criminal justice system than from being shot by an armed homeowner.[50] Kleck's research indicates that guns are used in self-defense against crimes between 645,000 and one million times a year.[51] Relying on Kleck's research the National Academy of Sciences report in 1992 concluded, "Self-defense gun use . . . is associated with a reduced risk of physical attack and injury."[52] Kates's study showed that 83 percent of private citizens who used a firearm to repel a criminal succeeded in preventing the crime and/or apprehending the criminal; the figure was only 68 percent for the police.[53] University of Massachusetts sociology professor James D. Wright used the money he received from a major federal grant earmarked for (presumably friendly) gun control research in interviewing prisoners for their perspectives. Wright and his colleagues discovered that while 76 percent of inmates did not worry about criminal prosecution when committing a crime, 57 percent agreed with the statement "Most criminals are more worried about meeting an armed victim than they are about running into the police." Fifty-six percent felt that "a criminal is not going to mess around with a victim he knows is armed with a gun." Nearly 40 percent stated that they had been deterred from committing at least one crime because they knew or thought that the victim was armed.[54]

This policy of armed community deterrence has been applied with varying rigor in two cities. In 1966, following a series of rapes in Orlando, Florida, the *Orlando Sentinel Star* ran a series of articles and editorials denouncing an ensuing gun-buying spree by area women. After the newspaper editors complained to the Orlando chief of police, both agreed to cosponsor a gun-training program for women. The *Sentinel Star* ran a front-page story announcing the time and location of the course. Orlando's offenders appeared to get the message. Orlando's rape rate subsequently plunged from 36 in 1966 to only 4 in 1967, a decrease that no other U.S. city with over 100,000 people enjoyed over the same period. Five years later rape was still well below the preprogram level, even though the rape rate had risen 308 percent in the surrounding metropolitan area and 64 percent in the nation.[55]

Kennesaw, Georgia, took a page right out of the Founders' statutes. In 1982 the town passed a city ordinance requiring every household to have a working firearm and stocked ammunition. Kennesaw experienced an 89 percent drop in the burglary rate in the seven months immediately following the law's passage.[56] This decrease continued for the following two years.[57]

While the drop in crime rates that followed these measures may well have been due to other factors, the apparent deterrent effect of these laws—probably attributable to sheer publicity—nonetheless suggests that maybe the Founders knew what they were doing after all. While they may have left us a political regime with latent centrifugal individualism and an unexplained role for a lawyer-intellectual Supreme Court, they did at least generously bestow on their descendants a permanent right to bear arms. It was a right that they knew from their own recent experience to be precious, and most helpful when statutorily put to affirmative use by requiring its public exercise. This right, while not absolute and thus not proscribing reasonable gun restrictions, was something that, when codified in tandem with a civic duty of community self-defense, provided the surest method of criminal deterrence and social cohesion.

The recent riots in Los Angeles have only shown in stark relief this freedom's necessity. Gun control may help society avoid, at least for a while, certain civic duties or the business of assigning blame for criminal misconduct. But as a policy for combating the Great Havoc, it has proved ill-conceived and dangerous. After all, when L.A. trucker Reginald Denny was dragged from his truck at Florence and Normandie and nearly murdered, the weapon of choice was not a gun, but a fire extinguisher and bricks. Repealing the right to bear arms in self-defense can only fuel such violence by eliminating the lone practical deterrent to crime that now exists in many parts of America. In the creeping war of all against all, it may be private defenders of the peace like Richard Rhee who do the most for halting this war's spread, and for dispelling the misconceptions that make gun control seem like a forceful statement against crime.

VICTIMS' RIGHTS: JOINING THE RIGHTS RACE

At first glance, the concept of victims' rights seems to present us with the closest thing yet to a consensus approach to the crime problem. There is certainly plenty of ideological common ground here. The idea of giving victims of crime certain essential rights after the fact, such as the right to testify at the criminal's trial and to speak at his sentencing, has attracted wide support as a means of balancing the rights granted offenders in recent years. It certainly looks like a harmless handout. Surely our recent cornucopia of rights can find a few crumbs for the victims of crime, who, after all, have suffered the most from extreme individualism and distended individual rights.

The ideological spectrum is speckled with the various reasons given for this new compact. Many on the Right follow the libertarian lead in endorsing a rights-based approach to crime control; others simply despair of reversing the recent expansion of offenders' rights and want to even things up somewhat. Those on the Left who reject ultraindividualism yet support victims' rights are generally moved by other concerns. For them, victims' rights is an act of reparation of sorts for how awry things have gone recently. Victims' rights presents a way of leveling the playing field of entitlements through an equal distribution of rights. Finally, some on the far Left oppose victims' rights because the proposed recipients, those incidentally harmed by what society arbitrarily depicts as crime, are not victims at all. The true victims, as Jessica Mitford and others would argue, are those who have been forced by an unjust society into a life of crime. To them, the differentiation of victims' rights and criminals' rights does not make sense. The two are one and the same.

Except for Ms. Mitford and others in this last camp, victims' rights has come to be seen as a transideological solution for crime. Victims' rights is emerging as a rough bargain between the two main groups. Most important from everyone's standpoint, victims' rights is very inexpensive. It costs very little in actual outlays of dollars to, for instance, make victims feel that their opinions count during the trial and sentencing of their assailants. And, as one professor observed, victims' rights carries a useful "placebo value . . . it creates the impression that 'something is being done'" about crime.[58]

Victims' rights provides a discouraging commentary on the present state of American criminal justice. Instead of grappling with the reasons for America's high crime rates, this new policy merely salves the mental wounds of crime's victims without helping to prevent other citizens from suffering a similar fate. Victims' rights is an unacceptable reaction to mushrooming crime rates from a society that can do better. Such rights reflect the growing popular belief that the "best" relative justice that can be had in modern America comes from standing in line at the national rights cafeteria and demanding a free serving. Society is thus looked upon as merely the sum total of individual rights. Civic life becomes a race to acquire and stockpile the most rights, which may then be used for self-gratification or for fortifying one's arsenal to keep out the losers in the competition. The devil take the hindmost.

Victims' rights has certain precedents in European history, but none that foreshadows the current tit-for-tat backlash against crime that this movement represents. Some of the related history of trial by battle was discussed earlier; the history of victims' rights is distinct and requires separate discussion. Victims' rights grew out of the medieval view of the community as the centerpiece of a private system of justice. This system took shape after the collapse of the Roman Empire, filling the justice void that this created. This vacuum of central authority for meting out just punishment to criminal offenders, as noted previously, meant that criminal justice in the Middle Ages usually devolved upon private parties. Justice was secured through various forms of vigilantism, the most common being the blood feud. Through the blood feud the victim or his kin exacted retribution against the offender, sometimes in the form of compelled monetary compensation. This tradition of the feud came well before the modern disintegration of the family, and therefore naturally expressed itself most commonly as strife between the disputants' relatives. The family feud lingered for centuries. One of the most famous feuds of later times was that between two American clans, the Hatfields and the McCoys. The blood feud, the family feud's direct ancestor, was the principal criminal justice system both in England and on the Continent for most of the Middle Ages.[59]

A corollary system augmented this attempt to deter and punish crime in the fragmented feudal countryside. Throughout Europe the popular principle of outlawry held that the entire community could punish a criminal collectively, both to gain justice and to ensure public safety. Long before Hobbes would formulate his theory in these express terms, the community invoking outlawry viewed the criminal as someone who had declared war against society. Under this system the community responded in kind. Neighbors would join together to deal with the menace as a unit—burning his home, plundering his possessions, hunting him down and either banishing or killing him. Outlawry was at best rough justice, and at worst mob rule. But lacking a central government capable of enforcing the basic laws of civilized living, society was left to enforce these primitive, unwritten edicts privately with either an individual/family (feud) or collective (outlawry) effort.

As the Norman kings and their descendants tightened their control and authority over the English nation, some of the first powers they sought to expropriate from the people were those of informal criminal justice. The Crown replaced the blood feud with the punishments of "bot" and "wer." This was a system of government-collected monetary compensation for crime victims or their kin. Another fine, "wite," was levied separately for the Crown. The government established the value of restitution for every crime. The acceptance of the concept of the "king's peace" in later centuries caused crime to be looked upon less as a personal affront to the victim than as an offense against the monarch. Outlawry was transformed from a collective private punishment to a process for compelling the accused's attendance at a government-sponsored trial by ordeal or battle.[60] The crime victim still retained the power to initiate the criminal process under this State-run criminal justice system. Through an appeal or indictment, the victim could allege orally or in writing, respectively, that another member of the community had committed a crime. An impartial judge appointed by the king then presided over a trial with both the accuser and accused present, often a trial by battle in which the victor was declared the successful litigant.

Out of the Middle Ages evolved a mixed system of public and private criminal justice that worked reasonably well. But as governments throughout Europe grew in power, the right of victims to mete out justice personally was sapped by a corresponding amount. Until the middle of the nineteenth century in England, the victim retained the right to initiate and manage the proceedings against the alleged offender, just as a modern plaintiff supervises his own civil case. In America this method of prosecution fell out of favor in the late eighteenth century, as the deputy attorneys general of each county assumed complete control over all prosecutions within their counties.[61] Previously, convention had allowed the victim to finance the prosecution and tack on a civil dimension to the case. Crime victims, who often did their own detective work, could hire attorneys to file a suit as part of the criminal case and recover monetary damages from the jury at the criminal trial. Certain offenses even flashed the prospect of treble damages before victims and newly amicable members of the bar.[62] Thus, just as modern statutes providing for treble damages attract much litigation, the criminal justice business similarly beckoned to early American attorneys, who saw that such cases had monetary possibilities. Private prosecutors were rented as hired guns to exact retribution from the miscreant.[63]

But lawyers, despite their extensive lobbying efforts,[64] were later forced to yield to an even bigger, more insatiable entity in the modern State. The growth of governmental power in later centuries meant a steady accretion of criminal justice sovereignty to the government. By the time of the American Revolution, the present system of public prosecution with little to no private participation was well entrenched in American courts.

The reemergence of victims' rights in the late twentieth century is a reaction to the breakdown of America's criminal justice regime. The overloaded system has spurred Americans to call for the reimposition of the rugged individualist's crime control strategy. In some extreme cases the community has reverted to outlawry again in its modern form, vigilantism. Neighbors frustrated by a sluggish and unpredictable criminal justice system increasingly organize to collectively pursue and punish wrongdoers pursuant to the *a priori* sense of justice that guided their medieval forefathers. The victims' rights movement represents the opposite, individualized reaction by the community. And victims' rights is, of course, the more logical reaction for a society whose preoccupation with rights is a primary reason for its predicament. As Sir James Fitzjames Stephen observed of the precursor of victims' rights, the former system of private criminal prosecutions, the result is a system that serves mainly to give "a legal vent to feelings in every way entitled to respect."[65]

Regrettably, however, victims' rights accomplishes little more than this, and is in fact harmful in some respects. Like the earlier private prosecutions, victims' rights can introduce greater inequality into criminal proceedings. Most victims' rights proposals, true to Stephen's recommendation, revolve around victim-impact statements. These are pieces of evidence to be admitted into criminal proceedings, designed to inform the judge and jury of the suffering the alleged offender has inflicted on the victim and his kin. This suffering can be described in physical, psychological and financial terms. Although victim-impact statements may gratify the wronged citizen somewhat by allowing a "legal vent" to his outrage, their potential for injustice and inequality outweighs their helpfulness. These statements are simply irrelevant to determining the guilt of the accused. Their introduction into evidence, while comforting to the victim, may very easily overwhelm and inflame the jury with distracting information that leads them to convict innocent people out of a confused pity. Criminal punishment under such a system can become contingent on how much grief is exhibited in the courtroom, and how much sympathy is wrung out of the jury.

Even when the accused is guilty, as most criminal defendants are, victim-impact statements unacceptably make the amount of suffering caused by a criminal a factor in determining the amount of punishment. Thus, a defendant who murders an elderly, childless widow presumably gets lighter punishment than an offender whose victim happens to have more numerous or vocal family members. By making this latter victim a more powerful dictator of justice, the victim-impact statement places a premium on the amount of dramatic anguish that can be displayed in a courtroom. The arbitrariness and unpredictability that this practice injects into criminal law are no help to a system already straining to provide a modicum of sentencing consistency for deterrence purposes. For there to be equal justice under law, punishment must be based not on who the offender or his victim is, but on the crime committed.

This system of judicially orchestrated emotions makes one yearn for a nobler ideal. Socrates, as we might expect, provided us with one. Recalling an earlier defendant who had "begged and entreated the judges, with many tears, to acquit him, and brought forward his children and many of his friends and relatives in court in order to appeal to [the jury's] feelings," Socrates declined to similarly parade his wife and children for histrionic effect. As remembered in Plato's *Apology,* Socrates explained his reasons for doing so to the jury that would hand him his death sentence:

> My friend, I have relatives, too, for, in the words of Homer, I am "not born of an oak or a rock, but of flesh and blood." And so, Athenians, I have relatives, and I have three sons, one of them nearly grown up, and the other two still children. Yet I will not bring any of them forward before you and implore you to acquit me. And why will I do none of these things? It is not from arrogance, Athenians, nor because I lack respect for you—but for my own good name, and for your good name, and for the good name of the whole state.[66]

For justice's sake, the law cannot afford to reward such behavior, no matter how much the victim has suffered. Rather than becoming subsidiary prosecutors or competing with criminals for rights, victims of crime would be much better off seeking restitution from criminals. Victims should have the right to seek compensation from their assailants by filing a civil claim against the criminal as part of the general criminal trial. This procedure is common throughout Europe, where the victim is termed a *partie civile*. In such so-called adhesive proceedings, the victim is allowed to present a civil case as part of the overall trial. The civil claim must be based on the same criminal act with which the defendant is charged, and allows for monetary compensation for the acts of the offender. The same jury weighs the evidence and delivers two verdicts, one regarding the defendant's guilt and one regarding his liability for civil damages.

This framework synthesizes the community's need for justice with the desire of the individual victim and kin to seek personal vengeance. The *partie civile* system demonstrates to the offender that he is accountable both to the community whose moral order he has offended and to the specific victim he has wronged. This system has the additional virtue of consolidating two trials into one, making the court system more efficient and ensuring that the criminal and civil decisions are the same. Attaching the civil suit to the main criminal case makes the victim's attempt to seek damages quicker, simpler and generally cheaper than initiating a separate civil proceeding. There is equality before the law because the presentation of the victim's case is overwhelmingly the responsibility of the government-employed prosecutor. The victim merely "piggy-backs" on the State's case; his own counsel is limited to presenting evidence of the extent of the damages caused. This evidence should be permitted only after the jury's verdict on the accused's guilt in order to shield the jury from irrelevant, inflammatory information. Since, under present common law, the commission of a crime generally constitutes negligence per se, a separate trial on the defendant's liability would rarely be necessary. The jury would merely be required to calculate the defendant's percentage of fault and the corresponding amount of damages owed the victim.

Because most criminals are self-made poor folk, such monetary compensation would mean little as a practical matter under the current system. However, if welded to a revived system of prison labor, whereby part of the prisoner's wages would be garnished and given to the victim, restitution would become feasible. Inmates would be obliged to pay their debt to society and to the individuals whom they have harmed. The *partie civile* system works in Europe, and it cannot make things much worse here.

The victim does indeed deserve to be heard. However, this right to be heard is greatest not in the courtroom after a crime has been committed but in the political arena, where politicians should satisfy his rightful cries for crime control. The most important victims' right is the right not to become a victim in the first place.

CHAPTER ELEVEN

Conclusion: Putting First Things First

Voltaire is a bigot; he believes in God.

—Anonymous

$\mathbb{A}$s Rousseau, Marx and the other authors of our current crisis can attest, it is far easier to criticize civilization than to improve it. Perhaps it is this basic human tendency that explains why so many philosophers and social commentators enumerate society's problems without deigning to recommend reforms. This is a venerable practice, to be sure, made famous by the ancient Greek Sophists and popularly bemoaned ever since. But while it makes for good fun for the critic, this intellectual habit provides little amusement for anyone else, especially those whose mouths are left agape at the enormity of their society's problems. This chapter is meant as a departure from this policy.

The following is a summary of proposals made implicitly throughout this book. In the interests of clarity, they are not touched up with euphemisms. This will enable better analysis, but with some risks: some of these proposals, standing alone without preceding justification, may well seem harsh or even radical. Fair enough. But those who take issue with these reforms owe us more than simply criticism. They must offer their own prescriptions if they are to earn our attention and credence, if only because the solution may lie somewhere in between. In any event, we must do better than shrugging our shoulders and complaining that the tasks ahead of us are too daunting or impractical to admit of implementation. Anything less than these measures, I submit, will simply postpone the date of reckoning or even exacerbate things. If we shrink from these responsibilities, and society continues to unravel at the current exponential rate, it is not hyperbole but a demonstrable fact that we will witness our country reduced to a vast transcontinental ghetto, probably sooner than we can imagine.

I must warn the reader of my own pessimism. In the eight years I have spent researching and writing this book, I have come to fear that we are already in the terminal stages of decay. We appear to have traveled too far down the road toward disintegration to have much hope of retracing our steps. The reader will be disappointed if he expects to find in this summary of proposals a magic potion or simple expedient that will save us from the just fruits of our misbehavior. Moreover, I also am convinced, in view of history and basic psychology, that religion is necessary for this national comeback; and I recognize the improbability of such a rebirth based on current trends. Still, we must try. It is nothing less than our patriotic duty.

Before turning to these reforms, let us briefly consider, without flinching or evasion, what will happen to this American Republic if such steps are not taken. There are several possible futures for our nation. All of them are admittedly hypothetical at present, yet all grow more plausible and apocalyptic with each passing day. One possible scenario, based on our recent history and trajectory, is national anarchy. This would mean, in the strict sense of the word, a political order in which the government does not provide for the right of personal security. Already this is essentially the political regime of America's inner cities. An America that looks like scenes from *Road Warrior* or *Escape from New York* may not be too far from the mark. More probable is what we already have in the nation's inner cities—an equally grim scene that, when applied to the United States as a whole, would make us a ghetto writ large.

This future, however, would appear relatively unlikely. While the white majority may tolerate anarchy in the inner cities, it would be unlikely to do so for general society. Whites love their own lives and property too much to trust them to the war of all against all. They would probably join together in some systematic fashion to gain protection. Moreover, whites, unlike blacks, have the voting power to enlist government in serious attempts to thwart this condition. Faced with such nationwide upheaval, American government would be forced to muster a better response than inner-city residents can command at present.

An alternative and more likely political order presents itself: a fascist or military takeover. Although this seems far-fetched today, so did the current Havoc thirty years ago. History teaches that in desperate, and especially in violent, times, people will rally around a strongman who promises to make things right again. Fascists have triumphed in Western countries this century for far lesser reasons than fear of criminal chaos. Napoleon's ascent following France's Reign of Terror presents one of the more obvious historical parallels. Countless other examples of this human inclination can be found in this century and every other.

Again, though, this outcome seems relatively improbable. Americans may well be too attached to the nation's political process, with all its kaleidoscope of individual rights, to ever hand it over to a dictator or junta. On the other hand, experience and human nature suggest that if given an ultimate, stark choice between the right of personal security and all other rights, even Americans will prefer order to a rights-induced suicide.

Rather than anarchy or a putsch, the most likely future of America would seem a gradual return to a sort of feudalism. Feudalism followed the fall of the Roman Empire as a mass attempt to ward off the ensuing onslaughts of barbarians and robbers. Peasants were protected by a wealthy landholder if they agreed to become economic vassals and/or soldiers who upheld the peace in the landholder's private army. The primeval desire for order determined the political and economic regime that replaced the empire. Government of sorts still existed, usually, but it was a mere shell, much like the government of U.S. inner cities today. Already the signs of this neofeudalism can be seen taking shape in modern America. The wealthy turn their homes into armed fortresses, defended by platoons of security personnel. The middle class increasingly band together in gated, guarded suburban housing developments, paying for private security out of a common fund. Only the poor must rely on government or their own firearms for safety. When things get bad enough and the lower and middle classes cannot fight off the criminal hordes with their own income, they will turn to those with the financial ability to protect them. The wealthy will enlist them for their own private armies in return, and things will be much as they were a thousand years ago during the Dark Ages. History repeats itself because though human knowledge and technology may improve, human nature does not.

If this nightmare is to be avoided, a nightmare infinitely *worse* than the Dark Ages because of the many remorseless psychotics in America's barbarian ranks, substantial reforms must be undertaken immediately. We must begin by acknowledging that the right of personal security is paramount. Order provides the foundation for all of civilization's later advances. Government therefore must secure this right above all others, with its legislation, court decisions and fiscal policies reflecting this hierarchy.

How much law enforcement is enough? This is impossible to answer quantitatively; a rigid dollar figure or precise number of cops becomes superannuated with each passing day of the current crisis. There is, though, a rough standard to guide policymakers. When someone commits a crime, his neighbors should be able to say to each other, with certitude, "He's gonna get it." As the recent rise in vigilantism attests, law-abiding citizens unable to trust the effectiveness of their criminal justice system will not remain law-abiding for long, especially in an age such as ours when almost all nongovernmental inhibitions to criminality have dissipated.

Toward this end, Americans must be willing to invest their tax money—if need be, substantially—to shore up the nation's criminal justice triad. More police must be hired; more courts staffed and opened for business; more prisons built. Police in urban areas must abandon the patrol-car strategy as their primary framework for expending these resources. Patrol cars are useful, but should play a supporting role to the beat system. Augmenting the beat system with mini-stations in high-crime areas will further deter street crime.

The community must reclaim its traditional role as the first line of defense against crime. Americans should remember that nations are born communal and die individualistic. The frankpledge must be reinstituted. All able-bodied adult males without a criminal record should be legally obliged to serve in a Neighborhood Watch–style surveillance capacity. In addition, a person who has knowledge of a serious crime and is able to report it without substantial risk of serious injury should be legally required to do so, with appropriate exceptions for family, the clergy and the like.

Vagrancy laws should be enforced once again. The community should reinstitutionalize vagrants who are mentally ill, and should expect the families of these individuals, depending on their financial means, to help pay the cost of their care. The rest should be given short-term assistance, but then be legally required not to revert to their former lifestyle.

The courts must be made more efficient and less costly so that they can better process accused offenders. To streamline the court system and free up resources for more criminal trials, a loser-pays rule should be enacted, making the losing party liable for the prevailing party's attorney fees. This rule by itself will substantially reduce the number of lawsuits filed in America. An individualized docket system should be implemented and publicized to increase judicial productivity. Other reforms would also probably deter, at least somewhat, litigation of questionable merits: repealing the collateral source exclusionary rule, which bars evidence that the plaintiff has already been compensated by his own or other insurance policies; abolishing joint and several liability, thereby disallowing suits against remote, but deep-pocket, corporate defendants; and capping damages on a sliding scale based on the type of injury or wrong suffered. More broadly still, we must give serious thought to phasing out the adversary system and supplanting it with the judge-centered communal-law model. If this suggestion is, at present, hopelessly naive, let us at least cut through the lawyer propaganda and recognize squarely that the current adversary system makes equal justice under law impossible.

The following exclusionary rules of evidence lack a credible rationale and effectively encourage crime; accordingly, they should be repealed through legislation or court rulings: the attorney-client privilege, the right against self-incrimination and its *Miranda* rules, the Fourth Amendment exclusionary rule and the bar on evidence of past criminality. Plea bargaining should be permitted only in exceptional circumstances (e.g., for obtaining information regarding accomplices).

Criminal punishment should be made stiffer across the board until our streets are reclaimed. We must settle on a firm *raison d'être* for America's penal system—retribution, or, as it was once known, justice itself. Only this philosophy of punishment can ensure equal treatment of all offenders. Federal laws effectively prohibiting prison labor must be taken off the books. Prison industries should be designed to undercut foreign labor costs and bring low-skilled manufacturing jobs back to America. Round-the-clock shifts would increase the amount of available prison space. Prisoners would thereby be relieved somewhat of the tedium and brutality of modern prison life; society would benefit financially by having a self-sufficient prison system. Crime victims should be allowed to attach a civil suit to criminal proceedings and to garnish a portion of an inmate's wages.

Indeterminate sentencing and parole should be eliminated in favor of truth-in-sentencing practices that enable better punishment and deterrence. Prisoners must be required to finish at least 90 percent of their sentences. The remaining 10 percent can serve as an incentive for good behavior. Monies must be spent to build enough prisons to quarter all criminals for their full sentence. This will be expensive, but ours is a wealthy nation. Selective incapacitation might allow the penal system to economize somewhat, except that such rationing may well lead to the consideration of sentencing criteria that have no place in our system of justice (race, employment history, etc.). This must be guarded against. "Three strikes and you're out" is fine if we are prepared to pay for it and recognize its limitations. On the other hand, one strike should be enough for certain violent offenses.

Instead of alternative sentencing policies that generally decoct in practice to less criminal punishment, such nonincarcerative punishment should be limited to inexpensive programs that shame the offender into not repeating his crimes. There have been ingenious applications recently of this philosophy of moral education: publicizing criminals' names and affixing bumper stickers to their cars and signs to their homes. There are other, even more controversial steps that could be taken if an exploding crime rate continues to exhaust our national patience—a return to the crime control practices of our Founding Fathers. By *publicly* incarcerating drug dealers and other criminals, displaying them before their neighbors in large, open-air holding pens with their names and crimes prominently displayed, a modified stockade program could provide specific deterrence at marginal cost and general deterrence for the community. Such a program would also tarnish the glamour and "coolness" too often associated with a life of crime. This may seem harsh given our modern sensibilities, but perhaps the skeptical reader has not yet stared down the barrel of a gun as have residents of the inner cities, where many of these facilities would be located.*

The family should be bolstered through the means at government's disposal. Fault requirements for divorce should be restored. Ours is a modern, caste-free society, and Americans may date whomever we want, for as long as we want. But when we ask society to memorialize our relationship by recognizing us as married, couples acquire reciprocal obligations not to treat this arrangement as a garden-variety contract terminable at will. Tax policies should reward joint parenthood and legitimate births. The State should also encourage one parent to stay home and raise the couple's children. Welfare should be humanely phased out by removing from the rolls all recipients who have any immediate family (parents, grandparents, siblings). Families are the original safety net, and can provide better short-term assistance in most cases than the State. Private charity should be encouraged and directed toward the poor whose family members are indifferent to their plight. To the extent that government aid is still relied upon, it must no longer come in the form of direct transfer payments to individuals. It should instead be funneled into private, community-based organizations that have shown themselves efficient and equal to the task. These groups must provide their visitors the necessities of life, and with great care and compassion. But they must also not make their accommodations and expectations such that public assistance becomes, as it is now for too many Americans, a way of life. The Salvation Army is a shining model of this sort of charity.

Juvenile offenders should be tried and sentenced according to their understanding of the crimes they have committed. They should also retain their juvenile records for life, and these should be admissible in future court proceedings. Schools must teach children to obey the law, a lesson preferably backed up with a religious exhortation of the type currently banned by the Supreme Court. To accom-

---

* If nothing else manages to stem the tide in the coming years, a modern Militia Act also deserves some consideration as a potentially effective deterrent to crime. Consistent with the Founders' policy, all heads of household without conscientious objection would be required to possess a specified firearm. Safe storage of such weapons would be legally mandated. Accompanying firearms registration as well as courses in the use and safety of firearms would also be obligatory. This approach would have to be tried first on an experimental basis in local jursidictions to determine if the deterrent effect on offenders is more apparent than real. A new Militia Act is, of course, such a radical departure from current practice and assumptions that it could and should be enacted *only* if violent crime rates remain resistant to all other crime control measures.

plish this and other reforms, it may be necessary for a modern Madison to draft, as it were, a Bill of Responsibilities—a set of new constitutional provisions for the law-abiding majority to repeal the various criminals' rights and other recent jurisprudence undermining civil unity. This bill would merely return the constitutional order to the *status quo ante* that preceded the current multiplication of criminals and individual rights. Corporal punishment should be administered in and out of schools, as an ultimate penalty, on children who will not respond to any other sanctions. Parents should be held legally responsible for the criminal acts of their children until they reach adulthood.

The community should regain the right to prevent the dissemination of media programming and material that it believes socially disastrous, a right it effectively lost in the Supreme Court's *Memoirs* decision. The question of censorship versus no censorship is a false choice; and in any event we must confront directly the consequences of the current absolute freedom of expression. We must harbor no illusions about the likelihood of banishing all violent and prurient material from society, given modern communications technology and the difficulty of enforcing comparable laws against drugs and other perennial vices. But there is much to be said for official disapproval of such practices by government and the community it represents. It is hard enough for people to do the right thing when custom and peer pressure encourage proper behavior; it is well-nigh impossible when government and society take a completely hands-off approach. At the very least, the State should levy a substantial tax on the sale or rental of material, or admission to businesses such as theaters providing access to material, that the community's representatives judge socially hazardous. These materials would range from violent movies to pornography. The revenue from these taxes should be earmarked for a public relations campaign modeled after California's recent successful antismoking effort, one that uses celebrities and commercials to discourage violence and premarital sex.

As a final obstacle to premarital intercourse, let us consider without chortling something that the rest of the world uses with great, historically proven effectiveness: chaperones and adult guidance. Ours is the first civilization in history to treat adolescents as independent, rational adults capable of making wise decisions about dating and sexuality with little to no adult supervision. If this proposal seems hopelessly out of date and prudish, such a reaction merely begs the question of why we have drifted so far, so fast from globally endorsed traditions that have no effective alternative.

Finally, but most important, we must reject the ideas that made the Great Havoc possible. People commit crimes out of extreme selfishness. Thus, when basic politeness and other conventions designed to enforce selflessness and concern for others begin to give way, as we see currently in America, we must interpret these signs as the first rumblings of a coming eruption of crime. Criminals, of course, choose to commit crimes, and are responsible for their actions. But these decisions are not made in a vacuum. Influencing them are the centuries-old theories and notions that, culminating in the current radical individualism, make rampant crime inevitable. Political reforms alone cannot solve this problem. Lawfulness ultimately must come from within.

This process must begin with some simple, unpopular realizations. For starters, life, contrary to present appearances, is not something on the order of a slow-motion, egoistic orgy. Other, older cultures, as well as our ancestors, may sound like spoilsports, but they are right: life is a series of obligations to be fulfilled as honorably as possible, with occasional interludes for moderate self-indulgence. True, lasting happiness can come only from learning to deny oneself, if only because this lays the foundation for order and security. Self-discipline is therefore the most important lesson that we can teach our children, and we do them no favors by indulging their misbehavior. Similarly, personal relationships entered into for self-interested reasons are sown on very rocky soil and inevitably end in disillusionment and bitterness.

Past generations were, in a sense, fortunate in not having so many choices to make. Because the necessities of life were at that time procured so precariously, people had to spend almost all of their waking hours eking out an existence. They thus had very little spare time in which to get into trouble. Our prosperity has helped to spoil us into thinking that the world is our oyster, that we must put ourselves ahead of all others lest we miss out on the fun. Instead of spending our spare time helping others—especially our children, who are at our mercy—we too often dedicate it to idle, self-centered pursuits. In the process, we have forgotten how unpleasant life can become if everyone else does the same. Such is the road to havoc.

Most will agree that America's crime surge can be solved, in the end, only through the creation or sharpening of a conscience, one receptive to appeals to duty over rights, family and community over selfishness, law over chaos. The secularism of our times makes us look, sometimes a bit desperately, for secular methods to bring this about. In doing so we join a long and distinguished Western tradition. The effort to replace religion with a natural ethic stripped of appeals to a punitive higher power is at least as old as Socrates, who sought to make the love of knowledge a religion-free basis of conscience. This intellectual enterprise finally blossomed in the French Enlightenment and Marxism.

But all these attempts failed. After centuries of intellectual toil, in which the West's most brilliant men have scrutinized and scratched their heads over this central issue of practical philosophy, we are today no closer to a substitute than when they began. It is in fact one of the sterling lessons of Western philosophy that conscience, the basis of all civilization, cannot be fostered on a broad scale without religion. Religion, to be sure, has given rise to its own fair share of chaos throughout history. We must deplore the bigotry, hidebound intolerance and outright war that far too often accompany organized worship. I myself am not insensitive to these concerns, having grown up a religious nonconformist in the Ozarks of southern Missouri, and having been occasionally ostracized as a threat to local morals because of my attempts at open-mindedness. But religion would not have been around so long—would not be considered socially indispensable by so many of the world's peoples—if it did not provide an earthly as well as ethereal service. Because religion smites our very souls, it is of course a sensitive subject. However, if we are to leave no stone unturned in searching for answers to our national undoing, let us give this enduring object of inquiry and reverence its due.

Clearly, that religion has historically helped to provide order and personal security does not imply that nonreligious people are all, or even predominantly, criminals. Nor does faith alone guarantee sainthood. On the other hand, nonreligious individuals frequently benefit from an income or self-discipline uncommon in the masses. Indeed, the level of schooling required for one's religious convictions to be shaken almost necessarily confines the rejection of religion to an educated elite generally lacking in criminal ambitions. For the rest of society, more prosaic social controls must be relied upon. Until we can come up with a better way of nudging the conscience and honing the supernatural fears of our less responsible fellow citizens, religion will continue to be our most important means of crime control. Accordingly, we must begin to recognize frankly the current denigration of religion by many of society's opinion leaders—academia, the press, the entertainment industry—as an enormous tragedy at the heart of our current intellectual straits.

Some of the most illuminating criticism of mistrust of and snobbery toward religion came from those who saw the disturbing effects of that mind-set's implementation in eighteenth-century France. Voltaire, for instance, never surrendered his essential faith in a higher power. This was so even though his intellectual colleagues said of him, "Voltaire is a bigot; he believes in God." He matter-of-factly defended religion as making his lawyer and butler less likely to mishandle his affairs or pick his pockets.[1] The Marquis de Sade drew different, equally forthright conclusions. He inferred that if religion is humbug, then there is no right and wrong and cruelty is the highest pleasure. Alfred de Musset, reviewing these events, posed a frightful question to the triumphant *philosophes:*

> But, if the poor man, once satisfied that the priests deceive him, that the rich rob him, that all men have rights, that all good is of this world, and that misery is impiety; the poor man, believing in himself and in his two arms, says to himself some fine day: "War on the rich! for me, happiness here in this life, since there is no other! for me, the earth, since heaven is empty! for me and for all, since all are equal!" Oh! reasoners sublime who have led him to this, what will you say to him if he is conquered?[2]

James Q. Wilson's review of nineteenth-century American crime statistics offers empirical support for the near-universal cultural presumption in favor of religion. He found a noticeable drop in crime rates in the century's latter half despite the high-crime trends of industrialization and mass migration to big cities. Wilson concluded that one of the main curbs on this disorderly individualism was the rise in evangelism, and, more generally, the popular promotion of Judeo-Christian values during that period.[3] We will never know by the harsh rigors of true science whether Wilson's findings are correct. What we do know from our own recent experience is that no amount of money or rights can appease offenders or mend their souls. We must find some other way of burning a conscience into the present and future stone killers of the land.

If Western philosophy teaches us anything, then, it is that only a renaissance of the spirit can halt the criminal chaos of our times. Crime, as the most extreme form of selfishness, can be reduced significantly only if humans feel accountable to an ever present

Leviathan that will penalize them for their more aggressive displays of egoism, a divine power that is there when a policeman cannot be. Hobbes was so convinced of this that he defined crime explicitly as "sin"; Locke, Blackstone and the Founders of our Republic all concurred in the necessity of religion for order. For some, religion may fulfill its social mission by cultivating love for our fellowman and the supremacy of duty and conscience over self-interest. For others, especially the men who form the bulk of potential criminals, less exalted appeals may be necessary—namely, appeals to self-love. Fear, as Hobbes tells us, will do the job in most cases.

Political programs such as those sketched above cannot restore the essential internal fear of divine punishment that religion instills in would-be offenders, and the selflessness that submission to a higher power implies. We see the futility of other schemes in the current efforts to ingrain a conscience in public school students through values education, an appeal to values divorced from religious conviction. To repeat: these attempts at teaching the libertarian rules of the game are like teaching table manners to cannibals. Indeed, if anyone can make these programs work, he will verily be one of the greatest philosophers in history, putting Socrates and Voltaire to shame. I regret that I cannot join this hypothetical scholar's ranks; I have no better solution for our national upheaval than these giants of Western thought do. We must once again know what it is like to worship something more sublime than ourselves.

There are a few encouraging developments that lately suggest that such hopes may not be as quixotic as they first appear. Polls show that 90 percent of Americans believe in God, overwhelmingly the Judeo-Christian Deity. This provides a foundation of faith that might allow for just such a spiritual rebirth should a great leader or movement emerge to build upon these beliefs. There are, in fact, some precedents for this. Alcoholics Anonymous has achieved vast success in treating a condition widely thought to be a disease, much as crime is sometimes regarded, by arguing that willpower and self-knowledge cannot overcome alcoholism; only faith in and submission to a higher power can. In the 1700s John Wesley founded the Methodist Church and started a religious movement that brought large numbers of the British lower class back to church, hard work and sobriety. Some historians credit this revival with restoring the discipline and vigor necessary for Great Britain's international paramountcy in the following century.

Irving Kristol once argued that what America needs is a black John Wesley. Since America has far more whites than blacks in need of his services, another white John Wesley would be welcome as well.

Without a celestial sovereign to answer to, individuals have little to lose from a life of pillage, especially when their society casts them adrift from their families and communities, as ours has done of late. A lack of corporal penalties for crime meted out by government certainly does not help matters. But in the end, crime is inevitable once religion is ridiculed as superstition and people's attachments to one another are bound by nothing more than vain appeals to respect one another's rights. As a practical sociological matter, it does not matter much if the religion leashing our egos is Christianity or Zoroastrianism. At minimum, however, it must prominently feature a ubiquitous policeman/judge who does not look favorably on man's plundering his neighbor. Parents are most responsible for this education, followed in decreasing order by churches, schools and the government.

To conclude, politics alone and the government reforms proposed above cannot solve the "crime problem." "Respect my rights" is a feeble substitute for "Love one another." The solution to the sacking of America lies within us all, and must be tackled by each individual. Until we confront directly these matters of the heart and spirit, improved governmental crime control will be of very limited value. The current appeals to ethics directed at the homegrown barbarians looting America will be as useless as those that greeted the many other successful conquerors of Western societies past.

If these proposals strike some as "turning back the clock," very well. Obviously not everything associated with the America of our parents and grandparents deserves veneration or restoration. But by the same token, social progress cannot be measured in minutes; history shows that civilization does not inevitably improve with the passage of time; and when change is for the worse, when it means the random rupturing of customs and institutions that all other societies recognize as essential for order and survival, then we must revisit and reverse such change no matter how onerous and impossible such reforms may seem. The choice before us is both manifest and simple: freedom practiced responsibly or no freedom at all. All the while our nation teeters on the edge of a calamity whose dimensions we cannot fully fathom, a State of Nature unknown to all but those speculative first humans who, we are told, scrambled to escape its conditions.

I believe that America still has the wherewithal to save itself. But if not, let us at least resolve that we will no longer bow to the gods that unleashed this carnage, and that we will feel no shame in shedding a tear over the passing of this Republic, God's most splendid, wayward gift to a prodigal race.

NOTES

INTRODUCTION: AMERICA'S MODEL CITY

1. Graciela Sevilla, "Basu's Blood Found on Suspect's Clothing, Police Witness Testifies," *Washington Post*, April 21, 1993, p. C3; Graciela Sevilla, "'Bloody Streak' Marked Path of Carjackers, Jury Told," *Washington Post*, April 15, 1993, p. B1.

2. Graciela Sevilla, "Basu Jurors Shown Videotape of Crime Scene," *Washington Post*, April 16, 1993, p. D1; Elisha King, "Lawyers Argue Defendant's Intentions in Carjacking that Turned Fatal," *Washington Post*, August 12, 1993, p. B3; Sevilla, "'Bloody Streak.'"

3. Serge F. Kovaleski, "Youth Opens Fire at Shaw Music Hall," *Washington Post*, July 11, 1993, p. B1.

4. DeNeen L. Brown and Ruben Castaneda, "Police Say Turf Wars Fueled Day of Violence," *Washington Post*, September 27, 1993, p. A1.

5. David Fritze, "Violence Gnaws at Souls of 2 Cities," *Arizona Republic*, October 10, 1993, p. A1.

6. Athelia Knight, "Of 1,286 Slaying Cases, 1 in 4 Ends in Conviction," *Washington Post*, October 24, 1993, p. A1.

7. Rene Sanchez, "D.C. Curfew Is Proposed by Barry," *Washington Post*, October 18, l990, p. Al.

8. Knight, "1 in 4 Ends in Conviction."

9. David Whitman, "Marion Barry's Untold Legacy," *U.S. News & World Report*, July 30, 1990, pp. 22ff.

10. Jerry Wilson, "D.C.'s Other Crime Crisis: Our Vanishing Veteran Cops," *Washington Post*, March 15, 1992, p. C1.

11. Tucker Carlson, "Washington's Inept Police Force," *Wall Street Journal*, November 3, 1993, p. A19.

12. Martin Well and Gabriel Escobar, "D.C. Sets Homicide Record," *Washington Post*, December 25, 1991, p. A1.

13. Gabriel Escobar, "Homicides Averaging 2 per Day," *Washinqton Post*, November 14, 1991, p. D1; "Our Local Killing Fields . . . ," *Washington Post*, December 31, 1991, p. A16.

14. Gabriel Escobar, "Rapes in the District Up 66 Percent," *Washington Post*, October 22, 1990, p. A8.

15. Jared Taylor, *Paved with Good Intentions: The Failure of Race Relations in Contemporary America* (New York: Carroll & Graf, 1992), p. 314.

16. Lewis Lord, "Murder in a 'Model' City," *U.S. News & World Report*, April 16, 1990, p. 13.

17. B. Drummond Ayres, Jr., "Washington Finds Drug War Is Hardest at Home," *New York Times*, December 9, 1988, p. A22.

18. Michael Isikoff, "D.C.'s War on Drugs: 1 Year Later," *Washington Post*, April 13, 1990, p. B1.

19. Tracy Thompson, "D.C. Children Coming Home to Violence," *Washington Post*, February 28, 1991, p. C1.

20. DeNeen L. Brown, "Getting Ready to Die Young," *Washington Post*, November 1, 1993, p. A1.

21. Paul Barrett, "Killing of 15-Year-Old Is Part of Escalation of Murder by Juveniles," *Wall Street Journal*, March 25, 1991, p. A1.

22. Athelia Knight, "Strategies to End the Carnage," *Washington Post*, October 27, 1993, p. A1.

23. Sari Horwitz, "Violent Gangs 'All Over City,' D.C. Chief Says," *Washington Post*, September 29, 1991, p. A1.

24. Gabriel Escobar, "Washington Area's 703 Homicides in 1990 Set a Record," *Washington Post*, January 2, 1991, p. A1.

25. Keith A. Harrison, "As Homicide Rate Climbs, D.C. Conviction Rate Falls," *Washington Post*, May 21, 1992, p. A1.

26. Nancy Lewis, "Delinquent Girls Take a Violent Turn," *Washington Post*, December 23, 1992, p. A1.

27. Jason DeParle, "Young Black Men in Capital: Study Finds 42% in Courts," *New York Times*, April 18, 1992, p. A1.

28. Ibid.

29. Barrett, "Killing of 15-Year-Old."

30. Carl Horowitz, "Finally Getting Tough on Crime?" *Investor's Business Daily*, October 26, 1993, p. A1; Charles Oliver, "Are More Prisons the Answer?" *Investor's Business Daily*, January 18, 1994, p. A1.

31. Federal Bureau of Investigation, *Uniform Crime Reports 1991* (Washington, D.C.: U.S. Government Printing Office, 1991), p. 279.

32. Ibid.

33. Ibid., pp. 62, 243, 267.

34. Arizona Juvenile Justice Advisory Council Minority Youth Issues Committee, *Equitable Treatment of Minority Youth*, Report (Phoenix: Governor's Office for Children, 1993), p. 34; Victoria Harker, "Study Finds High Minority Arrest Rate," *Arizona Republic*, June 5, 1993, p. A1.

35. Ellis Cose, "Breaking the 'Code of Silence,'" *Newsweek*, January 10, 1994, p. 23.

36. Scott Minerbrook, "A Generation of Stone Killers," *U.S. News & World Report*, January 17, 1994, p. 37.

37. Serge F. Kovaleski, "D.C. Suffers Surge in Homicides," *Washington Post,* December 18, 1993, p. A1.

38. Avis Thomas-Lester, "Fairfax Authorities Cite 'Disturbing' Increase in Juvenile Arrests," *Washington Post,* February 22, 1992, p. B8.

CHAPTER ONE: THE SLAIN LEVIATHAN

Epigraph: Thomas Hobbes, *Leviathan,* ed. Nelle Fuller, in vol. 23 of *Great Books of the Western World* (Chicago: William Benton, 1952), p. 99.

1. William J. Bennett, "Commuter Massacre, Our Warning," *Wall Street Journal,* December 10, 1993, p. A14.

2. Howard Fineman, "The Virtuecrats," *Newsweek,* June 13, 1994, p. 31.

3. Judith Gaines, "In Pursuit of the Unmarried Life," *Boston Globe,* June 24, 1993, p. A1.

4. FBI, *Uniform Crime Reports 1991,* p. 4.

5. William J. Bennett, "Quantifying America's Decline," *Wall Street Journal,* March 15, 1993, p. A12.

6. Rorie Sherman, "Crime's Toll on the U.S.: Fear, Despair and Guns," *National Law Journal,* April 18, 1994, p. A1.

7. National Academy of Sciences, *Understanding and Preventing Violence,* ed. Albert J. Reiss, Jr., and Jeffrey A. Roth (Washington, D.C.: National Academy Press, 1993), p. 3.

8. "One of Four Homes Hit by Crime in '88," *New York Times,* June 12, 1989, p. B8.

9. "83% To Be Victims of Crime Violence," *New York Times,* March 9, 1987, p. A13.

10. William J. Bennett, *The Index of Leading Cultural Indicators* (New York: Touchstone, 1994), pp. 23, 25.

11. William Tucker, *Vigilante: The Backlash Against Crime in America* (New York: Stein & Day, 1985), p. 42.

12. Bureau of Justice Statistics, *Sourcebook of Criminal Justice Statistics 1991* (Washington, D.C.: U.S. Government Printing Office, 1991), Table 3.6, p. 260.

13. National Academy of Sciences, *Understanding and Preventing Violence,* p. 4.

14. Bureau of Justice Statistics, *Sourcebook,* Table 2.3, p. 173.

15. Michael Bates, "Gang Violence Worse than Wild West Days, Kansas Historian Says," *Phoenix Gazette,* September 10, 1993, p. A18.

16. Terri Thompson, "Crime and the Bottom Line," *U.S. News & World Report,* April 13, 1992, p. 55ff.

17. National Academy of Sciences, *Understanding and Preventing Violence,* p. 4.

18. Michael J. Mandel et al., "The Economics of Crime," *Business Week,* December 13, 1993, p. 72.

19. "Crime Robs New York of Business Growth," *Wall Street Journal,* May 23, 1989, p. B1.

20. Bureau of Justice Statistics, *Sourcebook,* Table 2.30, p. 198.

21. Ibid.

22. Bureau of Justice Statistics, *Sourcebook,* Table 2.1, p. 172.

23. Theodore H. White, *The Making of the President 1968* (New York: Atheneum, 1969), pp. 219–60.

24. "A Nation Turns Expectant Eyes to Clinton," *U.S. News & World Report,* January 25, 1993, p. 32.

25. Sherman, "Crime's Toll on the U.S."

26. Biographical Note to Hobbes, *Leviathan,* p. 41.

27. Hobbes, *Leviathan,* p. 85.

28. Ibid., p. 86.

29. Ibid., p. 100.

30. Ibid., p. 101.

31. Ibid., p. 91.

32. Andrew R. Willing, "Protection by Law Enforcement: The Emerging Constitutional Right," *Rutgers Law Review* 35 (1982): 47. Mr. Willing provides a fine overview of the history of the right to governmental law enforcement in Anglo-American thought, although the thesis of his article, as stated in its title, is not constitutionally correct.

33. Willing, "Protection by Law Enforcement," p. 33.

34. John Locke, *An Essay Concerning the True Original Extent and End of Civil Government,* in vol. 35 of *Great Books of the Western World* (Chicago: William Benton, 1952), p. 29.

35. Ibid., p. 26.

36. Ibid., p. 53.

37. Ibid., p. 27.

38. Ibid., p. 28.

39. Ibid.

40. Raoul Berger, *Congress v. the Supreme Court* (Cambridge: Harvard Univ. Press, 1969), p. 30.

41. Sir William Blackstone, *Commentaries on the Laws of England* (Baton Rouge: Claitor's Publishing, 1976), vol. 1, bk. 1, pp. 124–25.

42. Amitai Etzioni, *The Spirit of Community: Rights, Responsibilities, and the Communitarian Agenda* (New York: Crown, 1993), p. 5.

43. Quoted in Charles Warren, *The Making of the Constitution* (New York: Barnes & Noble, 1967), pp. 30–31.

44. Clinton Rossiter, *1787: The Grand Convention* (New York: Macmillan, 1966), p. 56.

45. Gordon S. Wood, *The Creation of the American Republic, 1776–1787* (New York: W. W. Norton, 1969), p. 285.

46. Quoted in Warren, *The Making of the Constitution,* p. 31.

47. George Washington, Letter to David Humphreys, October 22, 1786, and letter to James Madison, November 5, 1786, in *The Writings of George Washington,* ed. John C. Fitzpatrick (Washington, D.C.: U.S. Government Printing Office, 1939), vol. 29, pp. 27, 51.

48. George Washington, Letter to Marquis de Lafayette, March 25, 1787, letter

to Henry Lee, October 31, 1786, and letter to Henry Knox, February 3, 1787, in ibid., pp. 184, 34, 151.

49. George Washington, Letter to James Madison, November 5, 1786, letter to Henry Knox, February 3, 1787, and letter to Marquis de Lafayette, March 25, 1787, in ibid., pp. 51–52, 122, 184.

50. James Madison, *The Records of the Federal Convention of 1787*, ed. Max Farrand (New Haven: Yale Univ. Press, 1966), vol. 1, pp. 18–19.

51. Ibid., p. 318.

52. Willing, "Protection by Law Enforcement," pp. 42–43.

53. Alexander Hamilton, James Madison and John Jay, *The Federalist Papers* (New York: New American Library, 1961), No. 6, p. 54; No. 3, p. 42; No. 51, p. 322; No. 43, p. 279.

54. See, e.g., Willing, "Protection by Law Enforcement."

55. Laurence Tribe, "Unraveling *National League of Cities:* The New Federalism and Affirmative Rights to Essential Government Services," *Harvard Law Review* 90 (1977): 1092.

CHAPTER TWO: THE POLICE: CRIME CONTROL BY OTHER MEANS

Epigraph: Douglas Southall Freeman, *Robert E. Lee: A Biography* (New York: Scribner's, 1934), vol. 2, p. 462.

1. Jeremy Bentham, *An Introduction to the Principles of Morals and Legislation*, ed. Lawrence J. Lafleur (New York: Hafner, 1948), pp. 309–35.

2. Karl von Clausewitz, *On War*, ed. Anatol Rapoport (New York: Penguin, 1986), p. 119.

3. Wilbur R. Miller, *Cops and Bobbies: Police Authority in New York and London, 1830–1870* (Chicago: Univ. of Chicago Press, 1977), p. 2.

4. Robert M. Fogelson, *Big-City Police* (Cambridge: Harvard Univ. Press, 1977), p. 54.

5. Ibid., p. 154.

6. Thomas A. Reppetto, *Blue Parade* (New York: Free Press, 1978), p. 152.

7. B. H. Liddell Hart, *Strategy* (New York: New American Library, 1967), p. 10.

8. Reppetto, *Blue Parade*, p. 21.

9. Ibid., p. 243.

10. Mark H. Moore and George L. Kelling, "'To Serve and Protect': Learning from Police History," *Public Interest*, Winter 1983, p. 55.

11. Albert J. Reiss, Jr., *The Police and the Public* (New Haven: Yale Univ. Press, 1971), p. 11.

12. George L. Kelling et al., *The Kansas City Preventive Patrol Experiment: A Summary Report* (Washington, D.C.: Police Foundation, 1974), p. 49.

13. Larry Tye, "Community Approach Shows Results in Michigan City," *Boston Globe*, December 3, 1990, p. A1.

14. Dean E. Murphy, "Barricades, Police Visits Give Hope to Crime-Plagued Neighborhood," *Los Angeles Times*, June 22, 1991, p. B3.

15. Tye, "Community Approach."

16. "As Crime Drops in Midtown, Even Criminals Credit Police," *New York Times,* April 24, 1991, p. A1.

17. L. Gordon Crovitz, "How Law Destroys Order," *National Review,* February 11, 1991, pp. 28ff.

18. Mark A. R. Kleiman et al., *Imprisonment-to-Offense Ratios,* Working Paper #89–06–02 (Cambridge: John F. Kennedy School of Government, Harvard University, Paper in Progress, August 5, 1988), Table 10.

19. 232 U.S. 383 (1914).

20. 367 U.S. 643 (1961).

21. See, e.g., Steven R. Schlesinger, "The Exclusionary Rule: Have Proponents Proven That It Is a Deterrent to Police?" *Judicature* 62 (1979): 404; Dallin H. Oaks, "Studying the Exclusionary Rule in Search and Seizure," *University of Chicago Law Review* 37 (1970): 665; Bradley Canon, "Testing the Effectiveness of Civil Liberties Policies at the State and Federal Levels: The Case of the Exclusionary Rule," *American Politics Quarterly* 5 (1977): 57.

22. James Spiotto, "Search and Seizure: An Empirical Study of the Exclusionary Rule and Its Alternatives," *Journal of Legal Studies* 2 (1973): 243.

23. Oaks, "Studying the Exclusionary Rule," pp. 721–22.

24. William A. Schroeder, "Deterring Fourth Amendment Violations: Alter-natives to the Exclusionary Rule," *Georgetown Law Journal* 69 (1981): 1383–84.

25. Oaks, "Studying the Exclusionary Rule," pp. 737–38.

26. Ibid., p. 746.

27. Ibid.

28. Jerome H. Skolnick, *Justice Without Trial: Law Enforcement in Democratic Society* (New York: John Wiley, 1975), p. 214.

29. Albert J. Reiss, Jr., and David J. Bordua, "Environment and Organization: A Perspective on the Police," in David Bordua, ed., *The Police: 6 Sociological Essays* (New York: John Wiley, 1967), pp. 33, 39.

30. 384 U.S. 436 (1966).

31. *Oregon v. Elstad,* 470 U.S. 298, 312 (1985).

32. See *Minnick v. Mississippi,* 111 S. Ct. 486 (1990).

33. U.S. Congress, Senate Committee on the Judiciary, Subcommittee on Criminal Laws and Procedures, *Controlling Crime Through More Effective Law Enforcement: Hearings Before the Subcomm. on Criminal Laws and Procedures of the Senate Comm. on the Judiciary,* 90th Cong., 1st Sess. (1967), pp. 200–1, 204–6 (Philadelphia study); pp. 1120, 1123 (New York study); Richard M. Seeburger and R. Stanton Wettick, "*Miranda* in Pittsburgh: A Statistical Study," *Univ. of Pittsburgh Law Review* 29 (1967): 1 (Pittsburgh study).

34. Malcolm K. Sparrow, Mark H. Moore and David M. Kennedy, *Beyond 911: A New Era for Policing* (New York: Basic Books, 1990), p. 51.

35. "Charleston Chief Is Chasing Crime," *Washington Times,* April 26, 1991, p. B4.

36. Peter Applebome, "Dallas Anguished by Killing of Officer," *New York Times,* January 27, 1988, p. A12.

37. Ibid.

38. Ibid.

39. President's Commission on Law Enforcement and Administration of Justice, *The Challenge of Crime in a Free Society: Report of the President's Commission on Law Enforcement and Administration of Justice* (New York: Avon, 1968), p. 257.

40. National Advisory Commission on Civil Disorders, *Report of the National Advisory Commission on Civil Disorders* (New York: Bantam, 1968), p. 299.

41. Peggy S. Sullivan, Roger G. Dunham and Geoffrey P. Alpert, "Attitude Structures of Different Ethnic and Age Groups Concerning Police," *Journal of Criminal Law and Criminology* 78 (1987): 178–79.

42. Reiss and Bordua, "Environment and Organization"; see also discussion of studies in Douglas A. Smith, Christy A. Visher and Laura A. Davidson, "Equity and Discretionary Justice: The Influence of Race on Police Arrest Decisions," *Journal of Criminal Law and Criminology* 75 (1984): 234.

43. Reiss, *The Police and the Public*, 1971, p. 147.

44. James Q. Wilson, *Thinking About Crime* (New York: Vintage, 1985), pp. 101–5.

45. National Advisory Commission on Civil Disorders, *Report*, p. 308.

46. Ibid., pp. 94–95.

47. Jesse Jackson, "Time to Invest in People," *Guardian Weekly*, May 10, 1992, p. 1.

48. Bill Stall and Douglas Jehl, "Bush Offers Message of Healing to the City," *Los Angeles Times*, May 8, 1992, p. A1.

49. Pamela Reynolds, "A Verdict Cheers South Bronx, and 'Us-Against-Them' Rift Grows," *Boston Globe*, December 6, 1988, p. A3.

50. Ibid.

51. James Baldwin, *Nobody Knows My Name: Notes of a Native Son* (New York: Dial Press, 1961), pp. 65–66.

52. Miller, *Cops and Bobbies*, pp. 19–20.

53. Douglas Greenberg, "Crime, Law Enforcement, and Social Control," *American Journal of Legal History* 26 (1982): 301.

54. Miller, *Cops and Bobbies*, p. 19.

55. Sparrow, Moore and Kennedy, *Beyond 911*, p. 51.

56. Reppetto, *Blue Parade*, p. 96.

57. Roger Lane, *Policing the City: Boston 1822–1885* (Cambridge: Harvard Univ. Press, 1967), p. 37.

58. Ibid., p. 38.

59. Miller, *Cops and Bobbies*, pp. 10–11.

60. John Stuart Mill, *On Liberty*, ed. Currin V. Shields (New York: Liberal Arts, 1956), p. 13.

61. This phrase is borrowed from Will Durant, *Our Oriental Heritage* (New York: Simon & Schuster, 1954), p. 25.

62. Fyodor Dostoevsky, *The Brothers Karamazov*, trans. Constance Garnett, vol. 52 of *Great Books of the Western World* (Chicago: William Benton, 1952), pp. 158–59.

63. St. Augustine, *City of God,* trans. Marcus Dods (New York: Modern Library, 1950), p. 693.

64. James Q. Wilson, *Varieties of Police Behavior: The Management of Law and Order in Eight Communities* (Cambridge: Harvard Univ. Press, 1968), pp. 30–31.

65. Wilson, *Thinking About Crime,* pp. 75–89.

66. 405 U.S. 156 (1972).

67. Ibid. at 164.

68. Jerome H. Skolnick and David H. Bayley, *The New Blue Line* (New York: Free Press, 1986), pp. 197–200.

69. *Oxford English Dictionary* (Oxford: Clarendon, 1989), vol. 7, p. 328.

70. Donald Black, *The Manners and Customs of the Police* (New York: Academic Press, 1980), p. 29.

71. Robert C. Ellickson, "The Homelessness Muddle," *Public Interest,* Spring 1990, pp. 54–55.

72. Ibid., pp. 45–47.

73. Celia W. Dugger, "Twice as Many Families Seek Space in City Shelters," *New York Times,* September 17, 1992, p. B3.

74. Gina Kolata, "Twins of the Streets: Homelessness and Addiction," *New York Times,* May 22, 1989, p. A1.

75. "Addiction in the Homeless Shelters," *New York Times,* February 20, 1992, p. A24.

76. Carl Horowitz, "Fast Shuffle on the Homeless?" *Investor's Business Daily,* March 23, 1994, p. A1.

77. Kolata, "Twins of the Streets."

78. Josh Barbanel, "Joyce Brown's Ascent from Anonymity," *New York Times,* February 15, 1988, p. B1; John T. McQuiston, "Joyce Brown Held in Drug Case," *New York Times,* September 8, 1988, p. B3.

79. Joseph Sobran, "Mitch Snyder's Last Guilt Trip," *Arizona Republic,* July 17, 1990, p. A11.

80. Ed Foster-Simeon, "Guilt Ploy Tried Again by Homeless," *Washington Post,* July 24, 1990, p. B1.

81. Quoted in Lawrence Friedman, *A History of American Law* (New York: Simon & Schuster, 1985), p. 580.

82. Robert D. McFadden, "Poll Indicates Half of New Yorkers See Crime as City's Chief Problem," *New York Times,* January 14, 1985, p. A1.

83. Tucker, Vigilante, pp. 19–20.

84. Dan Morain, "Get Involved in Singleton Case, Governor Told," *Los Angeles Times,* May 29, 1987, part 1, p. 22.

85. "Vigils by Officials, Volunteers Squelch 'Devil's Night,'" *Los Angeles Times,* November 1, 1992, p. A22.

86. Dorothy J. Gaiter, "More Stores Seek Camera Monitors," *New York Times,* October 20, 1982, p. A23.

87. Jack Wenik, "Forcing the Bystander to Get Involved: A Case for a Statute Requiring Witnesses to Report Crime," *Yale Law Journal* 94 (1985): 1787.

88. Herman Goldstein, *Policing a Free Society* (Cambridge: Ballinger, 1977), p. 62.

89. Wenik, "Forcing the Bystander," p. 1803.

CHAPTER THREE: The Courts: Dueling Proxies

Epigraph: Napoleon, Maximes (London: Arthur L. Humphreys, 1903), p. 151.

1. George C. Thomas III and David Edelman, "An Evaluation of Conservative Crime Control Theology," *Notre Dame Law Review* 63 (1988): 159.

2. Sir James Fitzjames Stephen, *A History of the Criminal Law of England* (New York: Burt Franklin, 1973), vol. 1, pp. 72–73.

3. Ibid., p. 61.

4. John H. Langbein, "The Criminal Trial Before the Lawyers," *University of Chicago Law Review* 45 (1978): 282.

5. Ibid., p. 307.

6. Quoted in Laurie S. Fulton, "The Right to Counsel Clause of the Sixth Amendment," *American Criminal Law Review* 26 (1989): 1600.

7. Gordon Van Kessel, "Adversary Excesses in the American Criminal Trial," *Notre Dame Law Review* 67 (1992): 408.

8. Ibid., pp. 408–9.

9. Ibid., p. 407.

10. *1991 Selected Standards on Professional Responsibility,* ed. Thomas D. Morgan and Ronald D. Rotunda (Westbury, N.Y.: Foundation, 1991), Model Rule of Professional Conduct 3.8, comment 1, p. 75.

11. Richard Wasserstrom, "Lawyers as Professionals: Some Moral Issues," *Human Rights* 5 (1975–76): 6.

12. United States v. Wade, 388 U.S. 218, 256–57 (1967) (White, J., dissenting).

13. Van Kessel, "Adversary Excesses," pp. 435–36.

14. Quoted in Albert W. Alschuler, "Plea Bargaining and Its History," *Columbia Law Review* 79 (1979): 38.

15. Quoted in Van Kessel, "Adversary Excesses," pp. 436–37.

16. Thomas Wolfe, *The Bonfire of the Vanities* (New York: Farrar, Straus, 1987), p. 106.

17. John Henry Wigmore, *Evidence in Trials at Common Law,* ed. John T. McNaughton (Boston: Little, Brown, 1961), vol. 8, § 2290, p. 543. (Emphasis deleted.)

18. Ibid.

19. Fred C. Zacharias, "Rethinking Confidentiality," *Iowa Law Review* 74 (1989): 358.

20. Jeremy Bentham, *Rationale of Judicial Evidence,* in *The Works of Jeremy Bentham,* ed. John Bowring (New York: Russell & Russell, 1962), vol. 6, p. 100; vol. 7, p. 473.

21. Graham Hughes, "English Criminal Justice: Is It Better than Ours?" *Arizona Law Review* 26 (1984): 591.

22. David Dolinko, "Is There a Rationale for the Privilege Against Self-Incrimination?" *UCLA Law Review* 33 (1986): 1065–66.

23. Charles Fried, "Privacy," *Yale Law Journal* 77 (1968): 475.

24. Richard Wasserstrom, "Privacy: Some Arguments and Assumptions," in *Philosophical Dimensions of Privacy* (1968), pp. 322–23, quoted in Dolinko, "Self-Incrimination," p. 1139.

25. Wigmore, Evidence, vol. 2, § 575, pp. 802, 809; vol. 8, § 2252, pp. 324–25.

26. Ibid., vol. 8, § 2251, p. 313.

27. Van Kessel, "Adversary Excesses," pp. 283–84.

28. Bentham, *Rationale of Judicial Evidence,* vol. 7, book, p. 504.

29. Mirjan Damaska, "Evidentiary Barriers to Conviction and Two Models of Criminal Procedure: A Comparative Study," *University of Pennsylvania Law Review* 121 (1973): 525.

30. Stephen, *History of Criminal Law,* vol. 1, pp. 70–71.

31. Wigmore, *Evidence,* vol. 1A, § 197, p. 1859.

32. Langbein, "The Criminal Trial," pp. 303–5.

33. See Chapter 4.

34. Sherman, "Crime's Toll on the U.S."

35. Marc Galanter, "The Day After the Litigation Explosion," *Maryland Law Review* 46 (1986): 5.

36. Patrick Atiyah, "Tort Law and the Alternatives," *1987 Duke Law Journal:* 1002–44.

37. Towers Perrin Company, "Tort Cost Trends: An International Perspective" (unpublished study, 1992), p. 3.

38. Robert J. Samuelson, "The Litigation Explosion: The Wrong Question," *Maryland Law Review 46 (1986):* 79.

39. Ibid.

40. Ibid., p. 80; Towers Perrin, "Tort Cost Trends," p. 3.

41. Towers Perrin, "Tort Cost Trends," p. 3.

42. R. Berman, ed., *Solzhenitsyn at Harvard: The Address, Twelve Early Responses, and Six Later Reflections* (1980), p. 8, quoted in Galanter, "The Day After," p. 11.

43. Foreword to Berman, *Solzhenitsyn at Harvard*, pp. viii–ix, quoted in Galanter, "The Day After," pp. 11–12.

44. Werner Pfennigstorf, "The European Experience with Attorney Fee Shifting," *Law and Contemporary Problems* 47 (1984): 37.

45. John Leubsdorf, "Toward a History of the American Rule on Attorney Fee Recovery," *Law and Contemporary Problems* 47 (1984): 9.

46. Ibid., pp. 16–17.

47. Ibid.

48. Walter K. Olson, *The Litigation Explosion: What Happened When America Unleashed the Lawsuit* (New York: Truman Talley, 1991), p. 45.

49. Roscoe Pound, *Criminal Justice in America* (1930), p. 184, quoted in Alschuler, "Plea Bargaining and Its History," p. 30.

50. Douglas A. Smith, "The Plea Bargaining Controversy," *Journal of Criminal Law and Criminology* 77 (1986): 949.

51. Matthew Hale, *History of the Pleas of the Crown,* ed. S. Emlyn (1736), p. 225, quoted in Alschuler, "Plea Bargaining and Its History," p. 7.

52. Blackstone, *Commentaries,* vol. 2, bk. 4, p. 329.

53. Alschuler, "Plea Bargaining and Its History," p. 10.

54. Ibid., pp. 9–10.

55. 99 U.S. 594 (1878).

56. *Swang v. State,* 42 Tenn. (2 Cold.) 212, 213–14 (1865).

57. *Pope v. State,* 56 Fla. 81, 85; 47 So. 487, 489 (1908).

58. *Wight v. Rindskopf,* 43 Wis. 344, 354–55 (1877).

59. Cited in Alschuler, "Plea Bargaining and Its History," p. 26.

60. Ibid., p. 33.

61. 404 U.S. 257 (1971).

62. Ibid. at 260.

63. Dallin Oaks and Warren Lehman, *The Criminal Justice System and the Indigent: A Study of Chicago and Cook County* (Chicago: Univ. of Chicago Press, 1968), pp. 53–81; Peter F. Nardulli, "The Caseload Controversy and the Study of Criminal Courts," *Journal of Criminal Law and Criminology* 70 (1979): 89; Michael L. Rubinstein and Teresa J. White, "Alaska's Ban on Plea Bargaining," *Law & Society Review* 13 (1979): 367; Milton Heumann and Colin Loftin, "Mandatory Sentencing and the Abolition of Plea Bargaining: The Michigan Felony Firearm Statute," *Law & Society Review* 13 (1979): 393; Moise Berger, "The Case Against Plea Bargaining," *American Bar Association Journal* 62 (May 1976): 621.

64. Alschuler, "Plea Bargaining and Its History," p. 38.

65. Bureau of Justice Statistics, *Sourcebook,* Table 2.33, p. 200 (poll regarding propriety of plea bargaining).

66. Van Kessel, "Adversary Excesses," pp. 501–2.

67. Ibid., p. 408.

68. John H. Langbein, "Torture and Plea Bargaining," *University of Chicago Law Review* 46 (1978): 3.

69. Benjamin R. Civiletti, "Zeroing In on the Real Litigation Crisis: Irrational Justice, Needless Delays, Excessive Costs," *Maryland Law Review* 46 (1986): 45–46.

70. Jonathan D. Casper, "Determinate Sentencing and Prison Crowding in Illinois," *University of Illinois Law Review* 1984: 235–236.

71. Ilene H. Nagel, Stephen Breyer and Terence MacCarthy, "Equality Versus Discretion in Sentencing," symposium discussion published in *American Criminal Law Review* 26 (1989): 1813.

72. John J. DiIulio, "Let 'em Rot," *Wall Street Journal,* January 26, 1994, p. A14.

73. Candace McCoy, "Determinate Sentencing, Plea Bargaining Bans, and Hydraulic Discretion in California," *Justice System Journal* 9 (1984): 256; Thomas and Edelman, "Conservative Crime Control Theology," p. 129.

74. *Maryland v. Craig,* 110 S. Ct. 3157, 3164 (1990) (Sixth Amendment "con-

stitutionalizes the right in an adversary criminal trial to make a defense as we know it"); *Miranda*, 384 U.S. at 460 (right against self-incrimination essential because it is "the essential mainstay of our Adversary System").

75. Van Kessel, "Adversary Excesses," pp. 474–77.

76. Quoted in Charles E. Wyzanski, Jr., "A Trial Judge's Freedom and Responsibility," *Harvard Law Review* 65 (1952): 1293.

77. Immanuel Kant, *The Metaphysical Elements of Justice,* trans. John Ladd (Indianapolis: Bobbs-Merrill, 1965), p. 101.

CHAPTER FOUR: THE PRISONS: SOCIAL BURIAL

Epigraph: Polybius, *Histories,* quoted in Jay M. Shafritz, *Words on War* (New York: Simon & Schuster, 1990), p. 326.

1. Michael Satchell, "The Toughest Prison in America," *U.S. News & World Report,* July 27, 1987, p. 24.

2. Nathaniel Hawthorne, *The Scarlet Letter,* in *The Novels and Tales of Nathaniel Hawthorne* (New York: Modern Library, 1937), p. 112.

3. Satchell, "The Toughest Prison in America."

4. Michael Ignatieff, *A Just Measure of Pain: The Penitentiary in the Industrial Revolution, 1750–1850* (New York: Pantheon, 1978), p. 15.

5. Adam J. Hirsch, "From Pillory to Penitentiary: The Rise of Criminal Incarceration in Early Massachusetts," *Michigan Law Review* 80 (1982): 1203–12.

6. Ibid., p. 1212.

7. Gustave de Beaumont and Alexis de Tocqueville, *On the Penitentiary System in the United States and Its Application in France* (Carbondale, Ill.: Southern Illinois Univ. Press, 1964), p. 41.

8. Ibid., pp. 47, 91.

9. Ted Gest, "The Prison Boom Bust," *U.S. News & World Report,* May 4, 1992, p. 28.

10. Leo Carroll, *Hacks, Blacks and Cons: Race Relations in a Maximum Security Prison* (Lexington, Mass.: Lexington, 1974).

11. Taylor, *Paved with Good Intentions,* pp. 274–75.

12. Kathleen Engel and Stanley Rothman, "The Paradox of Prison Reform: Rehabilitation, Prisoners' Rights and Violence," *Harvard Journal of Law and Public Policy* 7 (1984): 414.

13. Karl Menninger, *The Crime of Punishment* (New York: Viking, 1968); Michel Foucault, *Discipline and Punish: The Birth of the Prison* (New York: Vintage, 1979).

14. James Q. Wilson and Richard Herrnstein, *Crime and Human Nature: The Definitive Study of the Causes of Crime* (New York: Touchstone, 1985), p. 496.

15. Stephen, *History of Criminal Law,* vol. 2, pp. 81–82.

16. Ibid., p. 82.

17. Kant, *Metaphysical Elements of Justice,* p. 101.

18. Herbert Packer, *The Limits of the Criminal Sanction* (Stanford: Stanford Univ. Press, 1968), p. 62.

19. Quoted in Will and Ariel Durant, *The Age of Voltaire* (New York: Simon & Schuster, 1965), p. 621.

20. Ibid., pp. 701–5.

21. Edwin H. Sutherland, *Principles of Criminology* (Chicago: Lippincott, 1939), p. 51.

22. *Williams v. New York,* 337 U.S. 241, 248 (1949).

23. *Furman v. Georgia,* 408 U.S. 238, 295 (1972) (Marshall, J., concurring).

24. Blake McKelvey, *American Prisons: A History of Good Intentions* (Montclair, N.J.: Patterson Smith, 1977), p. 327.

25. Robert Martinson, "What Works? Questions and Answers About Prison Reform," *Public Interest,* Spring 1974, p. 29.

26. Robert Martinson, "New Findings, New Views: A Note of Caution Regarding Sentencing Reform," *Hofstra Law Review* 7 (1979): 243.

27. Martinson, "What Works?" p. 48.

28. A recent renaissance of pro-rehabilitation research has still not repaired the damage. See Steven P. Lab and John T. Whitehead, "From 'Nothing Works' to 'The Appropriate Works': The Latest Stop on the Search for the Secular Grail," *Criminology* 28 (August 1990): 405.

29. Jessica Mitford, *Kind and Usual Punishment* (New York: Alfred A. Knopf, 1973), p. 71.

30. Beaumont and Tocqueville, *On the Penitentiary System,* p. 87.

31. Bentham, *Principles of Morals and Legislation,* p. 1.

32. Ernest van den Haag, "The Proper Goals of Punishment," transcript of a symposium published in *American Criminal Law Review* 26 (1989): 1800.

33. Wilson, *Thinking About Crime,* pp. 117–44.

34. Ernest van den Haag and John P. Conrad, *The Death Penalty: A Debate* (New York: Plenum, 1983), p. 92.

35. Cesare Beccaria, *On Crimes and Punishments,* ed. Henry Paolucci (Indianapolis: Bobbs-Merrill, 1963), p. 43.

36. Bentham, *Principles of Morals and Legislation,* p. 170.

37. Gordon Tullock, "Does Punishment Deter Crime?" *Public Interest,* Summer 1974, p. 103.

38. Isaac Ehrlich, "Participation in Illegitimate Activities: A Theoretical and Empirical Investigation," *Journal of Political Economy* 81 (1973): 521.

39. Daniel Nagin, "General Deterrence: A Review of the Empirical Evidence," in Alfred Blumstein et al., eds., *Deterrence and Incapacitation: Estimating the Effects of Criminal Sanctions on Crime Rates* (Washington, D.C.: National Academy of Sciences, 1978), p. 111.

40. Wilson, *Thinking About Crime,* pp. 117–44.

41. See, e.g., Richard A. Posner, "An Economic Theory of the Criminal Law," *Columbia Law Review* 85 (1985): 1193; Steven Shavell, "Criminal Law and the Optimal Use of Nonmonetary Sanctions as a Deterrent," *Columbia Law Review* 85 (1985): 1232.

42. Edwin W. Zedlewski, "Making Confinement Decisions," *Research in Brief* (Washington, D.C.: National Institute of Justice, July 1987).

43. E.g., John J. DiIulio, Jr., *No Escape: The Future of American Corrections* (New York: Basic Books, 1991), pp. 73–74.

44. Richard B. Adell, "Beyond Willie Horton: The Battle of the Prison Bulge," *Policy Review*, Winter 1989, p. 32.

45. DiIulio, *No Escape*, p. 75.

46. John J. DiIulio, Jr., "The Value of Prisons," *Wall Street Journal*, May 13, 1992, p. A16.

47. Eugene Methvin, "Pay Now—Or Pay Later," *Reader's Digest*, June 1991, p. 61.

48. Morgan O. Reynolds, *Crime Pays: But So Does Imprisonment*, NCPA Policy Report No. 149 (Dallas: National Center for Policy Analysis, 1990).

49. Etzioni, *Spirit of Community*, p. 13.

50. Kendall J. Wills, "A Dose of Shame," *Phoenix Gazette*, February 2, 1993, p. A5.

51. Jacqueline Cohen, "The Incapacitative Effect of Imprisonment: A Critical Review of the Literature," in Alfred Blumstein et al., eds., *Deterrence and Incapacitation: Estimating the Effects of Criminal Sanctions on Crime Rates* (Washington, D.C.: National Academy of Sciences, 1978).

52. Marvin E. Wolfgang, Robert M. Figlio and Thorsten Sellin, *Delinquency in a Birth Cohort* (Chicago: Univ. of Chicago Press, 1972).

53. Joan Petersilia and Peter W. Greenwood, "Mandatory Prison Sentences: Their Projected Effects on Crime and Prison Populations," *Journal of Criminal Law and Criminology* 69 (1978): 604.

54. Wilson, *Thinking About Crime*, pp. 151–61.

55. Oliver, "Are More Prisons the Answer?"

56. Jacqueline Cohen, "Selective Incapacitation: An Assessment," *University of Illinois Law Review* 1984: 261–63.

57. Reuben Greenberg and Arthur Gordon, *Let's Take Back Our Streets* (Chicago: Contemporary, 1989), pp. 119–20.

58. Ernest van den Haag, "How to Cut Crime," *National Review*, May 30, 1994, p. 35.

59. Cohen, "Selective Incapacitation," p. 262.

60. Cited in Francis T. Cullen and Lawrence F. Travis III, "Work as an Avenue of Prison Reform," *New England Journal of Civil and Criminal Confinement* 10 (1984): 48–49.

61. Bureau of Justice Statistics, *Sourcebook*, Table 2.43, p. 210.

62. John Howard, *The State of the Prisons in England and Wales*, in *Prisons and Lazarettos* (Montclair, N.J.: Patterson Smith, 1973), vol. 1, p. 13.

63. Beaumont and Tocqueville, *On the Penitentiary System*, pp. 57, 89–90.

64. W. J. Michael Cody and Andy D. Bennett, "The Privatization of Correctional Institutions: The Tennessee Experience," *Vanderbilt Law Review* 40 (1987): 852–53.

65. Donald R. Walker, *Penology for Profit: A History of the Texas Prison System, 1867–1912* (College Station: Texas A&M Univ. Press, 1988), p. 65.

66. Cody and Bennett, "Tennessee Experience," p. 830.

67. McKelvey, *American Prisons,* p. 292.

68. Ibid.

69. "Factories Behind Bars," *U.S. News & World Report,* December 30, 1991/January 6, 1992, p. 30.

70. Ibid.

71. McKelvey, *American Prisons,* p. 13.

72. M. de Voltaire, *Candide,* trans. and ed. Robert M. Adams (New York: W. W. Norton, 1966), p. 77.

CHAPTER FIVE: THE NEW NOBLE SAVAGE

Epigraph: Samuel Johnson, "Vanity of Human Wishes," in *The Poems of Samuel Johnson,* ed. David Nichol Smith and Edward L. McAdam (Oxford: Clarendon, 1951), p. 38.

1. M. P. Mack, *Jeremy Bentham: An Odyssey of Ideas* (New York: Columbia Univ. Press, 1963), p. 441.

2. Ibid., p. 7.

3. Ibid., pp. 8–9, 347.

4. See Chapter 4.

5. Isaac Ehrlich, "The Deterrent Effect of Capital Punishment: A Question of Life and Death," *American Economic Review* 65 (June 1975): 398.

6. Walter Berns, *Crime and the Morality of the Death Penalty* (New York: Basic Books, 1979), p. 98.

7. William J. Bowers and Glenn L. Pierce, "What Is the Effect of Executions: Deterrence or Brutalization," unpublished paper, discussed in van den Haag and Conrad, *The Death Penalty: A Debate,* p. 140.

8. David Hume, *A Treatise of Human Nature,* ed. L. A. Selby-Bigge (Oxford: Clarendon, 1987), pp. 74, 156.

9. Quoted in John Hearsey, *Voltaire* (New York: Barnes & Noble, 1976), p. 225.

10. Paul Johnson, *Intellectuals* (New York: Harper & Row, 1988), pp. 52–81.

11. Allan Bloom, *The Closing of the American Mind: How Higher Education Has Failed Democracy and Impoverished the Souls of Today's Students* (New York: Simon & Schuster, 1987), pp. 180–84.

12. Johnson, *Intellectuals,* p. 1.

13. Mill, *On Liberty,* pp. 69–70, 78–80, 85.

14. Will Durant, *Caesar and Christ* (New York: Simon & Schuster, 1944), p. 556.

15. Clifford R. Shaw and Henry D. McKay, *Juvenile Delinquency and Urban Areas* (Chicago: Univ. of Chicago Press, 1942).

16. Robert K. Merton, "Social Structure and Anomie," in Robert K. Merton, *Social Theory and Social Structure* (New York: Free Press, 1957).

17. Richard A. Cloward and Lloyd Ohlin, *Delinquency and Opportunity* (New York: Free Press, 1960), p. 193.

18. Charles A. Murray, *Losing Ground: American Social Policy, 1950–1980* (New York: Basic Books, 1984), pp. 147–91.

19. Voltaire, *Candide*, p. 2.

20. See Edward C. Banfield, *The Unheavenly City: The Nature and Future of Our Urban Crisis* (Boston: Little, Brown, 1970), pp. 45–66.

21. National Academy of Sciences, *Understanding and Preventing Violence*, p. 132.

22. Robert Rector, "America's Poverty Myth," *Wall Street Journal*, September 3, 1992, p. A12.

23. Holman Jenkins, Jr., "The 'Poverty' Lobby's Inflated Numbers," *Wall Street Journal*, December 14, 1992, p. A10.

24. Quoted in Banfield, *Unheavenly City*, p. 117.

25. Ibid., pp. 119, 124. (Emphasis in original.)

26. George F. Will, "Looters in a Queue," in *The Morning After: American Successes and Excesses 1981–1986* (New York: Free Press, 1986), p. 44.

27. Banfield, *Unheavenly City*, pp. 124–25.

28. Cesare Lombroso and William Ferrero, *The Female Offender* (New York: Philosophical Library, 1958), pp. 90–91.

29. H. H. Goddard, *Feeble-Mindedness: Its Causes and Consequences* (New York: Macmillan, 1914), pp. 6–10.

30. William H. Sheldon, *Varieties of Delinquent Youth* (New York: Harper, 1949).

31. Wilson and Herrnstein, *Crime and Human Nature*, pp. 81–90.

32. Patricia A. Jacobs, Muriel Brunton and Marie M. Melville, "Aggressive Behaviour, Mental Sub-normality, and the XYY Male," *Nature*, December 25, 1965, pp. 1351–52.

33. Wilson and Herrnstein, *Crime and Human Nature*, p. 101.

34. See, e.g., Leon Kamin, "Is Crime in the Genes? The Answer May Depend on Who Chooses What Evidence," *Scientific American* 254 (1986): 22.

35. Wilson and Herrnstein, *Crime and Human Nature*, p. 66.

36. Kamin, "Is Crime in the Genes?," p. 24.

37. See, e.g., Wilson and Herrnstein, *Crime and Human Nature*, pp. 95 (twin studies supporting determinism are "too few to permit a decisive conclusion"), 100 (adoption studies do "not preclude environmental influences"), 166 (IQ's effect on criminality is unclear from police records because unintelligent offenders are more likely to get caught).

38. Ibid., pp. 61, 171, 177, 183, 201–2.

39. Allen J. Beck, Susan A. Kline and Lawrence A. Greenfield, *Survey of Youth in Custody, 1987*, Bureau of Justice Statistics Special Report (Washington, D.C.: U.S. Department of Justice, 1988), p. 2.

40. See, e.g., National Academy of Sciences, *Understanding and Preventing Violence*, p. 15 (control of economic "resources" may foster crime); pp. 14, 20 for poverty-causes-crime theory.

41. Ibid., pp. 7, 38–39.

42. Ibid., pp. 118–21, 124–25.

43. Ibid., pp. 15, 105, 122.

44. Nicholas Eberstadt, "Is Illegitimacy a Public-Health Hazard?" *National Review*, December 30, 1988, pp. 36ff.

45. "Pregnant Smoker Rate High," *Arizona Republic*, April 22, 1992, p. A2.

46. Edwin H. Sutherland, "Varieties of Delinquent Youth," in *The Sutherland Papers*, ed. Karl Schuessler, Alfred Lindesmith and Albert Cohen (Bloomington: Indiana Univ. Press, 1956), p. 286.

47. Wilson and Herrnstein, *Crime and Human Nature*, p. 72.

48. James Boswell, *The Life of Samuel Johnson* (New York: Random House, 1964), p. 348.

CHAPTER SIX: THE FLIGHT FROM PARENTHOOD

Epigraph: John Milton, *Paradise Lost*, ed. A. W. Verity (Cambridge: Cambridge Univ. Press, 1934), vol. 1, p. 258.

1. Sherman, "Crime's Toll on the U.S." (the breakdown of the family named as the "greatest cause" of crime); see also "The Tourist Murders," *Wall Street Journal,* September 16, 1993, p. A24: "There are, indeed, root causes of crime. One of them is the now-obvious breakdown of the family."

2. Sheldon and Eleanor T. Glueck, *Unraveling Juvenile Delinquency* (Cambridge: Harvard Univ. Press, 1950), pp. 281–82.

3. Wilson and Herrnstein, *Crime and Human Nature*, p. 236.

4. Travis Hirschi, *Causes of Delinquency* (Berkeley: Univ. of California Press, 1969).

5. Wilson and Herrnstein, *Crime and Human Nature*, p. 217.

6. Albert K. Cohen, *Delinquent Boys* (New York: Free Press, 1955).

7. D. Baumrind, "Child Care Practices Anteceding Three Patterns of Preschool Behavior," *Genetic Psychology Monographs* 75 (1967): 43–88, cited in Wilson and Herrnstein, *Crime and Human Nature*, p. 246.

8. Henry B. Biller and Richard S. Solomon, *Child Maltreatment and Paternal Deprivation* (Lexington, Mass.: Lexington Books, 1986), p. 221.

9. Urie Bronfenbrenner, "What Do Families Do?" *Family Affairs,* Winter/Spring 1991, p. 4.

10. Barbara Dafoe Whitehead, "Dan Quayle Was Right," *The Atlantic,* April 1993, p. 47.

11. Plato, *The Republic,* trans. and ed. Francis MacDonald Cornford (New York: Oxford Univ. Press, 1966), pp. 163–66.

12. Aristotle, *Politics,* trans. Benjamin Jowett, in vol. 9 of *Great Books of the Western World* (Chicago: William Benton, 1952), bk. 1, chap. 2, p. 445. (Emphasis added.)

13. Ibid., bk. 2, chap. 4, p. 457; bk. 2, chap. 3, p. 457.

14. "Drop in Early Marriages May Have Lasting Impact," *Wall Street Journal,* November 26, 1991, p. B1.

15. Michele Ingrassia, "Endangered Family," *Newsweek,* August 30, 1993, p. 17.

16. Douglas J. Besharov, "That Other Clinton Promise—Ending 'Welfare as We Know It,'" *Wall Street Journal*, January 18, 1993, p. A10.

17. Bill McAllister, "To Be Young, Male, and Black," *Washington Post*, December 28, 1989, p. A1.

18. Taylor, *Paved with Good Intentions*, p. 82.

19. Cited in George Gilder, *Men and Marriage* (Gretna, La. Pelican, 1989), p. 60.

20. U.S. Department of Health and Human Services, *HHS News Release*, February 25, 1993, p. 1.

21. "29% of Homes Run by 1 Parent, Census Study Says," *Arizona Republic*, April 23, 1992, p. A3.

22. Charles Murray, "The Coming White Underclass," *Wall Street Journal*, October 29, 1993, p. A14.

23. Tom Mashberg, "More Mothers Unwed, Unwistful," *Boston Globe*, July 15, 1993, p. A1.

24. Wilson and Herrnstein, *Crime and Human Nature*, p. 252.

25. Frank F. Furstenberg and Andrew J. Cherlin, *Divided Families: What Happens to Children When Parents Part* (Cambridge: Harvard Univ. Press, 1991), p. 31.

26. Bennett, "Commuter Massacre, Our Warning."

27. Barbara Kantrowitz et al., "Breaking the Divorce Cycle," *Newsweek*, January 13, 1992, p. 48ff.

28. Furstenberg and Cherlin, *Divided Families*, p. 14.

29. "More Divorces Involve Fewer Children Apiece," *Wall Street Journal*, July 19, 1991, p. B1.

30. Kantrowitz, "Breaking the Divorce Cycle."

31. David B. Wilson, "Is Marriage Obsolete?" *Boston Globe*, August 6, 1989, p. A31.

32. Furstenberg and Cherlin, *Divided Families*, p. 35.

33. Wilson and Herrnstein, *Crime and Human Nature*, pp. 248–49.

34. Myron Magnet, "The American Family, 1992," *Fortune*, August 10, 1992, pp. 42ff.

35. Bryce J. Christensen, "The Costly Retreat from Marriage," *Public Interest*, Spring 1988, pp. 60–62.

36. Ibid.

37. Magnet, "American Family."

38. Federal Bureau of Investigation, *Uniform Crime Reports 1991*, p. 279.

39. Dafoe Whitehead, "Dan Quayle Was Right," p. 77.

40. Judith S. Wallerstein and Sandra Blakeslee, *Second Chances: Men, Women and Children a Decade After Divorce* (New York: Ticknor & Fields, 1989), p. xvi.

41. Ibid., pp. 153–54.

42. David Whitman and Dorian Friedman, "The War over 'Family Values,'" *U.S. News & World Report*, June 8, 1992, pp. 35ff.

43. Magnet, "American Family."

44. Lenore J. Weitzman, *The Divorce Revolution* (New York: Free Press, 1985), p. 362.

45. Ibid., p. 359.

46. Ibid., p. 362.

47. Mary Ann Glendon, *The New Family and the New Property* (Cambridge: Harvard Univ. Press, 1981), pp. 81–91.

48. James Patterson and Peter Kim, *The Day America Told the Truth* (New York: Plume Books, 1992), p. 93.

49. Mark 10:1–12.

50. Quoted in John Leo, "Censors on the Left," *U.S. News & World Report,* October 4, 1993, p. 30.

51. Catharine A. MacKinnon, *Only Words* (Cambridge: Harvard Univ. Press, 1993), p. 3.

52. William Tucker, "Why We Have Families," in *Orthodoxy: The American Spectator's 20th Anniversary Anthology* (New York: Harper & Row, 1987), pp. 176–86.

53. Wilson and Herrnstein, *Crime and Human Nature,* p. 249.

54. Bob Baker, "Homeboys: Players in a Deadly Drama," *Los Angeles Times,* June 26, 1988, p. A1.

55. David Cannella, "Rogue Males: Boyfriends Blamed in Children's Deaths," *Arizona Republic,* February 26, 1993, p. A1.

56. Scott Burns, "Tax Policy Works Against Family Values," *Dallas Morning News,* July 11, 1993, p. 1H.

57. Bennett, *Index of Leading Cultural Indicators,* p. 103.

58. Ron Haskins, "Public School Aggression Among Children with Varying Day Care Experience," *Child Development* 56 (1985): 689.

59. J. C. Schwarz, R. G. Strickland and G. Krolick, "Infant Day Care: Behavioral Effects at Preschool Age," *Developmental Psychology* 10 (1974): 502.

60. Ron Haskins, "Public School Aggression," p. 700.

61. Michael Rutter, "Social-Emotional Consequences of Day Care for Preschool Children," *American Journal of Orthopsychiatry* 51 (1981): 4; Christopher Bagley, "Aggression and Anxiety in Day-Care Graduates," *Psychological Reports* 64 (1989): 250; Urie Bronfenbrenner, "Research on the Effects of Day Care on Child Development," in National Research Council, *Toward a National Policy for Children and Families* (Washington, D.C.: National Academy of Sciences, 1976), p. 117.

62. Charles Darwin, *The Descent of Man and Selection in Relation to Sex,* in vol. 49 of *Great Books of the Western World* (Chicago: William Benton, 1952), p. 308.

63. Bronfenbrenner, "What Do Families Do?" pp. 2–3.

64. Brenda Hunter, *Home by Choice: Facing the Effects of Mother's Absence* (Portland, Oreg.: Multnomah, 1991), p. 65.

65. James Lincoln Collier, *The Rise of Selfishness in America* (New York: Oxford Univ. Press, 1991), p. 253.

66. Wade Lambert, "Child Support Tied to Mother's Potential Salary," *Wall Street Journal,* May 11, 1994, p. B1.

67. Gilder, *Men and Marriage,* pp. 5–18.

68. Irving Kristol, "Men, Women, and Sex," *Wall Street Journal,* May 12, 1992, p. A12.

69. Quoted in Gilder, *Men and Marriage,* p. 29.

70. David Wessel, "Rep. Weber's Plan for a Term Limit on Welfare Draws Criticism from Some of His Usual Allies," *Wall Street Journal,* June 17, 1992, p. A18.

71. Dorian Friedman, "Why the Welfare Mess Gets Messier," *U.S. News & World Report,* November 25, 1991, p. 30.

72. "Clinton's Welfare Pickle: Plan Is in Place, Money Isn't," *Arizona Republic,* March 28, 1994, p. A5.

73. Blackstone, *Commentaries,* vol. 1, bk. 1, p. 463.

74. 430 U.S. 651 (1977).

75. 105 S.Ct. 733 (1985).

76. *State of Maine v. Thiboutot,* 448 U.S. 1 (1980).

77. William Celis III, "More States Are Laying School Paddle to Rest," *New York Times,* August 16, 1990, p. A1.

78. Ibid.

79. Cited in Michael Elliott, "Crime and Punishment," *Newsweek,* April 18, 1994, p. 18.

80. Cotton Mather, *A Family Well-Ordered; or, An Essay to Render Parents and Children Happy in One Another* (Boston: B. Green, 1699), pp. 118–19, on microfiche produced by American Antiquarian Society, Worcester, Mass., 1st series, no. 875.

81. Horace Bushnell, *Christian Nurture,* in *Horace Bushnell,* ed. H. Shelton Smith (New York: Oxford Univ. Press, 1965), pp. 385–86.

82. Benjamin Spock, *The Common Sense Book of Baby and Child Care* (New York: Duell, Sloan & Pearce, 1957), p. 363.

83. Michael Rutter et al., *Fifteen Thousand Hours: Secondary Schools and Their Effects on Children* (Cambridge: Harvard Univ. Press, 1979), discussed in Wilson and Herrnstein, *Crime and Human Nature,* pp. 280–82.

84. Wilson and Herrnstein, *Crime and Human Nature,* p. 285.

85. National Institute of Education, *Violent Schools—Safe Schools: The Safe School Study Report to the Congress* (Washington, D.C.: U.S. Government Printing Office, 1978).

86. "The High School vs. the ACLU," *Wall Street Journal,* February 1, 1994, p. A14.

87. Phyllis Schlafly, "Clinton and Family Values," *Wall Street Journal,* January 19, 1993, p. A12.

88. "'Cheaters Do Prosper': Youths Poke Hole in 'Moral Ozone,'" *Arizona Republic,* November 13, 1992, p. A12.

89. Bertrand Russell, *What I Believe* (New York: Dutton, 1925), p. 11.

90. See, e.g., *Lemon v. Kurtzman,* 403 U.S. 602 (1971) (separation of Church

and State precludes government aid to church-affiliated schools); *Abington School District v. Schempp*, 374 U.S. 203 (1963) (reading from Bible at start of school day is unconstitutional).

91. Abraham Lincoln, "The Perpetuation of Our Political Institutions," Address Before the Young Men's Lyceum of Springfield, Illinois, in *The Collected Works of Abraham Lincoln*, ed. Roy P. Basler (New Brunswick, N.J.: Rutgers Univ. Press, 1953), vol. 1, p. 109.

92. Ibid., p. 112.

93. Han Fei Tzu, *Readings in Chinese Legal Thought*, trans. Wejen Chang (unpublished manuscript at Harvard Law School, 1990), p. 494.

94. Blackstone, *Commentaries*, vol. 1, p. 451.

95. Barbara Kantrowitz, "Now, Parents on Trial," *Newsweek,* October 2, 1989, p. 54.

CHAPTER SEVEN: GANGS, DRUGS AND PLATO'S OTHER CHILDREN

1. "The Panama Blitz," *Newsweek,* January 1, 1990, pp. 16ff.

2. Ibid.

3. Thomas L. Friedman, "After Noriega: U.S. and Rome," *New York Times,* December 29, 1989, p. A13.

4. David Margolick, "Judge Rules Noriega Is Prisoner of War," *New York Times,* December 9, 1992, p. A18.

5. Tod Robberson, "DEA: Money Laundry Pressing on in Panama," *Washington Post,* February 13, 1993, p. A20.

6. "The Panama Invasion: A Newsweek Poll," *Newsweek,* January 1, 1990, p. 22.

7. Gaetano Mosca, *The Ruling Class,* trans. Hannah D. Kahn (New York: McGraw-Hill, 1939), p. 163.

8. Alexis de Tocqueville, *Democracy in America,* ed. Phillips Bradley (New York: Alfred A. Knopf, 1987), vol. 1, pp. 191–98.

9. National Academy of Sciences, *Understanding and Preventing Violence,* pp. 141–42.

10. Frederic M. Thrasher, *The Gang* (Chicago: Univ. of Chicago Press, 1963), pp. 46, 31.

11. Cohen, *Delinquent Boys.*

12. Sutherland, *Principles of Criminology,* p. 145.

13. Robert Agnew and Helen Raskin White, "An Empirical Test of General Strain Theory," *Criminology* 30 (November 1992): 493.

14. Ira M. Schwartz, *(In)justice for Juveniles: Rethinking the Best Interests of the Child* (Lexington, Mass.: Lexington Books, 1989), p. 26.

15. Fred Bayles, "Fewer Teens, More Crime, Study Says," *Phoenix Gazette,* October 15, 1992, p. A11.

16. Federal Bureau of Investigation, *Uniform Crime Reports 1991,* p. 279.

17. Adam Smith, *Theory of Moral Sentiments* (Boston: Wells, 1817), p. 1.

18. Bayles, "Fewer Teens, More Crime."

19. Barbara Kantrowitz, "Wild in the Streets," *Newsweek,* August 2, 1993, p. 43.

20. Tom Morgenthau, "It's Not Just New York . . . ," *Newsweek,* March 9, 1992, p. 25.

21. Gordon Witkin, "Kids Who Kill," *U.S. News & World Report,* April 8, 1991, p. 27.

22. "Their Drug War—and Ours," *New York Times,* January 12, 1990, p. A34.

23. Lee N. Robins, *Deviant Children Grown Up* (Baltimore: Williams & Wilkins, 1966).

24. Joan Petersilia, "Criminal Career Research: A Review of Recent Evidence," in Norval Morris and Michael Tonry, eds., *Crime and Justice: An Annual Review of Research* (Chicago: Univ. of Chicago Press, 1980), vol. 2, pp. 347, 349–50.

25. Barbara Boland and James Q. Wilson, "Age, Crime and Punishment," *Public Interest,* Spring 1978, p. 22.

26. See Federal Bureau of Investigation, *Uniform Crime Reports 1991,* pp. 60–67 (crime rates by region).

27. Bob Baker, "Chicano Gangs: A History of Violence," *Los Angeles Times,* December 11, 1988, p. A1.

28. Baker, "Homeboys."

29. National Academy of Sciences, *Understanding and Preventing Violence,* pp. 141–42.

30. Baker, "Chicano Gangs."

31. National Academy of Sciences, *Understanding and Preventing Violence,* p. 144.

32. Ibid., p. 143.

33. Louis Sahagun, "Gang Crimes Drop Sharply in South L.A.," *Los Angeles Times,* May 4, 1990, p. A1.

34. David Freed, "Policing Gangs: Case of Contrasting Styles," *Los Angeles Times,* January 19, 1986, part 2, p. 1.

35. Whitkin, "Kids Who Kill," p. 30.

36. Barry C. Feld, "The Juvenile Court Meets the Principle of the Offense: Legislative Changes in Juvenile Waiver Statutes," *Journal of Criminal Law and Criminology* 78 (1987): 476–77.

37. Ibid.

38. 387 U.S. 1 (1967).

39. Quoted in "Headline Tells All," *Wall Street Journal,* November 20, 1990, p. A20.

40. Blackstone, *Commentaries,* vol. II, bk. IV, p. 23.

41. Rita Kramer, "Juvenile Justice Is Delinquent," *Wall Street Journal,* May 27, 1992, p. A14.

42. Harold Finestone, *Victims of Change: Juvenile Delinquents in American Society* (Westport, Conn.: Greenwood Press, 1976); Robert G. Caldwell, "The Juvenile Court: Its Development and Some Major Problems," *Journal of Criminal Law, Criminology and Police Science 51* (1961): 493.

43. Charles Oliver, "'Drop and Give Me 20 Push-Ups,'" *Investor's Business Daily,* March 22, 1994, p. A1.

44. Boland and Wilson, "Age, Crime and Punishment," pp. 27–30.

45. David F. Musto, *The American Disease: Origins of Narcotic Control* (New York: Oxford Univ. Press, 1987), p. 7.

46. Ibid., p. 57.

47. Ibid., p. 7.

48. Ibid., p. 267.

49. Richard K. Willard, "Improving National Drug Policy," *American Criminal Law Review* 26 (1989): 1698 (quoting federal regulation).

50. Joseph B. Treaster, "U.S. Cocaine Epidemic Shows Signs of Waning," *New York Times,* July 1, 1990, part 1, p. 14.

51. Elijah Anderson, *Streetwise: Race, Class, and Change in an Urban Community* (Chicago: Univ.of Chicago Press, 1990), pp. 77, 84.

52. Ramsey Clark, *Crime in America* (New York: Simon & Schuster, 1970), pp. 85–100.

53. Ronald J. Ostrow, "Doubt Cast on Crime Rate's Tie to Drug War," *Los Angeles Times,* September 6, 1991, p. A20.

54. Bureau of Justice Statistics, *Sourcebook,* Table 6.63, p. 629.

55. Ibid., Table 6.65, p. 630.

56. National Academy of Sciences, *Understanding and Preventing Violence,* p. 186.

57. Bureau of Justice Statistics, *Sourcebook,* Table 2.40, p. 207.

58. Will Durant, *The Age of Faith* (New York: Simon & Schuster, 1950), pp. 931–35.

59. William of Ockham, *Philosophical Writings,* ed. and trans. Philotheus Boehner (New York: Thomas Nelson & Sons, 1959), p. 33.

60. James Q. Wilson, "Against the Legalization of Drugs," *Commentary,* February 1990, p. 25.

61. Ibid., p. 24.

62. Clinton Rossiter, *Conservatism in America: The Thankless Persuasion* (New York: Vintage, 1962), p. 130.

63. Mill, On Liberty, p. 116.

64. Milton Friedman, "Prohibition and Drugs," *Newsweek,* May 1, 1972, p. 104.

65. Wilson, "Against the Legalization of Drugs," p. 22.

66. Ibid., pp. 21–25.

67. Bureau of Justice Statistics, *Sourcebook,* Table 2.67, p. 231.

68. William J. Bennett, "Losing the Drug War Without a Fight," *Wall Street Journal,* April 6, 1994, p. A20.

69. Wilson, "Against the Legalization of Drugs," pp. 21, 25–26.

70. Peter Reuter, Gordon Crawford and Jonathan Cave, *Sealing the Borders: The Effects of Military Participation in Drug Interdiction,* RAND Corporation, Report No. R-3594-USDP (Santa Monica: RAND Corporation, January 1988).

71. Wilson, "Against the Legalization of Drugs," p. 23.

72. Oaks, "Studying the Exclusionary Rule," pp. 706–7.

73. "Addicted Parents Mean More Foster Kids," *Arizona Republic,* April 28, 1994, p. A8.

CHAPTER EIGHT: THE ROUGH JUSTICE OF BLACK CRIME

Epigraph: Malcolm X and Alex Haley, *The Autobiography of Malcolm X* (New York: Ballantine, 1992), p. 271.

1. Seth Mydans, "Homicide Rate Up for Young Blacks," *New York Times,* December 7, 1990, p. A26.

2. Daniel Goleman, "Black Scientists Study the 'Pose' of the Inner City," *New York Times,* April 21, 1992, p. C1.

3. "Study Shows Racial Imbalance in Penal System," *New York Times,* February 27, 1990, p. A18.

4. William Glaberson, "One in 4 Young Black Men Is in Custody, a Study Says," *New York Times,* October 4, 1990, p. B6.

5. Carleton R. Bryant, "Recession, Racism Double Trouble for Black Americans," *Washington Times,* January 9, 1991, p. A1.

6. Federal Bureau of Investigation, *Uniform Crime Reports 1991,* pp. 16–17.

7. Wilson and Herrnstein, *Crime and Human Nature,* p. 461.

8. Unpublished study cited in Henry N. Pontell, *A Capacity to Punish: The Ecology of Crime and Punishment* (Bloomington: Indiana Univ. Press, 1984), pp. 70–71.

9. National Advisory Commission on Civil Disorders, *Report,* p. 203.

10. Carol Kalish, *International Crime Rates,* Bureau of Justice Statistics Special Report (Washington, D.C.: U.S. Department of Justice, 1984), Table 4, p. 3; Charles Silberman, *Criminal Violence, Criminal Justice* (New York: Random House, 1978), p. 123.

11. Wilson and Herrnstein, *Crime and Human Nature,* p. 481.

12. Silberman, *Criminal Violence, Criminal Justice,* pp. 153, 165.

13. Federal Bureau of Investigation, *Uniform Crime Reports 1991,* Table 2.7, p. 17.

14. Jared Taylor, *Paved with Good Intentions,* p. 273.

15. John Dollard, *Caste and Class in a Southern Town* (New York: Harper & Brothers, 1949), pp. 279–80, 285.

16. Tucker, *Vigilante,* pp. 307–10.

17. X and Haley, *The Autobiography of Malcolm X,* pp. 40–41, 54.

18. Ibid., pp. 239, 243–44.

19. Ibid., pp. 271, 274.

20. Ibid., pp. 91, 121–22.

21. Richard Vigilante, "Winning in New York," *National Review,* January 18, 1993, pp. 18ff.

22. Dostoevsky, *Brothers Karamazov,* p. 165.

23. Richard Wright, *Native Son* (New York: Harper & Row, 1989), p. 68.

24. W. E. B. Du Bois, *The Souls of Black Folk* (New York: Bantam, 1989), p. 6.

25. Kenneth O'Reilly, *"Racial Matters": The FBI's Secret File on Black America, 1960–1972* (New York: Free Press, 1989), p. 306.

26. "Modern Gangs Have Roots in Racial Turmoil of '60s," *Los Angeles Times,* June 26, 1988, p. A28.

27. Louis Sahagun and Leslie Berger, "Riot Aftermath; Some Gang Members Agreeing to a Truce," *Los Angeles Times,* May 6, 1992, p. A9.

28. "Man Guilty in Huey Newton Death," *Los Angeles Times,* October 10, 1991, p. A22.

29. Arch Puddington, "The Question of Black Leadership," *Commentary,* January 1991, p. 27.

30. Taylor, *Paved with Good Intentions,* p. 116.

31. Dorothy J. Gaiter, "Diversity of Leaders Reflects the Changes in Black Community," *Wall Street Journal,* May 6, 1992, p. A1.

32. "Angry Illinois Voters Cast Out 3 Incumbents," *Arizona Republic,* March 18, 1992, p. A7.

33. Lorrin Anderson, "Crime, Race, and the Fourth Estate," *National Review,* October 15, 1990, pp. 55.

34. Martin Gottlieb, "Dinkins and Police Faulted in Report on Unrest in 1991," *New York Times,* July 21, 1993, p. A1.

35. Taylor, *Paved with Good Intentions,* p. 264.

36. Edwin M. Reingold, "Hard Times for Teflon Tom," *Time,* May 22, 1989, p. 35; "Snarled in Corruption Traffic," *Time,* February 21, 1983, p. 20; Constance Johnson, "The Hidden Perils of Racial Conformity," *U.S. News & World Report,* December 24, 1990, pp. 42ff.

37. Paul Glastris and Jeannye Thornton, "A New Civil Rights Frontier," *U.S. News & World Report,* January 17, 1994, p. 38.

38. Michael Kramer, "What to Make of the 'New' Jesse," *U.S. News & World Report,* November 16, 1987, pp. 34ff.

39. Anderson, "Crime, Race, and the Fourth Estate," p. 55.

40. "Tyson Victim: 'No' to Bribe, Would Have Taken Apology," *Arizona Republic,* February 21, 1992, p. A3.

41. Robert L. Woodson, "Blacks Who Use 'Racism' as Their Excuse," *Wall Street Journal,* March 20, 1992, p. A12.

42. X and Haley, *Autobiography,* p. 242–43.

43. Walter Williams, "Media Deception About King Beating," *Arizona Republic,* January 4, 1993, p. A9.

44. Paul Lieberman, "King's Showing in Court May Aid Both Sides," *Los Angeles Times,* March 11, 1993, p. A18.

45. Hobbes, *Leviathan,* p. 84.

46. "Rethinking Black Concerns," *Wall Street Journal,* July 16, 1992, p. A10.

47. Joseph Perkins, "Bush's Potential Black Voters," *Wall Street Journal,* March 10, 1992, p. A18.

48. Adam Clymer, "Most Americans Are Undecided on Court Nomination, Poll Finds," *New York Times,* September 10, 1991, p. A1.

49. Mark R. Thompson, "L.A.'s Black Poor Demand Law and Order," *Wall Street Journal,* May 23, 1989, p. A18.

50. Ibid.

51. Ellen J. Bartlett, "Abortion Rights a Tangled Issue for Minorities," *Boston Globe,* April 26, 1989, p. 37.

52. Priscilla Painton, "The Shrinking Ten Percent," *Time,* April 26, 1993, p. 28 (table citing findings).

53. Joseph M. Rothberg, Paul T. Bartone, Harry C. Holloway and David H. Marlowe, "Life and Death in the U.S. Army," *Journal of the American Medical Association* 264 (1990): 2241.

54. Wilson, *Thinking About Crime,* pp. 32–33; Taylor, *Paved with Good Intentions,* p. 354.

55. Taylor, ibid., p. 349.

56. Du Bois, *Souls of Black Folk,* pp. 8, 63.

57. Ibid., pp. 136, 139, 134.

58. Robert A. Jordan, "Churches Must Reassert Role," *Boston Globe,* December 1, 1990, p. 29.

59. Du Bois, *Souls of Black Folk,* p. 145.

CHAPTER NINE: ATOM BOMB, OR AMERICA'S CULTURE OF CHAOS

1. Quoted in Silberman, *Criminal Violence, Criminal Justice,* p. 21.

2. Ibid., pp. 21–47, 117–67.

3. Kalish, *International Crime Rates,* Bureau of Justice Statistics Special Report, Table 4, p. 3.

4. Sir Leon Radzinowicz and Joan King, *The Growth of Crime: The International Experience* (New York: Basic Books, 1977), pp. 4–5.

5. Wilson and Herrnstein, *Crime and Human Nature,* pp. 446–47.

6. David H. Bayley, "Learning About Crime—The Japanese Experience," *Public Interest,* Summer 1976, p. 64.

7. Paul Johnson, "Duty, Honor, Unpopularity," *U.S. News & World Report,* December 30, 1985, p. 46ff.

8. Walter C. Reckless, *The Crime Problem* (New York: Appleton-Century-Crofts, 1955).

9. Discussed in Wilson and Herrnstein, *Crime and Human Nature,* p. 460.

10. Wilson and Herrnstein, *Crime and Human Nature,* p. 128.

11. Peter Brimelow, "Time to Rethink Immigration?" *National Review,* June 22, 1992, p. 46.

12. Dan Weikel, "Crime and the Sound of Silence," *Los Angeles Times,* October 1, 1990, p. A1.

13. Ibid.

14. David Haldane, "Latino and Asian Gangs Engage in Deadly Warfare," *Los Angeles Times,* April 15, 1991, p. B1.

15. See, e.g., Nieson Himmel, "Cambodians Trade Shots with Blacks at Housing Project," *Los Angeles Times,* May 13, 1988, p. B3; Stephanie Chavez, "Housing Project Shooting Called 'an Isolated Act,'" *Los Angeles Times,* May 14, 1988, p. B3 (a shoot-out at a different project one day later).

16. Jesse Katz, "Once Allies, Latino, Black Gangs Fight for Turf," *Los Angeles Times,* December 26, 1993, p. A1.

17. Bayley, "Learning About Crime—the Japanese Experience," pp. 64–68.

18. Ibid., p. 64.

19. Lawrence M. Friedman, *Crime and Punishment in American History* (New York: Basic Books, 1993), pp. 464–65.

20. Madison, *Federalist Papers,* No. 10, p. 78.

21. Will and Ariel Durant, *Rousseau and Revolution* (New York: Simon & Schuster, 1967), pp. 669–71 (discussing scientific bent of Anglo-Saxons as primary catalyst of Industrial Revolution).

22. Wilson, *Thinking About Crime,* p. 245.

23. While the Framers of the Constitution quoted Rousseau and many others in their writings, such attributions were often, as Bernard Bailyn once observed, part of a "massive, seemingly random eclecticism," frequently serving as mere "window dressing with which to ornament a page or a speech and to increase the weight of an argument." Bernard Bailyn, *The Ideological Origins of the American Revolution* (Cambridge: Harvard Univ. Press, 1967), pp. 23–24.

24. Cf. Bloom, *Closing of the American Mind,* pp. 173–79.

25. 383 U.S. 413 (1966).

26. Attorney General's Commission on Pornography, *Final Report* (Washington, D.C.: U.S. Government Printing Office, 1986), vol. 1, pp. 337–38; see, e.g., Barbara Gamarekian, "Report Draws Strong Praise and Criticism," *New York Times,* July 10, 1986, p. B7.

27. Larry Baron and Murray A. Straus, "Sexual Stratification, Pornography, and Rape in American States," unpublished paper, 1985.

28. See National Academy of Sciences, *Understanding and Preventing Violence,* cited on p. 7 and elsewhere.

29. Ron Langevin, Daniel Paitich and Anne E. Russon, "Are Rapists Sexually Anomalous, Aggressive, or Both?" in Ron Langevin, ed., *Erotic Preference, Gender Identity, and Aggression in Men* (Hillsdale, N.J.: Lawrence Erlbaum Associates, 1985), pp. 17–38, 31, 34.

30. Ron Langevin et al., "Sexual Aggression: Constructing a Predictive Equation, A Controlled Pilot Study," in Ron Langevin, ed., *Erotic Preference, Gender Identity, and Aggression in Men* (Hillsdale, N.J.: Lawrence Erlbaum Associates, 1985), pp. 49, 66.

31. Martinson, "What Works?" pp. 35–36.

32. Graph accompanying "Liberalism Strikes Out," *Wall Street Journal,* February 18, 1994, p. A12.

33. E.g., *Jenkins v. Georgia,* 418 U.S. 153 (1974); *F.C.C. v. Pacifica,* 439 U.S. 883 (1978).

34. Bennett, "Commuter Massacre, Our Warning."

35. Bloom, *Closing of the American Mind,* pp. 68–81.

36. Jeffrey Arnett, "Heavy Metal Music and Reckless Behavior Among Adolescents," *Journal of Youth and Adolescence* 20 (1991): 585.

37. Hannelore Wass, M. David Miller and Carol Anne Redditt, "Adolescents and Destructive Themes in Rock Music: A Follow-Up," *Omega* 23 (1991): 199.

38. Wilson and Herrnstein, *Crime and Human Nature,* p. 337.

39. "California's Anti-Smoking Drive 'Worked,'" *Arizona Republic,* March 21, 1994, p. A3; "California Cuts Rolls of Smokers," *Arizona Republic,* January 15, 1992, p. A16.

40. Chuck Philips, "Beating the Rap of Concert Violence," *Los Angeles Times,* February 10, 1991, Calendar section, p. 63.

41. "2 Rappers Sought on Gun Charges," *Chicago Tribune,* September 18, 1993, p. 16; Ronald Smothers, "Rapper Charged in Shootings of Off-Duty Officers," *New York Times,* November 2, 1993, p. A8; "Performer Arrested in Bronx," *New York Times,* November 2, 1993, p. A8; Mathis Chazanov and Chuck Philips, "Rap Singer Faces Charges of Murder," *Los Angeles Times,* September 4, 1993, p. B3.

42. Philips, "Beating the Rap."

43. Nadine Brozan, *New York Times,* November 11, 1992, Chronicle section, p. B5.

44. Whitman and Friedman, "The War over 'Family Values.'"

45. Wilson and Herrnstein, *Crime and Human Nature,* p. 339.

46. David P. Phillips, "The Influence of Suggestion on Suicide: Substantive and Theoretical Implications of the Werther Effect," *American Sociological Review* 39 (1974): 340.

47. Leonard D. Eron, L. Rowell Huesmann, Monroe M. Lefkowitz and Leopold O. Walder, *Growing Up to Be Violent: A Longitudinal Study of the Development of Aggression* (New York: Pergamon, 1977).

48. L. Rowell Huesmann, "Cross-National Communalities in the Learning of Aggression from Media Violence," in L. Rowell Huesmann and Leonard D. Eron, eds., *Television and the Aggressive Child: A Cross-National Comparison* (Hillsdale, N.J.: Lawrence Erlbaum, 1986), p. 255.

49. National Academy of Sciences, *Understanding and Preventing Violence,* pp. 104–6.

50. National Institute of Mental Health, *Television and Behavior: Ten Years of Scientific Progress and Implications for the Eighties,* Summary Report (Rockville, Md.: NIMH, 1982), vol. 1, p. 6.

51. Wilson and Herrnstein, *Crime and Human Nature,* p. 353.

52. Victoria Harker, "Teen Pregnancy Soaring in Arizona," *Arizona Republic,* April 25, 1994, p. A1.

53. Barbara Vobejda, "Teens' Use of Birth Control Up, Study Says," *Arizona Republic,* June 7, 1994, p. A1.

54. Robert Byrd, "Poll: Half in High School Have Had Sex," *Arizona Republic,* January 4, 1992, p. A1.

55. Sonia L. Nazario, "Schools Teach the Virtues of Virginity," *Wall Street Journal,* February 20, 1992, p. B1.

56. Jill Smolowe, "Sex with a Scorecard," *Time,* April 5, 1993, p. 41.

57. "Initiation for Gang Girls: Sex with HIV-Positive Members," *Chicago Tribune,* April 26, 1993, p. 2.

58. Neil A. Lewis, "Friends of Free Speech Now Consider Its Limits," *New York Times,* June 29, 1990, p. B7.

59. Sherman, "Crime's Toll on the U.S."

60. Rimer, "Rap Band Members Found Not Guilty."

61. Wesley Newcomb Hohfeld, *Fundamental Legal Conceptions,* ed. Walter Wheeler Cook (New Haven: Yale Univ. Press, 1964).

62. Plato, *Crito,* trans. F. J. Church (Indianapolis: Bobbs-Merrill, 1956), p. 60.

CHAPTER TEN: PLACEBOS

Epigraph: Miguel de Cervantes, *The History of Don Quixote de la Mancha,* trans. John Ormsby, vol. 29 of *Great Books of the Western World* (Chicago: William Benton, 1952), p. 18.

1. Will Durant, *The Pleasures of Philosophy* (New York: Simon & Schuster, 1953), p. 269; Durant, *Our Oriental Heritage,* p. 222.

2. Durant, *Pleasures of Philosophy,* pp. 260, 262.

3. Will and Ariel Durant, *A Dual Autobiography* (New York: Simon & Schuster, 1977), pp. 366–67.

4. Edward Gibbon, *The Decline and Fall of the Roman Empire,* vol. 40 of *Great Books of the Western World* (Chicago: William Benton, 1952), pp. 501–2.

5. Quoted in Will Durant, *The Age of Faith* (New York: Simon & Schuster, 1950), p. 30.

6. Ashley Dunn, "King Case Aftermath: A City in Crisis," *Los Angeles Times,* May 2, 1992, p. A1.

7. Taylor, *Paved with Good Intentions,* p. 119.

8. Tom Mathews, "The Siege of L.A.," *Newsweek,* May 11, 1992, pp. 30ff.

9. Dunn, "King Case Aftermath."

10. Ibid.

11. Sheryl Stolberg, "King Case Aftermath: A City in Crisis," *Los Angeles Times,* May 2, 1992, p. A6.

12. Dunn, "King Case Aftermath."

13. Ted Rohrlich and Rich Connell, "Police Pullout, Riot's Outbreak Reconstructed," *Los Angeles Times,* May 5, 1992, p. A1.

14. Mathews, "The Siege of L.A."

15. T. W. McGarry, "Violence and Looting Spread into the Valley," *Los Angeles Times,* May 1, 1992, p. B1.

16. Timothy Egan, "Los Angeles Riots Spurring Big Rise in Sales of Guns," *New York Times,* May 14, 1992, p. A1.

17. George D. Newton and Franklin Zimring, *Firearms and Violence in American Life,* Staff Report of the Task Force on Firearms, National Commission on the Causes and Prevention of Violence (Washington, D.C.: U.S. Government Printing Office, 1969), p. xiii.

18. Ibid., pp. 128, 123.

19. Gary Kleck, "The Relationship Between Gun Ownership Levels and Rates of Violence in the United States," in Don B. Kates, ed., *Firearms and Violence: Issues of Public Policy* (Cambridge: Ballinger Press, 1984), pp. 104, 111.

20. Alan J. Lizotte and David J. Bordua, "Firearms Ownership for Sport and Protection: Two Divergent Models," *American Sociological Review* 45 (April 1980): 229.

21. Kleck, "Gun Ownership Levels," p. 104. (Emphasis in original.)

22. Cited in National Academy of Sciences, *Understanding and Preventing Violence,* p. 256.

23. Don B. Kates, Jr., ed., *Restricting Handguns: The Liberal Skeptics Speak Out* (Croton-on-Hudson, N.Y.: North River Press, 1979); Don B. Kates, Jr., "Handgun Banning in Light of the Prohibition Experience," *Firearms and Violence: Issues of Public Policy* (Cambridge, Mass.: Ballinger Press, 1984), p. 139.

24. Gary Kleck, "Handgun-Only Gun Control: A Policy Disaster in the Making," in Don B. Kates, *Firearms and Violence: Issues of Public Policy* (Cambridge, Mass.: Ballinger Press, 1984), pp. 167–99, 195.

25. Kates, "Handgun-Banning," p. 156.

26. Paxton Quigley, *Armed and Female* (New York: St. Martin's Press, 1989), p. 82.

27. Kates, "Handgun Banning," pp. 157–58.

28. Ibid., p. 159.

29. Bureau of Justice Statistics, *Sourcebook*, Table 2.54, p. 217.

30. Ibid., Table 2.56, p. 220.

31. National Academy of Sciences, *Understanding and Preventing Violence*, p. 269.

32. Kleck, "Gun Ownership Levels," p. 132.

33. David J. Bordua and Alan J. Lizotte, "A Subcultural Model of Legal Firearms Ownership in Illinois," *Law and Policy Quarterly* 2 (April 1979): 147.

34. Kates, "Handgun Banning," p. 159.

35. National Academy of Sciences, *Understanding and Preventing Violence*, p. 18.

36. Ibid., p. 268.

37. Roy Innis, "Gun Control Sprouts from Racist Soil," *Wall Street Journal*, November 21, 1991, p. A14.

38. Don B. Kates, Jr., "Toward a History of Handgun Prohibition in the United States," in Don B. Kates, ed., *Restricting Handguns: The Liberal Skeptics Speak Out* (Croton-on-Hudson, N.Y.: North River Press, 1979), pp. 15–22.

39. Leroy G. Schultz, "Why the Negro Carries Weapons," *Journal of Criminal Law, Criminology, and Police Science* 53 (December 1962): 479–80.

40. Rene Sanchez, "Shooting Doesn't Contradict Gun Control Stance, Rowan Says," *Washington Post*, June 16, 1988, p. A1.

41. Kates, "Handgun Banning," p. 154.

42. Beccaria, *Of Crimes and Punishments*, pp. 87–88.

43. Quigley, *Armed and Female*, pp. 8–9.

44. Carol Ruth Silver and Don B. Kates, Jr., "Self-Defense, Handgun Ownership, and the Independence of Women in a Violent, Sexist Society," in Don B. Kates, ed., *Restricting Handguns: The Liberal Skeptics Speak Out* (Croton-on-Hudson, N.Y.: North River Press, 1979), pp. 139–70, 141.

45. Don B. Kates, Jr., "Handgun Prohibition and the Original Meaning of the Second Amendment," *Michigan Law Review* 82 (1983): 216.

46. First Militia Act, 1 Stat. 271 (1792).

47. Blackstone, *Commentaries*, vol. 1, bk. 1, p. 144; vol. 2, bk. 4, p. 149.

48. Kates, "The Second Amendment," p. 265.

49. Bureau of Justice Statistics, *Sourcebook,* Table 3.10, p. 264.

50. Gary Kleck and David J. Bordua, "The Factual Foundation for Certain Key Assumptions of Gun Control," *Law & Policy Quarterly,* July 1983, pp. 271–298.

51. Cited in National Academy of Sciences, *Understanding and Preventing Violence,* p. 265.

52. National Academy of Sciences, *Understanding and Preventing Violence,* p. 266.

53. Unpublished study cited in Kleck and Bordua, "Assumptions of Gun Control," p. 284.

54. James D. Wright and Peter H. Rossi, *Armed and Considered Dangerous: A Survey of Felons and Their Firearms* (New York: Aldine de Gruyter, 1986), pp. 145–47.

55. Quigley, *Armed and Female,* pp. 15–16.

56. Kleck and Bordua, "Assumptions of Gun Control," p. 288.

57. Quigley, *Armed and Female,* p. 89.

58. Anthony Walsh, "Placebo Justice: Victim Recommendations and Offender Sentences in Sexual Assault Cases," *Journal of Criminal Law and Criminology* 77 (1986): 1139.

59. Lynne N. Henderson, "The Wrongs of Victims Rights," *Stanford Law Review* 37 (1985): 937–1021.

60. Ibid., p. 940.

61. Juan Cardenas, "The Crime Victim in the Prosecutorial Process," *Harvard Journal of Law and Public Policy* 9 (1986): 370.

62. Ibid., p. 367.

63. Ibid.

64. Henderson, "Wrongs of Victims Rights," p. 941.

65. Stephen, *History of Criminal Law,* vol. 1, p. 496.

66. Plato, *Apology,* trans. F. J. Church, in *Euthyphro, Apology, Crito, Phaedo,* ed. Robert D. Cumming (Indianapolis: Bobbs–Merrill, 1956), p. 41.

CHAPTER ELEVEN: CONCLUSION—PUTTING FIRST THINGS FIRST

1. Will Durant, *The Story of Philosophy* (Garden City, N.Y.: Garden City Publishing, 1938), pp. 262–64.

2. Alfred de Musset, *The Confession of a Child of the Century,* in *The Complete Writings of Alfred de Musset,* trans. Kendall Warren (New York: Edwin C. Hill, 1905), vol. 8, p. 22.

3. Wilson, *Thinking About Crime,* pp. 228–34.

Selected Bibliography

BOOKS AND ARTICLES

Adell, Richard B. "Beyond Willie Horton: The Battle of the Prison Bulge." *Policy Review,* Winter 1989, pp. 32–35.

Agnew, Robert, and Helen Raskin White. "An Empirical Test of General Strain Theory." *Criminology* 30 (November 1992): 475–500.

Alschuler, Albert W. "Plea Bargaining and Its History." *Columbia Law Review* 79 (1979): 1–43.

Anderson, Elijah. *Streetwise: Race, Class, and Change in an Urban Community.* Chicago: Univ. of Chicago Press, 1990.

Aristotle. *Politics.* Trans. Benjamin Jowett. In vol. 9 of *Great Books of the Western World.* Chicago: William Benton, 1952.

Arizona Juvenile Justice Advisory Council Minority Youth Issues Committee. *Equitable Treatment of Minority Youth.* Phoenix: Governor's Office for Children, 1993.

Arnett, Jeffrey. "Heavy Metal Music and Reckless Behavior among Adolescents." *Journal of Youth and Adolescence* 20 (1991): 573–92.

Atiyah, Patrick. "Tort Law and the Alternatives." *1987 Duke Law Journal:* 1002–44.

Attorney General's Commission on Pornography. *Final Report.* Washington, D.C.: U.S. Government Printing Office, 1986.

St. Augustine. *City of God.* Trans. Marcus Dods. New York: Modern Library, 1950.

Bagley, Christopher. "Aggression and Anxiety in Day-Care Graduates." *Psychological Reports* 64 (1989): 250.

Bailyn, Bernard. *The Ideological Origins of the American Revolution.* Cambridge: Harvard Univ. Press, 1967.

Baker, Bob. "Chicano Gangs: A History of Violence." *Los Angeles Times,* December 11, 1988, p. A1.

———. "Homeboys: Players in a Deadly Drama." *Los Angeles Times,* June 26, 1988, p. A1.

Baldwin, James. *Nobody Knows My Name: Notes of a Native Son.* New York: Dial Press, 1961.

Banfield, Edward C. *The Unheavenly City: The Nature and Future of Our Urban Crisis.* Boston: Little, Brown, 1970.

Baron, Larry, and Murray A. Straus. *Sexual Stratification, Pornography, and Rape in American States.* Unpublished paper, 1985.

Bayley, David H. "Learning About Crime—The Japanese Experience." *Public Interest,* Summer 1976, pp. 55–68.

Beaumont, Gustave de, and Alexis de Tocqueville. *On the Penitentiary System in the United States and Its Application in France.* Carbondale, Ill.: Southern Illinois Univ. Press, 1964.

Beccaria, Cesare. *On Crimes and Punishments.* Ed. Henry Paolucci. Indianapolis: Bobbs-Merrill, 1963.

Beck, Allen J., Susan A. Kline and Lawrence A. Greenfield. *Survey of Youth in Custody, 1987.* Bureau of Justice Statistics Special Report. Washington, D.C.: U.S. Dept. of Justice, 1988.

Bennett, William. "Commuter Massacre, Our Warning." *Wall Street Journal,* December 10, 1993, p. A14.

———. *The Index of Leading Cultural Indicators.* New York: Touchstone, 1994.

———. "Losing the Drug War Without a Fight." *Wall Street Journal,* April 6, 1994, p. A20.

———. "Quantifying America's Decline." *Wall Street Journal,* March 15, 1993, p. A12.

Bentham, Jeremy. *An Introduction to the Principles of Morals and Legislation.* Ed. Lawrence J. Lafleur. New York: Hafner, 1948.

———. *Rationale of Judicial Evidence.* In *The Works of Jeremy Bentham,* ed. John Bowring. 11 vols. New York: Russell & Russell, 1962.

Berger, Moise. "The Case Against Plea Bargaining." *American Bar Association Journal* 62 (May 1976): 621–24.

Berger, Raoul. *Congress v. The Supreme Court.* Cambridge: Harvard Univ. Press, 1969.

Berns, Walter. *Crime and the Morality of the Death Penalty.* New York: Basic Books, 1979.

Biller, Henry B., and Richard S. Solomon. *Child Maltreatment and Paternal Deprivation.* Lexington, Mass.: Lexington Books, 1986.

Black, Donald. *The Manners and Customs of the Police.* New York: Academic Press, 1980.

Blackstone, Sir William. *Commentaries on the Laws of England.* 2 vols. Baton Rouge, La.: Claitor's Publishing, 1976.

Bloom, Allan. *The Closing of the American Mind: How Higher Education Has Failed Democracy and Impoverished the Souls of Today's Students.* New York: Simon & Schuster, 1987.

Boland, Barbara, and James Q. Wilson. "Age, Crime and Punishment." *Public Interest,* Spring 1978, pp. 22–34.

Bordua, David J., and Alan J. Lizotte. "A Subcultural Model of Legal Firearms Ownership in Illinois." *Law & Policy Quarterly* 2 (April 1979): 147–75.

Boswell, James. *The Life of Samuel Johnson*. New York: Random House, 1964.

Brimelow, Peter. "Time to Rethink Immigration?" *National Review*, June 22, 1992, pp. 30–46.

Bronfenbrenner, Urie. "Research on the Effects of Day Care on Child Development." In National Research Council, *Toward a National Policy for Children and Families*. Washington, D.C.: National Academy of Sciences, 1976.

———. "What Do Families Do?" *Family Affairs* Winter/Spring 1991, pp. 2–4.

Bureau of Justice Statistics. *Sourcebook of Criminal Justice Statistics 1991*. Washington, D.C.: U.S. Government Printing Office, 1991.

Bushnell, Horace. *Christian Nurture*. In *Horace Bushnell*, ed. Shelton H. Smith. New York: Oxford Univ. Press, 1965.

Caldwell, Robert G. "The Juvenile Court: Its Development and Some Major Problems." *Journal of Criminal Law, Criminology and Police Science* 51 (1961): 493–511.

Canon, Bradley. "Testing the Effectiveness of Civil Liberties Policies at the State and Federal Levels: The Case of the Exclusionary Rule." *American Politics Quarterly* 5 (1977): 57–82.

Cardenas, Juan. "The Crime Victim in the Prosecutorial Process." *Harvard Journal of Law and Public Policy* 9 (1986): 357–98.

Carroll, Leo. *Hacks, Blacks and Cons: Race Relations in a Maximum Security Prison*. Lexington, Mass.: Lexington Press, 1974.

Casper, Jonathan D. "Determinate Sentencing and Prison Crowding in Illinois." *University of Illinois Law Review* 1984: 231–52.

Christensen, Bryce J. "The Costly Retreat from Marriage." *Public Interest*, Spring 1988, pp. 59–66.

Civiletti, Benjamin R. "Zeroing in on the Real Litigation Crisis: Irrational Justice, Needless Delays, Excessive Costs." *Maryland Law Review* 46 (1986): 40–48.

Clark, Ramsey. *Crime in America*. New York: Simon & Schuster, 1970.

Cloward, Richard A., and Lloyd Ohlin. *Delinquency and Opportunity*. New York: Free Press, 1960.

Cody, W. J. Michael, and Andy D. Bennett. "The Privatization of Correctional Institutions: The Tennessee Experience." *Vanderbilt Law Review* 40 (1987): 829–49.

Cohen, Albert K. *Delinquent Boys*. New York: Free Press, 1955.

Cohen, Jacqueline. "The Incapacitative Effect of Imprisonment: A Critical Review of the Literature." In Alfred Blumstein et al., eds., *Deterrence and Incapacitation: Estimating the Effects of Criminal Sanctions on Crime Rates*. Washington, D.C.: National Academy of Sciences, 1978.

———. "Selective Incapacitation: An Assessment." *University of Illinois Law Review* 1984: 253–90.

Collier, James Lincoln. *The Rise of Selfishness in America.* New York: Oxford Univ. Press, 1991.

Crovitz, L. Gordon. "How Law Destroys Order." *National Review,* February 11, 1991, pp. 28–33.

Cullen, Francis T., and Lawrence F. Travis III. "Work as an Avenue of Prison Reform." *New England Journal of Civil and Criminal Confinement* 10 (1984): 45–64.

Damaska, Mirjan. "Evidentiary Barriers to Conviction and Two Models of Criminal Procedure: A Comparative Study." *University of Pennsylvania Law Review* 121 (1973): 506–89.

Darwin, Charles. *The Descent of Man and Selection in Relation to Sex.* In vol. 49 of *Great Books of the Western World.* Chicago: William Benton, 1952.

DiIulio, John J., Jr. *No Escape: The Future of American Corrections.* New York: Basic Books, 1991.

———. "Let 'em Rot." *Wall Street Journal,* January 26, 1994, p. A14.

———. "The Value of Prisons." *Wall Street Journal,* May 13, 1992, p. A16.

Dolinko, David. "Is There a Rationale for the Privilege Against Self-Incrimination?" *UCLA Law Review* 33 (1986): 1063–1148.

Dollard, John. *Caste and Class in a Southern Town.* New York: Harper & Brothers, 1949.

Dostoevsky, Fyodor. *The Brothers Karamazov.* Vol. 52 of *Great Books of the Western World.* Chicago: William Benton, 1952.

Du Bois, W. E. B. *The Souls of Black Folk.* New York: Bantam, 1989.

Durant, Will. *The Age of Faith.* New York: Simon & Schuster, 1950.

———. *The Age of Voltaire.* New York: Simon & Schuster, 1965.

———. *Caesar and Christ.* New York: Simon & Schuster, 1944.

———. *Our Oriental Heritage.* New York: Simon & Schuster, 1954.

———. *The Pleasures of Philosophy.* New York: Simon & Schuster, 1953.

———. *The Story of Philosophy.* 2d ed. Garden City, N.Y.: Garden City Publishing, 1938.

Durant, Will and Ariel. *A Dual Autobiography.* New York: Simon & Schuster, 1977.

Eberstadt, Nicholas. "Is Illegitimacy a Public-Health Hazard?" *National Review,* December 30, 1988, pp. 36ff.

Ehrlich, Isaac. "The Deterrent Effect of Capital Punishment: A Question of Life and Death." *American Economic Review* 65 (June 1975): 397–417.

———. "Participation in Illegitimate Activities: A Theoretical and Empirical Investigation." *Journal of Political Economy* 81 (1973): 521–65.

Ellickson, Robert C. "The Homelessness Muddle." *Public Interest,* Spring 1990, pp. 45–60.

Engel, Kathleen, and Stanley Rothman. "The Paradox of Prison Reform:

Rehabilitation, Prisoners' Rights and Violence." *Harvard Journal of Law and Public Policy* 7 (1984): 413–20.

Eron, Leonard D., L. Rowell Huesmann, Monroe M. Lefkowitz and Leopold O. Walder. *Growing Up to Be Violent: A Longitudinal Study of the Development of Aggression*. New York: Pergamon, 1977.

Etzioni, Amitai. *The Spirit of Community: Rights, Responsibilities, and the Communitarian Agenda*. New York: Crown, 1993.

Federal Bureau of Investigation. *Uniform Crime Reports 1991*. Washington, D.C.: U.S. Government Printing Office, 1991.

Feld, Barry C. "The Juvenile Court Meets the Principle of the Offense: Legislative Changes in Juvenile Waiver Statutes." *Journal of Criminal Law and Criminology* 78 (1987): 471–533.

Finestone, Harold. *Victims of Change: Juvenile Delinquents in American Society*. Westport, Conn.: Greenwood Press, 1976.

Fogelson, Robert M. *Big-City Police*. Cambridge: Harvard Univ. Press, 1977.

Foucault, Michel. *Discipline and Punish: The Birth of the Prison*. New York: Vintage, 1979.

Fried, Charles. "Privacy." *Yale Law Journal* 77 (1968): 475–93.

Friedman, Lawrence M. *A History of American Law*. New York: Simon & Schuster, 1985.

———. *Crime and Punishment in American History*. New York: Basic Books, 1993.

Friedman, Milton. "Prohibition and Drugs." *Newsweek*, May 1, 1972, p. 104.

Fulton, Laurie. "The Right to Counsel Clause of the Sixth Amendment." *American Criminal Law Review* 26 (1989): 1599–1616.

Furstenberg, Frank F., and Andrew J. Cherlin. *Divided Families: What Happens to Children When Parents Part*. Cambridge: Harvard Univ. Press, 1991.

Gaiter, Dorothy J. "Diversity of Leaders Reflects the Changes in Black Community." *Wall Street Journal*, May 6, 1992, p. A1.

Galanter, Marc. "The Day After the Litigation Explosion." *Maryland Law Review* 46 (1986): 3–39.

Gibbon, Edward. *The Decline and Fall of the Roman Empire*. Vols. 40 and 41 of *Great Books of the Western World*. Chicago: William Benton, 1952.

Gilder, George. *Men and Marriage*. Gretna, La.: Pelican Press, 1989.

Glendon, Mary Ann. *The New Family and the New Property*. Cambridge: Harvard Univ. Press, 1981.

Glueck, Sheldon and Eleanor T. *Unraveling Juvenile Delinquency*. Cambridge: Harvard Univ. Press, 1950.

Goddard, H. H. *Feeble-Mindedness: Its Causes and Consequences*. New York: Macmillan, 1914.

Goldstein, Herman. *Policing a Free Society*. Cambridge, Mass.: Ballinger, 1977.

Greenberg, Douglas. "Crime, Law Enforcement, and Social Control." *The American Journal of Legal History* 26 (1982): 293–325.

Greenberg, Reuben, and Arthur Gordon. *Let's Take Back Our Streets.* Chicago: Contemporary Press, 1989.

Hamilton, Alexander, James Madison and John Jay. *The Federalist Papers.* New York: New American Library, 1961.

Haskins, Ron. "Public School Aggression Among Children with Varying Day Care Experience." *Child Development* 56 (1985): 689–703.

Hawthorne, Nathaniel. *The Scarlet Letter.* In *The Novels and Tales of Nathaniel Hawthorne.* New York: Modern Library, 1937.

Henderson, Lynne N. "The Wrongs of Victims' Rights." *Stanford Law Review* 37 (1985): 937–1021.

Heumann, Milton, and Colin Loftin. "Mandatory Sentencing and the Abolition of Plea Bargaining: The Michigan Felony Firearm Statute." *Law & Society Review* 13 (1979): 393–429.

Hirsch, Adam J. "From Pillory to Penitentiary: The Rise of Criminal Incarceration in Early Massachusetts." *Michigan Law Review* 80 (1982): 1179–1269.

Hirschi, Travis. *Causes of Delinquency.* Berkeley: Univ. of California Press, 1969.

Hobbes, Thomas. *Leviathan.* Ed. Nelle Fuller. In vol. 23 of *Great Books of the Western World.* Chicago: William Benton, 1952.

Hohfeld, Wesley Newcomb. *Fundamental Legal Conceptions.* Ed. Walter Wheeler Cook. New Haven: Yale Univ. Press, 1964.

Howard, John. *The State of the Prisons in England and Wales.* In *Prisons and Lazarettos.* 2 vols. Montclair, N.J.: Patterson Smith, 1973.

Huesmann, L. Rowell. "Cross-National Communalities in the Learning of Aggression from Media Violence." In L. Rowell Huesmann and Leonard D. Eron, eds., *Television and the Aggressive Child: A Cross-National Comparison.* Hillsdale, N.J.: Lawrence Erlbaum, 1986.

Hughes, Graham. "English Criminal Justice: Is It Better than Ours?" *Arizona Law Review* 26 (1984): 507–614.

Hume, David. *A Treatise of Human Nature.* Ed. L. A. Selby-Bigge. Oxford: Clarendon, 1987.

Hunter, Brenda. *Home by Choice: Facing the Effects of Mother's Absence.* Portland, Ore.: Multnomah, 1991.

Ignatieff, Michael. *A Just Measure of Pain: The Penitentiary in the Industrial Revolution, 1750–1850.* New York: Pantheon, 1978.

Innis, Roy. "Gun Control Sprouts from Racist Soil." *Wall Street Journal,* November 21, 1991, p. A14.

Jacobs, Patricia A., Muriel Brunton and Marie M. Melville. "Aggressive Behaviour, Mental Sub-normality, and the XYY Male." *Nature,* December 25, 1965, pp. 1351–52.

Johnson, Paul. *Intellectuals.* New York: Harper & Row, 1988.

Kalish, Carol. *International Crime Rates*. Bureau of Justice Statistics Special Report. Washington, D.C.: U.S. Dept. of Justice, 1984.

Kamin, Leon. "Is Crime in the Genes? The Answer May Depend on Who Chooses What Evidence." *Scientific American* 254 (1986): 22–27.

Kant, Immanuel. *The Metaphysical Elements of Justice*. Trans. John Ladd. Indianapolis: Bobbs-Merrill, 1965.

Kates, Don B. "Handgun Banning in Light of the Prohibition Experience." In Don B. Kates, ed., *Firearms and Violence: Issues of Public Policy*. Cambridge, Mass.: Ballinger Press, 1984.

———. "Handgun Prohibition and the Original Meaning of the Second Amendment." *Michigan Law Review* 82 (1983): 204–73.

———. "Toward a History of Handgun Prohibition in the United States." In Don B. Kates, ed., *Restricting Handguns*, p. 7–30.

———, ed. *Restricting Handguns: The Liberal Skeptics Speak Out*. Croton-on-Hudson, N.Y.: North River, 1979.

Katz, Jesse. "Once Allies, Latino, Black Gangs Fight for Turf." *Los Angeles Times,* December 26, 1993, p. A1.

Kelling, George L., et al. *The Kansas City Preventive Patrol Experiment: A Summary Report*. Washington, D.C.: Police Foundation, 1974.

Kleck, Gary. "Handgun-Only Gun Control: A Policy Disaster in the Making." In Don B. Kates, ed. *Firearms and Violence: Issues of Public Policy*. Cambridge, Mass.: Ballinger Press, 1984.

———. "The Relationship Between Gun Ownership Levels and Rates of Violence in the United States." In Don B. Kates, ed. *Firearms and Violence: Issues of Public Policy*. Cambridge, Mass.: Ballinger Press, 1984, pp. 99–135.

Kleck, Gary, and David J. Bordua. "The Factual Foundation for Certain Key Assumptions of Gun Control." *Law & Policy Quarterly,* July 1983, pp. 271–98.

Kleiman, Mark A. R., et al. *Imprisonment-to-Offense Ratios*. Working Paper #89-06-02. Cambridge: John F. Kennedy School of Government, Harvard Univ., Paper in Progress, August 5, 1988.

Knight, Athelia. "Of 1,286 Slaying Cases, 1 in 4 Ends in Conviction." *Washington Post,* October 24, 1993, p. A1.

Kolata, Gina. "Twins of the Streets: Homelessness and Addiction." *New York Times,* May 22, 1989, p. A1.

Kramer, Michael. "What to Make of the 'New' Jesse." *U.S. News & World Report,* November 16, 1987, pp. 34–44.

Kramer, Rita. "Juvenile Justice is Delinquent." *Wall Street Journal,* May 27, 1992, p. A14.

Kristol, Irving. "Men, Women, and Sex." *Wall Street Journal,* May 12, 1992, p. A12.

Lab, Steven P., and John T. Whitehead. "From 'Nothing Works' to 'The Appropriate Works': The Latest Stop on the Search for the Secular Grail." *Criminology* 28 (August 1990): 405–18.

Lane, Roger. *Policing the City: Boston 1822–1885*. Cambridge: Harvard Univ. Press, 1967.

Langbein, John H. "The Criminal Trial Before the Lawyers." *University of Chicago Law Review* 45 (1978): 263–316.

———. "Torture and Plea Bargaining." *University of Chicago Law Review* 46 (1978): 3–22.

Langevin, Ron, Daniel Paitich and Anne E. Russon. "Are Rapists Sexually Anomalous, Aggressive, or Both?" In Ron Langevin, ed., *Erotic Preference, Gender Identity, and Aggression in Men*. Hillsdale, N.J.: Lawrence Erlbaum Associates, 1985.

Langevin, Ron, et al. "Sexual Aggression: Constructing a Predictive Equation, A Controlled Pilot Study." In Ron Langevin, ed., *Erotic Preference, Gender Identity, and Aggression in Men*. Hillsdale, N.J.: Lawrence Erlbaum Associates, 1985.

Leubsdorf, John. "Toward a History of the American Rule on Attorney Fee Recovery." *Law and Contemporary Problems* 47 (1984): 9–36.

Lincoln, Abraham. "The Perpetuation of Our Political Institutions." In *The Collected Works of Abraham Lincoln,* ed. Roy P. Basler. 9 vols. New Brunswick, N.J.: Rutgers Univ. Press, 1953.

Lizotte, Alan J., and David J. Bordua. "Firearms Ownership for Sport and Protection: Two Divergent Models." *American Sociological Review,* 45 (April 1980): 229–43.

Locke, John. *An Essay Concerning the True Original Extent and End of Civil Government*. In vol. 35 of *Great Books of the Western World*. Chicago: William Benton, 1952.

Lombroso, Cesare, and William Ferrero. *The Female Offender*. New York: Philosophical Library, 1958.

Mack, M. P. *Jeremy Bentham: An Odyssey of Ideas*. New York: Columbia Univ. Press, 1963.

MacKinnon, Catharine A. *Only Words*. Cambridge: Harvard Univ. Press, 1993.

Madison, James. *The Records of the Federal Convention of 1787*. Ed. Max Farrand. New Haven: Yale Univ. Press, 1966.

Magnet, Myron. "The American Family, 1992." *Fortune,* August 10, 1992, pp. 42–47.

Martinson, Robert. "New Findings, New Views: A Note of Caution Regarding Sentencing Reform." *Hofstra Law Review* 7 (1979): 243–58.

———. "What Works? Questions and Answers About Prison Reform." *Public Interest,* Spring 1974, pp. 25–57.

Mather, Cotton. *A Family Well-Ordered; or, An Essay to Render Parents and Children Happy in One Another*. Boston: B. Green, 1699. Microfiche produced by American Antiquarian Society, Worcester, Mass. First series, no. 875.

McCoy, Candace. "Determinate Sentencing, Plea Bargaining Bans, and

Hydraulic Discretion in California." *Justice System Journal* 9 (1984): 256–75.

McKelvey, Blake. *American Prisons: A History of Good Intentions.* Montclair, N.J.: Patterson Smith, 1977.

Menninger, Karl. *The Crime of Punishment.* New York: Viking, 1968.

Merton, Robert K. "Social Structure and Anomie." In *Social Theory and Social Structure.* New York: Free Press, 1957.

Methvin, Eugene. "Pay Now—or Pay Later." *Reader's Digest,* June 1991, p. 61.

Mill, John Stuart. *On Liberty.* Ed. Currin V. Shields. New York: Liberal Arts, 1956.

Miller, Wilbur R. *Cops and Bobbies: Police Authority in New York and London, 1830–1870.* Chicago: Univ. of Chicago Press, 1977.

Mitford, Jessica. *Kind and Usual Punishment.* New York: Alfred A. Knopf, 1973.

"Modern Gangs Have Roots in Racial Turmoil of '60s." *Los Angeles Times,* June 26, 1988, p. A28.

Moore, Mark H., and George L. Kelling. "'To Serve and Protect': Learning from Police History." *Public Interest,* Winter 1983, pp. 49–65.

Mosca, Gaetano. *The Ruling Class.* Trans. Hannah D. Kahn. New York: McGraw-Hill, 1939.

Murray, Charles A. "The Coming White Underclass." *Wall Street Journal,* October 29, 1993, p. A14.

———. *Losing Ground: American Social Policy, 1950–1980.* New York: Basic, 1984.

Musset, Alfred de. *The Confession of a Child of the Century.* In *The Complete Writings of Alfred de Musset.* Trans. Kendall Warren. New York: Edwin C. Hill, 1905.

Musto, David F. *The American Disease: Origins of Narcotic Control.* New York: Oxford Univ. Press, 1987.

Nagel, Ilene H., Stephen Breyer and Terence MacCarthy. "Equality Versus Discretion in Sentencing." Symposium discussion published in *American Criminal Law Review* 26 (1989): 1813–38.

Nagin, Daniel. "General Deterrence: A Review of the Empirical Evidence." In Alfred Blumstein et al., eds., *Deterrence and Incapacitation: Estimating the Effects of Criminal Sanctions on Crime Rates.* Washington, D.C.: National Academy of Sciences, 1978.

Nardulli, Peter F. "The Caseload Controversy and the Study of Criminal Courts." *Journal of Criminal Law and Criminology* 70 (1979): 89–101.

National Academy of Sciences. *Understanding and Preventing Violence.* Eds. Albert J. Reiss, Jr., and Jeffrey A. Roth. Washington, D.C.: National Academy Press, 1993.

National Advisory Commission on Civil Disorders. *Report.* New York: Bantam, 1968.

National Institute of Education. *Violent Schools—Safe Schools: The Safe*

School Study Report to the Congress. Washington, D.C.: U.S. Government Printing Office, 1978.

National Institute of Mental Health. *Television and Behavior: Ten Years of Scientific Progress and Implications for the Eighties, Summary Report.* Rockville, Md.: NIMH, 1982.

Newton, George D., and Franklin Zimring. *Firearms and Violence in American Life.* Staff Report of the Task Force on Firearms, National Commission on the Causes and Prevention of Violence. Washington, D.C.: U.S. Government Printing Office, 1969.

Oaks, Dallin H. "Studying the Exclusionary Rule in Search and Seizure." *University of Chicago Law Review* 37 (1970): 665–757.

Oaks, Dallin H., and Warren Lehman. *The Criminal Justice System and the Indigent: A Study of Chicago and Cook County.* Chicago: Univ. of Chicago Press, 1968.

Olson, Walter K. *The Litigation Explosion: What Happened When America Unleashed the Lawsuit.* New York: Truman Talley, 1991.

O'Reilly, Kenneth. *"Racial Matters": The FBI's Secret File on Black America, 1960–1972.* New York: Free Press, 1989.

Packer, Herbert. *The Limits of the Criminal Sanction.* Stanford: Stanford Univ. Press, 1968.

Petersilia, Joan. "Criminal Career Research: A Review of Recent Evidence." In Norval Morris and Michael Tonry, eds., *Crime and Justice: An Annual Review of Research.* Chicago: Univ. of Chicago Press, 1980.

Petersilia, Joan, and Peter W. Greenwood. "Mandatory Prison Sentences: Their Projected Effects on Crime and Prison Populations." *Journal of Criminal Law and Criminology* 69 (1978): 604–15.

Pfennigstorf, Werner. "The European Experience with Attorney Fee Shifting." *Law and Contemporary Problems* 47 (1984): 37–124.

Phillips, David P. "The Influence of Suggestion on Suicide: Substantive and Theoretical Implications of the Werther Effect." *American Sociological Review* 39 (1974): 340–54.

Plato. *Apology* and *Crito.* In *Euthyphro, Apology, Crito, Phaedo.* Ed. Robert D. Cumming. Trans. F. G. Church. Indianapolis: Bobbs-Merrill, 1956.

———. *The Republic.* Ed. Francis MacDonald Cornford. New York: Oxford Univ. Press, 1966.

Pontell, Henry N. *A Capacity to Punish: The Ecology of Crime and Punishment.* Bloomington: Indiana Univ. Press, 1984.

Posner, Richard A. "An Economic Theory of the Criminal Law." *Columbia Law Review* 85 (1985): 1193–1231.

President's Commission on Law Enforcement and Administration of Justice. *The Challenge of Crime in a Free Society: Report of the President's Commission on Law Enforcement and Administration of Justice.* New York: Avon, 1968.

Puddington, Arch. "The Question of Black Leadership." *Commentary*, January 1991, pp. 22–28.

Quigley, Paxton. *Armed and Female*. New York: St. Martin's, 1989.

Radzinowicz, Sir Leon, and Joan King. *The Growth of Crime: The International Experience*. New York: Basic Books, 1977.

Reckless, Walter C. *The Crime Problem*. New York: Appleton-Century-Crofts, 1955.

Reiss, Albert J., Jr. *The Police and the Public*. New Haven: Yale Univ. Press, 1971.

Reiss, Albert J., Jr., and David J. Bordua. "Environment and Organization: A Perspective on the Police." In David J. Bordua, ed. *The Police: 6 Sociological Essays*. New York: John Wiley, 1967.

Reppetto, Thomas A. *The Blue Parade*. New York: Free Press, 1978.

Reuter, Peter, Gordon Crawford and Jonathan Cave. *Sealing the Borders: The Effects of Military Participation in Drug Interdiction*. The RAND Corporation, Report No. R-3594-USDP. Santa Monica, Calif.: RAND Corporation, January 1988.

Reynolds, Morgan O. *Crime Pays: But So Does Imprisonment*. NCPA Policy Report No. 149. Dallas: National Center for Policy Analysis, 1990.

Robins, Lee N. *Deviant Children Grown Up*. Baltimore: Williams & Wilkins, 1966.

Rossiter, Clinton. *Conservatism in America: The Thankless Persuasion*. New York: Vintage, 1962.

———. *1787: The Grand Convention*. New York: Macmillan, 1966.

Rothberg, Joseph M., Paul T. Bartone, Harry C. Holloway and David H. Marlowe. "Life and Death in the U.S. Army." *Journal of the American Medical Association* 264 (1990): 2241–44.

Rubinstein, Michael L., and Teresa J. White. "Alaska's Ban on Plea Bargaining." *Law & Society Review* 13 (1979): 367–83.

Russell, Bertrand. *What I Believe*. New York: Dutton, 1925.

Rutter, Michael. "Social-Emotional Consequences of Day Care for Preschool Children." *American Journal of Orthopsychiatry* 51 (1981): 4–28.

Rutter, Michael, et al. *Fifteen Thousand Hours: Secondary Schools and Their Effects on Children*. Cambridge: Harvard Univ. Press, 1979.

Samuelson, Robert J. "The Litigation Explosion: The Wrong Question." *Maryland Law Review* 46 (1986): 78–85.

Schlesinger, Steven R. "The Exclusionary Rule: Have Proponents Proven That It Is a Deterrent to Police?" *Judicature* 62 (1979): 404–9.

Schroeder, William A. "Deterring Fourth Amendment Violations: Alternatives to the Exclusionary Rule." *Georgetown Law Journal* 69 (1981): 1361–1426.

Schultz, Leroy G. "Why the Negro Carries Weapons." *Journal of Criminal Law, Criminology, and Police Science* 53 (December 1962): 476–83.

Schwartz, Ira M. *(In)Justice for Juveniles: Rethinking the Best Interests of the Child.* Lexington, Mass.: Lexington Books, 1989.

Schwarz, J. C., R. G. Strickland and G. Krolick. "Infant Day Care: Behavioral Effects at Preschool Age." *Developmental Psychology* 10 (1974): 502–6.

Seeburger, Richard M., and R. Stanton Wettick. "*Miranda* in Pittsburgh: A Statistical Study." *University of Pittsburgh Law Review* 29 (1967): 1–26.

Shavell, Steven. "Criminal Law and the Optimal Use of Nonmonetary Sanctions as a Deterrent." *Columbia Law Review* 85 (1985): 1232–62.

Shaw, Clifford R., and Henry D. McKay. *Juvenile Delinquency and Urban Areas.* Chicago: Univ. of Chicago Press, 1942.

Sheldon, William H. *Varieties of Delinquent Youth.* New York: Harper & Row, 1949.

Silberman, Charles. *Criminal Violence, Criminal Justice.* New York: Random House, 1978.

Silver, Carol Ruth, and Don B. Kates, Jr. "Self-Defense, Handgun Ownership, and the Independence of Women in a Violent, Sexist Society." In Don B. Kates, ed., *Restricting Handguns,* p. 139–70.

Skolnick, Jerome H. *Justice Without Trial: Law Enforcement in Democratic Society.* New York: John Wiley, 1967.

Skolnick, Jerome H., and David H. Bayley. *The New Blue Line.* New York: Free Press, 1986.

Smith, Adam. *Theory of Moral Sentiments.* Boston: Wells, 1817.

Smith, Douglas A. "The Plea Bargaining Controversy." *Journal of Criminal Law and Criminology* 77 (1986): 949–67.

Smith, Douglas A., Christy A. Visher and Laura A. Davidson. "Equity and Discretionary Justice: The Influence of Race on Police Arrest Decisions." *Journal of Criminal Law and Criminology* 75 (1984): 234–49.

Sparrow, Malcolm K., Mark H. Moore and David M. Kennedy. *Beyond 911: A New Era for Policing.* New York: Basic Books, 1990.

Spiotto, James. "Search and Seizure: An Empirical Study of the Exclusionary Rule and its Alternatives." *Journal of Legal Studies* 2 (1973): 243–78.

Spock, Benjamin. *The Common Sense Book of Baby and Child Care.* New York: Duell, Sloan & Pearce, 1957.

Stephen, James Fitzjames. *A History of the Criminal Law of England.* 3 vols. New York: Burt Franklin, 1973.

Sullivan, Peggy S., Roger G. Dunham and Geoffrey P. Alpert. "Attitude Structures of Different Ethnic and Age Groups Concerning Police." *Journal of Criminal Law and Criminology* 78 (1987): 177–96.

Sutherland, Edwin H. "Varieties of Delinquent Youth." In Karl Schuessler, Alfred Lindesmith and Albert Cohen, eds., *The Sutherland Papers.* Bloomington: Indiana Univ. Press, 1956.

Taylor, Jared. *Paved with Good Intentions: The Failure of Race Relations in Contemporary America.* New York: Carroll & Graf, 1992.

Thomas, George C., III, and David Edelman. "An Evaluation of Conservative Crime Control Theology." *Notre Dame Law Review* 63 (1988): 123–60.

Thrasher, Frederic M. *The Gang.* Chicago: Univ. of Chicago Press, 1963.

Tocqueville, Alexis de. *Democracy in America.* Ed. Phillips Bradley. 2 vols. New York: Alfred A. Knopf, 1987.

Tolluck, Gordon. "Does Punishment Deter Crime?" *Public Interest,* Summer 1974, pp. 103–11.

Tribe, Laurence. "Unraveling *National League of Cities:* The New Federalism and Affirmative Rights to Essential Government Services." *Harvard Law Review* 90 (1977): 1065–1104.

Tucker, William. *Vigilante: The Backlash Against Crime in America.* New York: Stein & Day, 1985.

———. "Why We Have Families." In R. Emmett Tyrrell, ed. *Orthodoxy: The American Spectator's 20th Anniversary Anthology.* New York: Harper & Row, 1987.

Tzu, Han Fei. *Readings in Chinese Legal Thought.* Ed. and trans. Wejen Chang. Unpublished manuscript at Harvard Law School, Cambridge, Mass.

U.S. Department of Health and Human Services. HHS News Release, February 25, 1993.

U.S. Congress. Senate. Committee on the Judiciary. Subcommittee on Criminal Laws and Procedures. *Controlling Crime Through More Effective Law Enforcement: Hearings Before the Subcomm. on Criminal Laws and Procedures of the Senate Comm. on the Judiciary.* 90th Cong., 1st Sess. Washington, D.C.: U.S. Government Printing Office, 1967.

van den Haag, Ernest. "How to Cut Crime." *National Review,* May 30, 1994, pp. 30–35.

———. "The Proper Goals of Punishment." Transcript of symposium published in *American Criminal Law Review* 26 (1989): 1789–1812.

van den Haag, Ernest, and John P. Conrad. *The Death Penalty: A Debate.* New York: Plenum, 1983.

Van Kessel, Gordon. "Adversary Excesses in the American Criminal Trial." *Notre Dame Law Review* 67 (1992): 403–551.

Vigilante, Richard. "Winning in New York." *National Review,* January 18, 1993, pp. 18–20.

Voltaire, M. de. *Candide.* Ed. and trans. Robert M. Adams. New York: W. W. Norton, 1966.

Walker, Donald R. *Penology for Profit: A History of the Texas Prison System, 1867–1912.* College Station, Tex.: Texas A&M Univ. Press, 1988.

Wallerstein, Judith S., and Sandra Blakeslee. *Second Chances: Men, Women and Children a Decade after Divorce.* New York: Ticknor & Fields, 1989.

Walsh, Anthony. "Placebo Justice: Victim Recommendations and Offender Sentences in Sexual Assault Cases." *Journal of Criminal Law and Criminology* 77 (1986): 1126–41.

Warren, Charles. *The Making of the Constitution.* New York: Barnes & Noble, 1967.

Washington, George. *The Writings of George Washington.* Ed. John C. Fitzpatrick. 39 vols. Washington, D.C.: U.S. Government Printing Office, 1939.

Wass, Hannelore, M. David Miller and Carol Anne Redditt. "Adolescents and Destructive Themes in Rock Music: A Follow-up." *Omega* 23 (1991): 199–206.

Wasserstrom, Richard. "Lawyers as Professionals: Some Moral Issues." *Human Rights* 5 (1975–76): 1–24.

Weitzman, Lenore J. *The Divorce Revolution.* New York: Free Press, 1985.

Wenik, Jack. "Forcing the Bystander to Get Involved: A Case for a Statute Requiring Witnesses to Report Crime." *Yale Law Journal* 94 (1985): 1787–1806.

White, Theodore H. *The Making of the President 1968.* New York: Atheneum, 1969.

Whitehead, Barbara Dafoe. "Dan Quayle Was Right." *The Atlantic,* April 1993, pp. 47–84.

Wigmore, John Henry. *Evidence in Trials at Common Law.* Ed. John T. McNaughton. 11 vols. Boston: Little, Brown, 1961.

Will, George F. "Looters in a Queue." In *The Morning After: American Successes and Excesses 1981–1986.* New York: Free Press, 1986.

Willard, Richard K. "Improving National Drug Policy." *American Criminal Law Review* 26 (1989): 1683–1708.

William of Ockham. *Philosophical Writings.* Ed. and trans. Philotheus Boehner. New York: Thomas Nelson & Sons, 1959.

Willing, Andrew R. "Protection by Law Enforcement: The Emerging Constitutional Right." *Rutgers Law Review* 35 (1982): 1–99.

Wilson, James Q., "Against the Legalization of Drugs." *Commentary,* February 1990, pp. 21–28.

———. *Thinking About Crime.* New York: Vintage, 1985.

———. *Varieties of Police Behavior: The Management of Law and Order in Eight Communities.* Cambridge: Harvard Univ. Press, 1968.

Wilson, James Q., and Richard Herrnstein. *Crime and Human Nature: The Definitive Study of the Causes of Crime.* New York: Touchstone, 1985.

Wolfe, Thomas. *The Bonfire of the Vanities.* New York: Farrar, Straus, 1987.

Wolfgang, Marvin E., Robert M. Figlio and Thorsten Sellin. *Delinquency in a Birth Cohort.* Chicago: Univ. of Chicago Press, 1972.

Wood, Gordon S. *The Creation of the American Republic, 1776–1787.* New York: W. W. Norton, 1969.

Wright, James D., and Peter H. Rossi. *Armed and Considered Dangerous: A Survey of Felons and Their Firearms.* New York: Aldine de Gruyter, 1986.

Wright, Richard. *Native Son.* New York: Harper & Row, 1989.

Wyzanski, Charles E., Jr. "A Trial Judge's Freedom and Responsibility." *Harvard Law Review* 65 (1952): 1281–1304.

X, Malcolm, and Alex Haley. *The Autobiography of Malcolm X.* New York: Ballantine, 1992.

Zacharias, Fred C. "Rethinking Confidentiality." *Iowa Law Review* 74 (1989): 351–411.

Zedlewski, Edwin W. "Making Confinement Decisions." In *Research in Brief.* Washington, D.C.: National Institute of Justice, July 1987.

CASES AND COURT OPINIONS

Abington School District v. Schempp, 374 U.S. 203 (1963).

Furman v. Georgia, 408 U.S. 238 (1972) (Marshall, J., concurring).

In re Gault, 387 U.S. 1 (1967).

Ingraham v. Wright, 430 U.S. 651 (1977).

Lemon v. Kurtzman, 403 U.S. 602 (1971).

Mapp v. Ohio, 367 U.S. 643 (1961).

Memoirs v. Massachusetts, 383 U.S. 413 (1966).

Minnick v. Mississippi, 111 S. Ct. 486 (1990).

Miranda v. Arizona, 384 U.S. 436 (1966).

New Jersey v. T.L.O., 105 S. Ct. 733 (1985).

Oregon v. Elstad, 470 U.S. 298 (1985).

Pope v. State, 56 Fla. 81, 47 So. 487 (1908)

Santobello v. New York, 404 U.S. 257 (1971).

State of Maine v. Thiboutot, 448 U.S. 1 (1980).

Swang v. State, 42 Tenn. (2 Cold.) 212 (1865).

United States v. Wade, 388 U.S. 218 (1967) (White, J., dissenting).

Weeks v. United States, 232 U.S. 383 (1914).

Whiskey Cases, 99 U.S. 594 (1878).

Wight v. Rindskopf, 43 Wis. 344 (1877).

Williams v. New York, 337 U.S. 241 (1949).

Index

About the Author

ANDREW PEYTON THOMAS received his B.A. in political science from the University of Missouri–Columbia and his law degree from Harvard Law School, with a concentration in political philosophy. During law school he served as a legal assistant for the Boston office of the NAACP. Following graduation, he worked as an attorney for a large corporate law firm in Phoenix, where he also was a member of the Maricopa County Sheriff's Posse, a citizens' law enforcement body for metropolitan Phoenix. Mr. Thomas is currently an assistant attorney general for the state of Arizona. He lives in Phoenix with his wife, Ann Estrada Thomas, and their daughter, Monica.

About the Author